"Alternative data is one of the hottest topics in the investment management industry today. Whether it is used to forecast global economic growth in real time, to parse the entrails of a company with more granularity than that offered by a quarterly report, or to better understand stock market behaviour, alternative data is something that everyone in asset management needs to get to grips with. Alexander Denev and Saeed Amen are able guides to a convoluted subject with many pitfalls, both technical and theoretical, even for those who still think Python is a snake best avoided."

— Robin Wigglesworth, Global finance correspondent, Financial Times.

"Congratulations to the authors for producing such a timely, comprehensive, and accessible discussion of alternative data. As we move further into the twenty-first century, this book will rapidly become the go-to work on the subject."

— Professor David Hand, Imperial College London

"Over the last decade, alternative data has become central to the quest for temporary monopoly of information. Yet, despite its frequent use, little has been written about the end-to-end pipeline necessary to extract value. This book fills the omission, providing not just practical overviews of machine learning methods and data sources, but placing as much importance on data ingestion, preparation, and pre-processing as on the models that map to outcomes. The authors do not consider methodology alone, but also provide insightful case studies and practical examples, and highlight the importance of cost-benefit analysis throughout. For value extraction from alternative data, they provide informed insights and deep conceptual understanding – crucial if we are to successfully embed such technology at the heart of trading."

— Stephen Roberts, Royal Academy of Engineering/Man Group Professor of Machine Learning, University of Oxford, UK, and Director of the Oxford-Man Institute of Quantitative Finance

"True investment outperformance comes from the triad of data plus machine learning plus supercomputing. Alexander Denev and Saeed Amen have written the first comprehensive exposition of alternative data, revealing sources of alpha that are not tapped by structured datasets. Asset managers unfamiliar with the contents of this book are not earning the fees they charge to investors."

— Dr. Marcos López de Prado, Professor of Practice at Cornell University, and CIO at True Positive Technologies LP

"Alexander and Saeed have written an important book about an important topic. I am involved with alternative data every day, but I still enjoyed the perspectives in the book, and learned a lot. I highly recommend it to everybody looking to harness the power of alt data (and avoid the pitfalls!)."

— Jens Nordvig, Founder and CEO of Exante Data

The Book of Alternative Data

A Guide for Investors, Traders, and Risk Managers

ALEXANDER DENEV

SAEED AMEN

Published by John Wiley & Sons, Inc., Hoboken, New Jersey.
Published simultaneously in Canada.

No part of this publication may be reproduced, stored in a retrieval system, or transmitted in any form or by any means, electronic, mechanical, photocopying, recording, scanning, or otherwise, except as permitted under Section 107 or 108 of the 1976 United States Copyright Act, without either the prior written permission of the Publisher, or authorization through payment of the appropriate per-copy fee to the Copyright Clearance Center, Inc., 222 Rosewood Drive, Danvers, MA 01923, (978) 750–8400, fax (978) 646–8600, or on the Web at www.copyright.com. Requests to the Publisher for permission should be addressed to the Permissions Department, John Wiley & Sons, Inc., 111 River Street, Hoboken, NJ 07030, (201) 748–6011, fax (201) 748–6008, or online at http://www.wiley.com/go/permissions.

Limit of Liability/Disclaimer of Warranty: While the publisher and author have used their best efforts in preparing this book, they make no representations or warranties with respect to the accuracy or completeness of the contents of this book and specifically disclaim any implied warranties of merchantability or fitness for a particular purpose. No warranty may be created or extended by sales representatives or written sales materials. The advice and strategies contained herein may not be suitable for your situation. You should consult with a professional where appropriate. Neither the publisher nor author shall be liable for any loss of profit or any other commercial damages, including but not limited to special, incidental, consequential, or other damages.

For general information on our other products and services or for technical support, please contact our Customer Care Department within the United States at (800) 762–2974, outside the United States at (317) 572–3993 or fax (317) 572–4002.

Wiley publishes in a variety of print and electronic formats and by print-on-demand. Some material included with standard print versions of this book may not be included in e-books or in print-on-demand. If this book refers to media such as a CD or DVD that is not included in the version you purchased, you may download this material at http://booksupport.wiley.com. For more information about Wiley products, visit www.wiley.com.

Library of Congress Cataloging-in-Publication Data:
Names: Denev, Alexander, author. | Amen, Saeed, 1982- author.
Title: The book of alternative data : a guide for investors, traders and
   risk managers / Alexander Denev, Saeed Amen.
Description: Hoboken, New Jersey : Wiley, [2020] | Includes bibliographical
   references and index.
Identifiers: LCCN 2020008783 (print) | LCCN 2020008784 (ebook) | ISBN
   9781119601791 (hardback) | ISBN 9781119601814 (adobe pdf) | ISBN
   9781119601807 (epub)
Subjects: LCSH: Investments | Financial risk management. | Big data.
Classification: LCC HG4529 .D47 2020 (print) | LCC HG4529 (ebook) | DDC
   332.63/204—dc23
LC record available at https://lccn.loc.gov/2020008783
LC ebook record available at https://lccn.loc.gov/2020008784

Cover Design: Wiley
Cover Image: © akindo/Getty Images

Printed in the United States of America

V10019210_062520

To Natalie, with all my love. –Alexander
For Gido and Baba, in life, in time, in spirit, your path is forever
my guide. –Saeed

Contents

Preface   **xv**

Acknowledgments   **xvii**

PART 1   INTRODUCTION AND THEORY   **1**

1   Alternative Data: The Lay of the Land   **3**

1.1   Introduction, 3
1.2   What Is "Alternative Data"?, 5
1.3   Segmentation of Alternative Data, 7
1.4   The Many Vs of Big Data, 9
1.5   Why Alternative Data?, 11
1.6   Who Is Using Alternative Data?, 15
1.7   Capacity of a Strategy and Alternative Data, 16
1.8   Alternative Data Dimensions, 19
1.9   Who Are the Alternative Data Vendors?, 23
1.10   Usage of Alternative Datasets on the Buy Side, 24
1.11   Conclusion, 26

2   The Value of Alternative Data   **27**

2.1   Introduction, 27
2.2   The Decay of Investment Value, 27
2.3   Data Markets, 29
2.4   The Monetary Value of Data (Part I), 31
     2.4.1   Cost Value, 34
     2.4.2   Market Value, 34
     2.4.3   Economic Value, 35

2.5   Evaluating (Alternative) Data Strategies with and without
       Backtesting, 35

      2.5.1   Systematic Investors, 36

      2.5.2   Discretionary Investors, 38

      2.5.3   Risk Managers, 39

2.6   The Monetary Value of Data (Part II), 39

      2.6.1   The Buyer's Perspective, 40

      2.6.2   The Seller's Perspective, 41

2.7   The Advantages of Maturing Alternative Datasets, 45

2.8   Summary, 46

3   Alternative Data Risks and Challenges   **47**

3.1   Legal Aspects of Data, 47

3.2   Risks of Using Alternative Data, 50

3.3   Challenges of Using Alternative Data, 51

      3.3.1   Entity Matching, 52

      3.3.2   Missing Data, 54

      3.3.3   Structuring the Data, 55

      3.3.4   Treatment of Outliers, 56

3.4   Aggregating the Data, 57

3.5   Summary, 58

4   Machine Learning Techniques   **59**

4.1   Introduction, 59

4.2   Machine Learning: Definitions and Techniques, 60

      4.2.1   Bias, Variance, and Noise, 60

      4.2.2   Cross-Validation, 61

      4.2.3   Introducing Machine Learning, 62

      4.2.4   Popular Supervised Machine Learning Techniques, 64

      4.2.5   Clustering-Based Unsupervised Machine Learning
              Techniques, 70

      4.2.6   Other Unsupervised Machine Learning Techniques, 71

      4.2.7   Machine Learning Libraries, 71

      4.2.8   Neutral Networks and Deep Learning, 72

      4.2.9   Gaussian Processes, 80

4.3   Which Technique to Choose?, 82

4.4   Assumptions and Limitations of the Machine Learning Techniques, 84

      4.4.1   Causality, 84

      4.4.2   Non-stationarity, 85

4.4.3   Restricted Information Set, 86

4.4.4   The Algorithm Choice, 86

4.5   Structuring Images, 87

4.5.1   Features and Feature Detection Algorithms, 87

4.5.2   Deep Learning and CNNs for Image Classification, 89

4.5.3   Augmenting Satellite Image Data with Other Datasets, 90

4.5.4   Imaging Tools, 91

4.6   Natural Language Processing (NLP), 91

4.6.1   What Is Natural Language Processing (NLP)?, 91

4.6.2   Normalization, 93

4.6.3   Creating Word Embeddings: Bag-of-Words, 94

4.6.4   Creating Word Embeddings: Word2vec and Beyond, 94

4.6.5   Sentiment Analysis and NLP Tasks as Classification Problems, 96

4.6.6   Topic Modeling, 96

4.6.7   Various Challenges in NLP, 97

4.6.8   Different Languages and Different Texts, 98

4.6.9   Speech in NLP, 99

4.6.10 NLP Tools, 100

4.7   Summary, 102

5   **The Processes behind the Use of Alternative Data**   **105**

5.1   Introduction, 105

5.2   Steps in the Alternative Data Journey, 106

5.2.1   Step 1. Set up a Vision and Strategy, 106

5.2.2   Step 2. Identify the Appropriate Datasets, 107

5.2.3   Step 3. Perform Due Diligence on Vendors, 108

5.2.4   Step 4. Pre-assess Risks, 109

5.2.5   Step 5. Pre-assess the Existence of Signals, 109

5.2.6   Step 6. Data Onboarding, 110

5.2.7   Step 7. Data Preprocessing, 110

5.2.8   Step 8. Signal Extraction, 111

5.2.9   Step 9. Implementation (or Deployment in Production), 112

5.2.10 Maintenance Process, 113

5.3   Structuring Teams to Use Alternative Data, 114

5.4   Data Vendors, 116

5.5   Summary, 118

6   Factor Investing   **119**

6.1   Introduction, 119

6.1.1   The CAPM, 119

6.2   Factor Models, 120

6.2.1   The Arbitrage Pricing Theory, 122

6.2.2   The Fama-French 3-Factor Model, 123

6.2.3   The Carhart Model, 124

6.2.4   Other Approaches (Data Mining), 125

6.3   The Difference between Cross-Sectional and Time Series Trading Approaches, 126

6.4   Why Factor Investing?, 126

6.5   Smart Beta Indices Using Alternative Data Inputs, 127

6.6   ESG Factors, 128

6.7   Direct and Indirect Prediction, 129

6.8   Summary, 132

PART 2   PRACTICAL APPLICATIONS   **133**

7   Missing Data: Background   **135**

7.1   Introduction, 135

7.2   Missing Data Classification, 136

7.2.1   Missing Data Treatments, 137

7.3   Literature Overview of Missing Data Treatments, 139

7.3.1   Luengo et al. (2012), 139

7.3.2   Garcia-Laencina et al. (2010), 143

7.3.3   Grzymala-Busse et al. (2000), 146

7.3.4   Zou et al. (2005), 147

7.3.5   Jerez et al. (2010), 147

7.3.6   Farhangfar et al. (2008), 148

7.3.7   Kang et al. (2013), 149

7.4   Summary, 149

8   Missing Data: Case Studies   **151**

8.1   Introduction, 151

8.2   Case Study: Imputing Missing Values in Multivariate Credit Default Swap Time Series, 152

8.2.1   Missing Data Classification, 153

8.2.2   Imputation Metrics, 154

8.2.3   CDS Data and Test Data Generation, 154

8.2.4   Multiple Imputation Methods, 157

8.2.5   Deterministic and EOF-Based Techniques, 160

8.2.6   Results, 164

8.3   Case Study: Satellite Images, 173

8.4   Summary, 176

8.5   Appendix: General Description of the MICE Procedure, 178

8.6   Appendix: Software Libraries Used in This Chapter, 179

9   Outliers (Anomalies)   **181**

9.1   Introduction, 181

9.2   Outliers Definition, Classification, and Approaches to Detection, 182

9.3   Temporal Structure, 183

9.4   Global Versus Local Outliers, Point Anomalies, and
        Micro-Clusters, 184

9.5   Outlier Detection Problem Setup, 184

9.6   Comparative Evaluation of Outlier Detection Algorithms, 185

9.7   Approaches to Outlier Explanation, 189

9.7.1   Micenkova et al., 189

9.7.2   Duan et al., 191

9.7.3   Angiulli et al., 192

9.8   Case Study: Outlier Detection on Fed Communications Index, 194

9.9   Summary, 201

9.10   Appendix, 202

9.10.1   Model-Based Techniques, 202

9.10.2   Distance-Based Techniques, 202

9.10.3   Density-Based Techniques, 203

9.10.4   Heuristics-Based Approaches, 203

10   Automotive Fundamental Data   **205**

10.1   Introduction, 205

10.2   Data, 206

10.3   Approach 1: Indirect Approach, 211

10.3.1   The Steps Followed, 212

10.3.2   Stage 1, 213

10.4   Approach 2: Direct Approach, 223

10.4.1   The Data, 223

10.4.2   Factor Generation, 224

10.4.3   Factor Performance, 225

10.4.4   Detailed Factor Results, 229

10.5   Gaussian Processes Example, 238

10.6   Summary, 239

10.7   Appendix, 240

     10.7.1   List of Companies, 240

     10.7.2   Description of Financial Statement Items, 241

     10.7.3   Ratios Used, 242

     10.7.4   IHS Markit Data Features, 243

     10.7.5   Reporting Delays by Country, 244

11   Surveys and Crowdsourced Data   **245**

11.1   Introduction, 245

11.2   Survey Data as Alternative Data, 245

11.3   The Data, 247

11.4   The Product, 247

11.5   Case Studies, 249

     11.5.1   Case Study: Company Event Study (Pooled Survey), 249

     11.5.2   Case Study: Oil and Gas Production (Q&A Survey), 252

11.6   Some Technical Considerations on Surveys, 254

11.7   Crowdsourcing Analyst Estimates Survey, 255

11.8   Alpha Capture Data, 256

11.9   Summary, 256

11.10 Appendix, 256

12   Purchasing Managers' Index   **259**

12.1   Introduction, 259

12.2   PMI Performance, 261

12.3   Nowcasting GDP Growth, 262

12.4   Impacts on Financial Markets, 263

12.5   Summary, 266

13   Satellite Imagery and Aerial Photography   **267**

13.1   Introduction, 267

13.2   Forecasting US Export Growth, 269

13.3   Car Counts and Earnings Per Share for Retailers, 271

13.4   Measuring Chinese PMI Manufacturing with Satellite Data, 277

13.5   Summary, 280

14 Location Data 283

14.1 Introduction, 283

14.2 Shipping Data to Track Crude Oil Supplies, 283

14.3 Mobile Phone Location Data to Understand Retail Activity, 287

    14.3.1 Trading REIT ETF Using Mobile Phone Location Data, 288

    14.3.2 Estimating Earnings per Share with Mobile Phone Location Data, 291

14.4 Taxi Ride Data and New York Fed Meetings, 295

14.5 Corporate Jet Location Data and M&A, 296

14.6 Summary, 298

15 Text, Web, Social Media, and News 299

15.1 Introduction, 299

15.2 Collecting Web Data, 299

15.3 Social Media, 300

    15.3.1 Hedonometer Index, 302

    15.3.2 Using Twitter Data to Help Forecast US Change in Nonfarm Payrolls, 305

    15.3.3 Twitter Data to Forecast Stock Market Reaction to FOMC, 308

    15.3.4 Liquidity and Sentiment from Social Media, 309

15.4 News, 309

    15.4.1 Machine-Readable News to Trade FX and Understand FX Volatility, 310

    15.4.2 Federal Reserve Communications and US Treasury Yields, 316

15.5 Other Web Sources, 320

    15.5.1 Measuring Consumer Price Inflation, 321

15.6 Summary, 322

16 Investor Attention 323

16.1 Introduction, 323

16.2 Readership of Payrolls to Measure Investor Attention, 323

16.3 Google Trends Data to Measure Market Themes, 325

16.4 Investopedia Search Data to Measure Investor Anxiety, 328

16.5 Using Wikipedia to Understand Price Action in Cryptocurrencies, 330

16.6 Online Attention for Countries to Inform EMFX Trading, 330

16.7 Summary, 333

17   Consumer Transactions   **335**

    17.1   Introduction, 335
    17.2   Credit and Debit Card Transaction Data, 336
    17.3   Consumer Receipts, 337
    17.4   Summary, 340

18   Government, Industrial, and Corporate Data   **341**

    18.1   Introduction, 341
    18.2   Using Innovation Measures to Trade Equities, 342
    18.3   Quantifying Currency Crisis Risk, 344
    18.4   Modeling Central Bank Intervention in Currency Markets, 346
    18.5   Summary, 348

19   Market Data   **351**

    19.1   Introduction, 351
    19.2   Relationship between Institutional FX Flow Data and FX Spot, 351
    19.3   Understanding Liquidity Using High-Frequency FX Data, 355
    19.4   Summary, 357

20   Alternative Data in Private Markets   **359**

    20.1   Introduction, 359
    20.2   Defining Private Equity and Venture Capital Firms, 360
    20.3   Private Equity Datasets, 362
    20.4   Understanding the Performance of Private Firms, 363
    20.5   Summary, 364

Conclusions   **365**

    Some Last Words, 365

References   **367**

About the Authors   **373**

Index   **375**

Preface

Data permeates through our world, in ever increasing amounts. This fact alone is not sufficient for data to be useful. Indeed, data has no utility, if it is devoid of information, which could aide our understanding. Data needs to be insightful for it to be of use and it also needs to be processed in the appropriate way. In the pre-Big Data age days, statistics such as averages, standard deviation, correlations were calculated on structured datasets to illuminate our understanding of the world. Models were calibrated on (a small number of) input variables which were often well "understood" to obtain an output via well-trodden methods like, say, linear regression.

However, interpreting Big Data, and hence alternative data, comes with many challenges. Big Data is characterized by properties such as volume, velocity and variety and other Vs, which we will discuss in this book. It is impossible to calculate statistics, unless datasets are well structured and relevant features are extracted. When it comes to prediction, the input variables derived from Big Data are numerous and traditional statistical methods can be prone to overfitting. Moreover, nowadays calculating statistics or building models on this data must be done sometimes frequently and in a dynamic way to account for the always changing nature of the data in our high frequency world.

Thanks to technological and methodological advances, understanding Big Data and by extension alternative data, has become a tractable problem. Extracting features from messy enormous volumes of data is now possible thanks to the recent developments in artificial intelligence and machine learning. Cloud infrastructure allows elastic and powerful computation to manage such data flows and to train models both quickly and efficiently. Most of the programming languages in use today are open source and many such as Python have a large number of libraries in the sphere of machine learning and data science more broadly, making it easier to develop tech stacks to number crunch large datasets.

When we decided to write this book, we felt that there was a gap in the book market in this area. This gap seemed at odds with the ever growing importance of data, and in particular, alternative data. We live in a world, which is rich with data, where many datasets are accessible and available at a relatively low cost. Hence, we thought that it was worth writing a lengthy book to address how to address the challenges of how to use data profitably. We do admit though that the world of alternative data and its use cases is and will be subject to change in the near future. As a result, the path we paved with this book is also subject to change. Not least the label "alternative data" might become obsolete as it could soon turn mainstream. Alternative data may simply become "data". What might seem to be great technological and methodological feats today to make alternative data usable, may soon become trivial exercises. New datasets from sources we could not even imagine could begin to appear, and quantum computing could revolutionise the way we look at data.

We decided to target this book at the investment community. Applications, of course, can be found elsewhere, and indeed everywhere. By staying within the financial domain, we could also have discussed areas such as credit decisions or insurance pricing, for example. We will not discuss these particular applications in this book, as we decided to focus on questions that an investor might face. Of course, we might consider adding these applications in future editions of the book.

At the time of writing, we are living in a world afflicted by COVID-19. It is a world, in which it is very important for decision makers to make the right judgement, and furthermore, these decisions must be done in a timely manner. Delays or poor decision making can have fatal consequences in the current environment. Having access to data streams that track the foot traffic of people can be crucial to curb the spread of the disease. Using satellite or aerial images could be helpful to identify mass gatherings and to disperse them for reasons of public safety. From an asset manager's point of view, creating nowcasts before official macroeconomic figures and company financial statements are released, results better investment decisions. It is no longer sufficient to wait several months to find out about the state of the economy. Investors want to have be able to estimate such points on a very high frequency basis. The recent advances in technology and artificial intelligence makes all this possible.

So, let us commence on our journey through alternative data. We hope you will enjoy this book!

Acknowledgments

We would like to thank our friends and colleagues who have helped us by providing suggestions and correcting our errors.

In first place, we would like to express our gratitude to Dr. Marcos Lopez de Prado who gave us the idea of writing this book. We would like to thank Kate Lavrinenko without whom the chapter on outliers would not have been possible; Dave Peterson, who proofread the entire book and provided useful and thorough feedback; Henry Sorsky for his work with us on the automotive fundamental data and missing data chapters, as well as proofreading many of the chapters and pointing out mistakes; Doug Dannemiller for his work around the risks of alternative data which we leveraged; Mike Taylor for his contribution to the data vendors section; Jorge Prado for his ideas around the auctions of data.

We would also like to extend our thanks to Paul Bilokon and Matthew Dixon for their support during the writing process. We are very grateful to Wiley, and Bill Falloon in particular, for the enthusiasm with which they have accepted our proposal, and for the rigor and constructive nature of the reviewing process by Amy Handy. Last but not least, we are thankful to our families. Without their continuous support this work would have been impossible.

The Book of Alternative Data

PART 1

Introduction and Theory

Chapter 1: Alternative Data: The Lay of the Land, 3
Chapter 2: The value of Alternative Data, 27
Chapter 3: Alternative Data Risks and Challenges, 47
Chapter 4: Machine Learning Techniques, 59
Chapter 5: The Processes behind the Use of Alternative Data, 105
Chapter 6: Factor Investing, 119

CHAPTER 1

Alternative Data: The Lay of the Land

1.1 INTRODUCTION

There is a considerable amount of buzz around the topic of alternative data in finance. In this book, we seek to discuss the topic in detail, showing how alternative data can be used to enhance understanding of financial markets, improve returns, and manage risk better.

This book is aimed at investors who are in search of superior returns through nontraditional approaches. These methods are different from fundamental analysis or quantitative methods that rely solely on data widely available in financial markets. It is also aimed at risk managers who want to identify early signals of events that could have a negative impact, using information that is not present yet in any standard and broadly used datasets.[1]

At the moment of writing there are mixed opinions in the industry about whether alternative data can add any value in the investment process on top of the more standardized data sources. There is news in the press about hedge funds and banks who have tried, but failed to extract value from it (see e.g. Risk, 2019). We must stress, however, that the absence of predictive signals in alternative data is only one of the components of a potential failure. In fact, we will try to convince the reader, through the practical examples that we will examine, that useful signals can be gleaned from alternative data in many cases. At the same time, we will also explain why any strategy that aims to extract and make successful use of signals is a combination of algorithms, processes, technology, and careful cost-benefit analysis. Failure to tackle any of these aspects in the right way will lead to a failure to extract usable insights from alternative data. Hence, the proof of the existence of a signal in a dataset is not sufficient

---

[1]A lot of applications of alternative data are being found today in insurance and credit markets (see e.g. Turner, 2008; Turner, 2011; Financial Times, 2017). We will not explicitly treat them here, although the alternative data generalities we will examine are also applicable to those cases.

to benefit from a superior investment strategy, given that there are many other subtle issues at play, most of which are dynamic in nature, as we will explain later.

In this book, we will also discuss in detail the techniques that can be used to make alternative data usable for the purposes we have already noted. These will be techniques belonging to what are labeled today as the fields of Machine Learning (ML) and Artificial Intelligence (AI). However, we do not want to give the upfront impression of being unnecessarily complex, with these "sophisticated" catchall terms. Hence, we will also include simpler and more traditional techniques, such as linear and logistic regression,[2] with which the financial community is already familiar. Indeed, in many instances simpler techniques can be very useful when seeking to extract signals from alternative datasets in finance. Nevertheless, this is not a machine learning textbook and hence we will not delve in the details of each technique we will use, but we will only provide a succinct introduction. We will refer the reader to the appropriate texts where necessary.

This is also not a book about the technology and the infrastructure that underlie any real-world implementations of alternative data. These topics encompassing data engineering are still, of course, very important. Indeed, they are necessary for anything found to be a signal in the data to be of any use in real life. However, given the variety and the deep expertise needed to treat them in detail, we believe that these topics deserve a book on their own. Nevertheless, we must stress that methodologies that we use in practice to extract a signal are often constrained by technological limitations. Do we need an algorithm to work fast and deliver results in almost real time or can we live with some latency? Hence, the type of algorithm we choose will be very much determined by technological constraints like these. We will hint at these important aspects throughout, although this book will not be, strictly speaking, technological.

In this book, we will go through practical case studies showing how different alternative data sources can be profitably employed for different purposes within finance. These case studies will cover a variety of data sources and for each of them will explore in detail how to solve a specific problem like, for example, predicting equity returns from fundamental industrial data or forecasting economic variables from survey indices. The case studies will be self-contained and representative of a wide array of situations that could appear in the real-world applications, across a number of different asset classes.

Finally, this book will not be a catalogue of all the alternative data sources existing at the moment of writing. We deem this to be futile because, in our dynamic world, the number and variety of such datasets increase every day. What is more important, in our view, is the process and techniques of how to make the available data useful. In doing so, we will be quite practical by also examining mundane problems that appear in sieving through datasets, the missteps and mistakes that any practical application entails.

This book is structured as follows. Part I will be a general introduction to alternative data, the processes and the techniques to make it usable in an investment strategy. In Chapter 1, we will define alternative data and create a taxonomy. In Chapter 2

---

[2]In fact, most of the ML/AI textbooks start with these simple techniques.

we will discuss the subtle problem of how to price datasets. This subject is currently being actively debated in the industry. Chapter 3 will talk about the risks associated with alternative data, in particular the legal risks, and we will also delve more into the details of the technical problems that one faces when implementing alternative data strategies. Chapter 4 introduces many of the machine learning and structuring techniques that can be relevant for understanding alternative data. Again, we will refer the reader to the appropriate literature for a more in-depth understanding of those techniques.

Chapter 5 will examine the processes behind the testing and the implementation of alternative data signals-based strategies. We will recommend a fail-fast approach to the problem. In a world where datasets are many and further proliferating, we believe that this is the best way to proceed.

Part II will focus on some real-world use cases, beginning with an explanation of factor investing in Chapter 6, and a discussion of how alternative data can be incorporated in this framework. One of the use cases will not be directly related to an investment strategy but is a problem at the entry point of any project and must be treated before anything else is attempted – missing data, in Chapters 7 and 8. We also address another ubiquitous problem of outliers in data (see Chapter 9). We will then examine use cases for investment strategies and economic forecasting based on a broad array of different types of alternative datasets, in many different asset classes, including public markets such as equities and FX. We also look at the applicability of alternative data to understand private markets (see Chapter 20), where markets are typically opaquer given the lack of publicly available information. The alternative datasets we shall discuss include automotive supply chain data (see Chapter 10), satellite imagery (see Chapter 13), and machine readable news (see Chapter 15). In many instances, we shall also illustrate the use case with trading strategies on various asset classes.

So, to start this journey, let's explain a little bit more about what the financial community means by "alternative data" and why it is considered to be such a hot topic.

1.2 WHAT IS "ALTERNATIVE DATA"?

It is widely known that information can provide an edge. Hence, financial practitioners have historically tried to gather as much data as is feasible. The nature of this information, however, has changed over time, especially since the beginning of the Big Data revolution.[3] From "standard" sources like market prices and balance sheet information, it evolved to include others, in particular those that are not strictly speaking financial. These include, for example, satellite imagery, social media, ship

---

[3] There is no precise date of when this revolution started, and certainly this has not been an instantaneous event. In *Thank You for Being Late: An Optimist's Guide to Thriving in the Age of Accelerations,* Thomas Friedman puts the starting year as 2007 because this is the year when major development in computational power, software, sensors, and connectivity happened. The term "Big Data" has been around since the 1990s and the father of the term is John Mashey, who was the chief scientist at Silicon Graphics at the time.

movements, and the Internet-of-Things (IoT). The data from these "nonstandard" sources is labeled alternative data.

In practice, alternative data has several characteristics, which we list below. It is data that has at least one of the following features:

- Less commonly used by market participants
- Tends to be more costly to collect, and hence more expensive to purchase
- Usually outside of financial markets
- Has shorter history
- More challenging to use

We must note from this list that what constitutes alternative data can vary significantly over time according to how widely available it is, as well has how embedded in a process it is. Obviously, today most financial market data is far more commoditized and more widely available than it was decades ago. Hence, it is not generally labeled as alternative. For example, a daily time series for equity closing prices is easily accessible from many sources and it is considered nonalternative. In contrast, very high frequency FX data, although financial, is far more expensive, specialized, and niche. The same is also true of comprehensive FX volume and flow data, which is less readily available. Hence, these market derived datasets may then be considered alternative. The cost and availability of a dataset are very much dependent on several factors, such as asset class and frequency. Hence, these factors determine whether the label "alternative" should be attached to it or not. Of course, clear-cut definitions are not possible and the line between "alternative" and "nonalternative" is somewhat blurred. It is also possible that, in the near future, what we consider "alternative" will become more standardized and mainstream. Hence, it could lose the label "alternative" and simply be referred to as data.

In recent years, the alternative data landscape has significantly expanded. One major reason is that there has been a proliferation of devices and processes that generate data. Furthermore, much of this data can be recorded automatically, as opposed to requiring manual processes to do so. The cost of data storage is also coming down, making it more feasible to record this data to disk for longer periods of time. The world is also awash with "exhaust data," which is data generated by processes whose primary purpose is not to collect or generate and sell the data. In this sense, data is a "side effect." The most obvious example of exhaust data in financial markets is market data. Traders trade with one another on an exchange and on an over-the-counter basis. Every time they post quotes or agree to trade at a price with a counterparty, they create a data point. This data exists as an exhaust of the trading activity. The concept of distributing market data is hardly new and has been an important part of markets for the ages and is an important part of the revenue for exchanges and trading venues.

However, there are other types of exhaust data that have been less commonly utilized. Take, for example, a large newswire organization. Journalists continually write news articles to inform their readers as part of their everyday business.

This generates large amounts of text daily, which can be stored on disk and structured. If we think about firms such as Google, Facebook, and Twitter, their users essentially generate vast amounts of data, in terms of their searches, their posts, and likes. This exhaust data, which is a by-product of user activity, is monetized by serving advertisements targets toward users. Additionally, each of us creates exhaust data every time we use our mobile phones, creating a record of our location and leaving a digital footprint on the web.

Corporations that produce and record this exhaust data are increasingly beginning to think about ways of monetizing it outside of their organization. Most of the exhaust data, however, remains underutilized and not monetized. Laney (2017) labels this "dark data." It is internal, usually archived, not generally accessible and not structured sufficiently for analysis. It could be archived emails, project communications, and so on. Once such data is structured, it will also make that data more useful for generating internal insights, as well as for external monetization.

1.3 SEGMENTATION OF ALTERNATIVE DATA

As already mentioned, we will not describe all the sources of alternative data but will try to provide a concise segmentation, which should be enough to cover most of the cases encountered in practice. First, we can divide the alternative data sources into the following high-level categories of generators:[4] individuals, institutions[5] and sensors, and derivations or combinations of these. The latter is important because it can lead to the practically infinite proliferation of datasets. For example, a series of trading signals extracted from data can be considered as another transformed dataset.

The collectors of data can be either institutions or individuals. They can store information created by other data generators. For example, credit card institutions can collect transactions from individual consumers. Concert venues could use sensors to track the number of individuals entering a particular concert hall. The data collection can be either manual or automatic (e.g. handwriting versus sensors). The latter is prevalent in the modern age, although until a couple of decades ago the opposite was true.[6] The data recorded can either be in a digital or analog form. This segmentation is summarized in Table 1.1.

We can further subdivide the high-level categories into finer-grained categories according to the type of data is generated. A list can never be exhaustive. For example, individuals generate internet traffic and activity, physical movement and location (e.g. via mobile phone), and consumer behavior (e.g. spending, selling); institutions generate reports (e.g. corporate reports, government reports), institutional

---

[4]Here we draw inspiration from the United Nations classification (see United Nations, 2015), although, in this text, we make the distinction between generators and collectors.

[5]By "institutions" we mean associations of individuals such as corporations, public entities, or governments.

[6]This consideration might be important if we want to enrich short time series with previous and old recordings (e.g. temperature or river levels time series going as far back as the 19th century), or loss on loans in banks in the 1990s for loss-given-default (LGD) modeling.

TABLE 1.1   Segmentation of alternative data.

Who Generates the Data?	Who Collects the Data?	How Is It Collected?	How Is It Recorded?
Physical processes	Individuals	Manually	Via digital methods
Individuals	Institutions	Automatically	Via analog methods
Institutions			

behavior (e.g. market activity); and physical processes collect information about physical variables (e.g. temperature or luminosity, which can be detected via sensors).

As individuals, we generate data via our actions: we spend, we walk, we talk, we browse the web, and so on. Each of these activities leaves a digital footprint that can be stored and later analyzed. We have limited action capital, which means that the number of actions we can perform each day is limited. Hence, the amount of data we can generate individually is also limited by this. Institutions also have limited action capital: mergers and acquisitions, corporate reports, and the like. Sensors also have limited data generation capacity given by the frequency, bandwidth, and other physical limitations underpinning their structure. However, data can also be artificially generated by computers that aggregate, interpolate, and extrapolate data from the previous data sources. They can transform and derive the data as already mentioned above. Therefore, for practical purposes we can say that the amount of data is unlimited. One such example of data generated by a computer is that of an electronic market maker, which continually trades with the market and publishes quotes, creating a digital footprint of its trading activity.

How to navigate this infinite universe of data and how to select which datasets we believe might contain something valuable for us is almost an art. Practically speaking, we are limited by time and budget constraints. Hence, venturing into inspecting many data sources, without some process of prescreening, can be risky and is also not cost effective. After all, even "free" datasets have a cost associated with them, namely the time and effort spent to analyze them. We will discuss how to approach this problem of finding datasets later and how a new profession is emerging to tackle this task – the data scout and data strategist.

Data can be collected by firms and then resold to other parties in a raw format. This means that no or minimal data preprocessing is performed. Data can be then processed by cleansing it, running it through quality control checks, and maybe enriching it through other sources. Processed data can then be transformed into signals to be consumed by investment professionals.[7] When data vendors do this processing, they can do it for multiple clients, hence reducing the cost overall.

These signals could be, for example, a factor that is predictive of the return of an asset class or a company, or an early warning indicator for an extreme event.

---

[7]There are potentially different degrees of the data being processed. In this sense, data can be also semi-processed. We will not use this fine distinction here, but this is something to bear in mind.

FIGURE 1.1　　The four stages of data transformation: from raw data to a strategy.

A subsequent transformation could then be performed to convert a signal, or a series of signals, into a strategy encompassing several time steps based, for instance, on determining portfolio weights at each time step over an investment horizon. These four stages are illustrated in Figure 1.1.

1.4　THE MANY VS OF BIG DATA

The alternative data universe is part of the bigger discourse on Big Data.[8] Big Data, and hence alternative data, in general, has been characterized by 3 Vs, which have emerged as a common framework to describe it, namely:

1. Volume (**increasing**) refers to the amount of generated data. For example, the actions of individuals on the web (browsing, blogging, uploading pictures, etc.) or via financial transactions are tracked more frequently. These actions are aggregated into many billions of records globally.[9] This was not the case before the rise of the web. Furthermore, computer algorithms are used to further process, aggregate, and, hence, multiply the amount of data generated. Traditional databases can no longer cope with storing and analyzing these datasets. Instead, distributed systems are now preferred for these purposes.

2. Variety (**increasing**) refers to both the diversity of data sources and the forms of data coming from those sources. The latter can be structured in different ways (e.g. CSV, XML, JSON, database tables etc.), semi-structured, and also unstructured. The increasing variety is due to the fact that the set of activities and physical variables that can be tracked is increasing, alongside the greater penetration of devices and sensors that can collect data. Trying to understand different forms of data can come with analytical challenges. These challenges can relate to structuring these datasets and also how to extract features from them.

---

[8]Defining the "Big" in "Big Data" is subjective and its lower bound is revised upwards continuously.

[9]The OECD estimates that in 2015, the global volume of data stood at 8 zettabytes (8 trillion gigabytes), an eight-fold increase compared to 2010. By 2020, that volume is forecast to increase up to 40 times over, as technologies including the Internet of Things create vast new datasets. See OECD, "Data-driven Innovation: Big Data for Growth and Well-being," OECD Publishing: 2015, page 20.

3. Velocity (**increasing**) refers to the speed with which data are being generated, transmitted, and refreshed. In fact, the time to get hold of a piece of data has decreased as computing power and connectivity have increased.

In substance, the 3 Vs signal that the technological and analytical challenges to ingest, cleanse, transform, and incorporate data in processes are increasing. For example, a common analytical challenge is tracking information about one specific company in many datasets. If we want to leverage information from all the datasets at hand, we must join them by the identifier of that company. A hurdle to this can be the fact that the company appears with different names or tickers in the different datasets. This is because a certain company can have hundreds of subsidiaries in different jurisdictions, different spellings with suffixes like "ltd." omitted, and so on. The complexity of this problem explodes exponentially as we add more and more datasets. We will discuss the challenges behind this later in a section specifically dedicated to record linkage and entity mapping (see Chapter 3).

These 3 Vs are more related to technical issues, rather than business specific issues. Recently 4 further Vs have been defined, namely Variability, Veracity, Validity, and Value, which are focused more on the usage of Big Data.

4. Variability (**increasing**) refers both to the regularity and quality inconsistency (e.g. anomalies) of the data streams. As we explained above, the diversity of the data sources and the speed at which data originates from them has increased. In this sense, the regularity aspect of Variability is a consequence of both Variety and Velocity.

5. Veracity (**decreasing**) refers to the confidence or trust in the data source. In fact, with the multiplication of data sources it has become increasingly difficult to assess the reliability of the data originating from them. While one can be pretty confident of the data, say, from a national bureau of statistics such as the Bureau of Labor Statistics in the United States, a greater leap of faith is needed for smaller and unknown data providers. This refers both to whether data is truthful and the quality of the transformations the provider has performed on the data, such as cleansing, filling missing values, and so on.

6. Validity (**decreasing**) refers to how accurate and correct the data is for its intended use. For example, data might be invalid because of purely physical limitations. These limitations might reduce accuracy and also result in missing observations; for example, a GPS signal can deteriorate on narrow streets in between buildings (in this case overlaying them onto a roadmap can be a good solution to rectify incorrect positioning information).

7. Value (**increasing**) refers to the business impact of data. This is the ultimate motivation for venturing into data analysis. In general, the belief is that overall Value is increasing but this does not mean that all data has value for a business. This must be proven case by case, which is the purpose of this book.

We have encountered other Vs, such as Vulnerability, Volatility, and Visualization. We will not debate them here because we believe they are a marginal addition to the 7 Vs we have just discussed.

In closing, we note that parts of the alternative data universe are not characterized by all these Vs if looked upon in isolation. For instance, they might come in smaller sample sizes or be generated at a lower frequency, in other words "small data." For example, expert surveys can be quite irregular and be based on a small sample of respondents, typically around 1000. The 7 Vs should, therefore, be interpreted as a general characterization of data nowadays. Hence, they paint a broad picture of the data universe, although some alternative datasets can still exhibit properties that are more typical of the pre–Big Data age.

1.5 WHY ALTERNATIVE DATA?

Now that we have defined what alternative data is, it is time to ask the question of why investment professionals and risk managers should be concerned with it. According to a recent report from Deloitte (see Mok, 2017):

> *"Those firms that do not update their investment processes within that time frame [over the next five years] could face strategic risks and might very well be outmanoeuvred by competitors that effectively incorporate alternative data into their securities valuation and trading signal processes."*

There is a general belief today in the financial industry, as witnessed by the quote above, that gaining access and mining alternative datasets in a timely manner can provide investors with insights that can be quickly monetized (a time frame in the order of months, rather than years) or can be used to flag potential risks. The insights can be of two types: either anticipatory or complementary to already available information. Hence, information advantage is the primary reason for using alternative data.

With regards to the first type, for example, alternative data can be used to generate insights that are a substitute for other types of more "mainstream" macroeconomic data. These "mainstream" insights may not be available on a prompt basis and at a sufficiently high frequency. However, they are nevertheless deemed to be important factors in portfolio performance. Investors want to anticipate these macro data points and rebalance their portfolios in the light of early insights. For example, GDP figures, which are the main indicator for economic activity, are released quarterly. This is because compiling the numbers that compose it is a labor-intensive and meticulous process, which takes some time. Furthermore, revisions of these numbers can be frequent. Nevertheless, knowing in advance what the next GDP figure will be can provide an edge, especially if done before other market participants. Central banks, for example, closely watch inflation and economic activity (i.e. GDP) as an input to the decision on the next rate move. FX and bond traders try in their turn to anticipate the move of the central banks and make a profitable trade. Furthermore, on an intraday basis, traders with good forecasts for official data can trade the short-term reaction of the market to any data surprise.

What can be a proxy for GDP, which is released at a higher frequency than quarterly? Purchasing Managers Indexes (PMI) that are released monthly could be one possibility.[10] They are based on surveys for sectors including manufacturing or service.[11] The survey is based on questionnaire responses from panels of senior purchasing executives (or similar) working in a sample of companies deemed to be representative of the wider universe. Questions could be, for instance, "Is your company's output higher, the same, or lower than one month ago?" or "What is the business perspective over a 6-month horizon?"

The information of the various components mentioned earlier is aggregated into the PMI indicator, which is interpreted based on its relative position to the value 50. Any value higher than the 50 level is considered to show expanding conditions while a value below the 50 mark potentially signals a recession.

The correlation between Real GDP growth rate and PMI is shown in Figure 1.2 for the US and Figure 1.3 for China. We can see that indeed an index like this, albeit not 100% correlated to GDP, is a good approximation to it. One explanation is the relative differences in what the measures represent. GDP measures economic output that has already happened. Hence, it is defined as hard data. By contrast, PMIs tend to be more forward-looking, given the nature of the survey questions asked. We define such forward-looking, survey-based releases as soft data. We should note that it can be the case that soft data is not always perfectly confirmed by subsequent hard data, even if they are generally correlated.

US ISM vs US GDP QoQ (Q1 2005–Q3 2019)

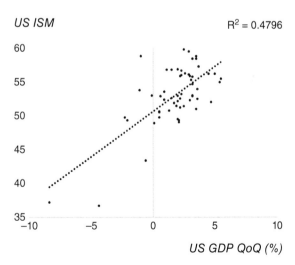

FIGURE 1.2   US GDP growth rate versus PMI; correlation 68%; time period: Q1 2005–Q1 2016.
Note. The dots indicate quarterly values.
Source: Based on data from PMI: ISM and Haver Analytics. GDP: Bureau of Economic Analysis and Haver Analytics.

---

[10] Another one could be measuring levels of pollution as a proxy for economic activity.
[11] The three principal producers of PMIs are the Institute for Supply Management (ISM), the Singapore Institute of Purchasing and Materials Management (SIPMM), and IHS Markit.

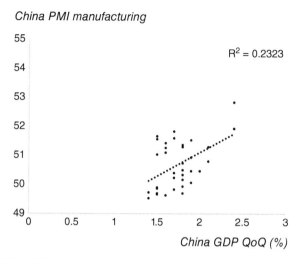

China PMI vs China GDP QoQ (Q1 2011–Q3 2019)

China PMI manufacturing

$R^2 = 0.2323$

China GDP QoQ (%)

FIGURE 1.3 China GDP growth rate versus PMI; correlation 69%; time period: Q1 2005–Q3 2019.
Source: PMI: China Federation of Logistics and Purchases and Haver Analytics. GDP: National Bureau of Statistics of China and Haver Analytics.

The PMI indicators are considered alternative data, in particular when we consider looking at them in a much more granular form. We will examine them more in detail in Chapter 12.

An alternative data source can be also used to anticipate the performance of a company, not only to forecast/nowcast the broader macroeconomic environment. Value investing, for example, is rooted in the idea that share prices should reflect company fundamentals in the long-term (which are also reflective of the macro environment), so the best predictors are the current fundamentals of a firm. However, maybe we can do even better if we knew (or could forecast) the current fundamentals in advance of the market? We will test this hypothesis later. An example of alternative data in this context is the aggregated, anonymized transaction data of millions of consumers' retail transactions that can be mapped to the shopping malls sales numbers where these purchases happened. The performance and hence the fundamentals of a mall can thus be forecasted relatively accurately long before the official income statement is released.

Alternative data can also be used as a complement, not just a replacement or substitute for other data sources as we have already mentioned. Thus, investors will be look at it for signals that are uncorrelated (or weakly correlated) to existing ones. For example, apart from company fundamentals disclosed in the financial statements, a good predictor for the future performance of an industrial firm could be examining the capacity and utilization of plants they operate or the consumer loyalty to the brand. Alternatively, we could collect data about their greenhouse gas emissions. Some of this information could be absent in balance a sheet but could be an indicator of the long-term performance of the company.

In Figure 1.4 we show some examples of alternative data usage by different market players.

Online price = inflation	App + credit card = performance	Social + search = earnings
Global FSI firm employs tech to track prices of 5 million products online to understand price shocks and monitor shift inflation across 70 countries (1)	Hedge fund looks at combination of alt data including credit card transactions, geo-location and app downloads to analyze burger chain performance (2)	90 bn USD AUM global asset manager mines search engine data combined with social media data to predict results of corporate events like quarterly earnings (3)
Mobile foot traffic = economy	**Satellite + ships = mispriced security**	**Web + Twitter = market moving event**
Hedge funds using location data pulled from mobile devices to predict outlook on economy and REIT values (4)	Hedge funds using satellite intelligence on ships and tank levels to identify upcoming impact to oil producers and commodity prices (5)	Data provider using 300m websites, 150m Twitter feeds in combination with FactSet reports to measure rise up media food chain (e.g. blogs to newswire) to highlight potentially market-moving events (6)

FIGURE 1.4 Examples of alternative data usage by different market players.
Source: Based on data from (1) "Innovative Asset Managers," Eagle Alpha; (2) "Foursquare Wants to Be the Nielsen of Measuring the Real World," Research Briefs, CBInsights, June 8, 2016; (3) Simone Foxman and Taylor Hall, "Acadian to Use Microsoft's Big Data Technology to Help Make Bets," Bloomberg, March 7, 2017; (4) Rob Matheson, "Measuring the Economy with Location Data," MIT News, March 27, 2018; (5) Fred R. Bleakley, "CargoMetrics Cracks the Code on Shipping Data," Institutional Investor, February 4, 2016; (6) Accern website.

1.6   WHO IS USING ALTERNATIVE DATA?

After a seminal paper in 2010 (see Bollen et al., 2011), the topic of alternative data started getting traction both in academia and in the hedge fund industry. The paper showed an accuracy of 87.6% in predicting the daily up and down changes in the closing values of the Dow Jones index when using Twitter mood data. This provided the spark for alternative data and, since then, quantitative hedge funds have been at the forefront of the usage of and investment in this space. However, at the beginning, only big banks and larger hedge funds could afford access to sentiment data as the annual cost of access, for instance, to the full Twitter stream was priced at around $1.5 million.[12] It should be noted that it is likely that some very sophisticated quants funds were using alternative data for a long time, well before the term *alternative data* came into vogue. Zuckerman (2019) discusses how a very sophisticated quant firm, Renaissance Technologies, had been using unusual forms of data for many years.

At time of press, several asset management firms are setting up data science teams to experiment with the alternative data world. To the knowledge of the authors, many attempts have been unsuccessful so far. This can be due to many reasons and some of them are not linked to the presence or absence of signals in the dataset they have acquired but to setting the right processes in place. As a cautious first step, many are using it as a confirmation of the information coming from more traditional data sources.

Fortado, Wigglesworth, and Scannell (2017) talk about many of the price and logistics barriers faced by hedge funds when using alternative data. Some of these are fairly obvious, such as the cost associated with alternative data. There are also often internal barriers, related to procurement, which can slow down the purchase of datasets. It also requires management buy-in to provide budget, not only for purchasing of alternative data, but also to hire sufficiently experienced data scientists to extract value from the data. In fact, there is evidence that only a small part of it is being currently analyzed, ~1% (see McKinsey, 2016).

The underusage of data could happen for a variety of reasons, as mentioned in the previous paragraph. Another reason could be coverage. Systematic funds, for example, try to diversify their portfolios by investing in many assets. While machine readable news tends to have an extensive coverage of all the assets, other datasets like satellite images may only be available for a small subset of assets. Hence, in many instances, strategies derived from satellite images could be seen as too niche to be implemented and they are thus defined as low capacity. Larger firms with substantial amounts of assets under management typically need to deploy capital to strategies that have large capacity, even if the risk-adjusted returns might be smaller compared to low-capacity strategies. We give a more detailed definition of what capacity is in the context of a trading strategy later in this chapter.

---

[12]Opimas expects (see Marenzi, 2017) that "alternative data will contribute significantly to a further shrinkage in the hedge fund population, as firms unable to exploit the information needed to compete effectively in the new world of intelligent investing will fall behind."

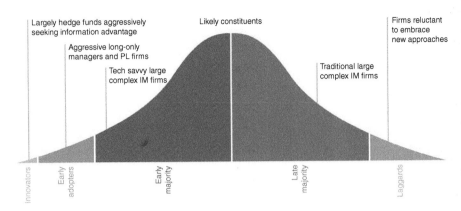

FIGURE 1.5   Alternative data adoption curve: investment management constituents by phase.

The decision of whether to buy a dataset is often based on a performance measure such as backtests. A quandary with alternative data is that, as we have mentioned, it tends to be characterized by a shorter history. In order to have an effective backtest, a longer history is preferred. A buy side firm could of course simply wait for more history to become available. However, this can result in a decay in the value of the data due to overcrowding. We tackle the problem of valuing alternative data in Chapter 2.

All these considerations point to the fact that – as with every innovation – only a few bold players have taken risks of starting to use alternative data, but further along the way, other firms might also get involved (e.g. less sophisticated asset managers). We illustrate a snapshot of our thinking in Figure 1.5.

We expect, of course, as technological and talent barriers decrease and the aware-ness of the market to alternative data increases, every investor to make use of at least a few alternative data signals in the next decade.

1.7   CAPACITY OF A STRATEGY AND ALTERNATIVE DATA

What do we mean when we talk about the capacity of a strategy? Essentially, we are referring to the amount of capital that can be allocated to it, without the performance of a strategy being degraded significantly. In other words, we want to make sure that the returns of our strategy are sufficiently large to offset the transaction costs of exe-cuting it in the market and the crowding out of the signal by other market participants, who are also trading similar strategies.

Trying to understand whether other market participants are trading similar strate-gies is challenging. One way to do it is to look at the correlation of the strategy returns against fund returns, although this is only likely to be of use for strategies that dom-inate a fund's AUM. We can also try to look at positioning and flow data collected from across the market. When it comes to transaction costs, at least for more liquid markets, the problem is somewhat easier to measure.

When we refer to transaction costs, we include not only the spread between where we execute and the prevailing market mid-price, but also the market impact, namely how much the price moves during our execution. Typically, for large orders we need to split up the risks and execute them over a longer period, during which time the price could drift against us. As we would expect, the transaction costs, which we incur, increase as we trade larger order sizes. However, this relationship is not linear. In practice, for example, doubling the size of the notional that we trade is likely to increase our transaction costs much more than a factor of 2. It has been shown with empirical trading data across many different markets, ranging from equities and options to cryptocurrencies, that there is a square root relationship between the size of our orders and the market impact (see Lehalle, 2019). The transaction costs are contingent on a number of factors as well as the size of the order, such as the volatility of underlying market, the traded volume in that asset, and so on. If the asset we are trading has very high volatility and low traded volume, we would expect the market impact to be very high.

Let us take for example a trading strategy that trades on a relatively high frequency, where on average we can make 1 basis point per trade in the absence of transaction costs. In this instance, if our transaction costs exceed 1 basis point per trade, the strategy would become loss making. By contrast, if a trading strategy has high capacity, then we can allocate large amounts of capital to it, without our returns being degraded significantly by increased transaction costs. Say, for example, we are seeking to make 20–30 basis points per trade. If we are trading relatively liquid assets such as EUR/USD, we could trade larger sizes and the transaction costs would be well below our target P&L per trade. Hence, we could conceivably allocate a much larger amount of capital to such a strategy. Note that, if we are trading a very illiquid asset, where typically transaction costs are much higher, then such a strategy could be rendered as low capacity.

One simple way to understand the capacity of a strategy is to look at the ratio of returns to transaction costs. If this ratio is very high, it would imply that you can allocate a large amount of capital to that strategy. By contrast, if that ratio is very low, then it is likely that the strategy is much lower capacity, and we cannot trade very large notional sizes with it.

It is too labor intensive to deploy large amounts of capital only to niche strategies because it would require a significant amount of research to create and implement many of them. Different types of strategies can require very different skillsets as well. For more fundamentally focused firms, having a dataset that is only available for a smaller subset of firms is less of an impediment. Typically, they will drill down into greater detail to investigate a narrower universe of assets. Hence, for smaller trading firms, niche strategies might be more attractive, as they are less impacted by capacity considerations. In other words, they are typically trading smaller notional sizes in the markets, given that they have less AUM, which are less impacted by transaction costs. Hence, they are able to run strategies that trade more often, such as high-frequency trading strategies, or those with more illiquid assets.

Below we summarize some of the properties that are typical of high-capacity strategies:

- Returns are less sensitive to increased transaction costs.
- Higher amounts of capital can be allocated without negatively impacting returns.
- Can be traded on a wide variety of tickers.
- Lower frequency.
- Lower Sharpe ratio.

Here we do the same for low-capacity strategies:

- Returns are sensitive to transaction costs.
- Higher amounts of capital will render the strategy loss making.
- Restricted to a small number of tickers.
- Higher frequency.
- Higher Sharpe ratio.

In Figure 1.6, we illustrate how transaction costs can impact a trading strategy. We show the risk-adjusted returns of Cuemacro's CTA (commodity trading advisor) strategy, dependent on different assumptions for transaction costs for a period between 2000 and 2019. These strategies are often known as CTA-type strategies, because originally firms trading them predominantly traded commodities. However, these days they trade these strategies across liquid futures in a number of different asset classes, including FX, fixed income, equity indices, and commodities. The CTA strategy involves trend following and typically also involves some sort of risk allocation based on vol targeting and positions are often leveraged.

Cuemacro's CTA strategy is designed to be proxy for the returns of a typical CTA. We note that increasing the transaction costs from 0 bp to 2.5 bp decreases the

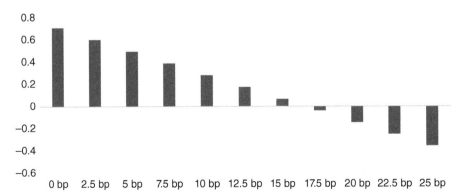

FIGURE 1.6   Impact of transaction costs on the information ratio of Cuemacro's CTA strategy.
Source: Based on data from Cuemacro.

information ratio from around 0.7 to 0.6, which is a relatively small difference. This perhaps isn't surprising given the strategy trades relatively infrequently, and relies upon identifying longer term trends. Hence, the returns per trade are typically quite large compared to the transaction costs. The various properties of the strategy suggest that we could label it as a higher-capacity strategy. Increasing the transaction costs for a low-capacity strategy would have a negative impact on both the information ratio and annualized returns.

Why is this concept of strategy capacity important in the context of alternative data? Once we know the approximate amount of capital we can deploy to a strategy, it enables us to understand the dollar value we can make, as opposed to purely the percentage returns. This in turn helps us when evaluating how much value to associate with a certain alternative dataset, if we are using it to generate trading signals. Let's say an alternative dataset enables us to develop a trading strategy that has returns of 25%. However, the capacity of the strategy is very limited. Hence, we can only allocate at most 1 million USD to it, without transaction costs significantly impacting our returns. Another dataset enables us to generate returns of 5%, but the capacity of the strategy is significantly more (say 1 billion USD), because it can be deployed on many assets. If we have lots of capital available for deployment, then the second dataset generates more value in dollar terms. Hence, we would likely be willing to pay more for the second dataset. By contrast if we have very limited capital available, it is unlikely we would be willing to pay as much for the second dataset, as we would be unable to use up much of the capacity of that strategy. As discussed elsewhere in the book, we also need to evaluate other costs associated with using the dataset too, such as the time taken to incorporate it within our investment process. In Chapter 2, we discuss the value of alternative data in more detail from the perspective of both buyers and sellers.

1.8 ALTERNATIVE DATA DIMENSIONS

So far, we have considered and analyzed in some detail different aspects of alternative data and its usage. Every time an investor ponders whether to purchase a dataset, they must bear in mind all these aspects together, along with other important issues such as the business use and technological limitations. We show in this section a summary of dimensions along which a potential data source should be projected in our view, ideally before it is purchased. Of course, the most important thing in the end is the amount of extracted alpha but before venturing into alpha research some prescreening should be carried out along the lines of these dimensions. A list of them follows:

Asset Class Relevance

- Equity
- Credit
- Rates
- Cash and cash equivalents
- FX
- Commodity

- Private markets
- Real estate
- Infrastructure
- Cryptocurrencies
- A mixture thereof

Coverage[13] within an asset class (score 1–10) e.g.

- Full – 10
- . . . . .
- None – 1

Breadth[14] within an asset class (score 1–10) e.g.

- Full – 10
- . . . . .
- None – 1

Depth[15] within an asset class (score 1–10) e.g.

- Full – 10
- . . . . .
- None – 1

Free data?

- Yes, the raw data only
- Yes, the processed dataset
- No

History (score 1–10) e.g.

- Short – 1
- . . . . .
- Medium – 5
- . . . . .
- Very long –10

Data Frequency

- Intra-daily
- Daily
- Weekly

---

[13]Coverage: how many instruments (e.g. stocks) are covered in the dataset, and also across which sectors, geographies, etc.

[14]Breadth: how many features can be generated by instrument (e.g. stock) in a dataset.

[15]Depth: how granular are the features generated by instrument (e.g. stock) in a dataset. For example, do we have information about the whole supply chain and assets of a manufacturing stock?

- Monthly
- Quarterly
- Yearly
- Other

Publishing lag (score 1–10) e.g.

- Real-time – 10
- .....
- Lagged – 5
- .....
- Substantially lagged – 1

Level of Processing

- Raw
- Semi-processed
- Fully processed

Level of Structuring

- Unstructured
- Semi-structured
- Structured

Research Cost (score 1–10)

- Research can rely on existing processes and requires minimal labor time – 10
- ...
- Needs some additional research work and computation cost – 5
- ...
- Heavily labor intensive and has very heavy computation costs – 1

Data Quality

- Amount of missing data (fraction %)
- Number of outliers (fraction %)

Data Bias

- Has an extensive panel, which is unbiased – 10
- ...
- Has an extremely limited sample and a narrow panel (e.g. individuals across limited geographies, income groups etc.) – 1

Data Availability (score 1–10) e.g.

- Public dataset – 10
- ...

- Widely sold against a subscription fee – 7
- …
- Exclusive – 1

Data Originality (score 1–10) e.g.

- Similar to many other datasets in the market – 1
- …
- Unique – 10

Technology (score 1–10) e.g.

- Available through an API – 10
- …
- CSV files – 1

Availability of trial

- Yes, against a fee
- Yes, free
- No

Legal (score 1–10) e.g.

- No legal limitations to use the data – 10
- …
- Limitations only in certain jurisdictions –5
- …
- Severe restrictions to use the data – 1

Portfolio effects – degree of orthogonality to other already purchased datasets (score 1–10)
Investment style suitability

- Macro
- Sector specific
- Asset specific

Time frequency of the investment strategy

- Intraday
- Daily
- Weekly
- Monthly
- Quarterly
- Yearly
- Other

Building a scorecard by considering some or all of these dimensions is an option to decide whether to purchase a dataset. If the score is higher than a certain threshold, a dataset might be considered further for acquisition. To some extent data brokers and scouts can help to outsource this type of scoring process. In many cases, financial firms will ask data firms to fill in questionnaires to answer similar questions to the above.

In building a scorecard, one must also consider rules that directly exclude (or include) a dataset for further consideration, for example, when there are severe legal restrictions when using the dataset. In this case, a dataset can be blacklisted directly without scoring it across the other dimensions.

1.9   WHO ARE THE ALTERNATIVE DATA VENDORS?

We have noted that alternative data has proliferated over years, increasing its supply to the market with this trend likely to accelerate over time. Indeed, statistics from Neudata (2020) show that the number of alternative datasets is now around 1000 (see Figure 1.7).

The alternative vendors can range significantly in size and what they do. They can include well-known existing market data companies such as Bloomberg, which sell their own alternative datasets, such as machine readable news (see Chapter 15), or IHS Markit, which sells alternative datasets related to crude oil shipping (see Chapter 14). A lot of these firms are also creating their own data markets to offer data from third-party alternative data vendors. At the other end of the spectrum, many alternative data vendors can be start-ups. Large corporates, not traditionally associated with this space, can also be alternative data vendors. They can sell their datasets derived from their exhaust directly to data users. These firms include MasterCard, which sells its consumer transaction data (see Chapter 17). In practice, many

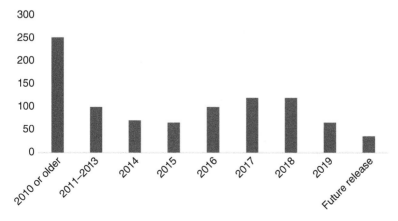

FIGURE 1.7   Alternative datasets released commercially per year.
Source: Based on data from Neudata.

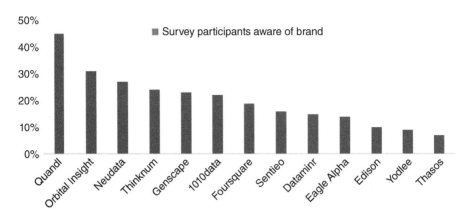

FIGURE 1.8   Brands most associated with alternative data.
Source: Based on data from Greenwich Associates.

corporates who wish to monetize their own exhaust data often work with an alternative data vendor or a consultancy to help them. These vendors can use their expertise
in alternative data processing to monetize these datasets, which include structuring
the data, creation of data products, marketing and selling the data to users, and so on.

Having an internal exhaust source requires a firm to engage in a large amount of
business tangential to selling data. As a result, many alternative data vendors source
their raw data from many different external sources, rather than being able to exclu-
sively use their own exhaust data.

In terms of the brands most associated with alternative data, we present a recent
survey of market participants from (Greenwich Associates, 2018) in Figure 1.8 based
on 36 total respondents. The poll is topped by Quandl, which is an aggregator and
marketplace of alternative datasets. It is followed by Orbital Insight, which sells its
own datasets related to satellite imagery. Neudata is an alternative data scouting firm
(see Chapter 5). Thinknum creates datasets based upon web data.

As we can see the most recognized alternative data vendors differ significantly
in terms of what they do and also in what the focus of their business is. We, of
course, acknowledge that the sample is relatively small, and given the fast-moving
nature of the alternative data landscape it is likely that these names may have changed
recently. Indeed, since publication a number of entrants have entered this space, such
as Bloomberg, which has launched its platform for distributing alternative data.

In Section 5.4 we will delve more into the details of how data vendors distribute
their data offerings.

1.10   USAGE OF ALTERNATIVE DATASETS ON THE BUY SIDE

While the supply of alternative data has increased, has the capacity for buy-side firms
to digest this data also increased? We mentioned in Section 1.5 that the usage of

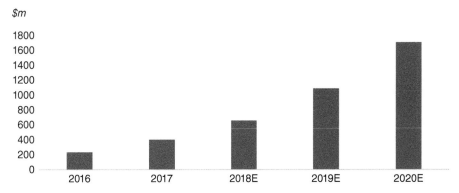

FIGURE 1.9   Total spend on alternative data by buy side.
Source: Based on data from alternativedata.org.

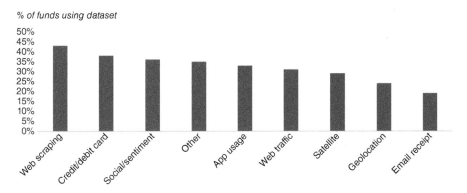

FIGURE 1.10   "Alternative datasets" derived from web scraping: most popular at funds at present.
Source: Based on data from alternativedata.org.

alternative data is overall still limited due to a variety of reasons but what is the trend in this space?

A survey from alternativedata.org (2019) shows that the number of full-time alternative data employees working in funds topped 1000 in 2017, and it is likely that this number has increased significantly by the time of print. Typically, these employees have more than a decade of experience, often from areas outside of asset management such as technology, academia, and working at data providers themselves. This increase in the capability of funds to process alternative datasets has perhaps unsurprisingly been accompanied by an increase in spending on the actual alternative datasets themselves. It is forecasted that spending by buy-side firms on alternative data is likely to increase to close to 2 billion USD for 2020 (see Figure 1.9). This compares with 232 million USD in 2016. We would expect continuing growth in alternative data spending by the buy side in the coming decade.

We noted that one of the main differentiating properties of alternative datasets is that they are not purely derived from financial markets. The usage of alternative datasets by funds varies significantly by type. Datasets derived from web scraping are most popular at present at funds (see Figure 1.10), closely followed by credit/debit card datasets. By contrast, those datasets from satellite imagery, geolocation, and email receipts are less popular, using the data available at the time of print.

1.11   CONCLUSION

We have briefly introduced what alternative data is and what some of the challenges in using it are. In doing so we have only scratched the surface of a big and complex world. In the next chapters we will dig more into the details of this world that under-pin practical applications. We will thus reexamine many of the concepts and topics introduced here. Later, in the second part of this book we will explore real-world case studies so that the reader can become further familiar with the concepts discussed in this chapter and also in the next few.

CHAPTER 2

The Value of Alternative Data

2.1 INTRODUCTION

One key question in the discussion about alternative data is how to assign value to it. This needs to be addressed from the perspectives of both data consumers and data producers. Data is only valuable from the perspective of a data consumer if it can be monetized, directly or indirectly. From the viewpoint of a data vendor, the cost of creating and distributing the dataset needs to be recouped when selling it. The data vendor would of course also want to add margin on it, when selling it.

In this chapter, we discuss this topic in some detail and show some directions to help value alternative data. We note that at the moment of writing there is still no solution to the problem of how to find the "right" price to assign to a dataset. The development of marketplaces where market participants can converge to one price is still at its infancy and, given the nature of what data is, many challenges still remain open, as we will shortly discuss. We will also show that having a standardized marketplace might not be the economically optimal solution for a data vendor.

2.2 THE DECAY OF INVESTMENT VALUE

Data, alternative or not, is ultimately used in investing and risk management to make predictions. In the investment space, if all or most of the market participants make the same prediction based on the same information, they can trade on it and opportunities could quickly disappear. The Efficient Market Hypothesis (EMH) in its semi-strong form reflects this point of view by asserting that public information is incorporated (almost) immediately in the prices of financial assets and hence any hope to outperform the market in the long-term based on that information is in vain. A direct result of this, if true, is that superior risk-adjusted returns are only available through insider information (or an exclusive or restricted access to a dataset in the sense of this book).

We will not debate the validity of this hypothesis[1] but what everybody would agree on is that if a piece of information has been available publicly for a while, then it has most probably lost a lot of its investment value.[2] In this sense data is a perishable asset. This could be a problem for data providers whose datasets then face the danger of quick obsolescence. In fact, in our experience, some of the alternative datasets that emerged first are now decreasing in their ability to generate alpha (e.g. news sentiment and earning calls transcripts for stocks).

All this reasoning might lead us to the conclusion that data, alternative or not, could be of little value unless exploited almost immediately after its release, and gains over the market can only be made by having a speed edge. However, there are some counterarguments to this. First, the variety and the multitude of data could make the decay of a signal less rapid. New data sources continuously appear. Hence, it becomes less probable that a large number of the market participants have access to all of them and have incorporated a given dataset into their processes once it is available, let alone the case that they have combined with exactly the same set of other data sources that other participants are using. There are many more alternative data sources than standardized financial market data and their types are much more diverse. Hence, it is less probable that two different market players will discover precisely the same datasets and gain access to them at the same time. It is also less likely that they will end up mining these datasets and combine them with other signals gleaned from other data sources. We can argue that essentially there are more degrees of freedom for the data sources used in general, with the advent of alternative data.[3]

Second, if two investors mine the same dataset, the techniques used to transform the raw data into a signal can be quite different. This could lead to different results, unless there is a very strong directional signal, in particular because they are likely to augment it with different datasets. A linear regression model, for instance, is not able to exploit nonlinear relationships in the data that a deep learning model is naturally incorporating. The two could lead to quite different predictions over the next investment horizon and hence point to different actions (e.g. buy versus sell).

Third, another factor that contributes to the persistence of the value of a dataset is the different investment mandates, horizons, styles, and risk appetite that investors have. Given this, the number of relevant features that can be extracted from

---

[1] Instead of checking the validity of the assumptions (which is very difficult), we can look at how active managers perform versus their relevant index. Soe and Poirier (2016, p. 1) claim that over the whole of 2016, 84.6%, 87.9%, and 88.8% of large-, mid-, and small-cap managers underperformed the S&P 500, S&P MidCap 400, and S&P SmallCap 600 respectively. It also states that, on a 5-year time horizon, 91.9%, 87.9%, and 97.6% of them underperformed their respective benchmarks. It is a similarly bleak story for the 10-year period: 85.4%, 91.3%, and 90.8% respectively.

[2] We also admit that, because of exactly the same reasons, investment clues derived from our case study results in this book can be self-defeating.

[3] Of course, much depends also on the distribution policy of a data seller. For example, is the data available on an exclusive or a restricted basis? Or is it available for every potential buyer? The relative availability of a dataset could impact on the subscription fee paid for the dataset. Even if a dataset is not available on an exclusive basis, a high cost adds an implicit barrier to the number of firms using it. We will discuss this point in Section 2.4.

a combination of orthogonal data sources is, therefore, further multiplied. For example, investors interested in directional trading will be looking at trends and features that can predict it. Volatility investors, on the other hand, will search for signals that drive the price of an asset in both directions. Styles like long-only, long-short, and so forth also determine what is relevant in the data and what is not. Sometimes datasets can be relevant for many different investment styles. We can take the example of machine-readable news. Longer term investors can aggregate the sentiment from machine readable news articles over a long period of time to inform their trading. By contrast high-frequency traders will use machine readable news at a much more granular level, using it to trigger very short-term trades, and also for risk management purposes, to identify when an asset is suspended from trading on an exchange.

Still the timeliness of the prediction and speed of the subsequent action are also of essence to make the most of a dataset. In fact, hedge funds have invested millions in servers physically located as close as possible to stock exchanges to gain a timing edge over their competitors. For latency-sensitive strategies, like high-frequency trading, this is very important. However, it is not the only thing that matters as we have just explained. It is also important to make an accurate prediction of at least the direction of the markets.

In summary, getting access to the right data at the right time is advantageous for the monetization of a dataset in the likely short opportunity window after it is released. Market players who are quick to discover valuable datasets will have an edge, before these datasets become more commoditized. However, whether a dataset has a positive investment value will also depend on other factors such as its price. We will turn to examine the delicate issue of pricing in the next sections.

We note in closing that arguments about decay of investment value can be time dependent. A dataset could cease to provide signals only temporarily if the economy enters an irrelevant period for the type of data it contains but could re-surface again in a future period. For example, a political news stream could bear almost no impact on financial markets in relatively calm periods but in times of political turbulence (e.g. Brexit) it could be the most important source of signals.

2.3 DATA MARKETS

The current exchanges of data between buyers and sellers are largely ad-hoc, with data trading performed through informal partnerships or private agreements. In these circumstances data pricing is often determined by the seller who does not provide visibility into the cost of collection, treating, and packaging to the buyer (see Heckman et al., 2015). According to Heckman, this asymmetry of information results in a lack of pricing transparency, hurting both the seller and the buyer. The former is unable to price optimally in the market, and the latter cannot strategically assess pricing options across data service providers. According to Heckman (2015), a more structured data market with standardized pricing models would improve the transaction experience for all parties.

Indeed, recently we have seen the rise of data marketplaces,[4] although we are still far from the adoption of standardized models. A data marketplace (also called Data as a Service, or DaaS) is essentially a platform in which data sellers and data buyers connect to buy and sell data from each other. A typical data market comprises three main roles: data sellers, data buyers, and a data marketplace owner. Data sellers supply data to the data marketplace and set the corresponding prices. Data buyers purchase the data that they need. The marketplace owner acts as the intermediary between sellers and buyers and sometimes negotiates the pricing mechanism with those providers and manages the data transactions. Typically, the marketplace owner will be compensated by the data seller in the transaction.

From a data user perspective, using a marketplace can help to simplify the process. Usually the marketplace will provide a common billing point and also access to data via common APIs, as well as making it easier to browse available datasets from many vendors. A data user just needs to sign one set of contracts, rather than having to negotiate separate NDAs and legal agreements with every data vendor before they engage. As a result, the onboarding process is likely to be quicker. Even for trials, data vendors are likely to be keen to have NDAs, to protect their data. Data users may also get other services from the data marketplace, such as research on the datasets that are carried by that marketplace or tools to help analyze the data.

The number of data marketplaces has been increasing with the growth of big data, as the amount of data collected by institutions has increased and as data has become increasingly recognized as an asset on its own. Data marketplaces are often integrated with cloud services. Examples of data markets include Quandl (now owned by Nasdaq), Eagle Alpha, Qlik Data Marketplace, D&B Data Exchange, BattleFin Ensemble, and AWS Public Dataset. There are also alternative data marketplaces from existing market data vendors. These include FactSet, which operates the Open:FactSet marketplace. Bloomberg also has a marketplace for alternative data with datasets from a number of vendors like Predata. With BattleFin Ensemble platform, clients can evaluate datasets directly on the platform, using Python on hosted Jupyter notebooks, and combine with reference data from Refinitiv.

Pricing models for data markets can be classified as follows (see Yu & Zhang, 2017; Muschalle, 2012):

1. Free models where data services can be used for free
2. Freemium models that combine free services and value-added services (In this pricing model, consumers have limited access to data for free and pay for the premium services.)
3. Packaging models, in which buyers purchase a certain amount of data at a fixed price
4. Pay-per-use models where buyers pay for data services based on their usage
5. Flat-fee models that involve data buyers paying a monthly subscription fee in return for unrestricted access to data services

---

[4]Both the private and the data market exchanges are largely unregulated.

6. Two-part-tariff models in which buyers pay a fixed basic fee that becomes supplemented by an additional fee when their usage exceeds some predefined quota

At the moment of writing, there are still issues concerning the trustworthiness (veracity) of data sold via data markets (and privately) to be addressed. While external data like weather or macroeconomic data can be trusted and easily verified through many sources, the same does not apply to many datasets available from third-party vendors, which may be relatively unique. Incorporating the latter into the decision-making process is more difficult because its truthfulness and authenticity cannot be assessed (although using proxies could be one approach, to corroborate datasets). This is why, in order to ensure trust in the marketplace, blockchain solutions, among others, are currently being proposed. The blockchain data is immutable, auditable, and completely traceable. There is still no clear solution for how this should work as there are hurdles inherent in how the blockchain currently operates. Speed and latency time are some of the concerns. The amount of data the blockchain can contain is limited and this is another big issue. Solutions based on only metadata being contained in the blockchain and the big datasets residing in separate data stores have been proposed but are still being experimented with. Currently there are exchanges running already on the blockchain technology such as Ocean Protocol and IOTA Protocol that enable users to connect to live sensors across the world and receive real-time streaming data for a subscription fee. We believe that this is an area that is evolving and more will be seen on this front once the blockchain technology has settled from what is believed by many to be hype.

In summary, as of today, data companies mostly use manual price discrimination to sell their data to their customers. Based on the information that can be gathered on the market, the data is typically priced according to the relative purchasing power of each customer. We also mentioned that the economics of information is imperfect: it is often hard to gather much information on customers and, as a consequence, pricing models can be inefficient in their task of maximizing revenue. This revenue management dilemma continues to apply today to different industries, which is why many of these industries keep updating their pricing models to make revenue collection more efficient and maximize profits (e.g., how Uber dynamically adjusts prices based on a wealth of information in real time to maximize revenue, through surge pricing). We also mentioned that data markets come with a desirable set of functionalities but also offer a platform where a price of a dataset can be made uniform across all customers. But is this really the way to maximize the revenue for a data vendor? Before answering this question, let's delve more into the details of data valuation.

2.4   THE MONETARY VALUE OF DATA (PART I)

Purchasing data comes at a price that includes the acquisition cost plus a seller's markup. Let's take for example a system to monitor temperature and humidity over a large geographical area, which could be used to estimate crop yields. There would be an initial cost for purchasing of temperature and humidity sensors. Then there would also be running costs such as electricity for the sensors and maintenance of the sensors, which could fail, especially in harsh climates. There would also be storage costs for the data collected. There would also be the costs of integration of the data into other systems and so on. There are essentially acquisition costs. If the data is exhaust, this doesn't mean the acquisition costs are zero, but it would imply that the business is already likely to be monetizing this data elsewhere. In our example, it could be that a farmer has set up this weather monitoring solution to help enhance the yields off their own crops. However, even with exhaust data, there are likely to be additional costs we would need to include, such as marketing, productionizing the data, legal costs of drafting contracts, and the like. It might also be the case that we could seek to enhance the data we are selling through the use of additional external datasets, which need to be purchased and joined to the existing dataset.

The seller's markup will depend on the pricing approach of the seller, which could depend on how unique this dataset is, and, hence, whether a monopolistic price is chargeable, and how many other buyers it is distributed to. Data could have quite a big range of price variation, from a couple of thousand (e.g. sentiment analysis) to millions of dollars (e.g. consumer transaction data).

On the other hand, the price a buyer would be willing to pay will depend on their utility (i.e. what is the value added for its business given the uncertainty of this estimate, what are the downside risks, etc.). Hence, the price of data is one of the components that will determine whether a data source will add value to an investment or a hedging strategy. Sometimes this value could be directly measurable as alpha – or excess returns over a benchmark – which directly translates into monetary terms. Sometimes, the value added is more difficult to quantify, such as in the case of cost savings (operational alpha). Obviously, while the price paid for a dataset is set in advance and fixed, the value derived from alpha generation is not known with absolute certainty beforehand, even if some tests are performed on a sample of the data before acquiring it. We should also, of course, note that the relative uniqueness of a dataset does not in itself mean that a dataset can be valuable for generating alpha.

Before venturing further into pricing, let's step back and examine the value of data in more general terms. The first question that we want to address is: if a company owns data, how can it determine its value if it wants to simply record it on its books? The answer to this question is difficult, because data is an intangible asset, like the value of a brand. It is not officially recorded on balance sheets, so it does not have accounting value. This might appear a strange fact considering that we live in the information age. For example, in the aftermath of 9/11, many companies located in the Twin Towers made claims to be indemnified for the loss of their information assets, but those claims were rejected by insurance companies arguing that information is not a tangible property and hence does not have value. At the time, extensive cloud infrastructure to back up data did not exist.

However, recording the value of data on the balance sheet is in principle possible and can be done indirectly, for example, by calculating the cost of acquisition. This may include the required capital expenditure to start recording the data (e.g. sensors) or the cost of buying it from a third party plus "installation" costs like the integration in a database. Running costs like maintaining the databases, the sensors, and the human processes behind this can be also incorporated. But there must be more than that to determining the value of data. A better question to ponder here is what the business impact of data is. The answer lies within departments such as legal, marketing, and the broader business. It can include different valuation components such as revenue potential, usage frequency, reputational, compliance, and legal risks. All these things can be very context specific. We will explain a simplified version of the cost value approach shortly.

Hence, valuing data assets is something that could be (and should be!) done regardless of whether they are commercialized externally. Indeed, having an understanding of the value of data within an organization will mean that it will become a better maintained and more useful resource. If data is undervalued within an organization, it is less likely that time and effort will be taken to store it or analyze it.

An MIT Sloan report[5] provides a suggestion on how companies should approach this task logistically. First, it suggests this can be done by developing firm-wide policies and, second, by acquiring and developing valuation expertise. Last, it suggests evaluating whether top-down or bottom-up valuation processes are the most effective within the company. In the top-down approach to valuing data, companies identify their critical applications and assign a value to the data used in those applications. A second approach is to define data value heuristically. In effect, this involves working up from a map of data usage across the core datasets in the company. Key steps in this approach include assessing data flows and linkages across data. From these steps, one can then produce a detailed analysis of data usage patterns. We refer to Short and Todd (2017) for more details on this topic.

Knowing the internal value of data assets is good but a trickier question to answer is how to determine the right price if a company wants to monetize this data externally. For example, Microsoft acquired LinkedIn for $26B back in 2016. The platform had at the time around 400M registered users, of whom approximately 100M were active. This translates into a $260 acquisition cost per active user. The announcement of the acquisition attracted the attention of the rating agencies and Microsoft's shares dipped immediately by 3%. The counterparties agreed on the deal, but was this a reasonable price to pay? The answer to this question is still unclear years after the acquisition.

Another example is the valuation of the customer database of Caesars Entertainment Corp. when they filed Chapter 11 in 2016. According to the some of the creditors, the value of the database was around $1B. This figure was derived by calculating the loss of earnings that some companies that sold off previously from Caesars Entertainment Corp. experienced and who no longer had access to the database. However, the bankruptcy report also noted that it would be difficult to integrate and use this dataset outside of Caesars Entertainment Corp. Hence, the value of their database was something extremely difficult to calculate and very much dependent on a variety of factors.

Laney (2017) suggests both a fundamental and a financial approach to data valuation. According to Laney, understanding the fundamental valuation of data is relevant for organizations that are not ready to prescribe monetary value to it, but are

---

[5] See Short (2017).

nevertheless interested in assessing its quality and potential. It can, hence, be used as a leading indicator of monetary value.

Financial valuation of data, on the other hand, can be done in three ways: by calculating the (1) cost value, (2) market value, and (3) economic value. We describe each of them in the following sections.

2.4.1   Cost Value

This method is preferred when there is no active market for the data. It reflects the annualized financial expense incurred to generate, capture, and collect the data according to the following formula:

$$CV = \frac{\sum_i Process\ Expense_i * Attribution\%_i * T}{t}$$

where T is the average life span of the data and t is the time period over which the process expense is measured. $Process\ Expense_i$ is the cost of the i-th process involved in capturing the data and $Attribution\%_i$ is the percent of $Process\ Expense_i$ attributable to the data capturing. An optional term that considers the impact on the business if information assets were rendered unavailable, stolen, or damaged could be also included in the formula.

There are, of course, elements of subjectivity in the cost value approach. These elements can include the percentage of the process that can be attributed to the capture of the data as well as the potential business damage in the case of data loss, if that term is included. Accountants, in general, prefer this approach to valuing intangibles as it is more conservative and less volatile.

2.4.2   Market Value

This approach looks at the potential monetary value of a data asset in a marketplace,[6] and hence cannot be applied to assets that are not for sale such as internal datasets. As we discussed in Section 2.3, there are already some fully operational online market platforms where datasets are being sold,[7] although they include only a small portion of the datasets in circulation, are unregulated, and do not have standardized pricing models.

A subtle clarification is that most of the time, the ownership of data (and the process behind its capture) is not actually sold but it is licensed. The number of licenses is potentially unlimited as data can be replicated with almost no costs. However, selling to many market participants results in decreased marketability, which means that its value is diminished the more investors trade on it.[8] A variable discount factor could be applied to the market price starting from an exclusive price (i.e. the price of the right of using the data by one client and not any others). A cost value or economic

---

[6]By this we will also mean on private exchanges.

[7]It is important to say that data can also be privately exchanged and bartered for goods, services, or contractual discounts.

[8]This, it can be argued, does not apply to domains outside trading. Jones (2019), for example, discusses the aspects of data and policies related to its widespread use to maximize social gains.

value (see further below) can be the starting point to determine such exclusive price to which a variable discount factor can then be applied. This is shown in the following formula:

$$MV = \frac{Exclusive\ Price * Number\ of\ Licensees}{Premium(Number\ of\ Licensees)}$$

Number of Licensees can be quantified through research of the market of potential buyers. It may also require a subjective estimate of the *Premium* discount factor based on an extensive market analysis and it depends on *Number of Licensees*.

2.4.3 Economic Value

The economic value approach takes into consideration the realized change in revenue minus the expenses when a data asset is incorporated into a revenue generating process. By change, we mean with respect to the case in which that data asset is not used. This is the traditional income approach in accounting. The expenses include the cost of acquiring, administering, and applying the data in the process as described in the Cost Value case. The calculation of such measure requires running a trial over a certain period t (A/B test), estimating the difference in revenue between the two alternatives and subtracting lifecycle cost of the information. In a nutshell:

$$EV = [Revenue_A - Revenue_B - Expenses] * T/t$$

where again T is the average life span of the data. As we will explain below, not A/B tests but backtesting is the preferred method in risk management and investing. Of course, a data vendor does not know the economic value to the data consumer and it is highly unlikely that two different data consumers will have the same economic value. We will show later that the valuation of a dataset depends on the exposure of an asset manager and this can vary widely, even by several orders of magnitude, between different players in the market.

In this section we took the point of view of a company that wishes to understand the value of its data assets both for internal purposes and for external monetization by selling to the market. However, what about the value of a dataset from a buyer's perspective? When considering whether to buy a dataset, investment and risk managers must estimate the additional economic value to their bottom line derived from that data. While, in general, it is difficult to measure the value of data, say, for branding, increased competitiveness, and other similar business uses, the impact of a dataset on an asset management firm can be directly measured in monetary terms. This sounds easy but, in reality, it comes with some ambiguity. We turn to discuss this in the next section.

2.5 EVALUATING (ALTERNATIVE) DATA STRATEGIES WITH AND WITHOUT BACKTESTING

We argued that in order to understand how much to pay for a dataset, if purchased externally, a business needs to quantify the additional value to their bottom line they can derive from its purchase. In asset and risk management, the most likely method of quantification is backtesting, although this is not always possible, as we will explain later. In essence, one wants to see how the business would have done had they incorporated that dataset in the past in their strategies. This test is performed on historical data, hence the name backtesting. What is usually then assumed is that the results of the backtest will hold in the future. There are, of course, limitations to such a method, as sometimes the future does not look like the past.

In particular, the value of a dataset for a systematic investor can be measured by estimating the enhanced returns the dataset unlocks over the investment horizon minus the costs. For a risk manager, its value can be quantified by assessing how much that dataset helps anticipate and mitigate negative extreme returns (e.g. by hedging, by divesting, etc.) that are outside the established risk tolerance levels. For a discretionary investor, a measure could be the value added in investment decisions. In practice, all these are always likely to be approximate estimates because there is no unique and deterministic way to perform such measurements. It very much depends on the choices underpinning the selected model to measure value and the underlying data, as we will now explain, addressing the different groups of systematic investors, discretionary investors, and risk managers.

2.5.1 Systematic Investors

For a systematic investor, a good way to quantify the improved predictive ability derived from a dataset is through an out-of-sample performance test calculated with or without using that dataset (Strategy A and Strategy B respectively).[9] For example, we can calibrate two models – Strategy A and Strategy B – in the period $(t - 15, t - 10)$, where t is the current time, and test their performance between $(t - 10, t - 9)$. The numbers 9, 10, 15 can be days, months – anything of our choice. Then we can roll over, recalibrate the models on $(t - 14, t - 9)$, and test them on $(t - 9, t - 8)$, and so on. In the end, we will have some measures to establish whether Strategy A is superior to Strategy B. These measures can be, for example, the Sharpe ratio, the compounded annual return (CAR), and so on. These type of backtests should be conducted across all the asset classes over which the dataset is expected to be implemented. For example, we can use the same dataset to generate enhanced strategies across equities, fixed income, FX, and the like. The combined value of these tests then should be used to assess the overall performance of Strategy A.

This might appear easy at first sight, but there are some methodological caveats one must bear in mind. First, the selected performance measure(s) could yield different results according to the time window chosen for the out-of-sample test (e.g. one week, one month, two years) as well as the time window chosen for the in-sample fit and the time step of the rollover. A winning strategy for certain

---

[9]This is very similar to the Economic Value approach of Section 2.4. However, what is described here is not an A/B test where different strategies are applied to different subgroups at the same time and the two impacts are then assessed and compared. Of course, nothing stops us from adopting such an approach by splitting the portfolio in two, but this could be hard to justify from business point of view. Backtesting is the preferred approach in investing.

in-sample and out-of-sample time window lengths could become losing if the lengths of those windows are changed. Second, the frequency of the input/output variables can have an impact, too (i.e. whether we are calibrating on data at daily, quarterly, or other frequencies). Third, different assumptions about transaction costs could lead to different conclusions as well. Finally, even if we have a clear winner over the first three dimensions, this might be due to the type of predicative model used. If the model functional form is changed, say, from a linear to a nonlinear, we can observe the performances of Strategy A and Strategy B to flip.[10]

These considerations apply in more general terms to models in the time series domain. Their predictive performance, as decided by the modeler through some measures, depends on the choice of (1) the time window used for the calibration (in-sample fit), (2) the time window used for the out-of-sample test, (3) the frequency of the data, (4) the chosen explanatory variables, and (5) the chosen model functional form. All these considerations indicate that having a clear-cut winning model is not always possible. Some variability in the conclusions can be removed by narrowing the hypothesis space of the choices based on economic reasoning or technological constraints. We might, for example, strongly believe that a linear model is the only suitable one for a strategy on a dataset based on our knowledge of the economics of the domain we are modeling. We can then limit ourselves only to exploring linear models. In other times, we will simply have no choice because the technological infrastructure, for example, could be able to ingest data at minimum, say, weekly frequency. Even after these types of restrictions, the choices left can still be too many. We will return to this point in Section 2.6.

In the end, we would ideally like to conclude that Strategy A is superior to Strategy B. Furthermore, we could like to say that it is better by a certain amount greater than a threshold we established beforehand. Sometimes this will not be the case, which means that the dataset contains no, or a very weak, signal and that it does not lead to a workable strategy. This does not mean, though, that if combined with other alternative datasets, the conclusions would be the same. In fact, in our experience, strong signals are usually detected when combining multiple data sources. Hence, discarding a data source after finding only a weak signal when used in isolation might be premature.

An additional complication is that the conclusions we draw from all the tests we discussed can be very much time dependent. Whatever findings are valid as of today might change in the future at the next date at which we will decide to retest the two strategies. This can be due both to overcrowding (everybody starts to use that data source and hence the investment value decays) and/or the always changing nature of financial markets (i.e. the lack of stationarity), which renders certain information obsolete.[11] If we can gain an understanding of the additional value a dataset provides, it can help us as a guideline of how much we would roughly pay for a dataset. Typically, as a rule of thumb, based on our various discussions with industry participants,

---

[10]There could also be a deterministic component in a model, meaning the rules used to rebalance the portfolio (e.g. go long the top 5% performers and short the bottom 5%, go long the top 10%, etc.). This also has impact on the conclusions.

[11]Additionally, the always evolving data protection regulations could make a certain data source completely unavailable. See Section 3.13.1 for a detailed discussion on the topic.

data buyers seek to make around 10 times the purchase price of a dataset, although the precise multiplier can vary between firms. In other words, if a firm believes they can make a million dollars from a dataset, this would imply that they'd be willing to pay around $100k for that dataset.

However, the costs associated with a dataset are not simply its purchase price. As we already mentioned, there is also the cost side to be factored in to the calculation, which consists not only of the purchase price of the dataset, but also the time spent to analyze it, and the expenses (CAPEX and OPEX) to incorporate it in a strategy.[12] These expenses could include data quality checks and transformations like filling missing data gaps, matching entities identifiers, and so on. If a strategy has a very large capacity strategy, then it is likely that costs of the data and developing a trading strategy are likely to be a smaller proportion of the returns than a very low capacity strategy.

We note in closing that if there are policies in an asset manager to have at least a certain number of years of backtesting to implement a strategy this can impede the adoption of alternative data as typically these sorts of datasets have shorter history. These firms could miss the informational advantages that come with the alternative data wave unless they accommodate their policies to be more reflective of this new reality. We could also suggest that one way to alleviate the problems associated with short histories is for data vendors to make a dataset broader – for example, to add more tickers. Ideally, of course, quants would prefer datasets that are both very long in history and very broad in the number of assets they cover.

2.5.2   Discretionary Investors

Sometimes alternative data can be used in different ways from the strategy we have discussed so far. It is not always the case that a buy or sell signal is necessarily the output of a particular alternative dataset. This is particularly the case for discretionary investors, who often want to make the final buy or sell decision themselves. Instead, in many instances, it is used as an additional input into the decision-making process by the investor. In particular, the use of alternative data might be done on more of a thematic basis, to dig down into a specific company or political event of interest.

In this context, one-off purchases of datasets are not infrequent, especially by fundamental discretionary investors who want some more information (e.g. about the condition of an asset they are monitoring, say, a factory). In this case, survey data can invariably help as we will show in Chapter 11. In this example, it is not possible to have a statistical assessment as the one-off dataset refers to one-off assessment and hence lacks repetition. But how can we put a price tag to a dataset in this case? This is clearly very difficult. However, one way to approach this is to ask whether this

---

[12]Because of this, running a proof-of-concept (POC) to detect signal on a sample of data before operationalizing a strategy is the best way to ensure that time and resources are not unnecessarily wasted. If a signal is detected at the POC stage, then an implementation of the strategy could be considered. The steps from POC to full operationalization and the subtleties around will be examined in detail in Chapter 6.

additional dataset has changed your view or not, or at least helped to add additional evidence. Has the dataset helped you to answer questions that you would have been unable to answer without it? The answers to questions of this type are very subjective[13] and hence the price variation that a buyer is willing to offer is substantial.

Other times an investor might be interested in repeated events. However, these events are not regularly distributed in time. For example, we might want to subscribe to an information service that monitors the military conflicts in a certain geography. These are certainly not regular in time. We need then a model (approximate) for the distribution in time of these events and their past impacts to come with an (approximate) valued added of that information.

Again, as in the case of systematic investors, much is left to the negotiation process between buyers and sellers to determine the price. However, competition – for example, in the market of survey/expert networks service providers – pushes down prices to slightly above cost. We note that what is offered by these types of firms are the services to collect the data, and costs of this can be more transparent than a data stream that leverages sensors, databases, platforms, and people. This leaves more negotiating power in the hands of the data buyer.

2.5.3   Risk Managers

Extreme events are rare, by definition, but they are one of the main concerns of risk managers. They tend to also be very irregular in time and very different in nature from each other. The failure of the LTCM, 9/11, and the Great Financial Crisis are fundamentally different from one another and the potential early warning indicators to look for to anticipate these events potentially reside every time in different data sources. Hence, a measure of the extent to which an alternative data source could be useful for the purposes of predicting extreme events is difficult and it might lack a statistical corroboration. In this sense, backtesting is not possible, and hence coming up with a price for a dataset could prove to be trickier. Again, in this case valuation must be done on subjective basis.

However, alternative data can give insights to risk managers to help forecast some risk metrics like short-term volatility, which can be used as inputs into broader-based risk controls. These forecasts can be backtested and hence the considerations of the previous section apply. See, for example, Chapter 15 for how news can be used to help forecast volatility around data events such as FOMC and ECB meetings.

2.6   THE MONETARY VALUE OF DATA (PART II)

As already stated, one of the biggest and most important challenges within the emerging market of data, as of today, is the lack of a widespread and accepted methodology

---

[13]We must note that even if in Section 2.5.1 we presented an "objective" and statistical approach, we pointed also to some elements of subjectivity, such as the choice of the time window, frequency, and so on. Another argument against "objectivity" in that case is that historical data might not be representative for the future and hence sometimes subjective tweaks in the backtests are necessary.

for valuing it. This makes the functioning of the data market even more difficult. In this section we will continue to bring some clarity to the subject and point to a solution, although much more research must be done on the topic in our view. We will put ourselves in the shoes of both the data seller and the data buyer.

2.6.1 The Buyer's Perspective

Asset pricing theory gives a hint of how to approach the problem of pricing data from the buyer's side, with some caveats that we will shortly explain.

In Section 2.5 we have been tacit about the price of data because we assumed it to be fixed and exogenous, and determined whether the benefits of using it outweigh the costs (which include the price) through backtesting. In what we have described so far, however, the price can be regarded as a free parameter to play with to determine the break-even point at which benefits equal the costs. This can be regarded as the maximum price a buyer should be willing to pay for it and it can be used as a negotiating argument to bring the offering price down if it is higher. In summary, the maximum price is simply the break-even price that would make a dataset profitable in an investment strategy compared to when that dataset is not used (Strategy A versus Strategy B). The break-even price will also depend on the average bet size of the positions in the portfolio. The larger the position we hold, the larger the potential profit and hence the amount we would be willing to pay for the dataset.

However, there is a problem with this line of reasoning. There are two sources of uncertainty in the procedure that we described and these must be incorporated in the price. These are (1) the uncertainty due to the potential stochastic nature of the models in the strategy and/or the features extraction; and (2) uncertainty due to the choice of hyperparameters of the models and the backtest (e.g. time window length, rollover).

The former arises because we will often use models to make predictions when devising a strategy and these models will have stochastic error terms.[14] The latter, as we have already mentioned, arises from the variety of choices that we have when selecting the hyperparameters. It is likely that we could have several layers of ML processing involved in terms of structuring a very complex unstructured dataset, each of which involves selecting different hyperparameters.

In summary, a strategy will yield a distribution of outcomes rather than a sharp point forecast. Let's describe uncertainty due to the choice of hyperparameters.

In general, given any investor, the time t price of an asset i according to this investor is given by the fundamental pricing equation:

$$p_t^i = E_t[m_{t+1} x_{t+1}^i] \tag{2.1}$$

with m_{t+1} the stochastic discount factor, and x_{t+1}^i the payoff at time $t + 1$. This payoff can be the distribution of the final payoff of Strategy A.

---

[14]If we use linear regression models, for example, they unavoidably contain a stochastic error term ε:
$y = \beta x + \varepsilon$.

We stress that this may be a nonequilibrium price (i.e. not the result of many participants acting in a market but a *private* valuation). As is well known and is discussed by Cochrane (2009), the stochastic discount factor is given by:

$$m_{t+1} = \frac{U'(w_{t+1})}{\gamma}$$

where $U'(w_{t+1})$ represents the derivative (with respect to wealth) of the utility function at wealth level w_{t+1}[15] achieved by starting from a wealth level w_0 at time $t = 0$. The stochastic discount factor is given by the product of the inverse of γ – a Lagrange multiplier – and the marginal utilities of wealth at time $t + 1$. It is a stochastic discount factor because the investor does not know exactly their wealth at time $t + 1$, w_{t+1}, which enters the (derivative of the) deterministic utility function. The utility function of an investor can be hard to determine but it essentially expresses their (nonlinear) attitude toward different magnitude of gains/losses.

The definition of the stochastic discount factor might seem unfriendly and complex although the assumptions behind this pricing theory are overly simplistic (e.g. two period economy), as discussed in Cochrane (2009). It involves determining the utility function (and a risk aversion coefficient inside it) of an investor and his impatience through γ. These are indeed difficult to quantify.[16] However, if the investor is able to quantify their impatience and their risk aversion and utility, then the price can be obtained through Equation (2.1). This is going to be their private valuation, which they can use in any negotiation or compare to a data market price if available.

Hence, an investor will be willing to accept any price below their private valuation. In reality, determining risk aversion and utility is difficult, on top of measuring and incorporating all the stochasticity of a strategy, although this is the most principled approach. Hence, shortcuts and rules of thumb, such as the one mentioned in Section 2.5.1, are applied where a subjective multiplier of the expected (i.e. without considering at all the stochasticity) monetary gain is used.

2.6.2 The Seller's Perspective

If data markets were liquid and perfect competition was in place, then the price of a dataset would be set by the market itself. However, most of the time datasets will be unique or almost unique, hence monopolistic pricing considerations should apply but always bearing in mind that overcrowding can decrease their value. We turn to discuss the case of data (quasi) monopoly shortly in this section.

---

[15]This wealth is essentially the sum of the payoffs of all the strategies in a portfolio.

[16]We must note, the effect of any potential overcrowding in the signal will be reflected in the price through this approach. If there is overcrowding it will be reflected in lower returns during the backtest, lower payoff of the dataset, and hence a lower price that a buyer is willing to pay. A caveat here is that this conclusion relies on historical data that also contains data about past overcrowding or the lack of it. Nobody guarantees that this is not going to change the horizon over which we agreed to pay a certain price to the data vendor.

But before that, we note that a monopoly is not a clear-cut definition in the case of the data world as it is for other markets, such as for electricity and water, even if there is only one supplier of a certain data stream. In fact, two data sources could easily contain overlapping information, even if the collection methods are very different. For example, mobile foot traffic in shopping malls and satellite images of car count pertain to very similar types of information. In that case, if satellite images are too expensive, buyers could switch to the potentially cheaper foot traffic tracking data. Hence, monopolistic pricing cannot be always strictly applied. Vendors must be aware of such situations because it might put them out of business quickly.

2.6.2.1 Monopoly
In the case that the dataset is unique, the data vendor can set the rules and apply a monopolistic pricing. In an ideal world, they try to maximize the revenue given by the following quantity:

$$Revenue = p_i x(p_i) \qquad (2.2)$$

where p_i is the price of dataset i and $x(p_i)$ is the quantity sold at that price that will be determined by demand. Quality of information also plays a role and can also be factored into the equation. In fact, we expect more highly cleansed datasets to cost more as higher-quality data implies more data processing and higher costs.

The question for a seller is then how to understand the value of p_i that maximizes Equation (2.2). This means the buyers in the market must somehow reveal their preferences. Unfortunately, this is not possible unless a survey or an auction for the data or another specifically engineered self-revelation mechanism is conducted. Figure 2.1 shows some pricing mechanisms that apply to different industries.

Constraining the number of consumers in an auction of high-value data feeds is a useful heuristic to prevent overexploitation. Dependent on the use case, artificial latency constraints can be used (or combined with other techniques) to support multiple consumers without overexploitation and consequent erosion of alpha generation opportunities. Auctions can be used to allocate licenses to a multiple but restricted set of winners. Data can be then sold with some latency to a fixed price to the rest of the market. There would need to be sufficient liquidity in the market such that there were a sufficient number of bidders in such an auction.

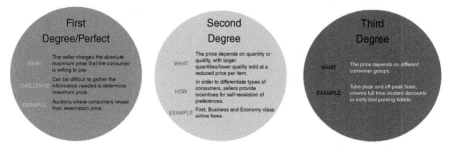

FIGURE 2.1   Different discriminatory pricing mechanisms.

The four main types of auction are the English auction, the Dutch auction, the First-Price Sealed-Bid auction, and the Vickrey auction. The Vickrey is praised for its property to induce bidders to reveal their true valuations, enabling sellers to apply a nearly perfect price discrimination strategy. The likes of Google and eBay have successfully embedded the Vickrey auction at the core of their business models.

At the time of writing, data auctioning is not a known pricing mechanism. However, we believe we will see some movement in this direction in the near future. As of today, the most preferred method is that of the differential pricing of data. This means that prices are adjusted by the seller according to the size of the buyer without room for much negotiation. Equation (2.1) shows that the private valuation of a buyer depends on the payoff, which is proportional to the exposure. Hence, the bigger the asset manager, the bigger the price they are willing to pay, and the seller is well aware of this fact. As a consequence, we have seen in practice different prices being offered to different client classes determined by their size.[17] As argued in the previous paragraphs though, an auction could be economically a better price-revealing mechanism as buyers know best the value to their portfolios and hence how much they would be willing to pay.

2.6.2.2   Sharing in the Upside of Data When Selling Externally

When selling data externally, we have assumed that the price of data is agreed and fixed beforehand. For example, a hedge fund will purchase a dataset for an agreed sum from a data vendor. The hedge fund will then seek to monetize that data through trading. Hence, the price of data is a known (and fixed) quantity that the data firm will receive. However, there can be another arrangement in place that could turn profitable to both sides.

If the dataset is particularly valuable, the hedge fund might make substantially more than the initial cost of data, yet the data firm will receive none of the upside. You could argue that this is fair, given that the hedge fund is paying a fixed price, which is paid regardless of how the dataset performs in the live trading environment. In a sense, we could argue that it is like the data vendor is selling an option and the hedge fund is buying the option (in the literature such concepts are often referred to as real options). The main caveat, however, is that the option seller here keeps the premium regardless of the final payoff.

What about having a different way to price data? For example, instead of having a fixed price agreed in advance, the data was priced according to the final trading outcome. In a sense, this is similar to how some traders are compensated. Traders can either be paid a fixed salary, or they can be paid as percentage of the profits they generate from their trading strategies.[18] The next question of course, is how you allocate this bonus within a team, who might have all had some role to play in the

---

[17] We have also seen cases where the price is influenced by the threshold above which a portfolio manager is required to go through an upper management approval process.
[18] The risk of this type of incentive is that it might encourage traders to take excessive risks, in particular, because their downside losses are capped (i.e. maximum downside is the loss of their job, rather than personal bankruptcy).

decision making. To simplify matters, for the sake of argument let us simply assume we have one trader who makes all the trading decisions for a single trading book.

Is there a way a data vendor can share in the upside in the same way? One way to do this is for the data vendor to sell trading signals to a fund. A percentage of profits related to this trading strategy can be returned to the data firm, which is fairly easy to define. In a sense, in this way, the data vendor is becoming a trader, but a fund is executing the trades. This, obviously, requires the data vendor to convert raw datasets into trading signals. In practice, this requires a different skill set, which data vendors don't typically have. This could potentially be the main sticking point of such approach. Furthermore, as we note in numerous places throughout the book, in some cases combining datasets together improves the predictability. A hedge fund is unlikely to allow an outside party to come in and look at their trading strategies to see which datasets they use and do analysis to understand which contributed the most.

One way to fix this problem is for an independent party to aggregate many datasets together to construct a trading strategy. Hedge funds can then buy the signal from the independent party to execute themselves. Alternatively, the independent party can execute them, effectively turning them into a mini-hedge fund, which is likely to push it toward a regulated entity.

The hedge fund will take most of the upside, given they are providing the capital for the transactions and taking the risk. The independent party will take a percentage for managing the process. The rest of the profits can be distributed to each data vendor. The breakdown of the payment to each data vendor is decided by the independent third party, based on their own analysis. A data vendor might also try to manage the process, although, clearly, it would be less independent, particularly when it comes down to how it would spread the P&L to other data vendors.

The "pricing" for having access to the signal could be done through a market-based approach, such as an auction along the lines of what we suggested in the previous section. We still face the issue that the skill set for creating trading signals is something that is most likely to be in a fund, rather than in a data vendor or other party. Hence, it could be the case that a trading strategy developed this way might not necessarily be as profitable as if the fund had developed it.

2.6.2.3 External Marketing Value in Data
In some instances, the data seller may judge that the pure monetary value of selling a dataset externally is not significant enough to "move the needle" when it comes to revenue. This could be the case for data sellers that are not primarily data vendors. These firms might be very large corporates looking to monetize their exhaust data externally. While the pure dollar value of selling their data could be insignificant when viewed against their primary revenues, there might be indirect ways of monetizing the data externally. One way might be to give out data for free externally as a marketing tool, which is something that, for example, ADP does.

ADP is a large US firm that provides software for HR and payrolls. As a result, they collect a large amount of data on US payrolls. Much of this data is clearly very sensitive, so it cannot be released externally without a significant amount of aggregation and anonymization. Once aggregated it can give us a picture of what the employment situation is like nationally, given the size of ADP's sample. ADP releases the ADP

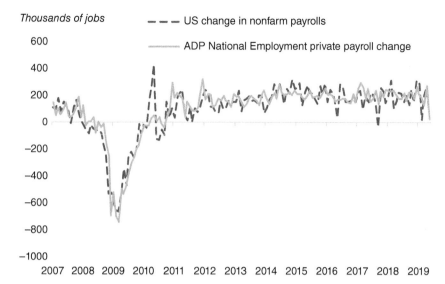

FIGURE 2.2   US change in nonfarm payrolls versus ADP private payroll change.
Source: Based on data from ADP, Bloomberg.

National Employment report at the start of each month, based upon this aggregated dataset. They have a headline figure for the national change in private payrolls, as calculated using ADP's data and model. Alongside this, there are a number of components for employment in different industries. It is specifically released before the official US employment report. It is often used by market participants as a nowcast for the official data release, which usually occurs later in the same week. The data is closely followed by financial market participants and also more broadly in the media, providing an opportunity to market the brand of ADP every month. In Figure 2.2, we plot the US change in nonfarm payrolls against the ADP National Employment private payroll change. We can see that by and large the time series do follow one another, although typically the official data tends to be more volatile.

Alternatively, the data could be distributed on a more limited basis to clients, by bundling it on a so-called "soft dollar" basis. The data would be paid for indirectly by the client through the consumption of other products and services. This helps to enhance service offerings to clients. However, a key part of MiFID II has been to unbundle the services that the sell side offers to buy side firms. Hence, buy-side firms now have to pay separately for services such as research. This could potentially make "soft dollar" arrangements more difficult for buy-side firms within the EU.

2.7   THE ADVANTAGES OF MATURING ALTERNATIVE DATASETS

Throughout the book we discuss many of the challenges associated with alternative data. Earlier in this chapter we discussed the potential for the alpha of an alternative dataset to decay over time. This might be particularly true of datasets that are most amenable for higher-frequency and lower-capacity strategies. However, we could argue that there are circumstances where a dataset might actually become more valuable or at the very least more usable over time.

One obvious advantage of a maturing dataset is the availability of more data history. The lack of data history is one of the barriers to the adoption of particular dataset. Without sufficient data history, it can be difficult to backtest trading strategies through different market regimes.

Over time, it is likely that data vendors will be also able to increase the coverage of a dataset so that it covers more assets and more geographies. If we take the example of satellite imagery for counting cars in retail car parks (see Chapter 13), typically the dataset not only needs access to the images themselves, but also mapping data. It also requires the construction of polygons (geo-fencing) to outline the car parks. This is a time-consuming process, which needs to be done for each car park. This increases its appeal to quant-focused accounts, who tend to trade a broader array of assets. Ideally, we would want a dataset to become sufficiently mature so that it has decent history and coverage, but before it becomes subject to significant alpha decay.

In general, the approaches and techniques associated with structuring data have improved over time. These newer techniques (or new applications of existing techniques) help us to understand unstructured content better. Much of the content on the web – which includes text, images, and video – is not structured. Machine learning algorithms in text to tag the topic of documents or understand sentiment, for example, have improved, as have those for understanding images (see Chapter 4). There are also more techniques available to clean data that have missing values (see Chapter 7). All this contributes to the increased maturity and hence usability of a dataset.

2.8 SUMMARY

We began the chapter by noting that we would expect the alpha decay associated with an alternative dataset to be slower than that of a more commoditized dataset. A key question for participants in the alternative data markets then is, what is the value of a dataset? From the perspective of a systematic investor, it is possible to backtest an alternative dataset to see how much additional value it brings to existing models. Even here, different investors are likely to attribute different values to the same dataset. For discretionary investors, it is more challenging to do a backtest. We talked about how to try to model the buyer's perspective. We discussed how various pricing schemes could be adopted from the seller's perspective. Lastly, we noted that maturing datasets can also have some advantages, in particular related to a longer data history. Over time, analytical techniques improve; hence, it is possible that we could find new insights from existing datasets. We turn now to discuss risks related to the usage of alternative data.

CHAPTER 3

Alternative Data Risks and Challenges

3.1 LEGAL ASPECTS OF DATA

Recently new legislation, like the EU General Data Protection Regulation (GDPR),[1] has been enacted. The aim of GDPR is to protect all EU citizens from privacy and data breaches and to give them control over their personal data. Hence, GDPR is already impacting how investors can obtain and use alternative data in those cases where data contains what is possibly considered the personal data of individuals in the European Union. Indeed, many alternative datasets contain personal information (e.g. credit card panel data and location). Therefore, their usage for investing must be always preceded by some due diligence checks.

Let's first more rigorously define what GDPR defines as "personal data." It is different and broader than the US definition of "personally identifiable information" (PII). In the EU, a key question to ask when defining "personal data" is whether a person can be identified based on that data. This means whether it is possible to reverse-engineer the data, maybe by combining it with other data sources, and to be able to uniquely identify that person. Hence, according to the European Commission definition, "For data to be truly anonymized, the anonymization must be irreversible." For example, if the name was removed from a dataset of individuals but the address remained, it would be fairly straightforward to derive the name (or least narrow it down to a household) by joining with a dataset of addresses and names.

If we take a very broad attribute, such as the sex of the individual, this will obviously split a population into two groups, and this will be insufficient to be a unique characteristic. However, if we then add more attributes, such as date of birth, then the combination of the attributes can become more unique, even if any particular characteristic is not in isolation. The more demographic attributes are associated with an individual, then the more "unique" that record would be. Furthermore, we need to

---

[1] It took effect on May 25, 2018.

ask whether collecting certain attributes is absolutely necessary and could be viewed as contentious and unwarranted.

Rocher, Hendrickx, and Montjoye (2019) flag various instances where supposedly anonymized datasets have been reverse engineered. They create a generative model to reidentify individuals from a dataset. Using their model, they note that with 15 demographic attributes, it is possible to render 99.98% of the people as unique in Massachusetts. Most of the attributes are relatively common, such as date of birth, gender, ZIP code, and so on, and wouldn't necessarily be classified as alternative data.

Montjoye, Hidalgo, Verleysen, and Blondel (2013) give an example of how uniqueness of individuals can be derived from an alternative dataset. They use a dataset of 15 months of human location data, derived from mobile phones. They note that when this location data is hourly and if it is of suitable resolution, it is sufficient to identify 95% of unique people.

In the United States, PII is more limited to categories such as names, addresses, telephone numbers, and the like, unlike GDPR, according to which personal data can also additionally include IP addresses, location, web cookies, photographs, and so on. Hence, all PII is personal data but not all personal data is considered PII.

Across the world, local laws regulate data protection to a different degree. We cannot detail all of them here, but Figure 3.1 shows the levels of enforcement of data protection laws in all the jurisdictions worldwide at the moment of writing.

Data protection laws restrict the amount of alternative data that can be used. Onboarding data must then come after a careful due diligence check of whether it contains personal data. Assurances from data vendors cannot offload this burden from the shoulders of the data buyers and appropriate procedures, and internal controls must be put in place to ensure that data protection laws are not breached. Insurance policies can be used as part of the risk mitigation methods to handle the financial costs of data breach risks. However, it should be noted that insurance may not offset all costs, which are difficult to quantify, such as reputational damage.

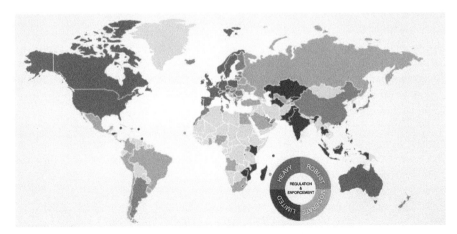

FIGURE 3.1   Comparison of data protection laws around the world.
Source: DLA Piper.

The limitations of what data we can use means that we cannot always have a complete picture in principle, say, of the potential earnings of an EU company or a non-EU company with regard to their operations in the EU,[2] if we use personal data to infer them (e.g. the people who bought the products of a company). Luckily, we do not always need to pinpoint information down to the person level. Instead, what we need is a more aggregated view. For example, the number of people who visited a shopping mall each day of the year is an aggregated metric that will suffice to predict sales and earnings. Therefore, whenever we do not need to buy person-level information, we can only require anonymized aggregated counts directly from the data vendor, instead of buying granular data and doing the aggregation ourselves. Whatever the caveat to get the information an investor needs, it is without doubt that data protection laws, in general, pose a constraint that could in principle reduce (but not eliminate!) the usability of alternative data.

Web scraping is another area where legal questions may arise. A lot of data on the web appears on private websites and behind paywalls. However, many web pages are publicly accessible. Does this mean that we can freely reuse the content that is viewable by users on a public website? Each website has its own terms of usage, which in some cases may prohibit web scraping of content. In many instances, firms seek to monetize the content of their websites by doing their own internal analysis, which is repackaged for clients to access. Alternatively, firms may be selling machine-readable access via APIs, either to the raw data or a structured representation. It is therefore perhaps unsurprising that many firms seek to prevent web scraping of their web content through their terms of usage. At the time of writing there is a lawsuit on the use of web-scraped data, which is being closely watched by hedge funds (Saacks, 2019). In September 2019, the Ninth Circuit Court of Appeals sided with hiQ against LinkedIn. LinkedIn had been seeking to prevent hiQ web scraping publicly accessible LinkedIn user pages (see Condon, 2019). hiQ had been using the data to provide services for HR professionals. Condon notes that the "judge concluded that, even if LinkedIn users had some interest in withholding their publicly-available data, those interests did not outweigh hiQ's interest in continuing its business." The ruling was seen as a positive development for firms sourcing data from the web.

Another legal issue associated with alternative data is whether a particular dataset constitutes material non-public information (MNPI). Deloitte (2017) notes that just because data might be accessible, such as certain content on the web, which might be tricky to find without the use of advanced coding techniques, does not necessarily make it public. In some cases, they note that certain firms might be less willing to purchase data that appears particularly predictable of information that is embargoed till official release time, such as quarterly earnings.

This leads us again to the concept of exclusivity for datasets. Theoretically, if a dataset is more exclusive, we might conjecture that it is less likely to suffer from alpha decay, particularly if it is most likely to be traded for strategies that have a low capacity. Hence, typically, such datasets are likely to be much more expensive. Fortado, Wigglesworth, and Scannell (2017) note that exclusive datasets can be a

---

[2] In the case of extra-EU companies, the amount of their EU operations could be limited so a better estimate of their earnings could be possible provided that the local data protection laws they operated under are not that stringent as the GDPR.

"double-edged sword," quoting Rado Lipuš of Neudata, and that some large funds prefer to avoid them. This is not only related to their expense of such datasets, but also to avoid any potential legal risks associated with them. They also note that in the past New York's attorney general has intervened to stop a data vendor distributing exclusive content to premium subscribers. We have already discussed auctioning datasets and giving to the winners of the auction a restricted access to the data (or low-latency access) to avoid overcrowding and maximize the revenues of the data vendor. It is important for a vendor to investigate if such auctions could be fit if data is considered MNPI. Currently this is still a legally blurred area.

The legal aspects of data do not purely govern whether data can be purchased. Data users often face legal restrictions in how they can use purchased data and this is related to the data license. Is the data license firm-wide, or only restricted to a small number of users? Does the data license restrict its redistribution in raw form or derived indices? All these contractual limitations can also influence the decision of whether to acquire a dataset.

3.2   RISKS OF USING ALTERNATIVE DATA

There are many risks associated with using alternative data, which are discussed by Deloitte (2017). Some of these risks are likely to be faced most by the early adopters. Some of these might be related to the legal risks, which we have discussed earlier. These might be related to privacy issues like GDPR. Alternatively, it could be the case that the data is being collected in a way that violates a website's terms of usage, such as through web scraping, as already mentioned. It should be noted that traditional datasets can also have similar issues. For example, a license may allow for internal usage of a certain common market dataset; however, this does not automatically mean it can be repackaged and used in datasets sold externally.

Other risks might relate to the quality of the data or its validity, a matter we touched upon when discussing the many Vs of Big Data. Admittedly, data quality and validity has also been an issue for traditional datasets. Even with market data, we might have fat-finger values, missing values, and so on. However, with alternative data, we face additional issues. In particular, if we think about social media, a large amount of content is not neutral and may be totally false. As with more traditional datasets, it can also be the case that certain alternative datasets disappear over time. If our models are heavily dependent on such datasets, it will make a strategy more difficult to maintain (see Section 5.2.10) and audit. There might be many reasons for this to happen, such as data vendors that close down. Or it can simply be the case that the raw data is no longer available because it has been discontinued by the vendor. There have been instances where changes in law, such as GDPR, have resulted in the disappearance of certain datasets.

Further risks include employee turnover, which can result in leakage of intellectual property. This has always been an issue with financial markets, where firms have sought to protect themselves from employees moving with particular knowledge of intellectual property. This has resulted in noncompete clauses being enforced. This is no different for dealing with alternative data, which requires specialist skills that are difficult to source. Potentially, one way to reduce employee turnover is to continually train employees so they can build their skillsets and also become more productive in the process. This is especially relevant in a fast-evolving area, such as alternative data.

However, those starting to use alternative data even after many of these issues have been resolved face other risks. Deloitte (2017) points out that these firms will essentially have to be playing catchup with established players in the field. As we noted earlier, developing a strategy for alternative data does not purely involve hiring a few data scientists. It requires data strategists, data scientists, and data engineers. It also requires the business to be able to utilize these resources and have the right processes in place. Creating such a framework takes time and cannot be done overnight. It is also difficult to execute successfully.

Those late to using alternative data might face "blind spots," as certain alternative datasets that they do not yet know how to use become common. Indeed, this can already be observed with some alternative datasets that have become more ubiquitous, such as consumer transaction data and estimated quarterly earnings for US retailers. For those firms late to the area, it could also result in a loss of assets under management, as investors see them as firms that are behind the curve. In substance, latecomers face a strategic extinction risk.

3.3 CHALLENGES OF USING ALTERNATIVE DATA

Starting to use alternative data might not be that straightforward. First, it could come in an unstructured form. If this is the case, being able to use it warrants first creating a structured dataset from which a model can be built and tested. Subsequently, unstructured data must be continuously converted into structured data in order to feed in the model at the production stage. Second, data might contain streaks of missing values, outliers, and other anomalies. These should be treated before any modeling is attempted unless we have a strong reason to believe that their amount is negligible. Third, in many applications, data from multiple sources must be integrated in order to enrich the feature set and hence do more powerful data mining and predictions than analyzing single sources in isolation. Aggregating diverse data sources comes with some practical challenges as well. Data from different sources is seldom in the same format and frequency; it could come with different delays, and identifiers between different data sources could require some treatment before being matched with a good level of confidence. Let's examine these issues in more detail.

In substance, the steps that data should be subjected to before the modeling stage (not necessarily in the following sequence) are:

1. Matching entity identifiers between different data sources
2. Treating missing data
3. Converting unstructured data into structured
4. Treating outliers in the data

In what follows, we examine these steps in more detail. We will dedicate separate chapters to missing data (Chapters 7 and 8) and outliers (Chapter 9).

3.3.1 Entity Matching

One of the biggest hurdles in matching different datasets is the fact that the name of an entity[3] can be different in different sources because of the multitude of ways to spell it or because of typographical errors. Take, for example, the simple case of the abbreviation for limited companies, which could have a number of different variations, such as limited, LTD, Ltd, or the like. This problem is not static and is not purely limited to the model training phase. Indeed, it will resurface live in production as new entities appear in the data sources (e.g. new companies being registered and as companies disappear through events such as takeovers). In the later section on natural language processing, we discuss many other examples to illustrate the importance of entity matching. Recently, advances have been made in the area of record linkage, especially since 2000, and now a variety of techniques and libraries are widely available. Luckily for tickers, there is the common CUSIP standard, which can be used to join together datasets by ticker. This can be particularly useful if we want to join up many different alternative datasets that might refer to a specific company.

However, for entities such as people and organizations, even once we might have detected them, many different standards might be used by data vendors. This makes it tricky to join together these datasets by entity. To alleviate this problem, Refiniv have open sourced their PermIDs for many different types of entities such as people and organizations. These are available from https://permid.org/. Very granular entries, such as subsidiaries, are available on a subscription basis.

As Christen (2012) explains, integrating data from different sources consists of three tasks. The first one is "schema matching." It is concerned with identifying database tables, attributes, and conceptual structures (such as ontologies, XML schemas, and UML diagrams) from disparate databases that contain data that correspond to the same type of information. The second is "data matching." It consists of identifying and matching individual records from disparate databases that refer to the same entities. The third task, known as "data fusion," is the process of merging pairs or groups of records that have been classified as matches (i.e. that are assumed to refer to the same entity) into a clean and consistent record that represents an entity. We should note, however, that some alternative data may have no particular schema, because it may be unstructured.

Data matching itself is divided into five steps: data preprocessing, indexing, record comparison, classification, and evaluation. There is also a human review step, if necessary.

The aim of data preprocessing is to ensure that that the attributes used for the matching have the same structure, and their content follows the same formats. This means cleaning and standardizing the data into well-defined and consistent formats. Inconsistencies in the way information is represented and encoded also need to be

---

[3] An entity can be a company, a person, a product, or a security, for example.

resolved. Data preprocessing thus deals with removing unwanted characters and words, expanding abbreviations and correcting misspellings, segmenting attributes into well-defined and consistent output attributes (e.g. splitting an address into street name, number, postcode etc.), and verifying the correctness of the attribute values (e.g. correcting company names from an external database).

Once the database tables have been cleansed and standardized, they are ready to be matched. This means potentially comparing each pair of records in the two tables. If each table contains one million records, this translates into one trillion records, which can take several days of computing time. Indexing is a way to reduce the number of comparison operations by filtering out pairs that are unlikely to be a match and by creating candidate records. Several techniques exist to do so, and blocking is one of the most used ones.

In the record comparison step, the candidate records generated in the previous step are compared more in detail by taking into account all the attributes (e.g. additional fields containing the address of the company or its activity). Rather than exact matching, which could miss many entities that are the same but appear slightly different due to things like typographical mistakes, an approximate matching is usually conducted. This is done by generating a similarity score between records, which is a number between 0 and 1. Similarity of 1.0 would correspond to an exact match between two values. By contrast, a similarity of 0.0 corresponds to a total dissimilarity between two values. Scores between 0.0 and 1.0 would correspond to some degree of similarity between two values. For each candidate record pair several attributes are generally compared, resulting in a vector of numerical similarity values for each pair. These vectors are called comparison vectors.

Once the comparison vectors have been calculated, pairs of entities have to be assigned to a class: match, non-match, or a potential match. In the latter, a human can be used to resolve the uncertainty and assign a match or non-match class manually. This can be done by thresholding the sum of the elements of the comparison vectors. For example, if the comparison vectors have 10 attributes, then the sum of their elements must be in the interval [0,10]. A thresholding can be defined as follows: [0,4] non-match, [4,6] potential match, [6,10] match. A potential match is escalated for manual review, but we must say that this can be a slow process and prone to errors. An external service such as Amazon Mechanic Turk can be used to outsource this process by crowdsourcing it. We must stress that any sort of manual process like this, whether done internally or externally, needs to have clear and definable criteria outlined, otherwise the accuracy is likely to be very low.

The last step is concerned with the evaluation of the quality of the matches and non-matches. Techniques like F-score borrowed from the machine learning field are commonly used. The quality of the matching is influenced by all the steps described above. The preprocessing step helps make two different values similar. The indexing step leaves out very dissimilar records. The algorithms in the data matching steps and the thresholds and the manual process in the classification steps also have an influence on the final results.

We also note that how we store the matching results is important, especially when it comes to backtesting investment strategies. In this case, we want to make sure that at any point in time of the backtest, we are not inadvertently using data from the future. This can introduce an upward bias to our results and make our backtest unrepresentative. Essentially, data can "leak" from the future to our backtest.

We will make the distinction at this point between *transaction time* and *belief time*. A transaction time denotes when a record was inserted into the database. It is usually recorded automatically as a timestamp by the database system and cannot be modified. Belief time refers to the time when the fact inserted into the database is valid.[4] For example, we might believe that country X has a GDP[5] figure for 2015 of, say, $1 trillion. We might have this belief and insert it as a record as of December 31, 2016. We might then update our belief on January 31, 2017, and insert it as a new record with the new GDP figure. Belief times, in general, can be intervals, points in time, or a series of points in time.

Constructing the database in such a (bi-temporal) way means that we can now find out what our belief time was for any given past transaction time (e.g. what was our belief as of January 15, 2016, with regard to the GDP of country X). Thus, bi-temporal databases of this kind allow retroactive updates coming into effect after the period of time the data is referencing. They also support proactive updates coming into effect before the period of time the data is referencing.

The results from entity matching should be stored in a way such that there are bi-temporal relationships between a permanent entity identifier and the entity attributes used in the matching process. This enables point-in-time or as-of queries to be used and allows for historical analysis without bias. This issue about point-in-time recording is also applicable to the underlying dataset itself, in addition to any history of the entity relationships.

3.3.2   Missing Data

Across many different fields, ranging from finance and economics to energy and transportation, to geophysical, meteorological, and sensor data, one of the challenges when working with data is that it is rarely complete. For instance, about 28% of publications in finance between 1995 and 1999 are reported to contain on average about 20% missing values (see Kofman, 2003). As analyzed in Rezvan et al. (2015), a sample of more than 100 papers in medical research between 2008 and 2013 typically contain missingness fractions exceeding 20%. The reasons for data to be incomplete are manifold and usually domain specific. Possibilities include faulty sensors or processes, incomplete records, mistakes in data collection, unavailability to report certain information, or other very specific reasons. Often it is also not known exactly why data is missing. In most cases it is not possible to recover missing values through additional data collection or measurements. Therefore, when building data applications, one has to accept incomplete data as the norm and devise appropriate strategies for dealing with it. We will dedicate one full chapter (Chapter 7) to missing data and will present detailed case studies in Chapter 8.

---

[4]This type of database is called temporal.
[5]Past GDP figures of countries are frequently revised months after they are first officially released.

3.3.3 Structuring the Data

According to widely cited statistics, 80%–95% of the data in the world comes in unstructured form: text, images, videos, and the like. Data can be also semi-structured like, for example, XML files containing both text and tags. Regardless of the origin of data (individuals, institutions, and sensors), making it useable requires it to be converted to a structured form, sharing a common format. Once it is in a structured form, it becomes easier to analyze.

There are some necessary steps for this to happen. Once data has been captured into a raw digital format, it needs to be preprocessed and validated at every step. Quite often, data can be of such low quality that it makes no sense to use it any further. Therefore, at each major stage of preprocessing it is logical to perform a validation check that would filter only the data that is good enough to proceed to more downstream tasks. When reading documents electronically, for example, it would be important to perform quality checks on PDFs first to assess whether they are "extractable." These checks can include assessing whether PDFs have sufficient contrast, reasonable DPI, lack of noise, and so on. If the quality is very bad, then it is logical to drop these specific observations. If the quality is average, then we can try to fix. If we assess that the quality is good enough after these various preprocessing steps, we can start doing Optical Character Recognition (OCR). After performing OCR and before trying to process the extracted information, we can do additional checks, this time, for example, on the tables/text specific to the business case at hand.

In the case of web text, preprocessing might also involve removing data that is superfluous for deciphering any meaning, such as HTML tags and other code. These parts of the text are primarily for a computer to interpret and do not aid human interpretation. It also means removing sections of the text that are human-readable but are unlikely to be of interest, such as the navigation bars, page numbers, and disclaimers. By the end of this step, we should be left with the body text of the article. This body text can be structured using NLP (Natural Language Processing) to add additional metadata to help with interpretation. Earlier stages of NLP will include steps such as word segmentation to pick out individual words. Downstream from that, part-of-speech tagging can be applied to identify which words are verbs and nouns, for example. The final structured output can be viewed as a summary of the raw data, which could be more easily stored in a database and analyzed than the original unstructured dataset.

Later on, the text may be classified to identify the overall topic. Name entity recognition is also key to identifying proper nouns of interest, such as people, places, and brands. This is usually combined with entity matching, too, so entities tagged in text can be mapped in tradable instruments. Sentiment analysis can be used to understand how positive or negative the text is. For speech data, we also have the additional step of applying speech recognition in order to transcribe the actual audio into written text.

The equivalent of NLP for images is computer vision. Just as with NLP, the goal of computer vision is to get an understanding of the data from a human perspective. It encompasses a number of different methods. Like text, images need to be cleaned before any further higher-level steps are taken for interpretation. The first step for images will include image processing, such as changing the contrast and sharpening, as well as the removal of noise. Other tasks include edge detection and image segmentation to split an image into various regions or to simplify it; these tasks are tackled by convolutional neural networks (CNN). These image preprocessing steps are essential preparation for higher levels of analysis later.

From a higher-level perspective, computer vision tries to interpret an image to add additional metadata to it and to structure it. These computer vision tasks include image recognition or classification for the entire image. It could also be to pick out specific objects in an image, namely object detection, where we seek to create a bounded box around objects. This includes object classification and object identification. One simple example of object classification could be to classify a "burger" and then identification of its specific type, such as "Whopper." We could view facial recognition as a very specific example of object identification. In recent years, machine learning, and in particular deep learning techniques, have become very suitable for tasks within computer vision such as image classification. The use of machine learning has not been confined to the higher-level tasks only. It has also been helpful for a number of image processing tasks, such as image colorization and removing blurring from an image. While many of the tasks associated with computer vision are also applicable for video, some are very specific to video, such as object movement tracking or lip reading.

Computer vision can also be used as part of an NLP task when our input text is not already in a digitized text format, but it is instead within an image. This can occur when the input text consists of handwriting. We can use OCR to pick out printed text not only from documents discussed earlier but also when reading road signs for self-driving cars. We discuss the structuring of images and computer vision in Section 4.5 and use cases in more detail in Chapter 13 and natural language processing in Section 4.6 and use cases in Chapter 15.

Even if data has a relatively common structure already, such as trade transaction data, we might still want to add other fields to help with additional classification of the dataset. In the case of transaction data, this is likely to involve adding tags to describe the general type of counterparties, such as understanding whether they are on the sell side, buy side, or a corporate firm, for example. As with many types of structuring, this will involve joining it with other datasets.

3.3.4   Treatment of Outliers[6]

Data, even if structured, is invariably fraught with records that could substantially deviate from expected patterns. As with missing data, the primary cause of such technical outliers could be faulty sensors, processes, or mistakes in data collection. These technical outliers can also be referred to as unwanted anomalies or noise. As Huber (1974) puts it, noise accommodation refers to immunizing a statistical model estimation against anomalous observations. Other outliers are not technical but something that is inherent in the data itself and that we actually want to model (e.g. credit card

---

[6]We will use the words "anomaly" and "outlier" interchangeably.

fraud transactions, insurance claims, extreme events in financial time series, or cyber-breaches).

Three types of outliers detection techniques exist[7] – supervised, semi-supervised, and unsupervised:

- Supervised anomaly detection assumes the existence of a labeled dataset of outliers versus normal observations on which a classifier can be trained. Then the model is used on new data records to determine which class they belong to.

- Semi-supervised anomaly detection assumes the existence of a labeled dataset only for the normal class. A model is then built for the class corresponding to normal behavior, and used to identify outliers in the test data.

- Unsupervised anomaly detection means that a labeled dataset is not required, which makes this the most widely used approach. The techniques in this category make the implicit assumption that normal instances are far more frequent than anomalies in the test data.

According to the domain and nature of the data, the type of anomaly, and the challenges associated with anomaly detection, different techniques may be applicable. We will discuss those in much greater detail in Chapter 9.

3.4 AGGREGATING THE DATA

Let's say we have already structured the data to some extent and we have already flagged and treated the outliers. Whatever input data we have, whether images or text, are now in a standardized format. Our dataset is also tagged with metadata fields to help describe the data. Some of these might be text based (like tickers) or numerical. The numerical fields might be car counts, sentiment, and so on.

The next step is to aggregate the data to make it more readily available for use in a trading strategy or a financial model. Typically, time series derived from our alternative data might be available on an irregular frequency while our financial model might be expecting data that has a regular frequency (e.g. every minute, or daily). Hence, we should think about resampling our dataset to fit. If we are getting high-frequency observations from news data, we can think about getting a summary statistic to describe the whole day, whether a mean, median, or some range. Obviously, this resampling will necessitate the loss of some information, but it is essential to creating useful information that can be incorporated into a comprehensive model. The final output is likely to be an index of some sort that can be used as an input into another model.

We could employ many other types of aggregation, in addition to frequency. Another common type of aggregation is that based upon the ticker and also the location or indeed any other category style tags. Indeed, many of the use cases later in the book employ alternative data that has been aggregated by category or ticker.

---

[7] See Chandola (2009).

In some cases, it might be a legal requirement to aggregate parts of the dataset, to ensure that specific people or counterparties are not identifiable, before distribution (see Section 3.1).

3.5 SUMMARY

In the alternative data investment-driven process, there are some potential risks and pitfalls that we have pointed out so far. First, many data sources could contain rapidly decaying signals, no signals at all, or are simply too expensive compared to the strength of the signal that can be extracted. Second, even if there is a signal as of today, there is no guarantee that it will persist long enough in the future to justify the initial investment (price of the data and infrastructure costs). Third, finding talent with the right skillset and domain knowledge is still a challenge at the moment of writing. This could be a significant source of model risk. Finally, in a rapidly evolving world, new laws could emerge daily in different geographies and this can all of a sudden preclude the use of some types of alternative data (e.g. personal data).

We will show in what follows that having the right approach and strategy to navigate the complexities deriving from the use of alternative data is an absolute necessity if one wants to reap rewards hidden in it. Although this sounds like a difficult journey, we believe that in the end it will be worth the effort. But before that let's turn to discuss some methodological challenges that can be encountered along the way.

In this chapter, we also talked about many of the challenges associated with alternative datasets. One of these is entity matching. This involves being able to convert references to entities such as brands or people to traded assets. These references need to be recorded in a point-in-time format. More broadly alternative datasets need to be structured. Often they can be in forms such as images and text, without a common format. We need to convert alternative datasets such as images and text into a more readily consumable form for investors, such as numerical time series. Other challenges we mentioned are not exclusive to alternative datasets, such as being able to deal with missing data and also being able to pick out outliers. We will discuss those in greater detail in Chapters 7, 8, and 9.

CHAPTER 4

Machine Learning Techniques

4.1 INTRODUCTION

In this chapter, we will discuss several topics centered on machine learning. The rationale behind discussing it is that machine learning can be an important part of utilizing alternative data within the investment environment. One particular usage of machine learning concerns structuring the data, which is often a key step in the investment process. Machine learning can also be used to help create forecasts using regressions, such as for economic data or prices, using various factors, which can be drawn from more traditional datasets, such as market data and also alternative data. We can also use techniques from machine learning for classification, which can be useful to help us model various market regimes.

To begin with, we give a brief discussion concerning the variance-bias trade-off and the use of cross-validation. We talk about the three broad types of machine learning, namely supervised, unsupervised, and reinforcement learning.

Then we have a brief survey of some of the machine learning techniques that have applications to alternative data. Our discussion of the techniques will be succinct, and we will refer to other texts as appropriate. We begin with relatively simple cases from supervised machine learning, such as linear and logistic regression. We move on to unsupervised techniques. There is also a discussion of the various software libraries that can be used such as TensorFlow and scikit-learn.

The latter part of the chapter addresses some of the particular challenges associated with machine learning. We give several use cases in financial markets, and which machine learning techniques could be used to solve them, ranging from forecasting volatility to entity matching. We talk about the difficulties that arise when using it with financial time series, which are by nature nonstationary. We also give practical use cases on how to structure images and also text, through natural language processing.

4.2   MACHINE LEARNING: DEFINITIONS AND TECHNIQUES

4.2.1   Bias, Variance, and Noise

This section discusses one of the most important trade-offs that must be considered when building a machine learning model. This trade-off is general and arises regardless of the domain and the task we are focused on. While it is methodological in nature, there are also additional trade-offs between methodology, technology, and business requirements. We will touch upon those in Section 4.4.4. What we can say at this point is that the choices we make here in regard to this trade-off can significantly impact on our investment strategy.

Imagine that we have a dataset $\mathfrak{D}$ and want to model the relationship $y = f(x) + \varepsilon$ with $x, y \in \mathfrak{D}$. As pointed out by Lopez de Prado (2018)[1] models generally suffer from three errors: bias, variance, and noise, which jointly contribute to the total output error. More specifically:

Bias: This error is caused by unrealistic and simplifying assumptions. When bias is high, this means that the model has failed to recognize important relations between features and outcomes. An example of this is trying a linear fit on data whose data-generating process is nonlinear (e.g. quadratic). In this case, the algorithm is said to be "underfit."

Noise: This error is caused by the variance of the observed values, like changes to external variables to the dataset or measurement errors. This error is irreducible and cannot be explained by any model.

Variance: This error is caused by the sensitivity of the model predictions to small changes in the training set. When the variance is high, this means that the algorithm has overfit the training set. Therefore, even minuscule changes in the training set can produce wildly different predictions – for example, fitting a polynomial of degree four to data generated by a quadratic data-generating process. Ultimately, rather than modeling the general patterns in the training set, the algorithm has mistaken the noise for signal. Hence, it was fit to the noise, rather than the underlying signal.

We can express this in mathematical terms as follows. Assume the data-generating process (unknown) is given by $y = f(x) + \varepsilon$ with $E[\varepsilon] = 0$ and $Var(\varepsilon) = \sigma_\varepsilon^2$. f is what we have to estimate. Let's denote by $\widehat{f}$ our estimate. The expected error of the fit by the function $\widehat{f}(x)$ at the point $x = \overline{x}$ is given by:

$$E[(y - \widehat{f}(\overline{x}))^2 | x = \overline{x}]$$
$$= \sigma_\varepsilon^2 + [E[\widehat{f}(\overline{x})] - f(\overline{x})]^2 + E[\widehat{f}(\overline{x}) - E[\widehat{f}(\overline{x})]]^2$$
$$= \sigma_\varepsilon^2 + Bias^2(\widehat{f}(\overline{x})) + Var(\widehat{f}(\overline{x}))$$

$$= Irreducible\ error + Bias^2 + Variance \qquad (4.1)$$

---

[1] See also Hastie (2009), Chapter 7.

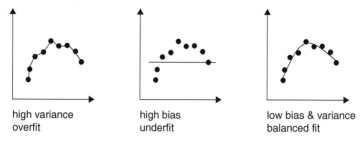

| high variance | high bias | low bias & variance |
| overfit | underfit | balanced fit |

FIGURE 4.1   Balance between high bias and high variance.
Source: Based on data from Towards Data Science (https://towardsdatascience.com/understanding-the-bias-variance-tradeoff-165e6942b229).

Typically, the bias decreases as model complexity[2] increases. The variance, on the other hand, increases.[3] If we assume that the data we are modeling is stationary over the training and test periods, then our aim will be to minimize the expected error of the fit (e.g. when trying to forecast asset returns). This error will then be an interplay between variance and bias and will be influenced by the complexity of the model we choose, as Equation (4.1) shows. Hence, we want to strike a balance between bias and variance. We don't want a model that has high bias or high variance (see Figure 4.1).

Of course, most of the time we will be (hopefully!) making models assumptions rooted in economic theory that will limit the model space, and hence typically reduce the model complexity. Other times we will make sacrifices, such as when required to deliver the results of a calculation on an unstructured dataset quickly and on a device that is slow, for example, a mobile phone – in this case a simpler model could be preferred but we should always keep in mind the trade-off of this section. In essence, we want to make the model simple enough to model what we want, but no simpler.

4.2.2   Cross-Validation

Cross-validation (CV) is a standard practice to determine the generalization capability of an algorithm. When calibrated on a training set it can yield very good fits but out-of-sample its performance can be drastically reduced. In fact, as Lopez de Prado (2018) argues, ML algorithms calibrated on a training set "are no different from file lossy-compression algorithms: They can summarize the data with extreme fidelity, yet with zero forecasting power." Lopez de Prado also argues that CV fails in finance as it is far-fetched to assume that the observations in the training and validation set are i.i.d. (independent and identically distributed). This could happen, for example, due to leakage when training and validation sets contain the same information.

In general, CV is also used for the choice of parameters of a model in order to maximize its out-of-sample predictive power. We do not want to fit parameters that

---

[2]We define complexity as the number of parameters in a model. The Vapnik–Chervonenkis (VC) theory provides a broader measure of complexity, see Vapnik (2013).
[3]The contrary can be observed in specific situations.

happen to simply work in a very short and specific historical period at the cost of poor out-of-sample performance.

For the purposes of an investment strategy, our CV will be determined by the back-testing method, where we specifically leave some historical data for out-of-sample testing. We discussed backtesting methodology in Section 2.5. We will also discuss it again in great length in Chapter 10, and in many of the later use cases in the book. We note that while backtesting has the general flavor of a CV method, it is not subject, at least to the same degree, to the criticisms made earlier. By design, it can better handle non-i.i.d. data, which is what we need.

4.2.3   Introducing Machine Learning

We have already mentioned machine learning a number of times in the text, with reference to many areas of relevance for alternative data, such as structuring datasets and anomaly detection. In the next few sections of the book, we give an introductory look at machine learning and discuss some of the most popular techniques used in this area. Later, we delve into more advanced techniques such as neural networks.

All of machine learning can be split into one of three groups: supervised learning, unsupervised learning, and reinforcement learning. In all types of machine learning, however, we are trying to maximize some score function (or minimize some loss function), whether this is a likelihood (from classical statistics) or some other objective function.

4.2.3.1   Supervised Learning

In supervised learning, for each data point, we have a vector of input variables, x, and a vector of output variables, y, forming a set of (x, y) pairs. The aim is to try to predict y by using x.[4] Within this predictive branch of supervised learning, there are two streams: regression and classification. Regression consists of trying to predict a continuous variable, such as $y \in (-\infty, \infty)$. An example might be predicting a stock's returns using the current interest rate, x_1, and a momentum indicator for the stock, x_2. For classification, we predict which group something belongs in, such as $y \in \{0, 1\}$. An example might be trying to predict whether a mortgage will default (belongs to class 1) given the recipient's credit score, x_1, and the current mortgage interest rate, x_2.

Classification problems are then further subdivided into two categories, generative and discriminative. Generative algorithms provide us with probabilities that the inputs belong to each class, such as P (mortgage will default|credit score of 670) and interest rate of 4% = 0.1. We must then decide how to use these probabilities to assign classes.[5] Discriminative algorithms merely assign a class to each of the input vectors.

In Chapter 14, for example, we use supervised learning in the form of a linear regression to fit earnings per share estimates with various alternative datasets, such as location data and news sentiment for specific US retailers.

---

[4]Our prediction for y is usually denoted $\hat{y}$.

[5]Typically, in binary output, we assign probabilities of more than 0.5 to group 1 and vice versa. For multiclass outputs, we usually assign to the class with the highest probability.

4.2.3.2 Unsupervised Learning

Rather than trying to predict the data, unsupervised learning is about understanding and augmenting the data. Here, instead of having (x, y) pairs, we simply have x vectors (i.e. there is nothing to predict). Outputs of unsupervised learning can often be good inputs to supervised learning models. Among the many subfields of unsupervised learning, the most popular are probably clustering and dimensionality reduction. Clustering is about grouping data points, but without prior knowledge of what those groups might be, whereas dimensionality reduction is about expressing the data using fewer dimensions.

A common example of clustering is in assigning stocks to sectors. This is particularly useful for diversification because it may not be particularly obvious at first that a stock should belong to a sector. By understanding how the elements of our universe form groups (i.e. sectors) we can ensure we don't give any one group too much weight within our portfolio.

4.2.3.3 Reinforcement Learning

For reinforcement learning, rather than map an input vector, x, to a known output vector that denotes some variable, y, either continuous or categorical, we instead want to map an input vector to an action. This is done without prior knowledge of which input vectors we want to map to which actions. These actions then lead to some reward, either immediately or later down the line, decided by some rule set or "environment."

If supervised learning is deciding which stocks will experience positive returns (which we would then decide to buy), then reinforcement learning is about teaching the model which stocks to buy (without explicitly stating so) by allowing it to learn that buying stocks that experience positive returns is a good thing. One way to do this is perhaps by giving it a "reward" proportional to end-of-day P&L and reinforcement learning, therefore, could be useful to derive trading strategies themselves, rather than us building the strategies around fixed rules where the inputs to those strategies come from models.

The difficulty with reinforcement learning is that, because our model starts off as being "dumb" and we often have many choices we could make at any point in time, it requires a very large amount of data to train, likely more than currently exists for any financial market. One way to overcome this is if we could set up a way to artificially generate real enough financial market simulations to allow the model to learn what to do in certain situations, much like how we can simulate games of chess or Go. Doing this, however, is not so simple, although there have been some attempts to address this problem in finance.

Reinforcement learning looks like it could be extremely powerful when applied to finance; however, at present, we are at very early stages. As such, we don't discuss reinforcement learning further in this text. For readers interested in methods of creating synthetic financial data, Pardo (2019) discusses the use of GANs (generative adversarial networks) to create such datasets. It shows how to create financial time series that exhibit similar characteristics to existing time series. For example, it shows how to create many synthetic time series that have similar behavior to the popular VIX index.

4.2.4   Popular Supervised Machine Learning Techniques

4.2.4.1   Linear Regression

Linear regression is probably the first model one should learn in one's attempt to expose oneself to machine learning. It is remarkably simple to understand, quick to implement, and, in many cases, extremely effective. Before attempting any other more complicated model, one should probably attempt a linear model first. This is also our approach in the use case chapters.

Linear regression, unsurprisingly, assumes a linear relationship between the dependent variable, y, and the explanatory variables, x_i. In particular, the model is usually denoted $y = \beta_0 + \sum_{i=1}^{n} \beta_i x_i + \varepsilon$ or $y = x^T \beta + \varepsilon$ with x augmented to include an element that is always 1 to represent the intercept β_0, and ε the error term.[6] In linear regression we are attempting to minimize the sum of the squared errors, $\sum_{i=1}^{n} \varepsilon^2$ (i.e. OLS, ordinary least squares) – see Figure 4.2 for an example. Other than linearity, we further assume that:

- The errors, ε, are:
  - Normally distributed with mean zero, and
  - Homoscedastic (all having the same variance)
- There is no (or suitably small) multicollinearity between the x_i, and
- Errors have no autocorrelation – knowledge of the previous error should not give any information about the next error.

Violations of these assumptions can lead to very strange results. It is, therefore, worth doing some quick checks beforehand to see if they seem to be roughly met. Variations, such as ridge regression, instead minimize a penalized version of the sum of squared errors. This approach is less susceptible to overfitting based on outlying points, making the model less complex, and also deals with some of the problems of multicollinearity between the various x_i.

Linear regression is often used in finance in the modeling of financial time series, given that we often have only small datasets for learning parameters. This is particularly the case if we are limited to using daily or lower-frequency data. This contrasts to techniques such as neural networks, which have many more parameters and hence need much more training data to learn these parameters. Another benefit of linear regressions is that we can often more easily explain the output (within reason, provided there are not too many variables).

This ability to explain the output of a model is important in areas such as finance, particularly if we are trying to do higher-level tasks, such as generate a trading signal. It tends to be less important where we are trying to automate relatively manual tasks, where we can more readily explain a "ground truth." These can include cleaning a dataset or doing natural language processing on a text.

For an example of how linear regression can be used specifically for alternative data models, see Chapter 10, where we use it to create trading strategies for automotive stocks, based on traditional equity ratios and also an alternative dataset based on

---

[6]Linear regression does **not always** assume a linear relationship between dependent and independent variables; we could have a model of $y = \beta_0 + \beta_1 \sin(x)$ and it is still considered to be linear regression.

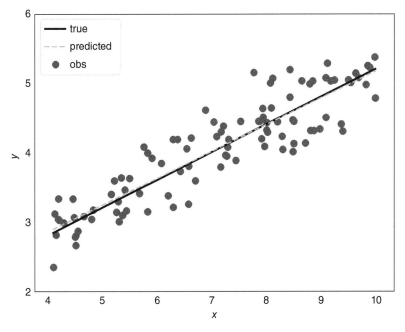

FIGURE 4.2 Visualizing linear regression.

automotive supply chains. Linear regression is also used in many other instances in this book, to help model estimates such as earnings per share, using input variables such as physical customer traffic data derived from location data (see Chapter 14), and using input variables like retailer car park counts derived from satellite imagery (see Chapter 13).

4.2.4.2 Logistic Regression

Logistic regression is to classification what linear regression is to regression. It is, therefore, one of the first machine learning methods one should learn. Like linear regression, logistic regression takes a set of inputs and combines them in a linear fashion to get an output value. If this output value is above some threshold, we classify those inputs as group 1 and otherwise as group 0 (see Figure 4.3). As doing things on a linear scale is slightly confusing, logistic regression converts this linear value to a probability through the use of the logistic function, $f(x) = \frac{1}{1+e^{-x}} = \frac{e^x}{1+e^x}$.

Putting this all together, we calculate the probability that the inputs belong to group 1 by calculating $p = f\left(\beta_0 + \sum_{i=1}^{n} \beta_i x_i\right)$, or $p = f(x^T \beta)$, and classify the inputs to group 1 if $p > 0.5$ and to group 0 otherwise.[7] Similar to linear regression, logistic regression assumes that there is little to no multicollinearity between the x_i. However, as we apply a nonlinear transformation here, instead of requiring a linear relationship

---

[7] It is this prediction (read regression) of probabilities where logistic regression derives its name. We are merely extending it to a classification technique by deciding to assign a class based on this regressed probability.

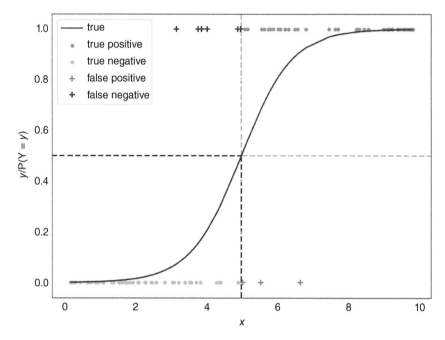

FIGURE 4.3   Visualizing logistic regression.

between the x_i and y, we instead require a linear relationship between the x_i and $\log\left(\frac{p}{1-p}\right)$, the log-odds. The only strict constraint is that an increase in each of the features should always lead to an increase/decrease in the probability of belonging to a class (i.e. increase always causes increase or increase always causes decrease). Like linear regression, logistic regression is likely the first model one should attempt when trying to classify something based on just a few inputs (i.e. not performing something like image classification, although it is possible in theory).

Logistic regression could be used in a variety of situations within finance. Some obvious areas could include classification of different market regimes. We could seek to create a model to classify if markets were ranging or trending. Typical inputs of such a model could include price data for the asset we were seeking to identify and also volatility. Typically, lower levels of volatility are related to ranging markets while increasing levels of volatility tend to be an indication of trend. A simple approach could be used to identify the various risk regimes of a market, using various risk factors as inputs. These risk factors could include credit spreads, implied volatility across various markets, and so on. We could also include alternative datasets such as news volume or readership figures. For example, in Chapter 15, we discuss how news volume can be a useful indicator to model market volatility and we also give specific examples around macroeconomic events like FOMC meetings.

4.2.4.3 Softmax Regression

Although powerful, logistic regression, in the form described above, does not handle the case of multiple classes. Say we want to predict whether a stock will experience returns below -2%, from -2% to 2%, or above 2%. How do we handle this with logistic regression? This is where softmax regression (aka multinomial logistic regression) comes in. We won't get into the mathematics of why softmax regression is the natural extension of logistic regression, but simply state its formula. In softmax regression, for n classes, we take:

$$P(x \in j) = \frac{\exp(w_j^T x)}{\sum_{i=1}^{n} \exp(w_i^T x)}$$

This allows us to predict the class of something in a very similar fashion to logistic regression, only this time with more than two classes. Here it is common to take the class with the highest "probability" as what we classify the inputs to.

4.2.4.4 Decision Trees

Unlike previously mentioned methods, decision trees can be used for both classification and regression. Essentially, decision trees boil down to a series of decisions, such as "Is $x_3 > 5$?" The results of these decisions instruct us on which branch of the tree to follow, left or right. In this way, we can arrive at a set of leaves at the end of our tree. These leaves can feed either to a class (i.e. classify something) or to a continuous variable (i.e. regress something).[8] Generally, for regression, the leaf node i outputs the average value of the dependent variable for all data points that pass the set of rules to arrive at leaf i. Because of their structure, decision trees can easily take in both categorical and continuous variables as inputs. Furthermore, decision trees have none of the linearity assumptions that linear and logistic regression have. Finally, they automatically perform what we call feature selection through their training. After we have trained our model, there may be features that are not used in our tree, an indication that these features are unnecessary.

4.2.4.5 Random Forests

Random forests are an extension of decision trees that make use of the "wisdom of the crowd" mantra, similar to the efficient market hypothesis. Although each individual decision tree is often not particularly performant in itself, if we can train lots of them, their average probably is, assuming we don't just have all trees predicting the same thing. To achieve this, we first perform what is called bagging. Bagging consists of training on only a random subset of the available data. This leads to different trees through different training sets. To further arrive at different trees, instead of randomly selecting data for each tree, at each new node, we only allow the algorithm to select from a random subset of the available features when deciding which to make a split

---

[8] Although, given that there are finite numbers of leaves on our trees, we cannot actually produce continuous predictions, but rather point out interval predictions along the real line.

on. This stops all trees deciding to split on, say, x_1 first, thus leading to an even more diverse set of trees. Finally, now that we have a group of, hopefully, different trees, we take their average prediction as our overall prediction. This group of trees is our random forest. For a use case of random forests in filling missing values in the case of time series data, see Chapter 7.

4.2.4.6 Support Vector Machines

Support vector machines (SVMs) essentially boil down to finding a line (hyperplane) that best separates two different classes of data points. In fact, SVMs are very similar to logistic regression in this sense. Where they differ, however, is how this is achieved. Logistic regression trains to maximize the likelihood of the sample. SVMs train to maximize the distance between the decision boundary (line/hyperplane) and the data points. Figure 4.4 shows an example of a decision boundary in black along with the distance of the nearest points for each class. Obviously, this cannot always be done by a straight line. If we would like to create a model to classify different market regimes, SVM can be considered as an alternative to using logistic regression, which has historically been used for such models.

An important point is that logistic regression is more sensitive to outliers than SVM due to the loss function used. Note that it isn't always the case that having less sensitivity to outliers is advantageous.

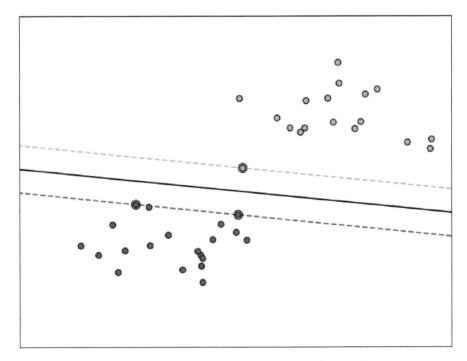

FIGURE 4.4   SVM example: The black line is the decision boundary.

While logistic regression outputs a probability of belonging to each class (it is generative), SVMs simply classify each data point (they are discriminative) and so we don't get a sense of whether data points were "obviously" in a class, such as $p = 0.99$, or somewhere between two classes (on the border), such as $p = 0.51$.

A benefit of SVMs, however, comes in how they deal with nonlinear relationships. Since their invention in 1963, mathematicians came up with the "kernel trick" so that SVMs can support nonlinear decision boundaries. Generally, a kernel is used to embed the data in a higher-dimensional space. In this new space, we may be able to find a linear decision boundary, after which we can transform back to the original space, resulting in a nonlinear decision boundary. In Figure 4.5, we illustrate the kernel trick. We first present a two-dimensional space. We can see that it is difficult to separate the two clusters from drawing a straight line. By converting to a higher-dimensional space, in this case of dimension three, we find that it is now possible to separate out the points with a linear hyperplane.

SVMs have been shown to perform well for image classification. While they do not perform as well as CNNs[9] when there is a large amount of training data at hand (e.g. for image recognition), for smaller datasets they tend to outperform them.

4.2.4.7 Naïve Bayes

The final supervised learning method we will mention is naïve Bayes. Naïve Bayes is a classification algorithm that uses the critical assumption that the value of each feature, x_i, is independent of the value of any other feature, x_j, given the class variable, y.

Using Bayes' theorem, we have that:

$$P(Y = y | X_1 = x_1, X_2 = x_2) = \frac{P(X_1 = x_1 | Y = y)P(X_2 = x_2 | Y = y)P(Y = y)}{P(X_1 = x_1, X_2 = x_2)}.$$

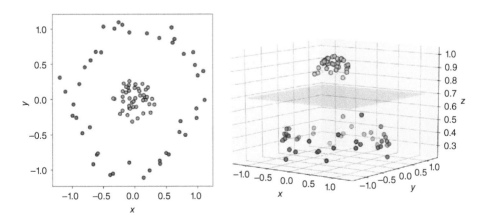

FIGURE 4.5 Kernel trick example.

---

[9]For an introduction on CNNs, see Section 5.3.2.2

In this formula the following assumption was made:

$$P(X_1 = x_1, X_2 = x_2 | Y = y) = P(X_1 = x_1 | Y = y)P(X_2 = x_2 | Y = y)$$

(i.e. the features are independent given the class y). There is not a single algorithm for training naïve Bayes classifiers, but rather a family of algorithms based on the aforementioned assumption.

If the assumption of naïve Bayes is satisfied, it generally performs very well; however, it still can perform well if it is violated. Naïve Bayes often only requires a small amount of data to train on; however, given enough data, it is often surpassed in its predictive ability by other methods, such as random forests.

Naïve Bayes has been shown to be useful for natural language processing and, therefore, can be useful for sentiment analysis. We discuss natural language processing in more detail in Section 4.6.

4.2.5   Clustering-Based Unsupervised Machine Learning Techniques

4.2.5.1   K-Means

K-means attempts to group data points into k groups/clusters. Essentially it randomly assigns k "means" in our data, groups each data point to a "mean" via some distance function, and recalculates the mean of each group. It iterates this process of assigning data points to a group/mean and recalculating mean locations until there is no change. As new data points arrive, we can, therefore, assign them to one of these groups. K-means is used in Chapter 7 to describe the missingness patterns within the data. We also use it in Chapter 9, in a case study based on Fed communication events. There, we find that K-means is particularly effective in identifying outliers in among the various Fed communication events.

As with other clustering algorithms, it also has applicability for identifying similar groups of stocks. As we noted earlier in this chapter, typically, stocks tend to be grouped together based on sectors that have been picked by experts. However, in practice, when using clustering algorithms based on their price moves, we might discover dependencies between stocks that are not necessarily explained by such sector classifications. Furthermore, such approaches are far more dynamic than arbitrary sector classifications, which rarely change over time.

4.2.5.2   Hierarchical Clustering

Rather than assume centroids/means for clusters, hierarchical cluster analysis (HCA) assumes either that all data points are their own cluster, or that all data points are in one cluster. It moves between these two extremes, adding or removing to the clusters based on some notion of distance. An example might be to start with all data points in separate clusters, linking them together according to whichever data point/cluster is nearest to another. This continues this until one ends up with one large cluster. This way one can have any number of clusters k according to the hierarchy one builds by linking clusters together.

If we think of portfolio optimization, Markovitz's critical line approach uses optimization based on forecasted returns, which is hard to estimate. The results can often be quite unstable and can sometimes concentrate risk in a specific asset. Risk parity, on the other hand, doesn't use covariance, and instead weights assets by the inverse of their volatility.

Instead, hierarchical clustering can be used in portfolio construction. Lopez de Prado (2018) introduces the hierarchical risk parity approach in order to do asset allocation and avoids the use of forecasted returns. It doesn't require having to invert a covariance matrix, but instead uses the covariance matrix to create clusters, and then diversifies the portfolio weights between the various clusters.

4.2.6 Other Unsupervised Machine Learning Techniques

Other than clustering, there are many other ways in which we can explore our unlabeled data.

4.2.6.1 Principle Component Analysis

Principle component analysis (PCA) consists of trying to find a new set of orthogonal axes for our data, with each successive axis explaining less of the variance than the previous. By doing this, we can select a small subset of our new axes to use while still being able to explain the majority of the variance in the data. PCA can, therefore, be seen as a sort of compression algorithm. One example of PCA within finance is in interest rate swaps (IRSs) where the first three principal components explain the level, slope, and curvature of the IRS curve, typically explaining 90–99% of the variance. Singular value decomposition, an extension of PCA called singular value decomposition (SVD), is used in Chapter 8 to reconstruct time series and images with missing points.

4.2.6.2 Autoencoders

Although we don't describe them fully now, autoencoders are similar to PCA in that they allow us to express our data via a different representation (encoding) and are typically used for dimensionality reduction. They are also useful in allowing models to learn which combinations of categorical inputs are similar. For more information on autoencoders, see Section 4.2.8.

4.2.7 Machine Learning Libraries

In this section, we describe two of the most popular machine learning libraries that we also use for the use cases we will explore later.

4.2.7.1 scikit-learn

The absolute go-to machine learning Python library for almost all of the above methods is scikit-learn. It offers a high-level API for a plethora of the most popular machine learning algorithms also offering preprocessing and model selection capabilities.

4.2.7.2 glmnet

As the name would suggest, glmnet is used for running general linear models. Originally written for the R programming language, there are now both Python and Matlab ports. It offers methods to train linear, logistic, multinomial, Poisson, and Cox regression models. It has a more statistics-focused set of algorithms than scikit-learn, offering p values and such for trained models.

4.2.8 Neutral Networks and Deep Learning

Now that we have been introduced to the basics of machine learning, let us discuss the current hot topic, neural networks. They have many applications, especially when dealing with unstructured data, which is essentially most of the alternative data world. Roughly speaking, a neural network is a collection of nodes (aka neurons), weights (slopes), biases (intercepts), directed edges (arrows), and activation functions. The nodes are sorted into layers, typically with an input layer, $n \geq 0$ hidden layers, and an output layer. For every layer other than the input layer, each node has nodes from previous layers fed into it (via the directed edges), each of which is multiplied by some weight, summed together and added to a bias.[10] The node output is generated by applying an activation function to this weighted sum.

Ultimately, we need to fit the various parameters of the neural network to the data. As with other machine learning techniques, this involves selecting a set of weights and bias in order to minimize a loss function. The first step is to randomly initialize the various weights of the model. We can then do forward propagation, to compute the node output from the inputs and randomized parameters. The output from this randomized model is then compared to the actual output we want by computing the loss function. In the context of a trading strategy, our model output could be the returns.

The next step is to select new weights, so that we can reduce the loss function. We could attempt to do this by brute force. However, this is typically not feasible given the number of parameters in many neural networks. Instead, we take the derivative of the loss function to understand this will give us the sensitivity of the various weights with respect to the loss function. We can then backpropagate the loss from the loss at the output to the input nodes. The next step is to update the weights, depending on the sign of the derivative. If the derivative is positive, it means that making the weight greater will increase the error, hence we need to reduce the size of that weight. Conversely, a negative derivative implies we should make the weight greater.

We then loop back to the beginning and start again, with our new updated weights, rather than the randomized weights. This exercise is repeated till our model converges to an acceptable tolerance. The learning rate will govern how much we "bump" the weight. The step size needs to be sufficiently small for the search not to skip over local optima. However, if the step size is too small, it will be computationally more expensive to find a solution, given that we will end up doing many more loops.

---

[10]Some architectures, such as recurrent neural networks, allow nodes to feed back into themselves, other nodes in the same layer, or nodes in previous layers.

We shall now follow with some examples of neural networks, and also how to represent other statistical models like linear regressions as neural networks.

4.2.8.1 Introductory Examples

4.2.8.1.1 Linear regression as a neural network In Figure 4.6 we have an input layer, an output layer, and no hidden layers. We have 2 nodes in our input layer, x_1 and x_2, and 1 node in our output layer, y. For the output layer, each node in the previous layer (here our input layer) has an associated weight, w_1 and w_2. We also have a bias, b. To "feed forward" from our input layer to our output layer, we multiply each input by its weight, sum all the results together, and add on the bias. In the case of Figure 4.2 we, therefore, have $y = b + w_1 x_1 + w_2 x_2$, or $y = w^T x + b$, our standard linear regression equation.

4.2.8.1.2 Single class logistic regression as a neural network You may notice that we originally mentioned activation functions, but we have not used them so far. To illustrate the use of an activation function, we now demonstrate logistic regression. Similar to before, we have 2 input nodes and 1 output node (see Figure 4.7). Here, however, instead of the output node having an associated bias and weights for the previous layer, it now also has an associated activation function, f, the logistic (also known as the expit) function, with $f(x) = \frac{1}{1+\exp(-x)}$. Here, the equation becomes $y = f(b + w_1 x_1 + w_2 x_2)$, or $y = f(w^T x + b)$, the standard logistic regression equation. We could say then that previously we used the identity function $f(x) = x$ as the activation function.

4.2.8.1.3 Softmax regression as a neural network Finally, we now show multi-class logistic regression (see Figure 4.8). Notice here that each node on the input layer now has **two** weights associated with it, each pertaining to a different node in the next layer. This is why it makes more sense to think of the weights

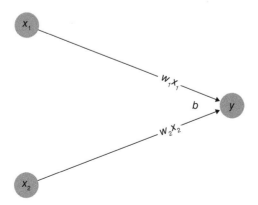

FIGURE 4.6 Visualizing linear regression as a neural network.

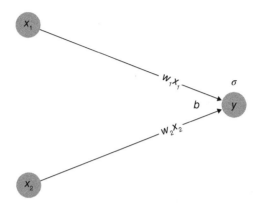

FIGURE 4.7   Visualizing logistic regression as a neural network.

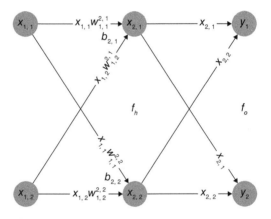

FIGURE 4.8   Visualizing softmax regression as a neural network.

as "belonging" to the node they feed into (and storing them in a vector). For the activation functions, however, they are all the same across this layer, $f_h(x) = \exp(x)$, as is usually the case. From this hidden layer, we then apply another "activation function" by normalizing our scores so that they sum to 1 to represent probabilities, $f_o^i(\mathbf{z}) = \frac{z_i}{\sum_{j=1}^{n} z_j}$. Alternatively, we could have represented this with just input and output layers with a slightly more complex activation function, the softmax function.

Hopefully, from these examples, we can see that, roughly speaking, a neural network is a system of layers of nodes, each of which feeds forward toward some output, whether that be continuous variables for regression, or class probabilities for classification. It is easy to see how more and more of these layers could be added to move further and further away from the "nice," "standard" functions we apply to an input and create highly nonlinear, difficult-to-describe relationships between our input and output vectors.

4.2.8.2 Common Types of Neural Networks

Linear, logistic, and softmax regressions are actually all types of *feed forward* neural network (NN). Although this is one of the most popular types of NN, many others exist. A few popular examples are:

- A **feed forward** neural network is a type of neural network where connections between the nodes do **not** form a cycle. In these networks, the information is only passed forward, from the input layer, through the hidden layers (if there are any), and to the output layer. All those shown in the previous sections are types of feed forward neural networks. Feed forward networks are generally further split into two main types:
  - A multi-layer perceptron (MLP) is the most standard form of neural network. It consists of an input layer, some number of hidden layers (at least one), and an output layer (see Figure 4.9). Each layer feeds to the next and through an activation function. Specifically, all those shown in the previous sections are MLPs. As shown, they can be used for both regression and classification.

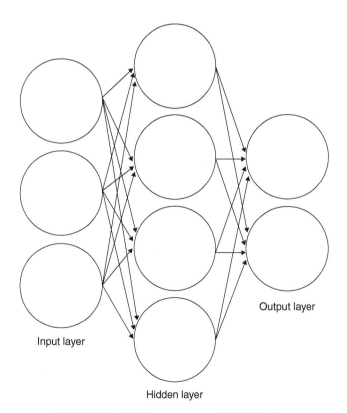

FIGURE 4.9 Multi-layer perceptron with 1 hidden layer.

- ○ **Convolutional** neural networks (CNNs) are popular for problems where there is some sort of structure between the inputs, such as in an image where adjacent pixels give information about the pixel in question. They are in fact a type of feed forward NN, but typically the 2D/3D structure is kept intact (see Figure 4.10). Generally, one passes some sort of "scanner" or "kernel" over the structure, which takes in some n-by-n(-by-n) subset of the image and applies a function to it, before moving one step right and doing the same. This process is repeated across the image from left to right, top to bottom, until we then have some new layer of transformed images. These layers are built up in a similar way to a standard feed forward NN to eventually yield an output layer. CNNs are particularly good at image detection, both in classifying an image and finding objects within an image. We discuss these in Section 4.5.2, in the context of structuring images.

- **Recurrent** neural networks (RNNs) are a class of artificial neural networks where connections between nodes do not have to point "forward" toward the output, but rather can point in any direction other than back to the input layer. This allows it to exhibit temporal dynamic behavior. Unlike feed forward neural networks, RNNs can use these loops (which act like memory) to process a sequence of inputs. As such, they are useful for tasks such as connected handwriting or speech recognition. Given their temporal nature, the hope is that they could provide a breakthrough in financial time series modeling. LSTMs (long short-term memory) are an extension of RNNs, which enable longer-term dependencies in time to be modeled.

- **Autoencoder** neural networks are designed for *unsupervised learning*. They are popularly used as a data compression model to encode input into a smaller dimensional representation, similar to principal component analysis (PCA).

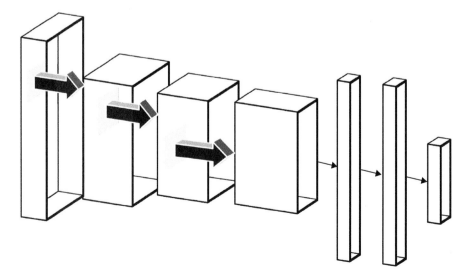

FIGURE 4.10   Convolutional neutral network with 3 convolutional layers and 2 flat layers.

They are trained by first converting to this lower-dimensional representation, before then being decoded to reconstruct the inputs back in the original dimensions, with the loss function increasing the more the reconstructed image deviates from the original. We can then take the layers that reduce the dimensionality of our inputs and use this new output (our encoding) as inputs in a separate model.

- **Generative adversarial** neural networks (GANs) consist of any 2 networks working together, typically a CNN and an MLP, where one is tasked to generate content (generative model) and the other to judge content (discriminative model). The discriminative model must decide if the output of the generative model looks natural enough (i.e. is classified as whatever the discriminative model is trained on). The generator attempts to beat the discriminator and vice versa. Through alternating training sessions, one hopes to improve both models until the generated samples are indistinguishable from the real world. GANs are a current hot topic and look as though they could be very useful for image/speech generation. A particular use within finance could be artificial time series generation as discussed by Pardo (2019), as discussed earlier in this chapter when talking about reinforcement learning. Hence, we can create time series that have the characteristics of specific assets (e.g. VIX or S&P 500). Generating these datasets would allow us to create unlimited training data to further develop reinforcement learning–based models.

4.2.8.3 What Is Deep Learning?

Deep learning (DL) involves the use of neural networks having many hidden layers (i.e. "deep" NNs). This depth allows them to represent highly nonlinear functions that pick up on nonobvious relationships within the data. This contrasts to more traditional types of machine learning, where we typically spend a large amount of time doing feature engineering, which relies upon our domain knowledge and understanding of the problem at hand. LeCun, Bengio, and Hinton (2015) give the example of when deep learning has been applied to the problem of image recognition. The problem of image recognition is often cited as being one of the major successes of deep learning. Typically, the first layer will try to pick up edges in specific areas of the image. By contrast, the second layer will focus on patterns made up of edges. The third layer will then identify combinations of motifs that could represent objects. In all these instances, a human hasn't made these features; they are all generated from the learning process.

Due to their large number of parameters, they require a very large training set in order not to overfit. However, it also allows them to be extremely flexible and pick up on highly nonlinear relationships, often resulting in less feature engineering being required, although there might still well be a certain amount of hand tuning involved, such as understanding the number of layers, which we should include in the model.

4.2.8.4 Neutral Network and Deep Learning Libraries

4.2.8.4.1 Low-level deep learning and neutral network libraries Theano and TensorFlow are to NN libraries as NumPy is to SciPy, scikit-learn, and scikit-image. Without NumPy, many popular scientific computing libraries would not exist today and, similarly, without either Theano or TensorFlow, many of the higher-level deep learning libraries popular today would not exist. Below we describe them in more detail and also outline PyTorch.

- **Theano.** Theano is a Python library used to define, optimize, evaluate, and analyze neural networks. Theano heavily utilizes NumPy while supporting GPUs in a transparent manner. Much like NumPy, although you could build a complete NN using Theano, you probably don't want to, in the same way that you usually don't want to build a logistic regressor from scratch in NumPy, but rather using scikit-learn. Instead, Theano is a library that is often wrapped around by other libraries providing more user-friendly APIs, at the cost of flexibility·

- **TensorFlow.** Like Theano, TensorFlow is another library that can be utilized to build NNs. Originally developed by Google, it is now open source and extremely popular.

- **PyTorch.** More recently, PyTorch has been developed as an alternative to Theano and TensorFlow. It uses a vastly different structure to the aforementioned that results in slower performance but is easier to read and, therefore, easier to debug code. PyTorch has become popular for research purposes, whereas Theano and TensorFlow are more popular for production purposes.

Next, we compare these various libraries in more detail.

- **PyTorch versus TensorFlow/Theano.** So why would one prefer PyTorch over TensorFlow/Theano? The answer is *static* versus *dynamic* graphs. We won't get into the nitty-gritty of what static and dynamic graphs are; however, in summary, PyTorch allows you to define and change nodes "as you go," whereas in TensorFlow and Theano, everything must be set up first and then run. This gives PyTorch more flexibility and makes it easier to debug but also makes it slower. Furthermore, some types of NN benefit from the dynamic structure. Take an RNN used for natural language processing (NLP). With a static graph, the input sequence length must stay constant. This means you would have to set some theoretical upper bound on sentence length and pad shorter sentences with 0s. With dynamic graphs, we can allow the number of input nodes to vary as is appropriate.

- **Theano versus TensorFlow.** If one has decided on Theano or TensorFlow over PyTorch, the next decision is, therefore, Theano or TensorFlow. When deciding between the two, it is important to consider a few things:
  - Theano is faster than TensorFlow on a **single** GPU, whereas TensorFlow is better for **multiple** GPUs/distributed systems, as many of those in production are today.
  - Theano is slightly more verbose, giving more finely grained control at the expense of coding speed.
  - Most importantly, however, the Montreal Institute for Learning Algorithms (MILA) have announced that they have stopped developing Theano since the 1.0 release. Indeed since 2017, there have only been very minor releases.

○ As such, the general consensus seems to be that people prefer TensorFlow, with TensorFlow having 41,536 users, 8,585 watchers, and 129,272 stars on GitHub to Theano's 5,659, 591, and 8,814 respectively at time of print.

It is somewhat a case of "horses for courses," however. TensorFlow is likely the safer bet if one must decide between the two. Another consideration when it comes to performance is the cloud environment one is using.

4.2.8.4.2 High-level deep learning and neutral network libraries For many purposes, users might prefer higher-level libraries to interact with neural networks, which strip away some of the complexity of dealing with low-level libraries like TensorFlow.

- **Keras.** As previously mentioned, there exist many equivalents to scikit-learn, but for NNs, the most popular of which is probably Keras. Keras provides a high-level API to either TensorFlow or Theano; however, Keras is optimized for use with Theano. Google have integrated Keras into TensorFlow from version 2 onwards.

- **TF Learn.** Like Keras, TF Learn is a high-level API, however, this time optimized for TensorFlow. Strangely, although TF Learn was developed with TensorFlow in mind, it is Keras that seems to be more popular on GitHub with 27,387 users, 2,031 watchers, and 41,877 stars to TF Learn's 1,500, 489, 9,121 respectively at the time of writing. In that sense, it is not as clear which of the two to use between Keras or TF Learn as it is with Theano and TensorFlow.

4.2.8.4.3 Middle level deep learning and neutral network libraries

- **Lasagne.** Lasagne is a lightweight library used to construct and train networks in Theano, being less heavily wrapped around Theano than Keras is, providing fewer restraints at the cost of more verbose code. Lasagne acts as a middle ground between Theano and Keras.

4.2.8.4.4 Other frameworks While TensorFlow has become one of the most dominant libraries for neural networks and has become a core part of many higher-level libraries, it is worth noting that there are frameworks available, some of which we discuss here.

- **(Apache) MXNet.** Although it offers a Python API, MXNet is technically a framework rather than a library. The reason we discuss it is that, although it does have a Python API, it also supports many other languages, including C++, R, Matlab, and JavaScript. Furthermore, MXNet is developed by Amazon and, as such, was built with AWS in mind. Although MXNet takes a bit more code to set up, it is well worth it if you plan to perform a large amount of distributed computing using, say, AWS, Azure, or YARN clusters. Finally, MXNet offers both an imperative programming (dynamic graph) structure, like PyTorch, and a declarative programming (static graph) structure, like Theano and TensorFlow.

- **Caffe.** Unlike the other frameworks previously mentioned, Caffe does not provide a Python API in the same way that the others do. Instead, you define your model architecture and solver methods in JSON-like files called .prototxt configuration files. The Caffe binaries use these .prototxt files as input and train your network. Once trained, you can classify new images using the Caffe binaries or through a Python API. The benefit of this is speed. Caffe is implemented in pure C++ and CUDA, allowing roughly 60 million images per day to be processed on a K40 GPU; however, it can make training and using models cumbersome, with programmatic hyperparameter tuning being particularly difficult.

4.2.8.4.5 Processing libraries   Another thing to consider when using alternative data is preparing your data. Although data vendors may provide you with the raw data you require, it may not be labeled or processed for you. Here we focus on general-purpose libraries. Later, in the book, we also discuss libraries specifically relevant for common tasks in structuring alternative data, namely image processing and natural language processing.

- **NumPy.** Although you probably know about NumPy already, many do not utilize it to its full extent. NumPy can be particularly useful when utilized properly due to its vectorized functions. Want to create an image mask? If your image is loaded into a numpy.ndarray, simply type `mask = image < 87`. Want to set pixels under that mask to white? `image[mask] = 255`. Although rudimentary, NumPy is very powerful and should not be overlooked.
- **Pandas.** Similar to NumPy, Pandas has an enormous arsenal of useful (vectorized) functions for us to use, making data preprocessing far easier than with standard Python alone.
- **SciPy.** What can be thought of as an extension of NumPy, SciPy offers another vast set of useful preprocessing functions. From splines to Fourier transforms, if there is some special mathematical/physical function you desire, SciPy is the first place you should look.

4.2.9   Gaussian Processes

In this section, we hint at another useful technique that has come to the fore recently – Gaussian processes (GP). GPs are general statistical models for nonlinear regression and classification that have recently received wide attention in the machine learning community. Given that any prediction is probabilistic when we use Gaussian processes, we can construct confidence intervals to understand how good the fit is. Murphy (2012) notes that having this probabilistic output is useful for certain applications, which include online tracking of vision and robotics. It is also reasonable to conclude that such probabilistic information is likely to be useful when it comes to making financial forecasts.

Gaussian processes were originally introduced in geostatistics (where they are known under the name "Kriging"). They can be also used to combine heterogeneous data sources, which occurs frequently in alternative (and non-alternative) data applications. Work has been done in this area by Ghosal et al. (2016), who use GPs to combine the following data sources: technical indicators, sentiment, option prices, and broker recommendations to predict the return on the S&P 500. Before discussing the paper of Ghosal (2016), we will briefly illustrate Gaussian processes based on that paper. For more details we refer the reader to Rasmussen (2003).

A Gaussian process is a collection of random variables, any finite subset of which has a joint Gaussian distribution. Gaussian processes are fully parametrized by a mean function and covariance function, or kernel. Given a real process, $f(x)$, a Gaussian process is written as:

$$f(x) \sim \mathcal{GP}(m(x), k(xx'))$$

with $m(x)$ and $k(x, x')$ respectively the mean and covariance functions:

$$m(x) = \mathbb{E}[f(x)]$$

$$k(x, x') = \mathbb{E}[(f(x) - m(x)) \times (f(x') - m(x'))]$$

with centered input set $X = \{x_1, \ldots, x_n\}$, output set $y = \{y_1, \ldots, y_n\}$. The Gaussian Process f, the distribution of $f = [f(x_1), \ldots, f(x_n)]^T$ is a multivariate Gaussian:

$$f \sim \mathcal{N}(0, K)$$

where $K_{i,j} = k(x_i, x_j)$. Conditional on f, we have:

$$y_i \mid f(x_i) \sim \mathcal{N}(0, \sigma_n^2)$$

where σ_n^2 parameterizes the noise. Due to the Gaussian distribution being self-conjugate, we have the following marginalization (independent of x, i.e. for a point in general, possibly where we have no observations):

$$y_i \sim \mathcal{N}(0, K + \sigma_n I)$$

When it comes to making a prediction, y^*, at some new unseen point, x^* (i.e. conditioning on the training data) we then have that:

$$y^* \mid x^*, X, y \sim \mathcal{N}(k^*(K + \sigma_n^2 I)^{-1} y, k^{**} - k^*(K + \sigma_n^2 I)^{-1} k^{*T})$$

where $K_{i,j} = k(x_i, x_j)$, $k^* = [k(x_1, x^*), \ldots, k(x_n, x^*)]$ and $k^{**} = k(x^*, x^*)$.

This setup allows us to encode prior knowledge of f through the covariance function $k(x, x')$ with observation data to create a posterior distribution based on our observations. The choice of k, often called a kernel, allows us to dictate what behavior we would expect from points based on their proximity to one another. One such as the Gaussian Radial Basis Function allows us to encode the fact that points nearby in vector space should realize similar values of f.

As Chapados (2007) points out, Gaussian processes differ from neural networks in that they rely on a full Bayesian treatment, providing a complete posterior distribution of forecasts. In the case of regression, they are also computationally relatively simple to implement. In fact, the basic model requires only solving a system of linear equations, albeit one of size equal to the number of training examples, that is, requiring $O(N^3)$ computation. However, one of the drawbacks of Gaussian processes is that they tend to be less well suited to higher-dimensional spaces.

As explained by Chapados (2007), a problem with more traditional linear and nonlinear models is that making a forecast at multiple time horizons is done through iteration in a multi-step fashion. Furthermore, conditioning information, in the form of macroeconomic variables, can be of importance, but exhibits the cumbersome property of being released periodically, with explanatory power that varies across the forecasting horizon. In other words, when making a very long-horizon forecast, the model should not incorporate conditioning information in the same way as when making a short- or medium-term forecast. A possible solution to this problem is to have multiple models for forecasting each time series, one for each time scale. However, this is hard to work because it requires a high degree of skill on the part of the modeler, and is not amenable to robust automation when one wants to process hundreds of time series. Chapados (2007) offers a GP-based solution to forecasting the complete future trajectory of futures contracts spreads arising on the commodities markets.

As for Ghoshal (2016), they analyze 12 factors that are thought to be signals for the next day's S&P 500 returns, split into technical, sentiment, price-space, and broker-data groups. They choose those deemed to have a significant correlation with the target to analyze further, namely; (1) 50-day SMA; (2) 12-day, 26-day, exponential MACD; (3) Stocktwits sentiment factor; (4) a "directionality" factor and; (5) a "viscosity" factor. Testing both stationary and adaptive Gaussian process models, they show that they can outperform their stationary/adaptive autoregressive model benchmarks in both cases, even when just using factors from one group. Furthermore, they also show how GP models can give us the relevance of a factor (either stationary over a whole period or adaptive over time). We will present an application of GPs in the case study in Chapter 10.

4.3   WHICH TECHNIQUE TO CHOOSE?

There is no general-purpose algorithm that can provide a best solution for all the problems at hand. Every problem, depending on its domain, complexity, accuracy, and speed requirements, might warrant a different methodological approach, and hence will result in different best-performing algorithms. The no-free-lunch (NFL) theorems have been stated and proven in various settings[11] centered on supervised learning and search. They show that no algorithm performs better than any other when their performance is averaged uniformly over all possible problems of a particular type. This means that we need to develop different models and different training algorithms for each of them to cover the diversity of problems and constraints we encounter in the real world.

With the mass advent of unstructured data, we may need to use more advanced techniques to those traditionally used within finance. For example, the analysis of unstructured data such as images cannot yield good results with the standard statistical tools. Logistic regression can be used for this task, but the classification accuracy is generally low. There have been recent developments in the machine learning field that now allow us to analyze images, text, and speech with a higher level of accuracy. Deep learning is one such development. Deep learning for a variety of image

---

[11] See Schaffer (1994) and Wolpert (2002).

recognition tasks, for example, has surpassed human performance.[12] We discussed deep learning in Section 4.2.8.

We itemize the techniques typically used to solve the most common types of problems, based on our experience (see Table 4.1). The list is not exhaustive and techniques different from the ones in the list could also fare well, so the reader should take this list as a starting map, not an absolute prescription. We will describe typical use cases that are of interest to the financial practitioner in the left column of

TABLE 4.1   Financial (and non-) problems and suggested modeling techniques.

Market regime identification	Hidden Markov Model
Future price direction of assets, basket of assets and factors	Linear regression, LSTM[13]
Future magnitude of price change of assets, basket of assets and factors	Linear regression, LSTM
Future volatility of assets, basket of assets and factors	GARCH (and variants), LSTM
Assets and factors clustering and how it changes over time	K-means clustering, SVM
Asset mispriced to the market	Linear regression, LSTM
Probability of an event occurring (e.g. market crash)	Random forests
Forecast company and economic fundamentals	Linear regression, LSTM
Forecast volume and flow of traded assets	GARCH (and variants), LSTM
Understanding market drivers	PCA
Events study (reaction of prices to specific events)	Linear regression
Mixing of multi-frequency time series	Gaussian processes
Forecasting changes in liquidity of trading	Linear regression, LSTM
Feature importance in asset price movements	Random forest
Structuring	
• Images	Convolutional neural networks
• Text	BERT,[14] XLNet[15]
• Speech	Deep neural networks–Hidden Markov model
• Video	Convolutional neural networks
Missing data imputation	Multiple singular spectral analysis
Entity matching	Deep neural networks

---

[12]See https://www.eff.org/ai/metrics for up-to-date performance benchmarks on different datasets. See Geirhos (2017) for different examples and comparisons of human vs machine performance under image degradations like contrast reduction, additive noise, or novel eidolon-distortions.

[13]Long Short-Term Memory is an artificial recurrent neural network.

[14]Bidirectional Encoder Representations from Transformers.

[15]XLNet is a generalized autoregressive model for natural language understanding based on Transformers-XL

the table. Corresponding suggestions are in the right column, many of which use models we have discussed earlier in this chapter. We also refer the reader to Kolanovic and Krishnamachari (2017), which has a larger list of various finance-based problems and potential machine learning methods that can be used to solve them.

In the latter part of this chapter we give some practical examples of using various techniques for structuring images and text.

In order to select the best method to analyze data, it is necessary to be acquainted with different machine learning approaches, their pros and cons, and the specifics of applying these models to the financial domain. In addition to knowledge of models that are available, successful application requires a strong understanding of the underlying data that are being modeled, as well as strong market intuition.

4.4   ASSUMPTIONS AND LIMITATIONS OF THE MACHINE LEARNING TECHNIQUES

Machine learning and, in general, quantitative modeling is based on assumptions and choices made at the modeling stage whose consequences we must be aware of. They seem trivial but in practice we have seen a lack of awareness about what these assumptions entail. First, there is difference between causality and correlation and it is the former we need most of the time when making predictions. Second, nonstationary data makes learning very difficult and unstable in time, yielding unreliable results. Third, it is important to bear in mind that a dataset we work on is always a subset of variables that might drive a phenomenon. Precious information that can complement a dataset might lie in other, different datasets, or even in our expert knowledge. Last, the choice of the algorithm must be determined given its known limitations, the data at hand, and the business case. We now turn to discuss these aspects in detail.

4.4.1   Causality

In the previous sections, we have provided a list of suggested different machine learning techniques according to the use case but there is a common aspect (and a potential problem) to many of the applications that we must be aware of. In classification (prediction) tasks we always try to learn the functional relationship between a set of inputs and an output(s). In doing so, we will likely encounter an old known problem – spurious correlations, or statistical coincidences. But even if a relationship between two variables is causal (i.e. there is no third variable acting as a confounder), a neural network, or even the much simpler linear regression, cannot tell the direction of causality, and hence input and output can be exchanged finding equally strong association.

Nevertheless, for certain tasks, in order to have a robust model, one that does not frequently need recalibration and whose results hold through time, solid domain-specific reasoning is warranted when building it.[16] This is to say that the causes must

---

[16]Sometimes, causality is not required, such as when counting cars in images or extracting sentiment from text. However, causality is necessary in macroeconomic forecasting, for example.

be the inputs to a model trying to predict an output (the effect). As Pearl (2009) points out, causal models have a set of desirable characteristics. To use his terminology, casting a treatment of a problem in terms of causation:

- Will make the judgments about the results "robust"
- Will make them well suited to represent and respond to changes in the external environment
- Will allow the use of conceptual tools that are more "stable" than probabilities
- Will also permit extrapolation to situations or combinations of events that have not occurred in history

When it comes to practicalities one must make sure that the processes by which the training data is generated are stable and that the relationships being identified are relationships that occur because of these stable causal processes. This can be a tricky task as most of the time causal relationships between variables are not known or nonexistent. However, we must be sure that we have inputted the best of our domain knowledge into the problem at hand. This leads us to another important point: stationarity.

4.4.2   Non-stationarity

The lack of stationarity is very tricky to deal with and in most cases machine learning models cannot cope with it. In fact, learning always assumes that the underlying probability distribution of the data from which inference is made stays the same. This is a condition that is hardly encountered in practice. We note that stationarity does not ensure good (or any) predictive power as it is a necessary but nonsufficient condition for the high performance of an algorithm. If we take the examples where deep learning has been particularly successful, it has typically been where the characteristics of the underlying dataset are relatively static, such as identifying cats in photos[17] or counting cars in parking lots or language translation.

The change in the distribution of data contained in development/test datasets versus the data in the real world on which a model is subsequently applied is called dataset shift (or drifting). Dataset shift could be divided into three types: (1) shift in the independent variables (covariate shift), (2) shift in the target variable (prior probability shift), and (3) shift in the relationship between the independent and the target variable (concept shift). Only the first type has been extensively studied in the literature (see e.g. Sugiyama, 2012) and there are some recipes of dealing with it while the other two are still being actively researched.

Financial time series exhibit non-stationarity, such that properties like their mean and variance can change significantly and the underlying probability distribution can change in a totally unpredictable way. This can be particularly observed during periods of market turbulence where there are structural breaks in the time series of many

---

[17]Cats do not change over time, especially after we observe them!

variables (e.g. volatility). These can be especially brutal for, say, managed currencies, where volatility is kept artificially low through central bank intervention and then explodes when central banks no longer have sufficient funds to keep the currency within a tight bound.

4.4.3   Restricted Information Set

Another important point is that any algorithm is trained on a restricted information set – both number of features and history – given by the specific dataset. Thus the insights that can be derived are inherently limited to what is contained in that dataset. In this sense, algorithms are blind to what happens outside of their narrow world. Essentially, data you have does not tell you about the data you do not have. To borrow the terminology popularized by Donald Rumsfeld, these are essentially known unknowns.

This could become quite problematic when trying to predict market crashes, which are rare events. Often early warning indicators can be found by looking outside the dataset and be integrated with the findings of an algorithm that operates on that dataset. However, the triggers for market crashes can vary significantly. For example, indicators within the emerging markets may have been useful for predicting many crises in the early 2000s and in particular the Asian Crisis in 1997. However, they would not have been as important for predicting the global financial crisis, which emanated from developed markets, such as in US subprime, before spreading. Variables related to developed market credit spreads would have been far more insightful in this instance than those related to emerging markets that moved later after the contagion. Commonly this can be done through a human-in-the-loop intervention to correct or complement the inputs/outputs of a model. In this case humans can exceed algorithms as knowledge of the context is sometimes more useful than tons of past data. Humans are sometimes extremely good at prediction with little data. We can recognize a face after seeing it only once or twice, even if we see it from a different angle or years after we last saw it. Deep learning algorithms, on the other hand, require hundreds if not thousands of images in the training set.

See Agrawal et al. (2018) for a more detailed reasoning on this topic. Of course, there are also the unknown unknowns. These elude both machines and humans. Last, in Agrawal et al.'s lingo (but not in Rumsfeld's), there are the unknown knowns where the algorithm gives an answer with a great confidence, but this can be spurious because the true underlying causality is not understood by it. We refer to Agrawal et al. for more details.

4.4.4   The Algorithm Choice

Finally, the choice of an algorithm – another assumption – will be important in the use case at hand and it must be guided by the nature of the problem we are trying to solve and the amount of data available. As already mentioned, there is no best-performing universal algorithm. Deep learning models do an excellent job counting cars in parking lots, or extracting sentiment from text, but they might not perform as well when predicting financial time series, in particular for lower-frequency data. Where data is particularly scarce, we could find that simpler machine learning techniques such as linear regression may be a better choice than more complicated deep learning approaches.

So what are the typical problems we face in finance? First, financial time series have a low signal-to-noise ratio. Image recognition systems are very sensitive to noise. Hence, for instance, adding some white noise to an image could completely alter the result of a classification. Second, the amount of data is sometimes not sufficient because deep learning is known to be data greedy. We can enlarge the sample to include more data points from the past. However, we may encounter the non-stationarity issues discussed in Section 4.4.2 given the continually changing nature of markets and the economy. For example, this approach is unlikely to be useful to backtest a high-frequency trading strategy, if we end up examining historical periods when the market was dominated by human market makers and had a very different market microstructure. These types of markets were very different from subsequent periods when electronic traders have come to dominate short-term price action.

We could use deep learning techniques, such as LSTM (long short-term memory) to explore time series from high-frequency order book data. As we noted earlier in this chapter, the benefit of LSTM over ordinary recurrent neural networks (RNNs) is that they can capture longer-term dependencies in the data while also forgetting less relevant events. Hence, LSTMs can learn over many time steps. The ability to be able to explain these longer-term dependencies is key to time series modeling. Indeed, without the ability to model longer term relationships in a time series, we would have difficulty modeling many patterns. These patterns would, for example, include those associated with seasonality (for example, time of day, day of the week, etc.).

In a high-frequency trading environment, we have very large amounts of data to train such a model, not only the number of trades executed but also the much larger dataset of all published quotes. Even in this instance, there are still likely to be multiple challenges, in particular making sure that once a model is trained, it can be executed quickly. If a high-frequency trading model cannot be run sufficiently quickly, then it will be impossible to monetize any of its trade recommendations. High-frequency trading strategies are often very latency sensitive.

Bearing all these issues in mind for the future, we now turn to discussing image and text structuring and understanding.

4.5 STRUCTURING IMAGES

4.5.1 Features and Feature Detection Algorithms

When interpreting an image, humans try to focus on important elements and often ignore much of the image. In a sense, we are subconsciously doing a dimensionality reduction of the data. The principle is similar in computer vision where we might seek to convert an image into a feature vector. Many alternative datasets that are relevant for finance are originally derived from images. While it might be possible for a human to interpret an image, when the volume of images becomes significant, this is not possible. Hence, having effective automated techniques to process these images is important. In Chapter 13, we specifically give use cases for satellite imagery for investors. These datasets can be derived from many thousands of images that would be very costly to process in a manual way and would also be prone to inconsistencies.

In image recognition, we essentially seek to extract important features from an image, which we hope are most useful for understanding its content. Salahat and Qasaimeh (2017) discuss some ideal properties of such features, which we summarize here. Some features within the image can be related to boundaries. Edges occur where there are sudden changes in the pixel intensity. Corners, meanwhile, occur where edges join. Some features are based on blobs or regions. Different blobs will be differentiated by differences in terms of brightness, color, and so on. Figure 4.11 presents a summary of various feature detector algorithms, breaking them down by their category and what their classifier is based on (Salahat and Qasaimeh, 2017).

So what are the ideal properties of features? Features should be distinctive so they can be distinguished from one another. They need to cover a relatively small area. In other words, they need to be local. It needs to be computationally efficient to compute the features. This is particularly relevant if we are using them for real-time applications, such as detecting objects in real-time video feeds.

Features should be repeatable, so should be relatively stable from frame to frame. For this to be the case, they need to be invariant to changes in perspective and rotation. A horse, for example, looks very different in profile compared to head on. Regardless of the angle of its image, it is still very much a horse. Furthermore, they shouldn't be affected by factors impacting image quality such as noise, blur, and compression

Category	Classification	Methods and Algorithms
Edge-based	Differentiation based	Sobel, Canny
Corner-based	Gradient based	Harris (and its derivatives), KLT, Shi-Tomasi, LOCOCO, S-LOCOCO
Corner-based	Template based	FAST, AGAST, BRIEF, SUSAN, FAST-ER
Corner-based	Contour based	ANDD, DoG-curve, ACJ, Hyperbola fitting, etc.
Corner-based	Learning based	NMX, BEL, Pb, MS-Pb, gPb, SCG, SE,tPb, DSC, Sketch Tokens, etc.
Blob (interest point)	PDE based	SIFT (and its derivatives), SURF (and its derivatives), CenSurE, LoG, DoG, DoH, Hessian (and its derivatives), RLOG, MO-GP, DART, KAZE, A-KAZE, WADE, etc.
Blob (key point)	Template based	ORB, BRISK, FREAK
Blob (interest region)	Segmentation based	MSER (and its derivatives), IBR, Salient Regions, EBR, Beta-Stable, MFD, FLOG, BPLR

Source: Based on data from Salahat and Qasaimeh (2017).

FIGURE 4.11   Various edge, corner, and blob-based feature detectors.

Features Detector	Invariance			Qualities			
	Rotation	Scale	Affine	Repeatability	Localization Robustness	Robustness	Efficiency
Harris	Y	–	–	+++	+++	+++	++
Hessian	Y	–	–	+++	++	++	+
SUSAN	Y	–	–	++	++	++	+++
Harris-Laplace	Y	Y	–	+++	+++	++	+
Hessian-Laplace	Y	Y	–	+++	+++	+++	+
DoG	Y	Y	–	++	++	++	++
Salient Regions	Y	Y	Y	++	+	++	+
SURF	Y	Y	–	++	+++	++	+++
SIFT	Y	Y	–	++	+++	+++	++
MSER	Y	Y	Y	+++	+++	++	+++

Source: Based on data from Salahat & Qasaimeh (2017).

FIGURE 4.12   Dominant feature detection algorithms and their properties.

artifacts. In Figure 4.12, we list some of the various feature detector algorithms and how they fare in terms of these various idealized feature qualities from Salahat and Qasaimeh (2017).

So how can we use these features in practice for a computer vision problem like image classification? The first step is to label the images we have, for example, "burger" and "other." Then we need to convert all the images into their respective feature vector representations by using a feature detector algorithm. The problem can then be solved as a classification-style supervised machine learning problem. In this instance, we are essentially trying to partition a high-dimensional hyperspace into areas for "burger" and "other." Our hyperspace consists of many points, each of which feature a vector representing an image. We could attempt to use a linear model, such as logistic regression to partition this space. However, it is likely that nonlinear techniques like SVMs (support vector machines) would yield better results.

4.5.2   Deep Learning and CNNs for Image Classification

Our discussion on computer vision has largely centered on constructing feature vector representations using feature detection algorithms related to edges, corners, and blobs. This approach seems intuitive given its similarity to the way we interpret an image. Is there a better way to extract features that could yield better accuracy for example for image recognition? Potentially can we automatically identify higher-level features? Would this do a better job than a feature detection algorithm where we preprocess an image for features based on intuitive features like corners?

We can use deep learning to "discover" appropriate features, as mentioned earlier in this chapter, as opposed to trying to create them ourselves by hand (i.e. feature engineering). In particular, convolutional neural networks have been successful in the area of image recognition, as we mentioned earlier. A CNN essentially skips the step where we apply a feature detection algorithm. Instead, it uses raw pixel data as an input feature map, where each pixel is basically a vector consisting of entries of red, green, and blue values. We can think of the convolution operation as a sliding tile, which sweeps over the original image. As the tile slides over the image on overlapping parts of the image, it creates an output feature map, constructing a dot product. In other words, it does a summation over the elementwise multiplications with a set of weights. The size of the "slide" is known as the stride. Dumoulin and Visin (2018) explains the impact of the stride and other factors in the convolution operation.

This matrix of weights is known as a filter. Traditionally, the filter would have been handcrafted to pick up specific relatively intuitive features, such as a horizontal, vertical, or diagonal edge. However, in this case, we instead start with randomized weights, which are later "fitted," so we can learn the important features, rather than prespecifying them.

It is common to have multiple filters applied, which increases the depth of the output. It is important to note that the convolution step allows us to keep some of the relationship between pixels that are near to each other. If this relationship was lost, it would make it much more difficult to make sense of the image. The more filters are used, the more features can be extracted by the CNN.

A nonlinearity is then introduced to the convoluted feature using a Rectified Linear Unit (ReLU). The ReLU outputs the maximum of each matrix element and zero. Recalling our introduction to neural networks, this is a prominent recent example of an activation function. Following this, there is the pooling step, where the convolution feature is downsampled. This reduces the number of parameters and hence reduces computation time necessary when training the network. There can be several convolutional and pooled layers after each other. The idea is that through these multiple steps we can capture the important parts of the image for classification purposes while discarding the less relevant parts.

After the convolutional and pooled layers, we flatten the image into a long vector. The next step is to have some fully connected layers, which perform the classification step for the N classes of objects we wish to identify. The final connected output layer will give a probability for the input image matching a classification such as "Is this a burger?" The network can be trained to fit the optimal weights through backpropagation. Typically, techniques based upon CNN are far more prevalent these days when it comes to image classification, compared to those using handcrafted features. The downside of such techniques is that it can sometimes be more difficult to understand why a certain output has been generated, because the features created may not always be intuitive. We could argue that for image recognition this is less of a concern, because the task they are performing is simply automating a task that a human can do and check.

4.5.3   Augmenting Satellite Image Data with Other Datasets

Recognizing objects from a satellite image can be done using the techniques described earlier. However, this is not the only step we need to structure image data in order for it to be useful for investing purposes. For each satellite image, there is associated geospatial data, such as GPS coordinates, the timestamp, and so on. This data can be joined with datasets containing addresses. As a result, the objects detected on the image can be annotated with additional tags. These tags can help us answer questions we can't answer from the satellite image alone. These questions can include whether the location is associated with a particular business, which particular city and country it is in, and so on. Typically, we might also wish to understand changes in a location over time, in particular if we wish to construct time series for use by investors. We give a use case later in the book in Chapter 13, where we discuss how investors can use satellite imagery of retailer car parks to help forecast earnings per share for these companies.

4.5.4   Imaging Tools

In practice, if we want to process images, there are many existing libraries that can help us, including:

- **scikit-image.** Another member of the scikit family, scikit-learn, while not offering anything particularly fancy, offers a clean and simple API that is quick to pick up with a plethora of useful functions. Want to find edges with a Sobel filter? `edges = skimage.filters.sobel(image)`.
- **SciPy.ndimage.** Probably one of SciPy's lesser known submodules is scipy.ndimage. Providing many functions that can be applied to numpy.ndarrays it certainly comes in handy now and then. Want to blur an image? `scipy.ndimage.gaussian_filter(image, sigma=1)`.
- **Matplotlib.** Although generally used in analysis/exploration, matplotlib offers a GUI to interact with images and can be used for centroid/bounding-box labeling by using its event handling capabilities.
- **Pillow.** Pillow, a fork from the now deprecated PIL, offers many basic image processing functions, such as brightness and contrast altering functions.
- **OpenCV.** Open CV is another framework that offers a Python API. A very powerful library with many pre-trained models, one could spend a lifetime learning all the ins and outs of OpenCV.
- **SimpleCV.** SimpleCV can be thought of as the Keras of image processing. It offers access to several computer vision libraries, such as OpenCV, but with a higher-level wrapper, resulting in a shallower learning curve.

4.6   NATURAL LANGUAGE PROCESSING (NLP)

4.6.1   What Is Natural Language Processing (NLP)?

Many alternative datasets consist of text. The web itself consists mostly of text. If we ignore text-based data on the web, we are essentially ignoring a lot of information that could potentially be useful from an investment perspective. In Chapter 15, we discuss many investment use cases for text, ranging from using social media to help make economic data estimates to using news sentiment to understand market sentiment. In order to make trading decisions using text data, we have to go through a number of steps. In particular, given the volume of text data, we need to have automated ways to analyze text. This is where natural language processing (NLP) can help us.

In a nutshell, NLP can be seen as a way for a computer to understand human language. However, in order to do NLP, we should first define the various parts of natural language. Briscoe (2013) describes the various components of natural or human language and gives an overview of NLP.

At the lowest level we have phonetics, which involves the specific sounds generated by a human. Built on top of this we have phonology, which examines the sounds of a particular language. The next level, morphology, looks at how words have been constructed and their decomposition. For example, the word "burgers" can be broken down into "burger" (which is a root) and "s" (which is a suffix showing plurality). We can have many other types of construction, such as different verbal forms like eating (verb), eating (adjective), and eating (noun). For certain languages, such as Arabic, morphology can be very important. At their root, Arabic verbs usually consist of three root letters (or sometimes four letters in certain cases) from which we can derive many different verb forms and related words, such as verbal nouns, which in other languages may have different roots. For example, in Arabic the verbs for "to teach" and "to learn," which have related meanings, have the same root. This contrasts with English where each word is totally different.

Syntax is the way in which words are combined to make sentences. The grammar will dictate how words can be combined together to form a grammatically correct sentence. Some languages, such as English, have the word order SVO (subject-verb-object). By contrast, Arabic tends to be VSO (verb-subject-object). However, for any particular set of words, there are likely to be several different grammatically correct word orders, each of which have different meanings. For example, both "Alex consumes burgers" and "Burgers consume Alex" are grammatically correct, but clearly they have totally different meanings. Indeed, in English, without any word order there would likely be a significant amount of ambiguity for the meanings of words. Potentially, though, we could have a more flexible ordering where words change depending on their place in a sentence, which is referred to as an inflected language. Latin is an example of such a language, where extensive use of case endings lets us tell whether, for example, a word is a subject or an object, without the need to adhere to a strict word order.

Semantics is about the meaning of language. We should be able to understand a sentence so we can answer questions like *who*, *what*, *why*, *where*, *how*, and *when*. Pragmatics refers to understanding the text with context, which often requires knowledge of information beyond the text itself.

NLP attempts to tackle problems at the various levels described above. Doing any sort of analysis of syntax first involves word tokenization/segmentation to identify words. We can then do other NLP tasks such as tagging the parts of speech (e.g. that words are nouns, verbs, adverbs, and so on).

At the semantic level, there are also a number of important NLP tasks. One of the most important is named entity recognition, to identify specific people, organizations, locations, and so on, and also being able to do relation extraction between their entities. An ability to extract the events and the temporal meaning is key. This is particularly true from the context of an investor, where we are likely to place more weight on forward-looking statements, compared to a review of historical market moves.

We also need to identify the semantic roles in the sentence, such as identifying the agent of the action and the target. More simply, an example of this can be asking, "Who is doing what to whom?" Again, this is very important for understanding the significance of a statement. If the president of the United States calls for sanctions against an oil-producing nation, this is of more relevance than a State Department spokesperson. Semantic role labeling is an automatic way to find these roles. We also have sentiment analysis to understand how positive or negative a text is. We might also wish to do topic recognition to identify the general subjects being discussed in a document.

NLP can therefore help us in our task of adding metadata to a particular text helping to identify the following:

- Topic of the content: What is it generally about politics, economy, the weather, and so on?
- Entities listed in the content: Are there any specific people mentioned, or companies, and in particular do they relate to any tradable assets?
- Sentiment of the content: Is it broadly positive or negative?

In the following sections, we briefly examine a few topics from NLP. For readers wishing to have an in-depth and more exhaustive look at NLP, we recommend reading Jurafsky and Martin (2019) and we have used that as a reference in this chapter. There are also many other tasks in NLP that are not related to understanding only. They can involve generation and summarization of text, too.

4.6.2 Normalization

Normalization involves breaking down the text into a more common form. Word segmentation or tokenization involves identifying separate words in text. In English, words are generally broken up by spaces, but we need to be aware of many exceptions. For example, "Burger King" could be considered a word despite having a space. At the same time, we also need to be aware of words that might be written in different ways, such as "KFC" instead of "Kentucky Fried Chicken," which are specific named entities. Other languages such as Chinese need different techniques for word tokenization. Jurafsky and Martin (2019) discuss using a maximum matching algorithm for word tokenization for Chinese, which requires a dictionary of Chinese. By contrast this algorithm has more difficulties in English. Sentence segmentation, as the name suggests, involves identifying separate sentences. Again, we might be able to utilize full stops as a marker, but need to be careful so we are not confused by full stops used in other contexts like initials. Once the words have been separated, we can put the words into more common forms, which involves lemmatization and stemming. The words "ate," "eaten," and "eats" are just different forms of the same verb. Lemmatization would involve normalizing them to the root form "eat." Stemming involves the simpler normalization of words like rendering plural nouns into their singular form. Obviously, what constitutes a word depends on the language!

A large number of common words are also unlikely to help with understanding the text and are simply used for grammatical reasons, such as "the" and "a." These are classified as stop words and are typically removed during the normalization stage. However, as in our previous example of "Burger King," we need to be wary of removing stop words, which could cause issues with named entity recognition. Let's take the example of the pop band "The 1975." We could use it in that specific context – for example, "The 1975 won a Brit award." However, another obvious context would be using it to refer to something that occurred in the year 1975, such as "The 1975 United Kingdom European Communities membership referendum resulted in entry to Europe." If we had removed the stop word of "The," it would have caused issues of understanding for the first sentence but not for the second sentence.

4.6.3   Creating Word Embeddings: Bag-of-Words

One of the simplest techniques to analyze a text involves using a technique known as bag-of-words. This ignores concepts like word order or grammar. Here we represent the words as a "bag," which consists of words and their associated frequency in the text. This is essentially a type of vectorized representation of our text, which is called word embedding.

There are many other ways to create word embeddings aside from bag-of-words. TF-IDF can also be used, which weights the importance of words. Another approach is to use n-grams. Here we look at n items in a text (such as words) together. However, this approach would still struggle with identifying a sentence such as "it was not at all good" as a negative statement. We can also extend such a vector into a matrix to work out similarities of words, counting the number of frequencies of co-occurrences, such as within the same sentence. However, in practice this is likely to result in a very sparse matrix. Young, Hazarika, Poria, and Cambria (2018) note that historically machine learning NLP has been trained on such very high-dimensional and sparse features. Furthermore, they can involve a combination of handcrafted features that can be labor intensive to complete.

4.6.4   Creating Word Embeddings: Word2vec and Beyond

While it can be argued that grammar can be codified in a systematic way, it is difficult to do so in a way that we make sure our rules are absolutely exhaustive, which makes it appealing to automate the process. There has been considerable success in using deep learning for understanding audio and image data. These naturally have dense representations (TensorFlow Tutorials). In order to apply similar approaches using deep learning to text, we need to somehow create word embeddings that are dense.

Instead of computing a word embedding using a technique like one we discussed earlier, such as the frequency of co-occurrences, which results in sparse representations, we can use an algorithm like word2vec introduced by (Mikolov, Chen, Corrado, and Dean, 2013). As the name suggests, it converts words to vectors. word2vec computes the probability that words are likely to be written near each other, essentially a probabilistic classifier. This will create a denser matrix representation of a text. Two underlying methods are used in word2vec, namely CBOW (continuous bag of words) and skip gram. Both of these are types of neural network, which we introduced earlier in this chapter, with three layers: an input layer, a hidden layer, and an output layer. CBOW tries to predict the target word from the context of what other words are around it. Skip gram works in the opposite direction, predicting the context from our target word. Hence the output of skip gram could be more than one word. In this instance, "context" basically means words near it within a specific sized window.

Mikolov, Chen, Corrado, and Dean (2013) note that these word embeddings or vector representations of words can be added to give outputs, which have interesting properties. They give an example showing that adding the vector representation of the Montreal Canadiens, a Canadian ice hockey team, to the vector for Toronto and then subtracting the vector for Montreal results in the vector for Toronto Maple Leafs, an ice hockey team based in Toronto. Another example often cited in the literature around word2vec is how the vector of king, take away the vector of man and with the addition of the vector of woman, results in queen. The fastText model extends word2vec, by looking at subwords; (see Bojanowski, Grave, Joulin, and Mikolov 2016). In fastText, each word is represented by a bag of character n-grams. The idea is that this approach can take advantage of morphology. At the same time, we do not have to explicitly define all the various rules for forming words, such as defining prefixes, suffixes, and so on. As discussed earlier, certain languages such as Arabic are heavily morphological.

Naili, Chaibi, Hajjami, and Ghezala (2017) discuss the difference between word2vec and another similar word embedding method, GloVe (Global Vectors for Word Representation), as well as discussing how CBOW compares to skip gram with some experimental examples in both English and Arabic. Rather than attempting to compute probabilities like word2vec, GloVe is based upon the ratios of how often words occur near each other. It involves first creating a co-occurrence matrix for words. However, this is then factorized to generate a vector representation for each word. In both word2vec and GloVe, words such as "bank" will have the same vector representation despite having different meanings within context such as "river bank" or "bank deposit."

Newer techniques such as BERT (Bidirectional Encoder Representations from Transformers), introduced by Devlin, Chang, Lee, and Toutanova (2018), can incorporate context within their word representations. In words, as a contextual model, it creates a representation based on other words in the sentence. As the name suggests, it is not a directional model, reading text input in one direction (left-to-right or right-to-left), but it can examine the context words in a bidirectional manner. We note that BERT is not unique in being a contextual model; there are many other models that also incorporate context such as XLNet.

4.6.5   Sentiment Analysis and NLP Tasks as Classification Problems

Let's say we want to do sentiment analysis on a text to get an understanding of how positive or negative it is. From an investor viewpoint this is likely to be a very useful exercise for a number of reasons. Perhaps the most obvious use case is to understand whether a particular news article on a company is good or bad. It can also be useful to ascertain how people are talking about certain brands and map these to an associated parent company.

We can give positive/negative scores for words. Words such as "like" would have a positive score while words such as "hate" would have a negative score. Typically, there are many existing semantic lexicons that classify words into positive and negative, which can be used. Once we have the frequencies of each word, and their corresponding sentiment score, we can aggregate together to form a sentiment score for the whole document. There are obviously many shortcomings to this bag-of-words approach, given that we are ignoring how words relate to one another, which can obviously change the meaning.

Jurafsky and Martin (2019) note many problems in NLP involve some element of classification. Sentiment analysis can be considered as a classification problem. Many other problems associated with the document level are classification problems, such as determining the author of a document by its style or its language. Tasks that are not at the document level, whether at the word level or at the sentence level, can also involve classification – take, for example, the tagging of stop words or part-of-speech tagging.

When explaining sentiment analysis above, we used a rules-based approach by constructing a weighted average sentiment score based upon how positive/negative words were in the text. As with dealing with word similarity or many other NLP tasks that are essentially classification problems, we don't have to use a rules-based approach. Instead, we could also use a probabilistic classifier, which we mentioned earlier in the context of more complicated word embeddings like word2vec. Ng and Jordan (2001) discuss the difference between two different classes of classifiers: generative and discriminative. Let's say we have inputs $x_1, \ldots, x_n$, which are text, and there is a label y, which, for example, could be a binary variable like "positive" or "negative." For a generative classifier like naïve Bayes, $P(Y = y | X = x)$ will be calculated using Bayes rules indirectly. A discriminative classifier, like logistic regression, instead models $P(Y = y | X = x)$ by directly mapping input x to y through learning.

4.6.6   Topic Modeling

So far we have mostly discussed words and documents; however, in between them we have the idea of topics. Topic modeling attempts to identify similarities at a higher level than purely at the word level. In a sense we can think of a document as being about a number of topics, and each topic is made up of a group of words. Latent Dirichlet Allocation (LDA) is a technique for extracting groups of words that are similar to one another, which we can group together as topics. It will also give us an indication of how each of these topics are weighted in a document. It is called "latent" because while we can observe the words, we don't actually observe the topics directly, which are latent variables. LDA essentially helps us find the distribution of the topics in a document, the number of topics, and how those words are distributed, given a corpus of documents.

Trying to find this joint posterior probability distribution for the topics in a document, number of topics, and so on, is tricky analytically. Instead, an approximation to this distribution is found using a variational inference as explained in the paper that introduced LDA; see Blei, Ng, and Jordan (2003). It should be noted that LDA applies unsupervised learning; hence, it does not require the manual assignment of topics to groups of words in documents beforehand. Although, we should note that "seeding" LDA can improve it, so it will increase the probability of a certain topic for chosen words. Other techniques such as NMF (non-negative matrix factorization) and LSA (latent semantic analysis) can also be used. In practice, NMF often outperforms LDA.

4.6.7   Various Challenges in NLP

Adding additional metadata using various NLP tasks to a text can involve very particular challenges. Let's take, for example, named entity recognition. For the purposes of trading, we often would like to do entity matching, in particular mapping a named entity to a traded instrument. In practice, we might have a product or a brand listed. We therefore need to augment our dataset so we can do entity matching from products or brands to companies. Consider a news article that discusses the launch of a new iPhone. iPhone is not a tradable financial instrument. However, Apple, which makes iPhones, is of course a tradable equity. Hence, we need to have a mapping between Apple and iPhone, in other words performing relation extraction. It is likely that an article would also mention Apple in any case.

In other instances, it can be complicated to identify the tradable instrument. For an investor, ultimately any signal needs to somehow map to a tradable signal in the end for it to be monetizable. In other words, we need to be able to do a profitable trade based on our trading signal for it to be of use for an investor. If a certain piece of analysis or signal cannot be used as part of an investor's decision-making process, then they can't monetize it.

Say we have a news article that refers to the launch of an Audi A8 luxury car. Audi as an entity is not tradable. However, the parent company of Audi, Volkswagen, is a traded equity. In this instance, a news article may well make no mention at all of Volkswagen, and hence we have to augment our machine-readable text dataset with a dataset that has a mapping between tradable companies and their subsidiaries. We could also have a mapping between companies, for example, the relationship between car manufacturers and their supply chain (see Chapter 10 for a detailed study on trading auto stocks based on automotive supply chain data). For automakers, we might argue there are not really that many brands. However, for many companies, it is likely to be extremely challenging. Take, for example, a company such as Unilever, the Anglo-Dutch consumer goods company; they alone have hundreds of different brands.

Hence, any sort of tagging of a news article or text in general needs to take these sorts of indirect mappings into account. Either we need to derive such relationships or we can use a premade set of mappings, such as TickerTags, which is a product from M Science. At present TickerTags contains over a million tags covering 3,000 public and private companies. Trying to reproduce such a mapping dataset is likely to be very challenging and also could be labor intensive. Furthermore, we need to note that this mapping needs to be recorded in a point-in-time fashion, because these brands and company relationships are not static. Hence, if we create a point-in-time history of such a mapping, which is likely to be used for backtesting, we would need to be careful not to induce any look-ahead bias.

In a sense, we can see a similar situation when we are trying to trade macro assets based on purely macro news. A macro news article might not even mention any traded assets (e.g. relating to economic data releases or central bank statements). We can use our domain knowledge to map the relationships between these macroeconomic events and the macro assets we are trading.

4.6.8   Different Languages and Different Texts

A word corpus is a collection of different texts that has been structured so it can be utilized to help with NLP tasks. The idea of a word corpus is that it should be representative of the type of language we are studying and can also include text that was originally speech.

We have already noted that different languages will often require applying different techniques for doing certain NLP tasks. Even in the same language, it is also the case that texts can be quite different. We can find English language in tweets, financial news articles, and the novels of Charles Dickens. However, there are likely to be very great differences in the style of English of each. It would not be representative to use a word corpus made up of Charles Dickens to do semantic analysis on tweets that contain a large amount of slang. Hence, if we are using word corpora in our NLP, it might be worth bearing in mind that we should try to select the one that is likely to be closest to our use case.

Many word corpora are freely available on the web. For example, the BYU corpus (https://corpus.byu.edu/) aggregates many different word corpora covering a large number of different sources, including a word corpus consisting of *Time* magazine articles from 1923 to 2006 (100 million words) to a more informal language in the Corpus of Contemporary American/COCA English (560 million words). The largest word corpus they have is the iWeb: 14 billion Word Web Corpus, which has been derived from 95,000 websites.

One of the simplest usages for a word corpus is for understanding the typical frequency of words. In Figure 4.13, we report the results of a search of COCA, for the frequency of the word "burger" and "king" in contemporary American English. The results are given for the number of instances of the word per million words of text.

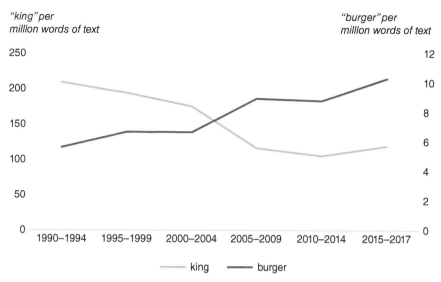

FIGURE 4.13   Frequency of the words "burger" and "king."
Source: Based on data from Corpus of Contemporary American English.

We see that on the whole "king" is more common than "burger" in the corpus. We note that the usage patterns have been different over time. Obviously, we would have to do more work to understand why the frequency might have changed.

4.6.9   Speech in NLP

Tasks involving speech are also part of NLP. For example, automatic speech recognition can also be considered as a part of NLP. Petkar (2016) discusses the many challenges associated with speech recognition. First, there is a difference between spoken language and written language. In some languages such as Arabic this can be very pronounced. There are large differences between the spoken dialects of Arabic and written text, which is in the form of Modern Standard Arabic. There are differences in pronunciation, vocabulary, and also grammar. However, even in English, spoken language tends to be less formal and generally less descriptive. The paper also notes the difficulties associated with continuous speech. Just as word segmentation needs to be performed on written text, for audio, speech segmentation is used to identify individual words, which can be challenging given that there aren't always clear pauses in human speech between words. There is also significant variability in speakers in terms of accent, gender, and speed of speech.

Speech recognition can often form the first step of solving an NLP problem, where our text is not in a written form. One example would be Siri, the Apple voice assistant on the iPhone, which takes the user's speech as an input. This is converted into written text, which is parsed for understanding using some of the techniques outlined earlier, into a structured form, so that we can understand things like the context. An answer is then generated based upon this structured input. The next step is natural language generation to create a human readable reply. Finally, text-to-speech synthesis is applied to this text to read aloud the output to the Siri user.

However, there are now new techniques that promise to apply advanced NLP techniques like translation from speech in one language into another, without intermediate conversion into written text and then application of text-to-speech synthesis. Jia and Weiss (2019) describe Translatotron, which uses a single sequence-to-sequence model for direct speech translation. The approach can even retain the style of speech from the original speaker, but in the foreign language, which would likely be more challenging to do using a traditional approach that requires a separate text-to-speech synthesis.

More broadly, we could argue that speech might have additional information that would be lost when converting into text. Speech has many different characteristics such as pitch, speed, and pronunciation that are not obvious from text. As a very simple example, it is far easier to determine the gender of the speaker from their speech than it is from reading their text. Features extracted from speech can be used to develop indicators for deception in speech and combined with text-based features. Hirschberg (2018) develops a machine learning–based approach for judging deception in speech, which outperforms humans.

From an investor viewpoint, many of these techniques are also relevant. Speech recognition could be used on events such as earnings conference calls and the question-and-answer sessions of central bank press conferences. Understanding deception in such situations would be extremely beneficial for investors, too! Text-to-speech could be used to provide automated alerts for traders, triggered by specific events like large price moves or economic events.

4.6.10 NLP Tools

What type of tools can we use to first get access to raw data from the web and then to structure it or to do tasks like automatic speech recognition? It is possible to develop libraries to do various NLP tasks such as generate word embeddings, word segmentation, sentiment analysis, and so on. However, it requires significant time and expertise to write these tools and then to train them.

In practice, there are many libraries and resources that can help us with different parts of the process that we can use as a starting point for our analysis of text. In many instances, these libraries also include models that have been pretrained on large corpora of text. Following is a list of some of the open-source Python tools available for the initial stage of gathering text data from the web and cleaning:

- **Scrapy:** Scrapy is a full framework for web crawling and web scraping. We can give it a URL and it will begin to crawl the various websites linked from that and help you save and download all that content.
- **BeautifulSoup:** BeautifulSoup focuses on parsing HTML data that has already been downloaded. Webpages have a large amount of formatting and script code, which are irrelevant for understanding the content. BeautifulSoup enables us to extract certain elements, remove superfluous information such as HTML tags, and so on. We can use Scrapy and BeautifulSoup together.

- **PDFMiner:** PDFMiner can extract text from PDF documents.
- **tablula-py:** tabula-py is a Python-based wrapper for the Java, Tabula library, specifically for reading tables from PDF documents. Use cases in finance could be reading from earning reports.
- **newspaper3k:** newspaper3k is a Python library for accessing articles from newspaper websites. It can, for example, extract the body text of articles and associated metadata such as the authors and publication date. It sits on top of some of the other libraries discussed here, like BeautifulSoup and NLTK.

Next, we list some of the libraries that are useful for higher-level natural language processing tasks, once we have gathered together and cleaned a text. We should also note that many of the general-purpose machine learning libraries such as TensorFlow and scikit-learn can also be used with text, although they are not specifically limited to dealing with text.

- **NLTK:** NLTK is one of the oldest Python libraries to do NLP tasks. It includes many trained models and word corpora to get you started, including a corpus of Reuters articles (from 1987). Bird, Klein and Loper (2009) guides users through using NLTK to a number of common NLP tasks ranging from processing raw text to text classification.
- **CoreNLP:** Stanford CoreNLP is accessible in a number of languages as well as Python. As with NLTK it performs a large number of NLP tasks, ranging from tokenization and sentence splitting to named entity recognition and sentiment tagging.
- **Gensim:** Gensim is a topic modeling library, which includes implementations of models such as Latent Dirichlet Allocation and Latent Semantic Analysis.
- **spaCy:** spaCy is written in Cython. It can do various NLP tasks such as tokenization, named entity recognition, and part-of-speech tagging. It also integrates with a number of Python machine learning libraries such as TensorFlow.
- **pattern:** pattern is a general-purpose web mining module for crawling the web and accessing sources like Twitter and Wikipedia via their APIs. It also contains a number of features to do NLP tasks, such as sentiment analysis based around words typically used in product reviews. It also includes functionality to perform simpler tasks such as part-of-speech tagging.
- **TextBlob:** TextBlob sits on top of NLTK and pattern. However, it provides an easier to use interface to access these libraries.
- **BERT:** BERT (Bidirectional Encoder Representations from Transformers) was developed by a team at Google; see Devlin, Chang, Lee and Toutanova (2018). Essentially, it is a method of pretraining language representations, which also incorporates context. It uses unsupervised learning, and as a result it can be trained on vast amounts of plain text. Google has a model that has been pretrained on text from Wikipedia and BookCorpus. The pretrained model can then be used for a number of NLP tasks such as question answering or

tokenization. The software implementation of BERT uses Google's TensorFlow machine learning library.

- **SpeechRecognition:** SpeechRecognition is a Python library that allows users to do speech recognition using a number of external online and offline services using a common API.

While we have focused on open source Python tools, there are many commercial tools available for doing NLP on text. Many of these are cloud based and can be used as pay-as-you-go-style services, where you upload the text you would like to analyze, and then NLP is performed on it.

- **Google Cloud Natural Language:** Google Cloud Natural Language can do a number of NLP tasks, including named entity recognition, sentiment analysis, and syntax analysis. While it has pretrained models, users can also train their own custom models. It can be accessed using a REST API to upload text for analysis or it can also read text stored on Google Cloud. It also supports the creation of own custom models, or it can be used on own training data for content classification.

- **Google Cloud Speech-to-Text:** Google Cloud Speech-to-Text is a cloud-based service that can convert audio to text using neural network models, which has a number of different APIs. It supports 120 languages.

- **Amazon Comprehend:** Amazon Comprehend performs different NLP tasks on the provided text, extracting properties such as entities, syntax, and sentiment. It also has a specific version trained on medical vocabulary to extract data from medical notes or similar texts.

4.7 SUMMARY

Machine learning encompasses a large number of individual techniques. At its core it can be split up into supervised learning, unsupervised learning, and reinforcement learning. When fitting these models, we need to be aware of the variance-bias trade-off. What may appear to work very well in-sample can end up performing poorly in-sample, because we have overfit it.

In the chapter, we discussed a number of machine learning techniques ranging from relatively simple examples such as linear regression, to logistic regression for classification, to more complicated models such as deep neural networks. We also gave a short summary of some of the machine learning libraries that can be used to fit these models.

Later we discussed some of the limitations associated with machine learning, in particular with reference to financial time series, which are nonstationary. We also discussed specific use cases for structuring images, using techniques like CNNs and we also included an introduction to natural language processing, where machine learning models tend to be used these days, in preference to more traditional rule-based approaches.

In Chapter 13, we shall use a dataset of satellite imagery that has been structured using CNNs to generate car counts for the car parks of European retailers. In addition, we had a detailed look at natural language processing that can enable a computer to understand human language. In Chapter 15, we shall have an extensive look at text data, and give several investor use cases for it. For readers interested in machine learning in finance more broadly, we refer the reader to Lopez de Prado (2018) and also Dixon et al. (2020).

CHAPTER 5

The Processes behind the Use of Alternative Data

5.1 INTRODUCTION

As explained in a lot of detail in the previous chapters, there are several potential pitfalls in the implementation of an alternative data strategy. In this chapter, we will discuss how to organize these implementation efforts in order to deliver a successful strategy. We must emphasize that the key to this success is to have the right processes, systems, and people in place. There are, of course, external constraints, such as the availability of talent in the marketplace, or internal ones, like budgeting and legacy systems. These will also determine how successful one can be in implementing an alternative data strategy.

We must also note that once a given strategy is deployed in production, that does not mark an end of the work. In fact, the signals generated from alternative data may begin to degrade. This means that the accuracy and performance achieved in model development and as measured through backtesting declines in time. Reasons for this can range from non-stationarity through technical implementation problems. While we cannot solve the problem of non-stationarity except under very special circumstances, we can address most other performance degradation issues by establishing and acting upon a suitable monitoring process. We will discuss this matter further.

We will divide the process of developing an alternative data process into a number of steps as follows:

- Set up the vision and strategy.
- Identify the relevant data asset(s) according to the investment strategy, mandate, and constraints.
- Perform due diligence on the vendors of those data assets.

- Pre-assess risks (e.g. technological, legal, cyber, etc.).
- Pre-assess the existence of signal(s) – run a proof-of-concept (POC) on a sample of data. If the outcome of the last step is positive, then one can proceed to the next steps.
- Perform data onboarding.
- Perform data preprocessing (if needed).
- Perform signal extraction (modeling).
- Implement the process (or deploy in production).

The sequence of steps may vary depending on the degree to which data has already been preprocessed.

5.2 STEPS IN THE ALTERNATIVE DATA JOURNEY

5.2.1 Step 1. Set up a Vision and Strategy

The first question an investor/risk manager can ask is: shall we begin to venture along the alternative data journey? This is a strategic question that involves the highest-level decision makers within an organization such as the chief investment officer (CIO), the chief risk officer (CRO), or the chief executive officer (CEO). The answer lies in their convictions that this kind of data has alpha after discounting for its price and the complexities behind its incorporation in the existing processes. It is a complex question to answer based on impressions and not on substantial quantitative analysis. As we remarked previously, the press has conveyed mixed messages and stories of success or the lack of it. Hopefully this book will provide more clarity in that direction.

Reading whitepapers by vendors is a good first step to be aware about the existence of signals in data and have a rough idea about the strength of the signal. However, running a small proof-of-concept (POC) along the lines of what we describe in the following could be a more convincing step for the decision makers in an organization. POCs are not costly to run because they neither require a complex infrastructure nor do they involve the complexities of a live implementation. The advantage of a POC is that decision makers can have a more tangible proof on their portfolio of whether or not a dataset is valuable.

Once the decision is made to attempt going along the alternative data path, a strategy must be put in place. In general, the strategy will depend on the type of investor. For example, one strategic choice could be whether to opt for raw data acquisition or for derived signals (see Section 5.4 on data vendors who provide this service). Quantitatively sophisticated investors (e.g. hedge funds) typically build their own analytics and hence prefer purchasing raw or lightly processed data.[1] For this purpose, they require access to good-quality raw data and the deployment of

---

[1] The conviction is that processing data (e.g. removing outliers) can throw away precious information.

cutting-edge technology and algorithms. Co-location of analytics and data could also speed up the research and deployment of signals.

More traditional but still quant-minded investors (e.g. large sell-side banks or big funds) are interested in derived analytics and more intuitive solutions. Smaller shops are less willing to employ technology, data science, and programming capabilities. They would opt for low-cost maintenance/build analytics platforms and sourcing on-demand of data science talent. Finally, there are small fintechs whose purpose is not to invest but to buy data and resell it in the form of a trading signal (e.g. CargoMetrics).

Hence, according to the type and size of the investor (or fintech), a strategy consists of defining a roadmap of data science capabilities and technology. In what follows, we will describe the full journey from raw data to signals. As we have just explained, an investor does not have to embark on all these steps as they might prefer the acquisition of curated signals. In other words, most of the steps that we will describe can be performed on the side of the data vendor.[2]

We note that regulatory, risk and reputational considerations should be monitored throughout the process we will describe to minimize the risk of investing in signal products that do not meet the buyer/vendor firm's relevant appetites.

5.2.2   Step 2. Identify the Appropriate Datasets

Once a strategic decision has been taken, the next step when starting an alternative data journey is to understand which data assets to pick up and test for a signal from a virtually infinite universe. Essentially, we are seeking to prune our search space. Most of the datasets will have potentially limited value, but this is not known upfront. This is a difficult task but new professions with the right skillset to perform it are starting to appear. In particular these new roles include those of data scouts or data strategists (we use the terms interchangeably). The role of the data scout is crucial for an organization wanting to have an edge. In fact, a lot of experience and common sense is needed to assess whether a data asset is worth purchasing and to make a decision how to test it. To make a judgment call with only a minimal amount of testing is difficult. However, it is necessary, given that it is too costly to do a thorough test for every single dataset on the market. There is obviously also a limited budget for purchasing datasets or samples of them. In this mission, the data scouts must be assisted by SMEs (subject matter experts) who deeply understand the markets and the investment portfolios and the risks of their institutions.

Organizations that have not established such highly specific roles can still rely on the experience of the chief data officer and their data scientists. There are also consulting firms such as Neudata, which can help outsource part of the data scout function to keep track of new alternative datasets. Neudata is compensated by data users, as opposed to data sellers. This is somewhat different to data markets discussed in Section 2.3, where typically the data marketplace owner is compensated in some form by the data seller. The emergence of outsourced data scouting services and data marketplaces is likely to help simplify the task of finding alternative datasets.

---

[2]This, however, restricts the options because curated signals might not be offered by all data vendors.

Depending on the stage of processing, the data scout/chief data officer has to approach the selection of a data asset differently (see Section 5.4). It is important to say that the bias on the vendor's side is to avoid advertising any omissions in the data. Hence, there are some checks to be performed upfront by the buyer in order to make sure that there aren't any gaps that could appear at a later stage or omissions that could become critical. This should be the case, even if the provider claims to be selling signals that are already "clean."

We described in Section 1.8 some dimensions on which a data asset can be projected. It is important to note that the asset classes required, the investment mandate and constraints that an asset manager has can help with preselecting a dataset. For example, is the asset manager investing only in fixed income instruments issued by governments and public entities? In that case, foot traffic data for only very specific shopping malls might be less useful at first glance. PMI indicators can be much more appropriate for this specific purpose. In this sense, a good approach to data asset selection can be both bottom-up and top-down. It can be bottom-up because one could start from the portfolio constituents and work out which data assets in the market could contain signals for the asset classes under management. It can also be top-down because one could start from a specific data asset (maybe a new entrant in the market) and cascade down on which asset classes it could have useful information about.

Coverage, breadth, and depth are also important considerations here. For example, sometimes it is better to try to increase coverage rather than focus on improving modeling techniques, such as adding extra complexity (which could even lead to overfitting). Whether this is possible must be considered at this stage.

5.2.3   Step 3. Perform Due Diligence on Vendors

As we mentioned previously and will again examine in detail in Section 5.4, there is a diverse spectrum of alternative data providers. Some of them can be big organizations with a long track record and history while others can be relatively new, small, and niche providers. Third-party due diligence is then needed to avoid risk of disappearance of these companies after subscribing to their data feeds. The risk of ceasing activity is, of course, an extreme issue but it is not the only one we have to be concerned about with respect to third parties. In general, organizations that create, gather, and/or distribute alternative data could often operate with immature risk and control frameworks. This means that the data they sell could be prone to errors and hence not truthful, or potentially obtained through processes that are not legally cleared. Hence, working with such vendors can be also a source of reputational and legal risk.

For example, third-party checks are performed by data aggregators for alternative datasets that they distribute to their clients. These are onboarded after a careful due diligence of their providers. If such a due diligence service is not available for a dataset we want to purchase, we have to make such checks ourselves, maybe through the help of external consultants. In any case, all these assessments should be performed before purchasing a dataset.

5.2.4 Step 4. Pre-assess Risks

There are many risks associated with alternative data, as we already discussed in Section 3.2. We discussed third-party due diligence in the previous section. The risks in this section are risks that are not associated with a third party. Some of this non-third-party risk assessment can be done at an early stage (i.e. before even purchasing a data asset by working with a sample of it or through metadata only). We must make sure that we do not expose ourselves to accuracy/validity risk of the data, privacy risk, and material non-public information (MNPI) risks.

From the metadata and the contractual agreement proposed by the vendor, we can also consider infrastructure risks connected to the frequency and the structure of the data. Can our infrastructure cope with the velocity of the data (e.g. millisecond ticks)? Is it also able to ingest the required volumes of data? This problem is present in many forms of unstructured data where volumes are typically bigger.

5.2.5 Step 5. Pre-assess the Existence of Signals

This step is a quick-and-dirty one to make sure that it is worth investigating the data asset further. As we explained, onboarding of data and processing it in a production environment might be costly so this step will help us to avoid committing time and resources that could lead to something that ultimately is of little use. Some data vendors already sell signals or evidence of a signal in the form of whitepapers (see Section 5.4 on data vendors) as we mentioned in Section 5.2.1. This could greatly facilitate the work of signal discovery if the asset manager wants to go their own route of working out a signal from the raw data. If they want to acquire a final signal, then this step can be skipped.

Getting a sample of the data and its metadata will be enough to assess (1) the quality of the data (e.g. missing values, anomalies), (2) what modeling techniques could be relevant and whether the data science team has expertise in them, and (3) possibly run some very simple transformations and models. Due to the requirement to identify signals quickly, coarser analyses techniques are typical (e.g. binned R^2 analyses for potential signal factors). Note that, with respect to the last point, the lack of a signal when attempting a very simple model is not sufficient to discard the dataset. A more sophisticated set of nonlinear models can be also attempted provided there is a solid justification to suspect nonlinearities in the data. Open source libraries make this last step straightforward even in the case of complex deep learning models. We also note that datasets in isolation may not yield a signal, but joining them with a number of other datasets could result in finding more usable signals.

Again, all this could happen without onboarding the data and setting up regular data feeds. A sample of a few thousand observations may be enough in many cases. It could be enough to create a very simple proof of concept to assess whether the data asset contains any alpha after subtracting costs.

At this stage it is also important to think about model risks and trade-offs. Does the model need to be interpretable by portfolio managers? If not, a deep learning model can, in principle, provide a better fit. But, is it overfitting? To check this, appropriate out-of-sample tests must be considered. Does it need to deliver results on a mobile device and also in real time? Hence, a simpler model that can deliver results even in the case of slow connectivity must be devised, typically by sacrificing some accuracy.

The list of datasets to explore should be prioritized according to the expected value likely to be added and also the business demands. Questions from the business can, for example, help us to focus on datasets relevant to particular asset classes, geographies, and so on. The experience of a data strategist could also prove useful in this regard.

5.2.6   Step 6. Data Onboarding

Even if the previous steps did not touch upon an implementation in production, there were still some overheads to be considered (e.g. infrastructure setup and legal arrangements with the data vendor). Once they have been dealt with and the presence of a stable signal has been proved, it is time to consider a fair price for which the dataset can be purchased. We discussed the delicate issue of pricing in Sections 2.4–2.6. If a price is agreed, the next step is to onboard the data in the local infrastructure.

Data sources often come with their own schema (or sometimes with no schema at all, which can make interpretation more challenging). This can affect how we work with the dataset. Any data we receive from an external (or indeed internal source) needs to be stored in a database. The nature of how we store the dataset will be dependent on its schema. For example, relatively well-structured high-frequency tick data could be stored in columnar databases like KDB. By contrast, other lower-frequency structured datasets might be better suited to SQL databases. A lot of alternative data, especially in its raw form, tends to be relatively unstructured; hence, it might make sense to store it in a data lake.

5.2.7   Step 7. Data Preprocessing

It is likely that a dataset requires some element of preprocessing when implementing in production. One common part of this is in tagging assets in a structured dataset. A data source describing firm-specific data might be tagged with Bloomberg tickers but without any other ticker identifiers. However, a fund might use ISIN codes internally as their common ticker mapping. Hence, the Bloomberg tickers would all need to be mapped to ISINs. This is done in order to facilitate joining it with other datasets. We would need to join market data for backtesting of trading strategies or indeed other alternative datasets to generate composite signals. For raw datasets, we would likely need to do entity matching from scratch. See Section 3.3.1 for a more detailed discussion on entity matching.

If datasets have time stamps with different time zones, it results in misaligned points when joining these datasets. All sorts of problems can ensue, such as using future data. It is possible to keep time stamps in their original time zone in each dataset (and keep track of that). However, it is much easier to convert them to a common time zone, such as UTC, during an earlier preprocessing stage.

In some instances, the time zone data might be missing, hence we would need to infer it. Typically, one way to infer it is by joining with another dataset, which is likely to have correlated points. For high-frequency data, we might be able to infer it by joining it with an indicator for major economic data releases. Typically, for important events, like the US employment report, FOMC, and so on, we would observe jumps in assets like FX, rates and equity futures. Hence, we can infer the time zone of our market data by observing where these jumps are in the month. Other important fields could also be missing, not purely the time stamp, that need to be inferred.

There might be other sorts of discrepancies in time stamps. For very high-frequency data, the time stamp between different sources might be slightly offset, which can prove problematic when aligning them.

There might also be the case where we need to fill in missing points in our dataset. The simplest way is to interpolate. In Chapter 7, we discuss more sophisticated ways of filling missing data points, which can help to preserve the properties of the dataset better (such as mean and variance). We give a specific example for CDS data, in Chapter 8, where data might be missing in certain tenors. If a dataset has very little structure, we may need to do a significant amount of preprocessing in order to make it usable for signal generation later. This is especially likely to be the case if our dataset consists of data types such as text or images.

In general, data quality is fraught with challenges such as:

- Clarity. Is there sufficient data definition clarity to support decision making with the data?
- Uniqueness. Is there a single source of truth, both globally and within a given dataset?
- Internal consistency. Is the data internally structurally sound, with datatype requirements obeyed throughout dimensions?
- External consistency. Is the data externally structurally sound, with no impossible combinations of data attributes?
- Timeliness. Is the data available at the required time for a given application?
- Completeness. Is data missing irrespective of time?
- Validity. Is the data an accurate reflection of the real-world event(s) it describes?
- Veracity. Is the data credible, and what confidence level can be attributed to the data, given its context (including any transformations it has undergone)?

Throughout data's usage lifecycle, machine learning techniques can enhance quality by both automating existing tasks and extending monitoring to previously resistant quality dimensions. We will show some examples in Chapters 7, 8, and 9.

5.2.8   Step 8. Signal Extraction

Once the dataset has been fully preprocessed after our initial testing suggested a dataset had some promise, the next step is to construct the signals. For trading this is likely to entail a number of steps, such as the construction of strategies or indices.

In some cases, the objective might be simple buy or sell signals, for example, for a quantitative hedge fund. Often this is done by combining the signal with those derived from other datasets. These signals are then fed into a portfolio optimizer to weight them. For discretionary traders, it may well simply be a forecast that is used as an input into the trading process. For economists, the signal is likely to be in the form of a forecast. For risk managers, a signal might involve the construction of volatility forecasts or other similar risk metrics, or signal to exit a certain market/asset class/asset. Whatever the purpose, we need to backtest any signal to see how it performed with historical data, if available and sufficient, as discussed in Section 2.5.

The signal extraction process is iterative and involves the use of SMEs and business analysts. Brainstorming sessions are a critical component of scaling the signals extraction process by generating testable hypothesis for data science resources. Hence, expertise in data and market trends is required to encourage full exploitation, and monetization, of the purchased data assets.

The end state of this step could be the lack of a signal or strong enough signal to justify implementation (even if Step 5 pointed in the opposite direction!). This will be judged by some pre-established success criteria or metrics such as the alpha generated by the signal averaged across a period of time minus the costs. If this is the case, a careful consideration must be made as to why this is the case. Is it because of mistakes – and hence this step should be repeated – or some other fundamental reason? The conclusion could be that there is indeed no signal. The findings should be archived and the process terminated here. In case of positive outcome of the signal extraction, the next step is to implement it in production.

5.2.9   Step 9. Implementation (or Deployment in Production)

So far, we have gone through a successful signal extraction stage and found a usable signal that has been validated in our analysis. We have also onboarded the dataset and preprocessed it. The final step is to create a production implementation of our model and to run it in a live environment.

For a POC, it is fine to receive data from a vendor in an ad-hoc way, such as via e-mail or USB key. However, in order to use data for production, we need to be able to retrieve it in an automated way. For high-frequency data, this will often require the writing of wrappers for APIs provided by the data provider, to ingest high-frequency data on a real-time basis. The time it will take to integrate such an API into a framework will depend on the format in which the data is provided to us. For lower-frequency data, such as daily or weekly data, we might potentially be able to download flat files (e.g. in CSV, XML, or Parquet format) on a batched basis, which is likely to be simpler to install.

From a production perspective, we need to make sure that our test infrastructure is also replicated, from ingesting the data, to preprocessing, generating the signal, and so on. This will require the rewriting of code, possibly even starting from scratch. For applications where high performance is required, this can mean shifting from languages used in data science such as Python and R, to languages like C++, Java, or Scala. It can also mean spending a significant amount of time making sure that any calculations are done on distributed infrastructure to speed up processing, if this wasn't already undertaken during the testing phase. For firms that have not dealt with such datasets before, it is likely that they will need to invest extra time and budget in developing such infrastructure.

At this stage, appropriate controls for risks must be put in place. For example, if one of the data feeds to the model disappears, we must receive a notification. If the trading signal is too strong and suggests high-volume trades that exceed trading limits, a "kill switch" control could be put in place.

5.2.10   Maintenance Process

Once a dataset is used as a production model, we need to monitor it. There are two types of live monitoring that can be put in place to detect dataset shifts and act accordingly. The first one follows the performance measures. This might be challenging in cases where there is not an established ground truth. For example, if it is a predictive classification model (e.g. stock going up or down), this could be a regularly generated confusion matrix. The second monitors the discrepancies between the distributions of the independent variables in the training dataset and the live data. We must stress that a model could also start producing poor forecasts because of purely mundane problems, such as one of the input features is missing due to a fault in the data flows or maybe because the sensors and the processes were reconfigured not to collect this information anymore, and the data vendor failed to inform us. Controls must be put in place to detect any such anomaly. Hence, alternative data variability which makes proactive quality monitoring and remediation much needed.

If deterioration in the model is detected, there are several actions that can be taken. First, we need to understand what caused the problem. Is it a mundane problem like the one mentioned above or is there evidence of a dataset shift? Second, we need to fix it. If the problem is technological, the remedy should be also technological. If it is due to a change in the processes that capture the data, the fix may not be that straightforward. There can be many reasons why this can occur. Data companies may shut down or they might simply stop publishing datasets, if the source data is no longer available, or they may simply change the format of the data. This will result in missing variables in our model. There is a reduction in the quality of data we receive from a data vendor, because the panel of data has changed significantly, which makes it less representative.

For more commoditized datasets, we may be able to substitute these easily with similar datasets. However, this might prove trickier for more unusual alternative datasets. Furthermore, within alternative data space, even for datasets within the same category, such as news, the way the dataset is generated and treated might differ significantly between vendors. Hence, we can't simply swap datasets without additional work and changes to the underlying model, like recalibration. If the missing variable has low marginal predictive power, for example, perhaps we could simply ignore that feature and not expect this to impact returns significantly. Of course, this is a temporary fix and a redevelopment of the model without that feature becomes necessary. If the problem is caused by a dataset shift, we must understand what type of shift that is. This can be challenging and also time consuming. It is not an exaggeration to say that detecting the reason for deterioration can take longer than model development itself.

There might well be other reasons why a model has stopped working as expected that are not related to data recording issues. It might be the case that the capacity of the trading strategy has been exceeded as more and more traders are replicating it and we start seeing alpha decay because of this. Furthermore, as mentioned in the introduction to this chapter, financial time series are often not stationary, whether we are referring to price data or macroeconomic data. Their properties can change over time. We can observe significant shifts in behavior of the market, such as when we observe changes in market regime. This change of regime may render the strategy loss making, as the market is no longer reacting to the factor we are modeling. Let's say we have had a model that aggregated Greek language news during the Greek debt crisis. At the time this was a major driver for EUR/USD. By contrast, once the worst turbulence had passed for the Greek debt crisis, such a dataset was unlikely to be as relevant for trading EUR/USD.

The maintenance process doesn't only encompass technical issues associated with the models. There is also a need to continually monitor any regulatory developments to make sure existing processes are compliant. This can also be useful, for example, in giving us prior warning about the discontinuation of datasets due to regulatory changes. Lastly, we need to make sure that we have sufficient manpower to run the maintenance process of our alternative data model. We are likely to need data scientists, data engineers, technologists, compliance officers, and others to help with such maintenance tasks.

5.3   STRUCTURING TEAMS TO USE ALTERNATIVE DATA

When structuring a team for dealing with alternative data, we note that in the long term, it is not sufficient purely to hire data scientists in isolation and ask them "do something with the data." Data can only be monetized in an investment firm if it is used to help make profitable investment decisions. In many large firms, there has been effort to centralize alternative data initiatives into central teams, which cover several different parts of the pipeline from identification and sourcing of data, to ingesting data, and then analyzing data.

Data scouts/strategists are an important part of any alternative data process, to help locate and identify datasets externally and to act as a bridge with internal teams. As we noted in Section 5.2.2, a data scout requires very specific skills. It is not possible to evaluate every dataset in existence given the constraints of time and cost. Hence this initial identification stage to choose which datasets to evaluate more closely is key. As a result, a data scout is an essential figure in the team.

Data engineers need to be hired to deal with the challenges of ingesting large quantities of data and storing them. The skillset for data engineers will be somewhat different than that for data scientists, and will involve understanding how to distribute processes and how to create data lakes.

Data scientists work to analyze the data. For fundamental firms, this might involve answering specific questions from the portfolio managers. In a sense, we can think of data scientists as generalists with skills in several different areas, including coding and statistics, as well as an element of domain knowledge, so similar in skillset to traditional financial quants.

Centralization of the process of data purchasing is also likely to reduce costs of purchasing datasets, rather than having individual teams negotiating separately, potentially for the same datasets. When data purchasing is centralized, it can make it easier to keep track of which datasets a firm can access. By creating a centralized pipeline for dealing with new datasets, it can reduce the time and cost of the evaluation process.

It is also incumbent on the business to leverage these resources. For example, in funds, if portfolio managers do not see alternative data as part of their investment process, then it is unlikely that a firm will be able to extract much value from the whole exercise of developing an alternative data pipeline. Data strategists and data scientists need guidance from the business to understand what investment questions are the most important and what metrics would be most useful for the business. This will help to guide them in identification of which datasets are most likely to be useful. Ultimately, communication between the various teams is critical to ensure the success of using alternative data within an investment firm. Otherwise, the data scientists end up working in an isolated environment, unable to provide the business with insights. Communication is important to ensure that data scientists have the right resources for their job. If a lack of communication and internal politics means that data scientists are unable to even have access to data, it is likely they will leave.

The creation of centralized data science teams can often be done gradually, in particular in firms that have a more discretionary focus. With these types of firms, often it is a good idea to start with smaller alternative datasets, which are less resource intensive to investigate and do not require massive team to support using it. Often resources might be reassigned internally at the early stages. As the business side sees benefits from using such datasets, it helps to justify additional spending of time and resources to grow the data team and buy additional datasets.

The "big bang" strategy of hiring a very large number of people externally to create a centralized data team all at once requires a substantial immediate upfront budget cost. If the business does not see immediate benefits of such an approach, it might be difficult to justify spending such large amounts of money. A strategy of obtaining small wins from using alternative data and gradually expanding the team may be more appropriate and more easily endorsed by the business.

We must say that creating a data science/engineering team capable of harnessing alternative data signals can be both expensive and time consuming. A diverse talent pool, typically not found within existing functions, is required to find, analyze, model, and productionize alternative insights. Large firms can set this up at a cost that is far below the benefits they will draw from alternative data. By contrast, smaller firms could opt for signals created by data vendors/fintechs and/or use platforms where the big infrastructure costs are avoided. From this point of view, smaller firms must shop around to see which data vendor's offering matches their requirements and demand.

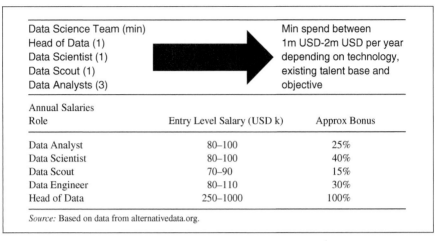

Data Science Team (min)		Min spend between
Head of Data (1)		1m USD-2m USD per year
Data Scientist (1)		depending on technology,
Data Scout (1)		existing talent base and
Data Analysts (3)		objective

| Annual Salaries | | |
Role	Entry Level Salary (USD k)	Approx Bonus
Data Analyst	80–100	25%
Data Scientist	80–100	40%
Data Scout	70–90	15%
Data Engineer	80–110	30%
Head of Data	250–1000	100%

Source: Based on data from alternativedata.org.

FIGURE 5.1   Cost of setting up a data science team.

We report in closing the approximate average spend to set up a data science team in an organization (see Figure 5.1). We note that the sums could vary between geographies and also the nature of the fund.

As we see, a spend of $1m–$2m can be a big ask for small or medium-size investor. We turn to discuss how the data vendor is responding to this and other challenges described in the previous steps.

5.4   DATA VENDORS

At the time of writing, the data vendor market remains fragmented; there are several hundred data vendors and thousands of datasets exist, and their number and variety continue to grow every month. The press often brands data as the new oil[3] (*Economist,* 2017), and the supply chain that data moves bears a significant similarity to the oil industry (Passarella, 2019). We can explore this analogy to better understand the data industry. There are many parts of the "data" supply chain.

Initially, data resides in the "ground," akin to crude oil; for example, this might be an actual corporate firm where the exhaust data was generated. Raw data providers, selling data with little to no preprocessing, populate the upstream portion of the supply chain. Here the burden of analysis is on the buyers' side, who must invest time and resources to make the data clean and usable. Buyers are likely to be other data companies themselves, who can ingest this dataset, or in some cases large quant hedge funds.

In the middle of the supply chain there are providers of processed data who clean and aggregate data from different sources to make it usable for a specific purpose such as equity markets signals, oil price movements, and so forth. An example dataset is the

---

[3]However, unlike oil, data is a nondepletable and non-rivalrous asset. It is in principle nonperishable, although its value can decay in time.

full geographical coverage of ship movements through aggregation and integration of data from different Automatic Identification System (AIS) systems.

Finally, at the end of the supply chain, there are providers of signals engineered specifically for the investment community, usually covering one or a few asset classes. This refinement process is similar to that performed by large chemical companies such as BASF in the oil refinery process. These providers often offer whitepapers to prove the existence of signals through specific case studies.

The data vendors' universe can also be segmented according to their offering, that is, the level of refinement of the data and the technological infrastructure used to deliver it. We can summarize this more explicitly as follows.

Most of the big data vendors provide Data-as-a-Service (DaaS) – minimally refined data supplied directly to customers. State of the art provides: (1) connected data, via a single point of access (SPV), and the ability to customize the data feed to a client's specific requirements, and (2) cleansed data with appropriate imputation and normalized data concepts and entities.

We also see a few cases of Infrastructure-as-a-Service (IaaS)/Platform-as-a-Service (PaaS) – flexible cloud infrastructure (and platforms) provisioned with simplified access to data. State of the art provides: (1) simplified access to data while improving usage monitoring, (2) co-located cloud infrastructure capable of supporting ultra-low-latency algorithmic decisions (and reducing communication infrastructure costs), and (3) access to cloud-based elastic/burst computing capabilities and a variety of price point storage solutions, presuming the co-location occurs in a cloud environment with sufficient scale. Given the complexities and costs, this option is typically reserved for the large data vendors such as Refinitiv.

We have not yet seen any data vendors fully capitalizing on the Analytics-as-a-Service (AaaS) space – where analytics data platforms hosted in IaaS/PaaS supply prebuilt environments at scale.[4] State of the art of this potential offering provides: (1) simplified access to data processing, providing off-the-rack data platform solutions that can be readily accessed, (2) app store engagement model that fosters agile fintech ecosystem, and (3) utility-based pricing. A key consideration here is the degree to which custom-built analytics platforms represent a differentiator for the data consumer. In most cases these represent a cost without any discernible market edge and hence the requirement is better solved through engagement with industry utilities.

Finally, some data vendors (or small startups that acquire data from different vendors) generate signals[5] that are sold to clients at a premium that target specific market segments and use cases.

The delivery model of a data vendor and the degree of transformation of the data must be driven by market research (and direct client outreach) and targeting appetite. We discussed in Section 5.2.1 that there are different types of data buyers that we ranked according to the level of sophistication. The question for the data vendor is what segments to target that will inform the most appropriate delivery model and the required investments.

---

[4]Generic analytics vendors (e.g. SAS, Cloudera, Pivotal) provide these capabilities.
[5]For example, Research Signals of IHS Markit.

5.5 SUMMARY

In this chapter, we discussed the general process for firms wishing to start using alternative data. The initial stages require a lot of organizational work and investment to get the right team hired. When it comes to selecting and evaluating datasets, as well as technical work to understand the value of a signal, a large amount of due diligence needs to be performed before any data is even ingested. This due diligence involves understanding how the data is produced. This also involves understanding the source of the raw data to assess whether it poses any legal and other risks. If the dataset passes these initial checks, and proves to be valuable in the backtesting (or another performance measurement) stage, it is then possible to move into production. However, the work does not stop there. It is also necessary to monitor the production process carefully and maintain the high quality of the model.

CHAPTER 6

Factor Investing

6.1 INTRODUCTION

Factor investing is a popular way to gain excess returns on top of market returns in the long run while offering a variety of different investment options. In general, a factor can be thought of as any characteristic relating to a group of securities that is important in explaining their returns. Alternative data sources can be used to devise or anticipate investment factors and hence, in principle, a strategy that can outperform other passive investing schemes, as we will show in the next chapters. In this chapter we will summarize the foundations of factor investing and point to how alternative data can be used to create or enhance factors. Nevertheless, we must say that factor investing is not the only way to make use of alternative data. Indeed, in Chapters 1 and 2, we noted that discretionary investors could also incorporate alternative data in their framework. They could, for example, use one-off surveys to confirm/disconfirm their belief about a position they hold.

6.1.1 The CAPM

Using Markowitz's work as their foundation,[1] Treynor (1962), Sharpe (1964), Lintner (1965), and Mossin (1966) all independently developed what is now referred to as the Capital Asset Pricing Model (CAPM).

On top of Markowitz's assumptions, the CAPM further assumes that (1) there exists a risk-free rate at which all investors may lend or borrow an infinite amount, and (2) all investors possess homogeneous views on the expected return and volatility of all assets. Under CAPM, all asset returns are explained by the market return plus

---

[1] We assume that the reader is familiar with the basics of Markowitz's portfolio theory. For those who are not, we advise the following literature: Markowitz (1991), Markowitz & Todd (2000).

some random noise specific to each asset and unrelated to any other common factor, in other words the idiosyncratic risk. In terms of expectations this is expressed as:

$$E[r_i] = r_f + \beta_{p,m} E[r_m - r_f] \qquad (6.1)$$

where r_i is the return of the asset i, r_m is the return of the market, r_f the risk-free rate, and $\beta_{p,m} = \rho_{p,m} \sigma_p / \sigma_m$, with $\rho_{p,m}$ the correlation between the portfolio and the market, and σ_p and σ_m the standard deviations of the portfolio and market returns respectively. Hence the CAPM is a one-factor model where the only factor is the market.

It is important to note that the CAPM can be derived more fundamentally from a two-period equilibrium model[2] based on investor optimization, consumption, and market clearing, so its simple form in Equation (6.1) could be misleading as to the depth of the economic theory behind it. Still the assumptions behind it are very simplified and stylized. Nevertheless, it has gained wide popularity and has worked pretty well for a long time.

However, a large amount of empirical evidence has been accumulated showing that it does not describe other sources of return beyond the movements of the market portfolio (Fama and French, 2004). Because of this, many researchers have proposed alternative multifactor models. We discuss some of them here, but before doing so, we will introduce more formally the notion of a factor model. One thing to note in this discussion is that, of course, what we define as the beta, or market factor, is not a "hard" fact, but more a proxy of what a typical market investor's returns would look like. In some assets, a proxy to the market is relatively easy to define; for example, in stocks we might choose S&P 500 while in bonds it might be an index such as the Bloomberg Barclays Global Agg. For other asset classes, like FX, there isn't a widely accepted notion of market index.[3]

6.2   FACTOR MODELS

Definition: (Factor Model) – Suppose we have a set of n observable random variables, $x_1, x_2, \ldots, x_n$. We say that the x_i follow a factor model if given another set of random variables F_j, with $i \in \{1, 2, \ldots, n\}, j \in \{1, 2, \ldots k\}$, and $k < n$, we have that:

$$x_i = a_i + \sum_{j=1}^{k} \beta_{i,j} F_j + \varepsilon_i = E[x_i] + \sum_{j=1}^{k} \beta_{i,j}(F_j - E[F_j]) + \varepsilon_i \qquad (6.2)$$

where the $\beta_{i,j} = cov(x_i, F_j)/\Sigma_F$, $E[\varepsilon_i] = 0\ \forall i$, F and ε are independent, that is, $cov(F_j, \varepsilon_i) = 0\ \forall i, j$, and the matrix Σ_F is non-singular. The x_i are most often associated with asset returns but can be prices or payoffs. Sometimes it is also assumed

---

[2]See Cochrane (2009) for a derivation of the CAPM in a fundamental equilibrium approach. The "prediction" of such an approach is essentially Equation (6.1).

[3]In theory, the market in Equation (6.1) must include all the asset classes. In practice, it is very difficult to construct such an index, so proxies are preferred.

that $cov(\varepsilon_i, \varepsilon_j) = 0 \ \forall i, j, i \neq j$ and, if this is the case, one says that the x_i follow a strict factor model.[4]

There are three main types of factors: macroeconomic, statistical, and fundamental (see Connor et al., 2010). Macroeconomic factors can, for example, be surprises in GDP, surprises in inflation, and so on. Statistical factors, on the other hand, are identified through data mining techniques on time series of asset returns. They could be devoid of any economic meaning. Finally, fundamental factors capture stock characteristics, such as industry membership, country membership, valuation ratios, and technical indicators. Some of these factors have become so commonplace that they can often be referred to as beta factors and are the basis of many so-called "smart beta" investing approaches; some particular examples of this can be momentum-based approaches, and indeed we shall discuss such a momentum factor later in this chapter.

Connor (1995) compares the fit of the three types of factor models – macroeconomic, statistical, and fundamental – on the same universe of assets (US equities). He finds that the macroeconomic model performs poorly compared to the other two. This seems intuitive, given that macroeconomic factors are more likely to be suited to macro-based assets, such as equity indices or FX, rather than for trying to explain the behavior of single stocks. While macroeconomic factors do impact stocks as a whole, they are unlikely to be able to explain the idiosyncratic behavior of specific stocks. The fundamental model outperforms the statistical, which at first sight might appear surprising as statistical models are designed to maximize the fit. Connor attributes this to the larger number of factors used in the fundamental model. In fact, the statistical model is focused on the returns dataset only while the fundamental one incorporates extra factors, such as industry identifiers.

According to the type of model and the way we choose to calibrate it, the number of parameters we have to estimate differs, and sometimes having a parsimonious model is highly desirable. Suppose we have time series of length T. Then we will have the following sets of parameters to estimate for each type of model[5] (suppose a strict factor model):

1. **Statistical:** We have to estimate $\beta, \Sigma_F, \Sigma_\varepsilon, F$[6] (time series/cross-sectional regression), which translates into:

$$nk + kT + \frac{1}{2}k(k+1) + n \tag{6.3}$$

parameters, using the nT panel dataset of returns.

---

[4]In the case of well-diversified portfolios, one can indeed argue that the idiosyncratic errors can be neglected. However, such assumption does not always hold in practice. In fact, network effects (i.e. non-vanishing correlations) can be present among the ε and they might be non-negligible (see Billio, 2016; Ahelegbey, 2014).

[5]See Connor (2010).

[6]We drop the subscripts here.

2. **Macroeconomic:** We have to estimate $\beta, \Sigma_F, \Sigma_\epsilon$ (time series regression), which translates into:

$$nk + \frac{1}{2}k(k+1) + n \tag{6.4}$$

parameters, using the nT panel dataset of returns and kT set of macroeconomic factor innovations.

3. **Fundamental:** We have to estimate $\Sigma_F, \Sigma_\epsilon, F$ (cross-sectional regression), which translates into:

$$kT + \frac{1}{2}k(k+1) + n \tag{6.5}$$

parameters, using the nT panel dataset of returns and nk set of asset characteristics.

For large n the fundamental model has fewer parameters than the other two. However, it uses the most data as the nk dimensional cross-section of fundamental characteristics is usually larger than the kT dimensional dataset of macroeconomic factors. This means that the fundamental model has more information per parameter in case of large n. Compare all three cases to a situation where one has to estimate directly the covariance matrix of the asset returns (i.e. no factor model involved). This means estimating n^2 parameters, which for large n is a number significantly higher that those of the strict factor models we have discussed.

Connor (1995) also experiments with hybrid models, for example, macroeconomic and fundamental. The results show that both statistical and fundamental factors can enrich the macroeconomic model. The opposite is not true in his findings – macroeconomic factors add little to the explanatory power of the statistical and fundamental factors. Miller (2006) shows on a dataset consisting of Japanese equities that at weekly and monthly frequency fundamental models outperform statistical ones. However, he shows that, at daily frequency, a hybrid model of the two can show better performance.

6.2.1   The Arbitrage Pricing Theory

Stephen Ross (1972, 1973, 2013) proposed a purely statistical model to explain asset returns based on the multi-factor formulation of Equation (6.2) without the economic structure behind the CAPM. Using the law of one price in Equation (6.2) and neglecting the error term leads (given it has a mean of zero) to:[7]

$$E[r_i] = r_f + \sum_{j=1}^{k} \beta_{i,j} E[F_j - r_f] \tag{6.6}$$

---

[7]See Cochrane (2009) for the derivation of Equation (6.6) both in the absence of stochastic error terms and in their presence. In the latter case, the argument goes that diversification can remove idiosyncratic risk as error terms are uncorrelated with one another and with the factors. This, of course, might not hold because in reality, for finite portfolios, the residuals' small risk can still be priced in, or even for very large portfolios where some assets could represent large portions of the market. See again Cochrane (2009), Chapter 9, and Back (2010), Chapter 6, for a discussion on the topic.

with $cov(\varepsilon_i, \varepsilon_j) = 0 \; \forall i, j$, that is, the APT imposes a strict factor model on the returns. It is worth noting that, unlike CAPM, APT tells us nothing about what these factors should be or about the sign of each factor's excess return $E[F_j - r_f]$.[8] The number and nature of these factors could potentially vary over time and across markets. As a direct influence of the APT, many new multi-factor models were proposed after its publication. We will now examine the most famous of them – the Fama-French model.

6.2.2 The Fama-French 3-Factor Model

Fama and French (Fama and French, 1992) developed a widely accepted model and the most successful one so far. We can say that it belongs to the class of hybrid models based on both macroeconomic (the market) and fundamental factors.

Fama and French showed that the CAPM fails to adequately explain asset returns cross-sectionally for portfolios consisting of small/large stocks, and of portfolios consisting of high/low book-to-market[9] ratio stocks. It tends to underestimate returns for small or high-value stocks and overestimate them for big or low-value stocks.[10] Fama and French used portfolios based on these ratios and time series regression analysis to show the significance of these factors. More specifically they proposed the following model to explain the returns of the portfolios over the risk-free rate:

$$r_{i,t} - r_{f,t} = \alpha_i + \beta_{mkt,i}(r_{m,t} - r_{f,t}) + \beta_{SMB,i} * r_{SMB,t} + \beta_{HML,i} * r_{HML,t} + \varepsilon_{i,t} \quad (6.7)$$

where r_i is the return of portfolio i, r_f the risk free rate, r_m the market return (calculated as the return on the market cap weighted portfolio of all stocks), r_{SMB} the returns of small stocks over big stocks, r_{HML} returns of high-value stocks over low-value stocks, and ε stochastic error term. The r_{SMB} and r_{HML} are constructed as follows. The stocks universe is partitioned by book-to-market ratio into 3 groups and by market-cap into 2 groups. Then the following further partitions are created as a Cartesian product; that is, $\{high, medium, low\} \times \{big, small\} = \{high - big, \ldots, low - small\}$. Then the following quantities are calculated:

$$r_{SMB}(t) = \frac{1}{3}(r_{high-small}(t) + r_{medium-small}(t) + r_{low-small}(t))$$

$$- \frac{1}{3}(r_{high-big}(t) + r_{medium-big}(t) + r_{low-big}(t)) \quad (6.8)$$

$$r_{HML}(t) = \frac{1}{2}(r_{high-small}(t) + r_{high-big}(t)) - \frac{1}{2}(r_{low-small}(t) + r_{low-big}(t)) \quad (6.9)$$

in which r_{SMB} and r_{HML} are calculated monthly.

---

[8]Could be regarded as a risk premium in case of positive sign of $E[F_j - r_f]$.
[9]The book-to-market ratio is defined as the book value of a company divided by its market capitalization (a stock's price times shares outstanding). The book value is defined as the net asset value of a company (i.e. the difference between total assets and total liabilities).
[10]Low-value stocks are also called growth stocks; high-value stocks are simply sometimes called value stocks.

Throughout Fama and French (1992), Fama and French (1993), and Fama and French (1995) it is shown that the Fama-French 3-factor model explains cross-sectional asset returns better than CAPM. In fact, their 3-factor model yields adjusted R^2 above 0.9 for 21 out of 25 examined portfolios. In contrast, by using only CAPM, just 2 out of 25 cases yield such good results (Fama and French, 1993, pp. 19–25).

Hence, rather than taking an equilibrium-based approach as the one on which the CAPM is founded, Fama and French based their model on purely empirical findings in the spirit of APT. A lot of explanations have been attempted ever since to understand why these factors fit empirical data so well. Are they proxy for some macroeconomic variables? Although in this way they would be easier to motivate, attempts to explain in this way the *HML* and *SMB* factors have not been extremely successful. However, research went also in the direction of complementing the *HML* and *SMB* factors with other factors with which their correlation is low. Momentum is such a factor, and this motivated the Carhart model, which we now describe.

6.2.3   The Carhart Model

There is empirical evidence that a long portfolio of long-term bad performers and short previous long-term high performers does better than the opposite (see Fama and French, 1996). The performance is calculated over a long period – that is, in the interval $(-5, -1)$ years before the rebalancing date. This may sound intuitive because stocks that have done too well in the past might be overpriced and vice versa. Fama and French, however, manage to explain the outcome of this strategy in terms of their *HML* factor (i.e. bad performers have higher $\beta_{HML,i}$).

However, if performance is calculated over the last 12 months – that is, not in the interval $(-5, -1)$ years – the picture is the opposite: good performers tend to continue to perform well and vice versa. This behavior cannot be explained by the Fama-French factors. This led Carhart (see Carhart, 1997) to propose a 4-factor model, which, in addition to the Fama-French factors, includes a momentum factor:

$$r_{i,t} - r_{f,t} = \alpha_i + \beta_{mkt,i}(r_m - r_f) + \beta_{SMB,i} * r_{SMB,t} + \beta_{HML,i} * r_{HML,t}$$
$$+ \beta_{UMD,i} * r_{UMD,t} + \varepsilon_i \qquad (6.10)$$

in which $r_{UMD,t}$ is constructed as the equal-weighted average of stocks with the highest 30% 11-month returns lagged one month minus the equal-weighted average of stocks with the lowest 30% eleven-month returns lagged one month. Carhart proves the significance of this regression on a dataset of funds returns. However, he also shows that after accounting for transaction costs, such a strategy is not necessarily winning. The Fama-French and Carhart models are not the only ones (although the most famous and tested!) that we can use in practice. There is no fundamental reason to believe, though, that the factors they propose are the only viable ones, neither to strictly adopt the sorting approach it is based upon. A more data-mining-based approach, which we will now discuss, is also perfectly justifiable.

6.2.4 Other Approaches (Data Mining)

Investors have long been in search of factors that indicate high or low average returns, seeking to construct portfolios based on those. These factors should not necessarily be constructed from the financial statements alone. Indeed, the case for using alternative data is that we can gain something on the top of accounting variables.[11]

We must note that there are some caveats to a pure data mining approach though. As pointed out by Yan and Zheng (2017), an important debate in the literature is whether the data-mined abnormal returns that can be generated by a strategy are compensation for systematic risk. One example of this is the carry-based factor model, which typically involves sorting assets by their carry (e.g. dividends in stocks). Long positions are taken in higher carry assets, funded by short positions in low carry assets. Typically, those assets with higher levels of carry are also more prone to large drawdowns. Hence, the strategy effectively harvests a risk premium, which is subject to periodic episodes of stress during market turbulence.

While data mining can uncover evidence of market inefficiencies, it is also prone to detecting patterns that are completely spurious and unstable through time. In other words, are we simply fitting to statistical noise? For example, in the case many variables are considered, then by pure chance this could lead to abnormal returns even if these variables do not genuinely have any predictive ability for future stock returns. An important test to perform in this case is whether the uncovered signals are due to sampling variation. Other desirable properties of the factors to be looked for are, for example, persistence over time, large enough variability in returns relative to individual stock volatility, and application to a broad enough subset of stocks within the defined universe (Miller, 2006).

Yan (2017), having first shown in their research that the fundamental-based anomalies they discover are not due to random chance, investigate whether they are consistent with mispricing or risk-based explanations. They conduct three tests for this purpose. We refer the reader to Yan (2017) for details around these tests but what is important to note is that their results indicate that a large number of fundamental factors exhibit genuine predictive ability for future stock returns. That evidence suggests that fundamental-based anomalies are more consistent with mispricing-based explanations.

While some of their factors have been explored in previous studies by other authors, many of the top fundamental signals identified in the Yan (2017) study were new at the time of publication and had received little attention in the prior literature. For example, they find that anomaly variables constructed based on, for example, interest expense, tax loss carry-forward, and selling, general, and administrative expense are highly correlated with future stock returns. They argue that it is reasonable to assume that these variables may predict future stock returns because they contain value-relevant information about future firm performance and the market fails

---

[11] Factors other than those based on accounting variables or alternative data can be of value as well. The momentum factor in the Carhart model, for example, is constructed from past stock returns, which is neither accounting nor alternative data.

to incorporate this information into stock prices in a timely manner. They conclude that limited attention is a more plausible reason of why investors fail to fully appreciate the information content of the fundamental variables documented in their study. We will leverage the approach and the findings of Yan (2017) later in Chapter 10.

An important test that we could perform is how the newly discovered factors correlate with the Fama-French factors. This will show us whether the former are a proxy for the latter and hence redundant, or whether they indeed contain some additional signals. In the same spirit, Fama and French (1996) analyzed strategies based on factors different from the *HML* and *SMB* and found that the strategies are mostly explained by their factors, and not purely by the market beta. Indeed, a key point of using alternative data is the hypothesis that by using an unusual dataset we are less likely to find a signal that correlates with existing factors.

6.3   THE DIFFERENCE BETWEEN CROSS-SECTIONAL AND TIME SERIES TRADING APPROACHES

Throughout this chapter, the trading rules we have discussed include ranking assets based upon a specific factor. We then take positions in these assets depending on their ranking. In other words, we are constructing cross-sectional trading rules. Hence our position in one asset is impacted by the position in another one. While cross-sectional rules are popular in equities, they can also be found in other asset classes when a factor-driven approach to trading is used, based, for example, on carry, which can be applied to many asset classes including FX. Sometimes these can be used to create market-neutral portfolios or alternatively to adjust the weightings on a long-only portfolio.

This contrasts to purely time-series-driven trading rules, such as those adopted by many managed futures trend-following funds. Typically, they trade futures in various macro-based assets, including sovereign bonds, FX, equity indices, and commodities, as opposed to single stocks. They take long or short positions in a particular future, purely based upon the trend in that asset, which is calculated based on the time series of a specific asset. This contrasts to a cross-sectional approach, where we use some sort of ranking approach across many assets at the same time.

6.4   WHY FACTOR INVESTING?

At this point, it is natural for one to ask what is the empirical evidence of performance when using factor-based strategies? There is some evidence that in good market conditions, indices based on extra factors do tend to outperform a simpler passive approach such as being long a market-cap index. We do of course note that, while such approaches are typically referred to as passive, in practice, such indices do have rebalancing rules associated with them, which tend to favor the larger cap stocks over time. Hence, "passive" strategies might be more active than investors believe.

In bad conditions, however, factor-based strategies can underperform the market (see Ang, 2014). Particular examples of this are those that harvest a risk premium, like carry, as we have noted. In general, however, markets seem to grow and have longer periods of strength than of weakness. In the long run then, it would make sense that market returns occurring in growth periods more than compensate for poor returns occurring during market declines and beat the market index. In fact, this is exactly what we have seen. Since 1973, there have been multiple periods in which factor indices[12] have underperformed the market. Overall, however, \$1 invested in the MSCI World index from 1973 to 2015 would have risen to \$34, whereas \$1 invested in their value index would have risen to \$49, or to \$98 in their momentum index[13] (see Authers, 2015). In the long run, then, it seems that the benefits outweigh the costs, at least given the current empirical evidence.

Given the historical evidence of outperformance of these factors over the market, a new type of passive investing has appeared. Rather than investing in the whole market weighted by market cap, investors decided to incorporate these findings by selecting subsets of the market to invest in, based on these factors (factor investing) or using alternative weighting systems to the market cap (smart beta investing). The benefits of these methods are similar to those of passive investing:

- Large investment capacity: Due to investing in indices, the market cap of the chosen investment universe is very large. It would, therefore, take an extreme amount of capital to move the market in some way (i.e. not to be a price taker). This is very attractive to large funds (e.g. pension funds), because many smaller strategies do not scale well when dealing with portfolio values in the high millions/billions.

- Low costs: As these methods are quite simple and can be readily automated, little effort is required to execute them. Thus, costs are low in terms of both factor selection and execution. In the past many of these smart beta strategies were typically only available to investors who allocated to hedge funds while these days variants of these factors are available through lower-cost wrappers such as ETFs.

- Diversification: As these methods are based on index investing, we still experience, given a large enough universe to invest over, a very good level of diversification among stocks.

Clarke et al. (2005) show that, with the addition of factor investment strategies, one can expand the efficient frontier and push/rotate it northwest, thus offering higher returns for the same level of risk.

6.5 SMART BETA INDICES USING ALTERNATIVE DATA INPUTS

For many years, financial indices have been used to benchmark market performance and are frequently tracked by institutional investors. The index market has evolved in

---

[12]Indices constructed with weights according to some risk factor (e.g. the value factor).
[13]These are the equivalent of roughly 8.8%, 9.7%, and 11.5% compound annual returns, respectively.

the last few years with the introduction of thematic and factor-based indices (smart beta), but they have not evolved too much to leverage the abundance of alternative data. However, recently, some index providers have started considering incorporating alternative data into a new generation of indices.

For example, a company named Indexica[14] provides indices such as Severity, Opportunity, Complexity, and Futurity. Futurity, for example, analyses through NLP and assigns a score regarding how much a company is referred to in the past and future tenses. Indexica found that if it ranked the constituents of the S&P 500 by their futurity score, the top decile has had between a 60% and 70% return over the past three years while the lowest decile had a 20% return over the same period.

Refinitiv created sector-based news sentiment indices, which track, for a given industry or sector, the media sentiment about this sector. Borovkova et al. (2017) empirically investigate the relationship between the Refinitiv sector sentiment indices for 11 sectors and the stocks trading in that sector. They show that this relationship is particularly significant at times of market downturns.

Indices are based on a set of underlying factors. For example, the main factor driving the S&P 500 is market capitalization. We shall see in Chapter 10 that by using automotive data factors other than the market cap can be predictive for companies' performance. We shall show results when weighting the companies by market cap or equally, comparing them to results using automotive data, including some alternative datasets relating to the automotive supply chain. Later, in Section 6.8, we give a broader overview of how to incorporate alternative data into the process of creating indices.

6.6 ESG FACTORS

Typically, when we think of developing factor indices, such as trend, our main objective is to maximize some type of return statistic, whether that is the Sharpe ratio, annualized returns, or others. However, there are some scenarios where we might wish to incorporate other criteria into our model. One such situation involves ESG-based factors for equities portfolios. In this instance, we want to select firms that adhere to various ethical standards, related to the environment, social, and governance concerns. This initiative to use ESG has been driven by investors, including some of the world's largest funds, such as Norges Bank Investment Management (Norges Bank Investment Management, 2018). There are no widely accepted definitions of what precise criteria to quantify companies through an ESG score. However, we can try to give a broad definition.

On the environment side, we can look at a number of factors, such as firms' usage of energy, how they handle waste, and so on. As we might expect, oil companies are unlikely to score very high on such criteria. By contrast, firms involved in more sustainable industries score highly.

For the social part, it is possible to look at how the company interacts with its clients, workers, and local community. It is unlikely that tobacco firms score highly

---

[14]https://www.indexica.com/.

on this scale, given that their products are harmful to their users. What are workers' conditions like and is a high priority given to their safety? Do they have policies for diversity? When we look at governance, we need to see what their decision-making process is like. Do they listen to the concerns of shareholders? Does their board have oversight? Do they have policies in place to manage conflicts of interest? Have they been accused of unethical and illegal practices such as bribery? Do board members have any significant conflicts of interest?

We could argue that given climate change, firms that score poorly on environmental issues are unlikely to be as good long-term investments in the coming decades. Hence there is likely to be a link with long-term returns and a firm's environmental score. One example might be an oil company that is not preparing for renewable energy. The same is also true of governance. A poorly governed firm is unlikely to be a good investment, as it could be subject to increased risks, whether related to litigation or also fraud. From the perspective of social concerns, we could also argue that firms that restrict their recruiting pool to a very small subset of the population are unlikely to be getting the best employees. Furthermore, the lack of diversity could also foster a large amount of groupthink. If firms treat their employees poorly, they are also unlikely to be productive as they could be.

It can be difficult to quantify the criteria for ESG. After all, most of the questions we ask are qualitative. However, we are ultimately interested in creating a time series of quantifiable results on which to rank companies. At present there are a number of alternative data vendors developing data products that give ESG data for companies. These include firms such as Engaged Tracking. Firms developing metrics for ESG can use a variety of techniques to harvest this information, ranging from parsing news to delving into annual reports of firms, essentially combining a mixture of data sources from within and outside the firm. RobecoSAM created an annual Corporate Sustainability Assessment (CSA) for over 4800 companies based on ESG criteria. RobecoSAM has partnered with S&P to create factor-based indices for common factors, such as momentum, which also incorporate ESG information derived from CSA.

6.7   DIRECT AND INDIRECT PREDICTION

Given our ultimate goal of predicting asset returns by making use of alternative data, we have three ways to proceed. We can either directly predict asset returns from the alternative data at hand; or we can use it to first predict some fundamentals and then make the link from the fundamentals to asset returns; or we can predict asset returns by jointly using alternative data and fundamentals. In the case of a company, the fundamentals can be financial ratios, such as book-to-market, leverage, earnings per share, or the like. There might be instances where the alternative dataset we are examining is already in a relatively structured form, which makes it intuitive to hypothesize that it has a direct relationship with returns. However, this might not always be the case.

In the case of investing macro-based assets, such as bonds or FX, we may seek to forecast macro data. These could be budget deficits or labor markets, for example.

We could also seek to track central bank communications to understand how they will likely change monetary policy, in reaction to shifting fundamentals. There is no way to say which one is better because it depends on the specificity of the problem and of the data. In practice, even if we are trading single stocks, we might also wish to have a broader-based macro overlay, as equity sector performance can be very sensitive to the various stages of the economic cycle.

One can argue in favor of first predicting fundamentals. In fact, there is economic intuition of why, say, company fundamentals should drive equity returns. If, for example, revenues-to-expenses decreases, our intuition suggests that this will negatively impact the equity price. If leverage increases, we also expect the credit spread to go up. We can also conjecture that macroeconomic fundamentals are likely to impact macro assets such as sovereign bond markets or currency markets. If economic data becomes weaker, it is likely that central banks will be more dovish. Hence, bond yields are likely to fall as the market prices in a more dovish outlook. Conversely, when economic data is consistently strong and pointing to higher inflation, it is likely that yields could rise. The rationale is that the market is pricing in a more hawkish central bank. The shift in monetary policy expectations often also ripples into the way currency markets trade.

Then we can use alternative data to predict such ratios. The approach would differ between industry sectors. In the case of revenue forecasting of, say, shopping centers, satellite images from parking lots could be a good predictor. For a firm such as Apple, we would need to try different approaches to forecast revenues. In this case, their revenues are heavily related to iPhone sales, and one way to do this could be through tracking mentions of iPhone in social media (Lassen, Madsen, & Vatrapu, 2014). We can also try to trade our fundamental forecast predictions around specific short-term events, such as quarterly company equities releases or economic data releases. Admittedly, there are likely to be some capacity constraints around such short-term strategies.

Hence, the modeling path we are opting for in this case (Model A)[15] is shown in Figure 6.1.

Contrast this with the direct approach (Model B) in Figure 6.2.

A third approach in which both alternative and fundamental data are used directly to predict asset returns is shown in Figure 6.3.

FIGURE 6.1   Probabilistic Graphical Model (PGM) showing a potential modeling sequence (Model A) where AD = Alternative Data, F = Fundamentals, AR = Asset Return.

---

[15]In this section we will make use of the language of Probabilistic Graphical Models (PGM). For an introduction see Koller et al. (2009).

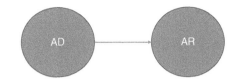

FIGURE 6.2   Another potential modeling sequence (Model B).

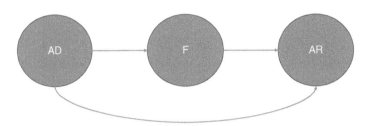

FIGURE 6.3   A third potential modeling sequence (Model C).

It is important to understand what all these alternatives mean. Assume for the sake of simplicity that we have only one variable in the alternative dataset trying to predict only one fundamental ratio, and let's focus on the case of linear regression models. In terms of equations, Model A translates into:

$$AR = \beta_{AR,F}F + \varepsilon_{AR} \tag{6.11}$$

$$F = \beta_{F,AD}AD + \varepsilon_F \tag{6.12}$$

with the assumption that $cov(\varepsilon_{AR}, \varepsilon_F) = 0$. For Model B we have:

$$AR = \beta'_{AR,F}AD + \varepsilon'_{AR} \tag{6.13}$$

and for Model C:

$$AR = \beta''_{AR,F}F + \beta''_{AR,AD}AD + \varepsilon''_{AR} \tag{6.14}$$

$$F = \beta''_{F,AD}AD + \varepsilon''_F \tag{6.15}$$

where it is assumed that $cov(\varepsilon''_{AR}, \varepsilon'_F) = 0$. There is no way to conclude upfront which is the best model but each modeling sequence we choose comes with assumptions with regard to the correlation (of lack thereof) between residual error terms.

We must say that practical considerations will also guide the modeling choice, like the availability of data. For example, assume that we have alternative data only for a short amount of time, say, 2 years of daily observations. Company fundamentals, on the other hand, are only available at quarterly frequency or perhaps semi-annual frequency, depending on the country. This means that over the 2 years' time window, the equations used to predict F (Model A and Model C) will have very low statistical power. In Model C, this also means converting AD to quarterly frequency, thus losing potential variation due to lower time granularity. If the asset returns are available daily, then a better option could be to use directly Model B but with the caveat that we might sacrifice some economic intuition. We will test the three approaches in Chapter 10 on a dataset consisting of global automotive stocks, alongside an alternative dataset from IHS Markit on the automotive supply chain.

We also point readers to other literature on this subject. This includes Guida (2019), who applies machine learning for factor investing. Their study uses a machine learning technique (XGBoost) to incorporate features based on equity ratios into a factor model that trades single stocks. Alberg and Lipton (2018), meanwhile, use deep learning to forecast traditional company fundamental ratios. These forecasts are used as inputs into an equity factor trading model. We shall elaborate on this paper in Chapter 10, in our own analysis of a trading strategy on automotive stocks.

6.8 SUMMARY

In this chapter, we gave a brief introduction to factor-based investing, discussing some of the most common factor models. While factors such as trend and value are very well established and form the basis of various smart beta indices, we noted that alternative data could be used within the process to enhance existing factors and also create new ones. As we might expect, factor-based investing is usually focused on improving the return statistics for an investor. However, it is possible that investors may have other objectives, over and above purely examining returns. We cited the example of ESG datasets that could be used by factor investors to include in their investment process, considerations related to environmental, social, and governance firms. In general, firms that score highly on ESG criteria are also likely to be good investments. For example, it is unlikely that a firm that is seen as having governance issues and significant conflicts of interest would be seen as a plus by markets.

PART 2

Practical Applications

Chapter 7: Missing Data: Background, 135
Chapter 8: Missing Data: Case Studies, 151
Chapter 9: Outliers (Anomalies), 181
Chapter 10: Automotive Fundamental Data, 205
Chapter 11: Surveys and Crowdsourced Data, 245
Chapter 12: Purchasing Managers' Index, 259
Chapter 13: Satellite Imagery and Aerial Photography, 267
Chapter 14: Location Data, 283
Chapter 15: Text, Web, Social Media, and News, 299
Chapter 16: Investor Attention, 323
Chapter 17: Consumer Transactions, 335
Chapter 18: Government, Industrial, and Corporate Data, 341
Chapter 19: Market Data, 351
Chapter 20: Alternative Data in Private Markets, 359

CHAPTER 7

Missing Data: Background

7.1 INTRODUCTION

As we discussed in Section 3.3.2, dealing with missing data – a ubiquitous problem – is one of the crucial steps in making data useful at all. In this chapter we will describe the problem of missing data imputation in more general terms. We will present a specific case study that focuses on filling gaps in multivariate financial time series in the next chapter.

Providing a general recipe for tackling missing data is not possible, given that the problem arises in many different-in-nature practical applications. For example, filling gaps in financial time series can be quite different from filling gaps in satellite images or text. Nevertheless, some techniques can be widely reused over different domains, as we will show in this chapter and the next. Techniques to fill missing data are applicable regardless of whether or not a dataset is alternative, so in what follows we will not make such distinction. We only remark that, in general, we expect to have more missing data and data quality problems in the alternative data space. This is due to the increased variety, velocity, and variability of alternative data compared to more standardized traditional datasets.

Treating missing data is something that must be performed before any further analysis is attempted. A predictive model (e.g. an investment strategy) can then be calibrated on the treated dataset as a second step. We must be careful, though, to understand whether the missing data in the training set was something accidental (e.g. deleted records in the historical database by mistake) or is a recurrent and unescapable characteristic of the data that will reappear in live feeds, hopefully with the same patterns when later deployed in production. In the latter case, the missing data algorithms must be implemented in production as well. It is also important to understand whether the missing data algorithms we built in the preprocessing stage are applicable in a live environment. This will depend on constraints such as how those algorithms are implemented, what is the maximum computational time tolerated for the execution of the missing data treatment step, and the like.

However, as we already mentioned in Chapter 5, if missing data is not something accidental in the training set but reappears in production, it could start to appear in a completely different pattern due to a variety of reasons. These could be a temporary technical glitch that must be fixed. Alternatively, it might be because certain information is no longer collected and hence the associated data feed is interrupted. In the latter case this might call for a complete revision of the algorithms – both for the investment strategy and for the missing data treatment step. Another possibility is that the missing data pattern has changed compared to the training set due to the changing nature of the input data. With market data, one obvious example can be changes in trading hours or the holiday calendar. In this case, this calls for a revision and update of the algorithm used to fill the missing data and maybe those of the investment strategy. A careful analysis is necessary according to each individual case to assess the best course of action. Last, non-stationarity (see Section 4.4.2) or regime changes can also impact the data collection and hence the missingness pattern. For example, when consensus estimates are collected, say, for credit default swap prices, they are not published if the dispersion of the analysts' estimates is too big. A disagreement between analysts is more likely to happen in periods of market turmoil, which could thus add different missingness patterns to the data.

7.2 MISSING DATA CLASSIFICATION

Patterns of missingness can appear in very different forms, which can impact the imputation strategy, as we will describe in the following sections. Hence, it is useful to first analyze possible missing mechanisms as well as common patterns.

In the statistical literature one usually considers the data being generated by a distribution function, $g(X|\theta)$, with unknown parameters θ. The functional form of g may or may not be known. It is then of interest to clarify how the missingness pattern M is generated and how it is related to the observed data – that is, what general form the conditional distribution function $f(M|X, \phi)$ has where ϕ is a collection of unknown parameters. Formally, we can separate the data into observed and missing parts, $X = (X^{obs}, X^{miss})$. This is meant to be understood as follows: there exists a complete dataset X, but we only observe values X^{obs}. The values X^{miss} are not observed, so usually we would not know them. However, for the following reasoning it is very useful to consider their values and their relation to the missingness patterns as well. In the literature typically the following distinction is made:[1]

1. **Missing Completely at Random (MCAR):** Missingness patterns do not depend on any observed or non-observed data values:

$$f(M|X, \phi) = f(M|\phi) \tag{7.1}$$

---

[1] See Little (2019).

2. **Missing at Random (MAR):** Missingness patterns depend on observed but not on non-observed data values:

$$f(M|X, \phi) = f(M|X^{obs}, \phi) \qquad (7.2)$$

One may find the term MAR confusing, since the missingness pattern M is not random, but rather depends on the observed values. It is, however, commonly used in the literature.

3. **Missing Not at Random (MNAR):** Missingness patterns depend on both observed and non-observed data values:

$$f(M|X, \phi) = f(M|X^{obs}, X^{miss}, \phi) \qquad (7.3)$$

An example for MAR is a survey where income quotes are missing for respondents above a certain age. An example for MNAR would be that in a survey income values are more likely to be missing if these values are below a certain threshold and age (observed) is above a certain value. In other words, respondents leave out income if they are old and earn little. The distinction has the following consequences: MCAR and MAR belong to a class of missingness that is called ignorable and that makes it applicable for multiple imputation (MI) approaches, which we will describe later. Roughly speaking, the non-observed values can be integrated out in these cases. In contrast, treating MNAR carefully is more difficult since in principle we cannot predict the missing values only from the observed ones. In these situations, extra data collection or additional insights from domain experts can be useful. Formally, one can then introduce suitable priors to deal with the imputation. Some of the MI packages allow for that.

7.2.1 Missing Data Treatments

In general, there are three methods to deal with missing data: (1) deletion, (2) replacement, and (3) predictive imputation. The first two are very simple and rudimentary, but they could be used in cases where the impact of their application is small or building a predictive imputation model could be too costly. We describe the three methods in the following.

7.2.1.1 Deletion

Deletion is the simplest method. It consists of simply removing records. This can be done listwise or pairwise. Listwise deletion means that any record in a dataset is deleted from an analysis if there is missing data on any variable taken into consideration in the analysis. In certain cases, this can be a viable option, but more often this constitutes a very costly procedure because a lot of data is discarded. Dropping records reduces the sample size and hence the statistical power of the results unless the remaining sample is still substantial. Moreover, this approach only works if the data is MCAR. If it is not, incomplete records that are dropped will differ from the complete cases still in the sample. Then the remaining selected random sample is no longer reflective of the entire population. This could lead to biased results. In some cases, listwise deletion is entirely impractical; for instance, for the credit default swap data discussed in the next chapter, we would lose a lot of valuable data.[2] Therefore, listwise deletion nowadays is usually dismissed in favor of more sophisticated techniques.

In pairwise deletion, missing data is simply ignored and only the non-missing variables are considered for each record. Pairwise deletion allows the use of more of the data. However, each computed statistic may be based on a different subset of cases and this could cause problems. For instance, using pairwise deletion may not yield a proper positive semidefinite correlation matrix.

More flexible and powerful strategies are ones where we predict missing data from the observed one. Generally, one can distinguish deterministic from stochastic approaches for data imputation.

7.2.1.2   Replacement

A basic deterministic approach is to impute missing values for a particular feature by a simple guess, such as the mean of the observed values of this feature or the majority value (mode). This can be a successful strategy if the missing fraction is very small. There are, however, two problems with this approach: (1) mean or mode imputation can be inaccurate, and (2) as discussed extensively in the literature (see Little & Rubin, 2019; Schafer, 1997), this simple imputation technique alters the statistical properties of the data. For instance, the variance of a variable is decreased through mean imputation. For missing values in a time series, we also need to be careful not to use a mean that is computed using future values, and only use a mean computed on historical values.

7.2.1.3   Predictive Imputation

To overcome the limitations of the simpleminded approaches, like mean imputation, a statistical framework has emerged over the last 30 years, which is termed multiple imputation (MI). The general idea of this framework is to deduce joint distribution functions from which the imputed data can be sampled. The data imputation is then nondeterministic, and multiple imputation sets can be generated. For predictive analytics on a completed dataset, statistics for the predicted quantities can be computed. Hence, the uncertainty about the imputation can be properly accounted for. Moreover, these imputation techniques ensure that statistical properties of the data, such as the underlying distribution, mean, and variance are not altered by the imputation.

This will be also one of the approaches we will use in the case examined in the next chapter. But before that, let's turn to provide a literature review of some missing data treatments that fall in the predictive imputation class.

---

[2] In any application, a judgment on whether we will lose a lot or a small amount of data depends on the aim of the application. In the case study in the next chapter, the data can be used for the calculation of the Expected Shortfall (ES), for example. The calculation of ES requires recent and plentiful data, which induces a low tolerance to long streaks of missing data.

7.3   LITERATURE OVERVIEW OF MISSING DATA TREATMENTS[3]

According to Wang (2010), inappropriate handling of missing data can introduce bias, leading to misleading conclusions and limited generalizability of research findings. Barnard (1999) argues that the most frequent types of associated problems with the lack of missing data treatment are: (1) loss of efficiency; (2) complications in handling and analyzing the data; and (3) bias resulting from differences between missing and complete data. This points to the fact that treating missing data is of crucial importance to practical applications.

In what follows we will review some of the important papers, in our view, on missing data imputation. We will substantiate the fact that – as expected by virtue of the no-free-lunch theorem – we cannot have a best-performing imputation algorithm for every problem. Instead, the "best" algorithm must be chosen for the specific problem we are examining.

7.3.1   Luengo et al. (2012)

The first paper we will summarize is that of Luengo et al. (2012), which compares the effects of 14 different imputation techniques on data on which 23 classifiers are subsequently trained. The classifiers fall into these three categories:

1. **Rule Induction Learning.** This group refers to algorithms that infer rules using different strategies. Those methods that produce a set of more or less interpretable rules belong in this category. These rules include discrete and/or continuous features, which are treated by each method depending on their definition and representation. This type of classification method has been the most used in cases of imperfect data.

2. **Approximate Models.** This group includes artificial neural networks, support vector machines, and statistical learning. Luengo et al. include in this group those methods that act like a black box. Hence, those methods that do not produce an interpretable model fall under this category. Although the naïve Bayes method is not a completely black box method, the paper considers that this is the most appropriate category for it.

3. **Lazy Learning.** This group includes methods that are not based on any model but use the training data to perform the classification directly. This process implies the presence of measures of similarity of some kind. Thus, all the methods that use a similarity function to relate the inputs to the training set are considered as belonging to this category.

The classification methods falling into the rule induction learning group are C4.5 (C4.5); Ripper (Ripper); CN2 (CN2); AQ-15 (AQ); PART (PART); Slipper (Slipper); scalable rule induction (SRI); Rule induction two in one (Ritio); and Rule

---

[3]The reader can also take a look at Graham (2009), who provides an exhaustive introduction to missing data problems.

extraction system version 6 (Rule-6). The classification methods falling into the approximate models group are multilayer perceptron (MLP); C-SVM (C-SVM); v-SVM (v-SVM); sequential minimal optimization (SMO); radial basis function network (RBFN); RBFN decremental (RBFND); RBFN incremental (RBFNI); logistic (LOG); naïve Bayes (NB); and learning vector quantization (LVQ). The classification methods falling into the lazy learning group are 1-NN (1-NN); 3-NN (3-NN), locally weighted learning (LWL), and lazy learning of Bayesian rules (LBR).

Finally, the imputation techniques they employ are do not impute (DNI), case deletion or ignore missing (IM), global most common/average (MC), concept most common/average (CMC), k-nearest neighbor (KNNI), weighted k-NN (WKNNI), k-means clustering imputation (KMI), fuzzy k-means clustering (FKMI), support vector machines (SVMI), event covering (EC), regularized expectation kmaximization (EM), singular value decomposition imputation (SVDI), Bayesian principal component analysis (BPCA), and local least squares imputation (LLSI).

They first apply each imputation technique before applying each classification method to each of the 21 (imputed) datasets. Each imputer-classifier combination is then given a rank on how it performed over the given dataset. The Wilcoxon signed rank test is then used to assign each imputer-classifier a single rank,[4] which can be seen in Figure 7.1. The lower the value of the rank, the better that imputation technique performs in combination with that classifier.

7.3.1.1 Induction Learning Methods
Luengo et al. come to the conclusion that, for the rule induction learning classifiers, the imputation methods FKMI, SVMI, and EC perform best, as can be seen in Figure 7.2. These three imputation methods are, therefore, the most suitable for this type of classifiers. Furthermore, both FKMI and EC methods were also considered among the best overall.

7.3.1.2 Approximate Models
In the case of approximate models, differences between imputation methods are more evident. One can clearly select the EC imputation technique as the best solution (see Figure 7.3), as seen by its average rank of 4.75, almost 1 lower than the next nearest technique, KMI, which stands as the second best with an average rank of 5.65. Next, we see FKMI with an average rank of 6.20. In this family of classification methods, EC is, therefore, the superior imputation technique.

7.3.1.3 Lazy Learning Methods
For this set of methods (Figure 7.4) Luengo et al. find that MC is the best imputation technique with an average rank of 3.63, followed by CMC with an average ranking of 4.38. Only the FKMI method can be compared with the MC and CMC methods with an average rank of 4.75, with all other techniques having an average rank at or above 6.25. Once again, the DNI and IM methods obtain low rankings, with DNI coming 13th of 14, with only the BPCA method performing worse.

---

[4]See Section 4.1 in Luengo et al. (2012).

	RBFN	RBFND	RBFNI	C4.5	1-NN	LOG	LVQ	MLP	NB	ν-SVM	C-SVM	Ripper	PART	Slipper	3-NN	AQ	CN2	SMO	LBR	LWL	SRI	Ritio	Rule-6	Avg.	RANKS
IM	9	6.5	4.5	5	5	6	3.5	13	12	10	5.5	8.5	1	4	11	6.5	10	5.5	5	8	6.5	6	5	6.83	7
EC	1	1	1	2.5	9.5	3	7	8.5	10	13	1	8.5	6.5	1	13	6.5	5.5	2	9	8	6.5	6	1	5.7	2
KNNI	5	6.5	10.5	9	2.5	9	7	11	6.5	8	5.5	2.5	6.5	11	5.5	11	5.5	5.5	9	8	11.5	11	11	7.76	10
WKNNI	13	6.5	4.5	11	4	10	10	4.5	6.5	4.5	5.5	2.5	6.5	7	5.5	6.5	1	5.5	9	8	11.5	6	11	6.96	8
KMI	3.5	2	7	5	12	3	11	3	4.5	8	5.5	2.5	6.5	3	5.5	6.5	5.5	9	9	2.5	9.5	12	7.5	6.24	5
FKMI	12	6.5	10.5	7.5	6	3	1.5	4.5	11	4.5	5.5	2.5	6.5	10	1.5	2	5.5	3	9	2.5	1	2	3	5.26	1
SVMI	2	11.5	2.5	1	9.5	7.5	3.5	1.5	13	8	11	5.5	6.5	7	9	1	5.5	9	3	8	6.5	6	2	6.09	3
EM	3.5	6.5	13	13	11	12	12.5	10	4.5	4.5	10	12	6.5	7	5.5	12	13	11.5	9	2.5	3	6	4	8.37	11
SVDI	9	6.5	7	11	13	11	12.5	8.5	3	11.5	12	11	6.5	12	12	10	12	11.5	1	12	9.5	10	11	9.72	12
BPCA	14	14	14	14	14	13	7	14	2	2	13	13	13	7	14	13	14	13	13	13	13	13	13	11.87	14
LLSI	6	6.5	10.5	11	7.5	7.5	7	6.5	9	4.5	5.5	5.5	6.5	7	5.5	6.5	11	9	9	8	3	6	7.5	7.22	9
MC	9	6.5	10.5	7.5	7.5	3	7	6.5	8	11.5	5.5	8.5	6.5	2	1.5	6.5	5.5	5.5	3	2.5	3	6	7.5	6.11	4
CMC	9	13	2.5	5	1	3	1.5	1.5	14	14	5.5	8.5	12	13	5.5	3	5.5	1	3	8	6.5	1	7.5	6.28	6
DNI	9	11.5	7	2.5	2.5	14	14	12	1	1	14	14	14	14	10	14	5.5	14	14	14	14	14	14	10.61	13

FIGURE 7.1 Average rank for all the classifiers. Column "Avg." is the average of all ranks for a given imputation technique.
Source: Based on data from Luengo et al. (2012).

	C45	Ripper	PART	Slipper	AQ	CN2	SRI	Ritio	Rules-6	Avg.	RANKS
IM	5	8.5	1	4	6.5	10	6.5	6	5	5.83	4
EC	2.5	8.5	6.5	1	6.5	5.5	6.5	6	1	4.89	3
KNNI	9	2.5	6.5	11	11	5.5	11.5	11	11	8.78	11
WKNNI	11	2.5	6.5	7	6.5	1	11.5	6	11	7	8
KMI	5	2.5	6.5	3	6.5	5.5	9.5	12	7.5	6.44	6
FKMI	7.5	2.5	6.5	10	2	5.5	1	2	3	4.44	1
SVMI	1	5.5	6.5	7	1	5.5	6.5	6	2	4.56	2
EM	13	12	6.5	7	12	13	3	6	4	8.5	10
SVDI	11	11	6.5	12	10	12	9.5	10	11	10.33	12
BPCA	14	13	13	7	13	14	13	13	13	12.56	14
LLSI	11	5.5	6.5	7	6.5	11	3	6	7.5	7.11	9
MC	7.5	8.5	6.5	2	6.5	5.5	3	6	7.5	5.89	5
CMC	5	8.5	12	13	3	5.5	6.5	1	7.5	6.89	7
DNI	2.5	14	14	14	14	5.5	14	14	14	11.78	13

FIGURE 7.2 Average rank for the rule induction learning methods.
Source: Based on data from Luengo et al. (2012).

	RBFN	RBFND	RBFNI	LOG	LVQ	MLP	NB	v-SVM	C-SVM	SMO	Avg.	RANKS
IM	9	6.5	4.5	6	3.5	13	12	10	5.5	5.5	7.55	10
EC	1	1	1	3	7	8.5	10	13	1	2	4.75	1
KNNI	5	6.5	10.5	9	7	11	6.5	8	5.5	5.5	7.45	9
WKNNI	13	6.5	4.5	10	10	4.5	6.5	4.5	5.5	5.5	7.05	6
KMI	3.5	2	7	3	11	3	4.5	8	5.5	9	5.65	2
FKMI	12	6.5	10.5	3	1.5	4.5	11	4.5	5.5	3	6.2	3
SVMI	2	11.5	2.5	7.5	3.5	1.5	13	8	11	9	6.95	5
EM	3.5	6.5	13	12	12.5	10	4.5	4.5	10	11.5	8.8	11
SVDI	9	6.5	7	11	12.5	8.5	3	11.5	12	11.5	9.25	12
BPCA	14	14	14	13	7	14	2	2	13	13	10.6	14
LLSI	6	6.5	10.5	7.5	7	6.5	9	4.5	5.5	9	7.2	7
MC	9	6.5	10.5	3	7	6.5	8	11.5	5.5	5.5	7.3	8
CMC	9	13	2.5	3	1.5	1.5	14	14	5.5	1	6.5	4
DNI	9	11.5	7	14	14	12	1	1	14	14	9.75	13

FIGURE 7.3   Average rank for the approximate methods.
Source: Based on data from Luengo et al. (2012).

	1-NN	3-NN	LBR	LWL	Avg.	RANKS
IM	5	11	5	8	7.25	7
EC	9.5	13	9	8	9.88	12
KNNI	2.5	5.5	9	8	6.25	4
WKNNI	4	5.5	9	8	6.63	5
KMI	12	5.5	9	2.5	7.25	8
FKMI	6	1.5	9	2.5	4.75	3
SVMI	9.5	9	3	8	7.38	9
EM	11	5.5	9	2.5	7	6
SVDI	13	12	1	12	9.5	11
BPCA	14	14	13	13	13.5	14
LLSI	7.5	5.5	9	8	7.5	10
MC	7.5	1.5	3	2.5	3.63	1
CMC	1	5.5	3	8	4.38	2
DNI	2.5	10	14	14	10.13	13

FIGURE 7.4   Average rank for the lazy learning methods.
Source: Based on data from Luengo et al. (2012).

7.3.1.4   *Overall*

Overall, conclusions are not that straightforward (see Figure 7.5). FKMI obtains the best final ranking; however, the EC method has a very similar average ranking (5.70 for EC, 5.26 for FKMI). There are some additional methods that obtain similar average rankings, not far off of FKMI and EC. SVMI, KMI, MC, and CMC have average rankings between 6.09 and 6.28 and we cannot, therefore, firmly establish one best method from among them all, as already anticipated.

	Ranking Rule Ind	Approx	Lazy
EC	3	1	12
KMI	6	2	8
FKMI	1	3	3
SVMI	2	5	9
MC	5	8	1
CMC	7	4	2

FIGURE 7.5   Best imputation methods for each group. The three best rankings per column are stressed in bold.
Source: Based on data from Luengo et al. (2012).

7.3.2   Garcia-Laencina et al. (2010)

Similar to Luengo et al. (2012), Garcia-Laencina et al. (2010) deal with the problem of handling missing values and subsequent classification on the imputed data. Rather than making a grouping by classifier, Garcia-Laencina aims to review a variety of approaches to handling missing data grouped into one of four following broad categories (see Figure 7.6):

1. Deletion of incomplete cases and classifier design using only the complete data portion.
2. Imputation or estimation of missing data and learning of the classification problem using the edited set (i.e. complete data portion and incomplete patterns with imputed values). In this category, we can distinguish between statistical procedures, such as mean imputation or multiple imputation, and machine learning approaches, such as imputation with neural networks
3. Using model-based procedures, where the data distribution is modeled by some procedure, such as by expectation–maximization (EM) algorithm. The PDFs of these models are then used with Bayes decision theory for the classification.
4. Using machine learning procedures designed to allow inputs with incomplete data (i.e. without a previous estimation of missing data).

The imputation methods that Garcia-Laencina et al. consider are mean imputation, regression, hot and cold deck imputation, multiple imputations, and machine learning imputation methods, including KNN, self-organizing maps (SOM), multi-layer perceptron (MLP), recurrent neural networks (RNN), auto-associative neural networks (AANN), and multi-task learning (MTL).

For model-based procedures (category 3), they also cover model-based Gaussian mixture models (GMM), expectation-maximization (EM) with k-means initialization, robust Bayesian estimators, neural networks ensembles, decision trees, support vector machines, and fuzzy approaches.

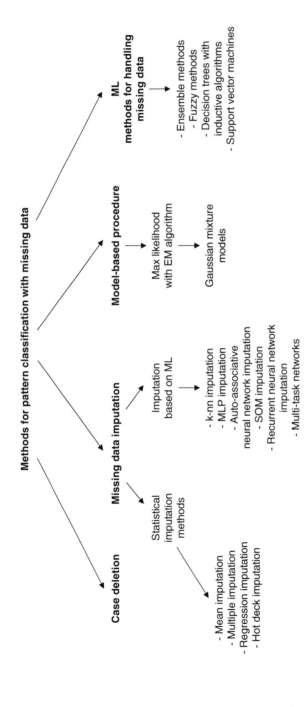

FIGURE 7.6 Methods for pattern classification with missing data. This scheme shows the different procedures that are analyzed in Garcia-Laencina et al. (2010).
Source: Adapted from Garcia-Laencina et al. (2010).

They assess all these methods by comparing mean classification errors across 20 simulated datasets over varying amounts of missingness along with a real medical dataset pertaining to thyroid disease.

Of the machine learning methods used for imputation, they find, similar to Luengo et al. (2012), that it is very much a case of "horses for courses" with different methods performing better in different classification domains, as can be seen in Figures 7.7, 7.8, and 7.9. They conclude that, generally, there is not a unique solution that provides the best results for each classification domain. Thus in real-life scenarios, a detailed study is required in order to evaluate which missing data estimation can help to enhance the classification accuracy the most.

Missing data in x_1 (%)	Missing data imputation			
	KNN	MLP	SOM	EM
5	9.21 ± 0.56	9.97 ± 0.48	9.28 ± 0.84	8.29 ± 0.24
10	10.85 ± 1.06	10.86 ± 0.79	9.38 ± 0.52	9.27 ± 0.54
20	11.88 ± 1.01	11.42 ± 0.44	10.63 ± 0.54	10.78 ± 0.59
30	13.50 ± 0.81	12.82 ± 0.51	13.88 ± 0.67	12.69 ± 0.57
40	14.89 ± 0.49	13.72 ± 0.37	15.55 ± 0.66	13.31 ± 0.56

FIGURE 7.7 Misclassification error rate (mean ± standard deviation from 20 simulations) in a toy problem (for more information on the dataset see Garcia-Laencina et al., 2010) after missing values are estimated using KNN, MLP, SOM, and EM imputation procedures. A neural network with six hidden neurons is used to perform the classification stage.
Source: Based on data from Garcia-Laencina et al. (2010).

Missing data in x_2 (%)	Missing data imputation			
	KNN	MLP	SOM	EM
5	15.92 ± 1.26	15.84 ± 1.13	16.32 ± 1.13	16.19 ± 0.99
10	16.88 ± 1.16	16.87 ± 1.16	16.97 ± 1.18	16.85 ± 1.03
20	18.78 ± 1.29	19.09 ± 1.29	19.30 ± 1.23	19.23 ± 1.12
30	20.58 ± 1.31	20.76 ± 1.34	22.04 ± 1.01	21.22 ± 1.12
40	22.61 ± 1.30	22.76 ± 1.23	24.06 ± 1.29	23.11 ± 1.37

FIGURE 7.8 Misclassification error rate (mean ± standard deviation from 20 simulations) in Telugu problem (a well-known Indian vowel recognition problem) after missing values are estimated using KNN, MLP, SOM, and EM imputation procedures. A neural network with 18 hidden neurons is used to perform the classification stage.
Source: Based on data from Garcia-Laencina et al. (2010).

	Missing data imputation			
	KNN	MLP	SOM	EM
Misclassification error rate (%)	3.01 ± 0.33	3.23 ± 0.31	3.49 ± 0.35	3.60 ± 0.31

A neural network with 20 hidden neurons is used to perform the classification stage.

FIGURE 7.9 Misclassification error rate (mean ± standard deviation from 20 simulations) in sick-thyroid dataset after missing values are estimated using KNN, MLP, SOM, and EM imputation procedures. A neural network with 20 hidden neurons is used to perform the classification stage.
Source: Based on data from Garcia-Laencina et al. (2010).

7.3.3 Grzymala-Busse et al. (2000)

Grzymala-Busse et al. (2000) tests how 9 methods of dealing with missing data affect the accuracy of both naïve and new LERS (Learning from Examples based on Rough Sets) classifiers across 10 different datasets.

The missing data methods used are: most common attribute value; concept most common attribute value; C4.5 based on entropy and splitting the example with missing attribute values to all concepts; method of assigning all possible values of the attribute; method of assigning all possible values of the attribute restricted to the given concept; method of ignoring examples with unknown attribute values; event-covering method; a special LEM2 algorithm; and method of treating missing attribute values as special values. More in-depth details of these methods can be found in the paper itself. They use classification error rates and the Wilcoxon signed rank test to assess which methods perform best over the 10 datasets.

Figures 7.10 and 7.11 show us the error rates of each classifier after imputing values using each of the given methods for each dataset.

	Methods								
Data file	1	2	3	4	5	6	7	8	9
Breast	34.62	34.62	31.5	28.52	31.88	29.24	34.97	33.92	32.52
Echo	6.76	6.76	5.4	-	-	6.56	6.76	6.76	6.76
Hdynet	29.15	31.53	22.6	-	-	28.41	28.82	27.91	28.41
Hepatitis	24.52	13.55	19.4	-	-	18.75	16.77	18.71	19.35
House	5.06	5.29	4.6	-	-	4.74	4.83	5.75	6.44
Im85	96.02	96.02	100	-	96.02	94.34	96.02	96.02	96.02
New-o	5.16	4.23	6.5	-	-	4.9	4.69	4.23	3.76
Primary	66.67	62.83	62	41.57	47.03	66.67	64.9	69.03	67.55
Soybean	15.96	18.24	13.4	-	4.1	15.41	19.87	17.26	16.94
Tokt	31.57	31.57	26.7	32.75	32.75	32.88	32.16	33.2	32.16

FIGURE 7.10 Error rates of input datasets by using LERS new classification.
Source: Based on data from Grzymala-Busse et al. (2000).

| | | | | Methods | | | | |
Data file	1	2	4	5	6	7	8	9
Breast	49.3	52.1	46.98	47.32	48.38	52.8	52.1	47.55
Echo	27.03	25.68	-	-	31.15	29.73	33.78	22.97
Hdynet	67.49	69.62	-	-	65.27	69.21	56.98	61.33
Hepatitis	38.06	28.39	-	-	32.5	37.42	41.29	34.84
House	10.11	7.13	-	-	9.05	10.57	12.87	11.72
Im85	97.01	97.01	-	97.01	94.34	97.01	97.01	97.01
New-o	11.74	11.74	-	-	11.19	11.27	10.33	10.33
Primary	83.19	77.29	53.16	60.09	81.82	80.53	82.1	79.94
Soybean	25.41	22.48	-	4.86	24.06	24.1	21.82	22.15
Tokt	63.62	63.62	62.82	62.82	64.15	63.36	63.62	63.89

FIGURE 7.11   Error rates of input datasets by using LERS naïve classification.
Source: Based on data from Grzymala-Busse et al. (2000).

Grzymala-Busse et al. first conclude that the new extended LERS classifier is always superior to the naïve one. They then compare the different imputation methods concluding that the C4.5 approach and the method of ignoring examples with missing attribute values are the best methods among all nine approaches, whereas the "most common attribute value" method performs worst. They also find that many methods do not differ from one another significantly.

7.3.4   Zou et al. (2005)

Zou et al. (2005) aims to assess 9 different methods of handling missing data by testing the improvement they give to each of the C4.5 and ELEM2 classifiers across 30 datasets, compared to ignoring data points with missing values. They further come up with meta-attributes for each dataset that are used in a rule-based system (i.e. decision tree) to decide under which circumstances one should use each imputation method over the others.

Similar to the other papers, and as the need for a rule-based system would suggest, there is no "clear winner" in terms of imputation techniques. The efficacy of each very much depends on the type of data and meta attributes of the data. As for their system to select which imputation technique to use, they conclude (after testing on a validation set) that this rule-based system is superior to simply selecting one imputation method for all datasets.

7.3.5   Jerez et al. (2010)

Jerez et al. (2010) tests a variety of imputation techniques to impute missing values on a breast cancer dataset. They compare the performance of different statistical methods, namely, mean, hot deck, and multiple imputation, against machine learning methods, namely, multi-layer perceptrons (MLP), self-organizing maps (SOM) and k-nearest neighbors (KNN). For multiple imputation, a variety of algorithms/software are used; Amelia II (bootstrapping-based EM); WinMICE

AUC	LD	Mean	Hot-deck	SAS	Amelia	Mice	MLP	KNN	SOM
Mean	0.7151	0.7226	0.7111	0.7216	0.7169	0.725	0.734	0.7345	0.7331
Std. dev.	0.0387	0.0399	0.0456	0.0296	0.0297	0.0301	0.0305	0.0289	0.0296
MSE	0.0358	0.0235	0.0324	0.0254	0.1119	0.1119	0.024	0.0195	0.0204

FIGURE 7.12   Mean, standard deviation, and MSE values for the AUC (area under the ROC curve) values computed for the control model and for each of the eight imputation methods considered. *Source:* Based on data from Jerez et al. (2010).

(multiple imputation by chained equations based); and MI in SAS (Markov chain Monte Carlo based). Performance was measured via the area under the ROC curve (AUC) and the Hosmer-Lemeshow goodness of fit test.

They find that, for this dataset, the machine learning methods were the most suitable for imputation of missing values and led to a significant enhancement of prognosis accuracy compared to imputation methods based on statistical procedures, as can be seen in Figure 7.12. In fact, only the improvements of these methods were deemed statistically significant in predicting breast cancer relapses compared to the method of removing entries with missing values.

7.3.6   Farhangfar et al. (2008)

Farhangfar et al. (2008) studies the effect of 5 imputation methods, across 15 datasets at varying levels of artificially induced missingness (MCAR), on 7 classifiers. The imputation techniques tested are: mean imputation, hot deck, naïve Bayes (the latter two methods with a recently proposed imputation framework), and a polytomous regression-based method. The classifiers used are; RIPPER, C4.5, k-nearest-neighbor, support vector machine with polynomial kernel, support vector machine with RBF kernel, and naïve Bayes.

The results show that imputation with the tested methods on average improves classification accuracy when compared to classification without imputation. However, there is no universal best imputation method. They also note a few more general cases in which certain imputation techniques seem to perform best. The analysis of the quality of the imputation with respect to varying amounts of missing data (i.e. between 5% and 50%) shows that all imputation methods, except for the mean imputation, improve classification error for data with more than 10% of missing data. Finally, some classifiers such as C4.5 and naïve Bayes were found to be missing data resistant. In other words, they can produce accurate classification in the presence of missing data while other classifiers such as k-nearest-neighbor, SVMs, and RIPPER benefit from the imputation. As C4.5 and naïve Bayes classifiers were found to be missing data resistant, any missing data imputation actually worsened their performance.

7.3.7   Kang et al. (2013)

Kang et al. (2013) proposes a new single imputation method based on locally linear reconstruction (LLR) that improves the prediction performance of supervised learning (classification and regression) with missing values. They compare the proposed missing value imputation method (LLR) with six well-known single imputation methods – mean imputation; hot deck; KNN; expectation conditional maximization (ECM); mixture of Gaussians (MoG); k-means clustering (KMC) – for different learning algorithms (logistic regression; linear regression; KNN regression/classification; artificial neural networks; decision trees; and the proposed LLR) based on 13 classification and 9 regression datasets, across a variety of amounts of (artificially induced) missing data.

Kang claims that: (1) all imputation methods helped to improve the prediction accuracy compared to removing data points with missing values, although some were very simple; (2) the proposed LLR imputation method enhanced the modeling performance more than all other imputation methods, irrespective of the learning algorithms and the missing ratios; and (3) LLR was outstanding when the missing ratio was relatively high and its prediction accuracy was similar to that of the complete dataset.

7.4   SUMMARY

As we have seen, each of the previous 7 papers draws different, and in some cases conflicting, conclusions about a variety of imputation techniques. Aside from LLR in Kang (2013), most methods are deemed to be superior in certain situations and not in others. As such, the general consensus seems to be that there is no clear choice of imputation technique that outperforms all others, other than possibly LLR. Due to the lack of papers reporting on LLR's use for data imputation, though, we are hesitant to categorically state it as the imputation technique of choice, rather than suggest trying a variety of methods based on the particulars of the dataset at hand. Hence, it is most likely that, as with all machine learning algorithms, each has its own benefits and drawbacks. Hence, there is no one algorithm that works in all cases in line with the no-free-lunch theorem.

The literature review in this chapter is by no means exhaustive. It can also be the case that none of these algorithms is applicable for alternative data treatment where, for example, spatial information (e.g. satellite images) can be important to use. We will show how to apply spectral techniques in this case in the next chapter. Also, time series could contain important temporal information that can be leveraged. Again, we will show a case study in the next chapter where information about the temporal ordering is used for the imputation.

CHAPTER 8

Missing Data: Case Studies

8.1 INTRODUCTION

In this chapter we will present real-world case studies on imputing missing values based on multivariate time series of credit default swap (CDS) data and satellite images. But before delving into it, let's start by introducing some notation.[1]

For the case study in this section, we use a description in terms of a standard data matrix $X_{N \times P}$ with N observations and P features. This means that X has observations along the first index (rows) and different features along the second index (columns). Since we are dealing with multivariate time series, P corresponds to the number of time series components and time stamps increase along the columns. It is noteworthy that a lot of what we discuss also applies to data in different formats such as heterogeneous data with P different features. Image data, for example, can be represented with either $N \times P$ pixel values.

All observations for a given time series component p can be written as a column vector $\boldsymbol{x}_p$. The row vector $(x_{n1}, \ldots, x_{nP})$ collects all values of the components for a particular observation and we define an observation vector by $\boldsymbol{x}^{(n)} = (x_{n1}, \ldots, x_{nP})^T$. Explicitly, the matrix X has the following form:

$$X = \begin{pmatrix} x_{11} & x_{12} & x_{13} & \cdots & x_{1P} \\ x_{21} & x_{22} & x_{23} & \cdots & x_{2P} \\ \vdots & \vdots & \vdots & \ddots & \vdots \\ x_{N1} & x_{N2} & x_{N3} & \cdots & x_{NP} \end{pmatrix} \tag{8.1}$$

---

[1] The case study for this chapter can be found in Bauer (2017), which one of us has co-authored.

A typical matrix with missing data (na) then looks like this:

$$X = \begin{pmatrix} x_{11} & na & x_{13} & \cdots & x_{1P} \\ x_{21} & x_{22} & na & \cdots & na \\ \vdots & \vdots & \vdots & \ddots & \vdots \\ x_{N1} & na & x_{N3} & \cdots & x_{NP} \end{pmatrix} \tag{8.2}$$

It is useful to define a missing matrix M to describe the position of missing data points; for the example above it is of the following form:

$$M = \begin{pmatrix} 0 & 1 & 0 & \cdots & 0 \\ 0 & 0 & 1 & \cdots & 1 \\ \vdots & \vdots & \vdots & \ddots & \vdots \\ 0 & 1 & 0 & \cdots & 0 \end{pmatrix} \tag{8.3}$$

This matrix helps to keep track of the position of the missing data and can also be used to analyze all the missingness patterns appearing. For a large number of features P, we can see that one of the challenges of filling missing data is that a large number of missing data patterns can appear, and it is not clear a priori which variables to use to predict the missing ones, since the predictors might as well contain missing values. As we will discuss below for the CDS data discussed in this chapter, we will have $P = 11$.

8.2   CASE STUDY: IMPUTING MISSING VALUES IN MULTIVARIATE CREDIT DEFAULT SWAP TIME SERIES

Before we jump into the case study, let's discuss some generalities. In literature, time series are often dealt with by deterministic techniques that, for instance, extract trend and seasonal behavior. We can split time series data into the univariate and the multivariate cases. Typical imputation techniques for univariate time series include linear interpolation, moving average smoothing and imputation, low pass filters, ARIMA decomposition, splines, wavelet expansion, Kalman filters, or singular spectrum analysis (SSA). These techniques are particularly successful when the stretches of missing data are short and if the time series has a good signal-to-noise ratio.

Imputation for multivariate time series can in principle also be performed by these techniques. However, when available, it can be particularly beneficial to use correlations for imputation. These can be taken into account by matrix decomposition techniques such as data interpolation with empirical orthogonal functions (DINEOF) or its extension, multiple singular spectral analysis (MSSA). Importantly, MI imputation techniques also provide multivariate time series imputation support using lags, leads, and explicit time covariates. We point out that imputations in this case study focus on working directly with the levels (values) and not on returns (first differences). Working with returns requires a different sort of analysis and reconstruction of the levels may require stitching the integrated series or approaches like Brownian bridge.

Preliminary analysis of this alternative approach did not suggest a strong performance for this case study.

The purpose of this section is twofold: (1) we introduce a systematic approach to deal with missing data for multivariate time series, and (2) we benchmark a number of advanced techniques for imputation. The approach is relatively general and with minor modifications can also be applied in other domains.

As a first step in our procedure we analyze missingness patterns in the data. In principle, there can be systematic reasons that particular data points are not reported, or data can be missing without any pattern (i.e. essentially at random). Thus, as a first step we test for the missingness mechanism. Then we extract features of the missingness patterns and perform a cluster analysis of the missingness patterns. This is very important to provide an overview of the missingness space and it also feeds into the generation of a realistic train/validation set. This is done by superimposing the different classes of observed missingness patterns on completed data.

Once the test data has been generated, we benchmark the performance of different imputation techniques. We use state-of-the-art MI techniques based on IP (impute-posterior, like multiple imputation with chained equations, or MICE) and EM (expectation maximization, like the R package Amelia) versus state-of-the-art multivariate time series techniques (DINEOF) and multiple singular spectral analysis (MSSA) on multivariate time series data. We will discuss advantages and disadvantages of the different methods. Depending on the application and the underlying data, one might prefer one over the other. For instance, deterministic techniques such as DINEOF and MSSA may be able to more accurately reconstruct a certain pattern in the data and hence fill values with higher accuracy. However, MI approaches preserve the statistical properties more accurately.

8.2.1 Missing Data Classification

Missingness patterns can appear in very different forms, which can impact the imputation strategy. Hence, it is useful at first to analyze possible missing mechanisms, as well as common patterns to understand whether they can be collected into similar groups (clusters). In this section, we describe a framework for doing that. The following procedure can be applied to find and characterize missingness patterns. As a first step we extract features of the missing data. The following numerical quantities were found to be useful in our case:

1. Total fraction of missing values.
2. Fraction of missing data in particular features; hence, for instance, for the CDS data consider the missingness fractions in short, medium, or long-term maturities separately.
3. Statistics about the length of runs of consecutive missing values for the different features (min, max, mean, standard deviation).
4. Other data-specific measures.

Once the feature space is constructed, dimensionality reduction (e.g. principal component analysis, or PCA) can be performed, followed by clustering (e.g. K-means). We will present the results for the clustering for the CDS data in the next section but before that let's define some performance metrics.

8.2.2 Imputation Metrics

In order to quantify the quality of data imputations, we define the following metrics:

Root mean square error (RMSE): This is an absolute measure, which is frequently used in the literature. We denote by S_p the set of missing observations for component p, $N_m = \sum_p | S_p |$,[2] and x_{np} the true and $\widehat{x}_{np}$ the imputed value and $| S_p |$ refers to the number of elements in the set; then RMSE is:

$$d_{RMSE} = 1/N_m \sum_{p=1}^{P} \sum_{n \in S_p} | (x_{np} - \widehat{x}_{np})^2 | \qquad (8.4)$$

Mean relative deviation (MRD): This is a relative measure, which can be more suitable when the values under consideration vary over different magnitudes:

$$d_{RMSE} = \sqrt{1/N_m \sum_{p=1}^{P} \sum_{n \in S_p} (x_{np} - \widehat{x}_{np})^2} \qquad (8.5)$$

In situations where x_{np} may take zero as a value or values close to zero, one needs to be very careful when using this metric. In the literature this quantity is sometimes referred to as mean absolute percentage error (MAPE). In the performance analysis in Section 8.2.6 we will focus on MRD.

True versus predicted R squared coefficient: R squared is a measure that appears frequently in linear regression analysis and is also often used to gauge the accuracy of data imputations. It is best to split it into separate quantities for each component p, so that values of different magnitudes do not get mixed:

$$d_{R^2,p} = 1 - \frac{\sum_{n \in S^p} (x_{np} - \widehat{x}_{np})^2}{\sum_{n \in S^p} (x_{np} - \mu_p)^2} \qquad (8.6)$$

Note that for the multiple imputation techniques all these metrics have multiple values, one for each realization. One can analyze the mean, standard deviation, best, or worst result for each of them.

8.2.3 CDS Data and Test Data Generation

We use credit default swap (CDS) time series data to test the performance of imputation techniques.[3] We started with a collection of over 4000 CDS entities for different

---

[2] We denote by $| S |$ the number of elements of a set S.

[3] The data was sourced from IHS Markit; more information about it can be found at http://www.markit .com/Product/Pricing-Data-CDS.

maturities and doc clauses over a period of nearly two years. In order to produce a comparable sample, we narrowed the data down by focusing on tickers based in the United States, which are traded in USD and occupy a higher-seniority tier. This resulted in a sample of 741 tickers with 11 maturities, 6 months to 30 years (6M–30Y). Data samples will be shown in Section 8.2.6. Missing values appear quite frequently for longer maturities (15Y, 20Y, 30Y), and occasionally also for short maturities (6M, 1Y, 2Y), whereas the central maturities (5Y, 7Y) are usually observed. As discussed below, this comes from the fact that missingness is related to the liquidity. The central maturities are the ones most commonly traded in the market. While we are using CDS data, we can imagine that a similar approach could be used for other asset classes such as rates and FX implied vol, where different tenors are likely to have different levels of liquidity.

For data characterization, we performed standard multivariate normal (MVN) tests (Henze-Zirkler, Royston, Mardia) for a subsample of 200 tickers with very small missingness fractions. We found that the data is not consistent with the MVN hypothesis, and instead shows considerable deviations from being MVN distributed.

We also investigated the missingness mechanism of the data (see Section 7.2). Generally, it is unfortunately not possible to determine unambiguously the missingness class for a given dataset without additional insights. It is, however, possible to run Little's test (Little, 1988) to assess whether the missingness patterns of the data are consistent with the MCAR hypothesis. We ran Little's test on the actual missingness patterns and the MCAR hypothesis was rejected in the majority of the cases with a very low p-value. This can be partly attributed to deviations from the MVN distribution assumed in Little's test, but it is also a clear indication that the missingness patterns mostly do not occur completely at random. The cases where the missingness pattern was found consistent with the MCAR hypothesis usually correspond to a low missingness fraction ($< 1\%$). In such cases it can be difficult to distinguish MCAR from non-MCAR. We further consulted with domain experts about the reasons for missing data. The main underlying cause quoted was liquidity (i.e. insufficient trading data to produce reliable price quotes). There was no particular evidence that the missingness mechanism is MNAR and we concluded that MAR, and in some cases MCAR, is a suitable assumption for the CDS dataset.

Then we performed the feature extraction and clustering analysis as introduced above. After some exploratory work we focused on the following four features: percentage of missing data in the four longest maturities, percentage of missing data in the four shortest maturities, a standard measure of the length of consecutive missing streaks for the four longest maturities, and the variance of this quantity. We then used Gaussian mixture models (see Murphy, 2012, for clustering in this four-dimensional space). The results are summarized in Figure 8.1.

We show different tickers in vertical bars, ordered by increasing maturity (6M–30Y) within each bar. The black regions indicate missing values. We identified five different clusters: (1) relatively small fraction of missing values, (2) missing values mainly for long maturities and with relatively short and alternating stretches of consecutive missing values, (3) missing values in long streaks for longer maturities, (4) patterns with considerable amounts of missing data and substantial variation, and

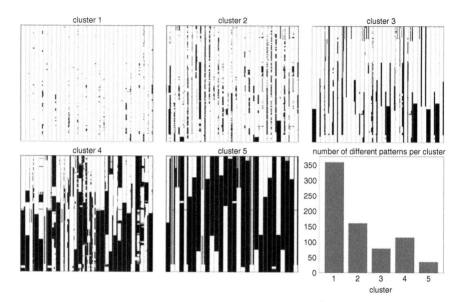

FIGURE 8.1   Clustering for CDS time series data: (1) relatively small fraction of missing values, (2) missing values mainly for long maturities and with relatively short stretches of consecutive missing values, (3) missing values in long streaks for longer maturities, (4) patterns with considerable amount of missing data and substantial variation, (5) patterns with large amounts of missing data with uniform long stretches, often covering all maturities. Histogram of number of occurrences of missingness patterns for the different clusters.

(5) patterns with large amounts of missing data with uniform long stretches, often covering all maturities. As we can see in the histogram in Figure 8.1 the majority of the patterns (around 70%) lie within clusters 1 and 2. For the patterns in the first three clusters, we will show the imputation results in Section 8.2.6. For cluster 1, about 15% of the samples were found to be consistent with the MCAR hypothesis. These usually possess a very low missingness fraction. For clusters 2 and 3, none of the samples were found to be consistent with the MCAR hypothesis.

An important question for the evaluation of the performance of data imputation techniques is how to produce a suitable training and validation set. Using data with actually missing values would be favorable in the sense that it contains realistic missingness patterns; however, it is problematic because it does not allow us to estimate how close the imputed values are to the true values, since they are not known. For MAR, ideally one would start with a complete dataset and use a missingness generator of the form $f(M|X^{obs}, \phi)$ to create realistic missingness patterns M. Then imputation routines can be applied to the training data and the imputed and true data can be compared. However, it is generally not easy to build such a generator; moreover, we are usually not in the possession of a complete dataset.

We approached the problem as follows: we extracted a subset of the tickers that have very few missing values (all 11 maturities with less than 1% missing fraction). The values that were missing were imputed by linear interpolation in order not to introduce a particular bias. This data serves as ground truth for testing. With this procedure we generated 200 samples of ground truth CDS data, each with 11 maturities.

As a next step we had to impose a missingness pattern. A simple procedure, often found in the literature, is to randomly remove data points; however, that is problematic, since the Little test discussed above showed that the data is not consistent with MCAR. Therefore, our procedure was to impose realistic missingness patterns M on this data (i.e., we remove values according to those predefined patterns). As discussed, we found five prevalent patterns. Here we focus on the imputation of clusters 1, 2, and 3, as clusters 4 and 5 contain longer stretches of completely absent data that would be better filled by a proxy. The test sets for each cluster are generated by applying the patterns on the 200 ground truth examples. In the case where the cluster does not contain enough different patterns, we draw from the available patterns with repetition. A typical block for cluster 2 (ticker number 1) is shown in the bottom of Figure 8.3. In this case the long maturities (10Y, 20Y, and 30Y) are missing for a considerable amount of the time steps. The described combination of the complete underlying dataset and imposed missingness pattern leads to semi-synthetic datasets on which we can run the imputation routines, and since we have the ground truth, all the performance metrics can be computed. This procedure leads to a relatively realistic missingness representation for test purposes, which can be generated with little effort. The described framework can be applied in other domains with minor modifications.

8.2.4 Multiple Imputation Methods

We briefly hinted at multiple imputation (MI) in Section 7.2. MI is a statistical framework for data imputation (see Little & Rubin, 2019; Schafer, 1997). The objective is to determine a good approximation for the joint distribution function for the data $f(X)$, both observed and unobserved. This is usually achieved by an iterative mechanism. Once $f(X)$ is found, imputations can be generated by sampling from the conditional distribution functions for the various missingness patterns that occur. The conditional distributions can be derived from the general joint distributions, either explicitly or made accessible implicitly by a Monte Carlo sampling procedure.

A particular framework is termed multiple imputations by chained equations (MICE). Chained equations refer to an iterative procedure through which data values and parameter values are generated in a series of steps. The general assumption is that the (complete) data is generated from a multivariate distribution function, $p(X|\theta)$, where θ is a collection of parameters, which is not known. In certain cases, the distribution function p can be assumed to have a particular form. For instance, a common assumption is that the complete data is generated by an MVN distribution. Then all the distribution functions can be given explicitly, and the procedure becomes a bit more transparent (see Enders, 2010). We focus on the description of this case in this section. The general description based on a Markov Chain Monte Carlo sampling approach can be found in Buuren and Groothuis-Oudshoorn (2010). We provide more details around the MICE procedure in Appendix 8.5.

8.2.4.1 The MVN Case

The basic assumption of this section is that the data (both observed and missing) is described by a multivariate normal distribution with mean vector $\boldsymbol{\mu}$ and covariance matrix Σ, formally:

$$X \sim N(\boldsymbol{\mu}, \Sigma) \tag{8.7}$$

Then the conditional distribution functions used to impute data are also MVNs (Murphy, 2012). The collection of parameters is written as $\theta = (\boldsymbol{\mu}, \Sigma)$.

The algorithm for the data imputation has an explicit form and does not rely on Gibbs sampling. It has the **imputation** (I) - **posterior** (P) form. First, based on an initial estimate, the generating distributions for the covariance matrix Σ, $p(\Sigma|v, \Lambda)$, and for the mean vector, $\boldsymbol{\mu}$, $p(\boldsymbol{\mu}|\boldsymbol{\mu}^*, \Sigma^*)$, are specified. We can draw initial parameters $\theta^{(1)} = (\boldsymbol{\mu}^{(1)}, \Sigma^{(1)})$ from these distributions.

I-step: We can impute data based on these parameters and from the generating distribution functions. We have to do this for all missingness patterns separately. To predict missing values for the variable X_k, we have to determine the conditional distribution

$$p(X_k|X_{-k}, \boldsymbol{\mu}^{(1)}, \Sigma^{(1)}) \tag{8.8}$$

where X_{-k} denotes the collection of observed variables excluding X_k. This can be achieved in two equivalent ways: (1) We can sample from Equation (8.8) to impute values for X_k, and so on for the other variables. (2) Instead of sampling from the conditional MVN in Equation (8.8), we can also derive the missing values from linear regression equations on $\boldsymbol{\mu}^{(1)}$ and $\Sigma^{(1)}$, which include a stochastic variance term. There are different ways of doing this regression. The ones that are most commonly used are (a) Bayesian linear regression (called norm in the MICE package), and (b) predictive mean matching (PMM). Once all values are imputed, the I-step has finished and the so-called P-step (for posterior in the Bayesian framework) follows.

P-step: In this step, new distribution functions for the parameters θ are estimated. This is usually done entirely in a Bayesian framework. Certain assumptions are made for the priors, and the likelihood and posterior functions are computed from the observed and previously imputed data. In the MVN case discussed here, the posterior distribution for the covariance matrix Σ has the following form (Enders, 2010):

$$p(\Sigma|v, \Lambda) = W^{-1}(\Sigma, v = N - 1, \Psi = \Lambda) \tag{8.9}$$

where W^{-1} is the inverse Wishart function, v is the number of degrees of freedom, Ψ is a positive definite scale matrix, and Λ is the sample covariance matrix of the completed dataset. If we denote the drawn matrix by Σ^*, then the new distribution function for $\boldsymbol{\mu}$ is (Enders, 2010):

$$p(\boldsymbol{\mu}|\boldsymbol{\mu}^*, \Sigma^*) = N(\boldsymbol{\mu}, \boldsymbol{\mu}^*, \Sigma_0) \tag{8.10}$$

with $\boldsymbol{\mu}^*$ the vector of sample means using the completed data and $\Sigma_0 = \Sigma/N$. Once the distributions are specified, new parameters θ can be obtained by sampling. We can see that the parameters for these distribution functions are estimated iteratively from previous imputation results, which in turn depend on previous parameter estimates. The procedure is iterated until stationary distributions are found.

8.2.4.2 Expectation Maximization (EM) Procedure

Instead of the I-P procedure discussed in the last section, the parameters $\theta = (\mu, \Sigma)$ can also be estimated by maximum likelihood estimation (MLE) using the expectation maximization (EM) algorithm. We use the assumption of the data being MVN distributed again.

The procedure is as follows. The data collected into a matrix X, can be split into observed and missing, $X = (X^{miss}, X^{obs})$. The log-likelihood can be written as:

$$l = \log p(X^{obs}|\theta) = \sum_n \log \sum_{x^{miss,(n)}} [p(x^{obs,(n)}, x^{miss,(n)}|\theta)] \quad (8.11)$$

This is difficult to maximize directly, but it is a situation that can be treated with EM. The idea is to compute the parameters $\theta = \theta^{(t)}$ iteratively. We first need an initial estimate to compute θ, either by just using complete data rows, or by using a simple imputation scheme, for example, mean imputation. Then we can compute $\theta^{(0)}$ from the MLE.

E-step: Once we have some estimate for $\theta^{(t-1)}$ we can compute the expectation:

$$Q(\theta^{(t)}, \theta^{(t-1)}) = E\left[\sum_n \log N(x^n|\mu, \Sigma)\right] | (X, \theta^{(t-1)}) \quad (8.12)$$

where the expectation value is conditioned on $(X, \theta^{(t-1)})$. This can be simplified and reduced to computing expectations of the form $\sum_n E[x^{(n)}]$ and $\sum_n E[x^{(n)}[x^{(n)}]^T]$ where we omitted the conditioning for notational simplicity. These are called expected sufficient statistics. In order to calculate those, we need to use relations of multivariate normal conditional probability densities (see Murphy, 2012, p. 374).

M-step: In the maximization step, we compute new parameters $\theta^{(t)}$. This is done by computing appropriate derivatives of the function Q and solving for μ and Σ, $\nabla Q = 0$. The result is:

$$\mu^{(t)} = \frac{1}{N} \sum_n E[x^n] \quad (8.13)$$

and

$$\Sigma^{(t)} = \frac{1}{N} \sum_n E[x^{(n)}[x^{(n)}]^T] - \mu^t[\mu^t]^T \quad (8.14)$$

Note that this approach is quite careful to take into account the variance of the data. Once this is computed, we can return to the E-step and iterate.

Once the parameters $\theta = (\mu, \Sigma)$ are estimated, missing values can be imputed by sampling from the appropriate conditional distribution. A data vector can usually be split up into missing and observed parts $x = (x^{miss}, x^{obs})$. Missing values x^{miss} can be predicted by sampling from the conditional distribution function:

$$p(x^{miss}|x^{obs}, \theta) \quad (8.15)$$

as in Equation (8.9). To account for the uncertainty in the parameters θ a bootstrap approach can be used, which is done in the implementation of the R package Amelia (see Honaker et al., 2011).

8.2.5 Deterministic and EOF-Based Techniques

As already discussed in Section 8.2, rather than using the MI frameworks, data imputation can also be achieved by deterministic techniques. One approach is to use machine learning techniques to predict missing data from the observed data. We used one popular approach based on random forests. Some details about the algorithm and the software library that was used can be found in Appendix 8.6. Other deterministic approaches are those based on spectral decompositions and empirical orthogonal functions (EOFs). We will give a brief introduction to those techniques.

8.2.5.1 Brief Recap of Singular Value Decomposition (SVD)

Consider the matrix $X_{N \times P}$. Then there exist orthonormal matrices $U_{N \times N}$, $V_{P \times P}$ such that:

$$X = USV^T \tag{8.16}$$

where $S_{N \times P}$ is a matrix with values $\sqrt{\lambda_i}$ on the diagonal (called singular values), and all other entries are zero. A common convention is to list the singular values in descending order. The matrix U can be written as a collection of column vectors:

$$U = [\boldsymbol{u}_1, \boldsymbol{u}_2, \dots, \boldsymbol{u}_N] \tag{8.17}$$

and similarly for V. They satisfy:

$$XX^T\boldsymbol{u}_i = \lambda_i\boldsymbol{u}_i \text{ with } i = 1, \dots, P \tag{8.18}$$

and:

$$X^TX\boldsymbol{v}_i = \lambda_i\boldsymbol{v}_i \tag{8.19}$$

We call $\boldsymbol{v}_i$ the right eigenvectors of X and $\boldsymbol{u}_i$ the left eigenvectors. These vectors are referred to as empirical orthogonal functions (EOF), since they span a space related to the empirical data. We can write the SVD decomposition explicitly as:

$$X = \sum_{k=1}^{q} \sqrt{\lambda_k}\boldsymbol{u}_k\boldsymbol{v}_k^T \tag{8.20}$$

where q is the number of non-zero singular values. This expression is a sum of rank 1 matrices.

8.2.5.2 Data Interpolation with Empirical Orthogonal Functions (DINEOF)

The DINEOF approach was introduced in the context of time resolved geological data (see Beckers & Rixen, 2003). For instance, consider a spatiotemporal field $f(t_i, \boldsymbol{r}_j)$ and relate it to the data matrix X by:

$$X_{ij} = f(t_i, \boldsymbol{r}_j) \tag{8.21}$$

The strategy to fill missing data is in the spirit of matrix completion via a decomposition of the form:

$$X = AB \qquad (8.22)$$

where A is an $N \times K$ matrix and B is a $K \times P$ matrix. K corresponds to a latent dimension carrying the essential information about the data. In the DINEOF approach this matrix factorization is constructed iteratively using the EOF basis obtained via SVD. We start by imputing a first guess for the missing values (e.g. mean values), and then compute the EOFs for the completed data matrix. The reconstruction in the DINEOF is based on a subset of the EOFs:

$$X^{(n_{EOF})} = \sum_{k=1}^{n_{EOF}} \sqrt{\lambda_k} u_k v_k^T \qquad (8.23)$$

where $n_{EOF} = 1, \ldots, N_{max}$, and N_{max} is an upper bound on the number of EOFs to be used. For a given number of EOFs, n_{EOF}, one has an inner loop to iterate to convergence for the imputed values. One typically measures the convergence of the imputations by initially removing a small random subset of otherwise known data points and computing RMSE (true versus predicted); see Equation (8.4). Convergence is assumed when RMSE does not decrease any further. A problem with this convergence assessment is that the randomly removed points might follow a quite different pattern than the data that actually needs to be imputed. Hence, the imputation may therefore not be optimal.

This approach works quite well when there is enough structure in the data, and P must not be too small. For illustration, we give an example of DINEOF imputation for synthetic two-dimensional data field[4] in Figure 8.2.

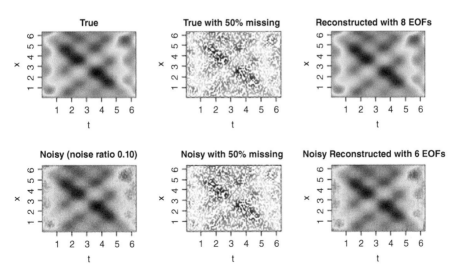

FIGURE 8.2   Example of DINEOF imputation for synthetic 2D data.

---

[4]This example is reproduced from http://menugget.blogspot.co.uk/2012/10/dineof-data-interpolating-empirical.html with the synthetic data introduced in Beckers (2003).

Two comparisons are shown. The first one has the true data from which randomly 50% of the pixels are removed. With $n_{EOF} = 8$ basis functions we can get an accurate reconstruction. In the second case, additional noise is added to the data and again a good reconstruction can be achieved. Note that the DINEOF approach aims to include EOFs only as long as they add signal. However, achieving a clear signal/noise separation is numerically not easy. We will show an example that is more in the spirit of this book – imputation on satellite images – in Section 8.3.

8.2.5.3 *Multiple Singular Spectral Analysis (MSSA)*

Singular spectral analysis (SSA) is a more advanced decomposition technique than the matrix factorization and it has been very successfully applied for time series analysis as well as images (see Golyandina et al., 2013 and references therein). We describe the technique for time series, but the extension to images is formally relatively straightforward. The basic idea is to account for time-lagged covariances up to a certain window length L. For these objects we perform SVD and then the time series can be decomposed and reconstructed with the dominant modes and EOFs.

First consider the case of a univariate time series $X = X_t$, $P = 1$. We first describe how to do the time series decomposition for a complete dataset formally. For a given window size $L \leq N$ and $K = N - L + 1$, construct the trajectory matrix T_X as follows:

$$T_X = \begin{pmatrix} x_1 & x_2 & x_3 & \cdots & x_K \\ x_2 & x_3 & x_4 & \cdots & x_{K+1} \\ \vdots & \vdots & \vdots & \ddots & \vdots \\ x_L & x_{L+1} & x_{L+2} & \cdots & x_N \end{pmatrix} \tag{8.24}$$

which is an $L \times K$ matrix with the same time series points on the anti-diagonals. Note that for the transformation $L \to K$, $K \to L$, the corresponding trajectory matrices satisfy $T_X \to T_X^T$. The trajectory matrix can be used to compute the time-lagged covariance matrix:

$$C = T_X T_X^T \tag{8.25}$$

This is a symmetric matrix and has the explicit form:

$$C = \begin{pmatrix} \sum_{i=1}^{K} x_i^2 & \sum_{i=1}^{K} x_i x_{i+1} & \cdots & \sum_{i=1}^{K} x_i x_{i+L-1} \\ \sum_{i=1}^{K} x_i x_{i+1} & \sum_{i=2}^{K+1} x_i^2 & \cdots & \cdots \\ \vdots & \vdots & \ddots & \ddots \\ \sum_{i=1}^{K} x_i x_{i+L-1} & \sum_{i=2}^{K+1} x_i x_{i+L-1} & \cdots & \sum_{i=K}^{N} x_i^2 \end{pmatrix} \tag{8.26}$$

We can see from this how time lags up to length L are considered. In other words, modes with maximal period L can be identified. The time-lagged covariance matrix is just used for illustration of which time correlations are picked up by SSA. The approach works directly with the trajectory matrix T_X. The next step is to perform SVD on T_X, such that the following reconstruction can be given:

$$T_X = \sum_{k=1}^{q} \sqrt{\lambda_k} u_k v_k^T \tag{8.27}$$

Typically, one groups eigenvalues into certain subsets $I_1 \ldots, I_m$; for instance, oscillatory modes appear as paired eigenvectors with very similar singular values. The partial reconstruction is then written as:

$$T_X = \sum_{h=1}^{R} \sum_{k \in I_h} \sqrt{\lambda_k} u_k v_k^T \qquad (8.28)$$

for a particular choice of $\{I_h\}$. There is some subjectivity involved in this step. For instance, in time series analysis, one might want to focus on a trend and only two oscillatory modes.

The final step is to map the reconstructed trajectory matrix back to the time series. We do this by averaging over the antidiagonals. Denote by Δ_k the set of anti-diagonal index pairs (i, j) such that $\Delta_1 = \{(1, 1)\}$, $\Delta_2 = \{(2, 1), (1, 2)\}$ etc., and $|\Delta_k|$ the number of elements. Then the reconstructed time series reads $k = 1, \ldots, N$:

$$x_k^{rec} = \frac{1}{|\Delta_k|} \sum_{(i,j) \in \Delta_k} [T_X^{rec}]_{ij} \qquad (8.29)$$

The data imputation based on SSA follows the same logic as for time series decomposition, except that the EOF basis for the reconstruction and the imputed values are determined iteratively. One starts by filling the missing values by an initial guess. Then T_X is constructed and the SVD computed. A partial reconstruction with n_{EOF} EOFs:

$$T_X = \sum_{k=1}^{n_{EOF}} \sqrt{\lambda_k} u_k v_k^T \qquad (8.30)$$

is used to fill the missing values for the reconstructed time series. This is iterated for convergence for a fixed n_{EOF} as above in the DINEOF approach. The algorithm successively adds more EOFs until no further improvement for the imputations can be achieved or a maximal number of EOFs is reached. The improvement is typically measured by randomly removing a small set of otherwise known data points and computing RMSE (true versus predicted). Like DINEOF, the method is subject to potential problems arising from different missingness patterns.

The multivariate case (MSSA) is formally very similar to the univariate case, but numerically more involved. For each time series $\{X_{n,p}\}$ a trajectory matrix T_{X_p} can be computed:

$$T_{X_p} = \begin{pmatrix} x_{1p} & x_{2p} & x_{3p} & \cdots & x_{Kp} \\ x_{2p} & x_{3p} & x_{4p} & \cdots & x_{K+1p} \\ \vdots & \vdots & \vdots & \ddots & \vdots \\ x_{Lp} & x_{L+1p} & x_{L+2p} & \cdots & x_{Np} \end{pmatrix} \qquad (8.31)$$

These trajectory matrices are stacked together into a combined trajectory matrix:

$$T_X = [T_{X_1}, T_{X_2}, \ldots, T_{X_p}] \qquad (8.32)$$

This is an $L \times P$ matrix. Note that the corresponding lagged covariance matrix accounts for correlations between the different time series. Once the trajectory matrix is defined, the formalism proceeds essentially as described above in the univariate case. Data imputation based on MSSA was proposed and tested in Kondrashov and Ghil (2006).

8.2.6 Results

We will now discuss the performance of the different imputation techniques on the CDS time series data introduced in Section 8.2.3. An example of a completed ground truth series is displayed in Figure 8.3. It belongs to an issuer in the consumer goods sector and possesses a "modified restructuring" doc clause.

We can see the daily quotes for a period of nearly two years. We observe a hierarchy of values, which are ordered by the maturity. Since the CDS price is a kind of measure for the market view on the probability of default of a certain underlying asset within a defined time period (maturity), this is expected to be the case. There are no strong trend or seasonality patterns, but the time series are also not strictly stationary. We can see that the values for the different maturities are relatively well correlated. It is therefore intuitive that if values for some of the maturities are missing, they can be inferred from the others. A typical missingness pattern in cluster 2 is shown in the lower part of Figure 8.3. Stretches of values for longer maturities are missing in certain intervals, some values of shorter maturities are missing as well, whereas the central maturities are complete. For the test data generation introduced in Section 8.2.3, we can think of this as a mask, which blocks out the respective values.

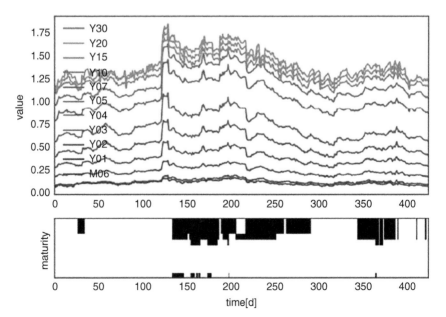

FIGURE 8.3   Top; Example of complete time series data (ticker 1, cluster 2). The lower part shows the missingness pattern that is imposed on the complete data.

Before we provide a detailed comparison of imputed values with the true values for the different imputation techniques, we first give a full overview of the results for the imputation performance in the different clusters. For each method, we did extensive initial testing to identify suitable hyper-parameters and input data adjustments. We have used several techniques (see also Appendix 8.6). The multiple imputation techniques are MICE, based on chained equations and conditional sampling, and Amelia, which uses the EM algorithm to determine the joint data distribution function. As discussed in Section 8.2.4.2, Amelia uses the assumption of the data being MVN distributed; however, we have seen in Section 8.2.3 that this is not the case. As pointed out in Honaker et al. (2011) and Schafer (1997), and illustrated by the following results, the MVN violation does not hamper imputations with good performance. For MICE, we manually included one step time leads and lags in the imputation procedure. We checked both the Bayesian linear regression option (norm) as well as predictive mean matching (PMM), but report results only for the former here, which showed better performance. In Amelia we used the options to include time-lagged and lead data and explicit time covariates to second order. For both MI techniques, we computed five imputations and took the average values as predictions to evaluate the performance metrics.

As deterministic routines we tested Random Forest (missForest R Package), DINEOF, and MSSA. We added an explicit time variable in the RF imputation, but no leads and lags. When all values were missing for a particular time step, we first interpolated the four central maturities linearly. This was also done for the DINEOF approach. In DINEOF, we first subtracted the mean for each time series and then added it again after the imputation. For MSSA we did not perform any prior linear interpolation. We chose the window length for the patterns in cluster 1 to be 10 time steps and for the ones in clusters 2 and 3 to be 40 time steps for better performance. It is noteworthy that both EOF-based techniques are sometimes very sensitive to the starting values. We also tested an approach where MSSA was initialized with Amelia results (Amelia+MSSA). This avoids the usual inaccurate starting values.

With these choices we computed the imputations for 200 cases of missingness patterns overlaid on the ground true values for each cluster 1, 2, and 3, enough to get reliable statistics. In this section we focus on the MRD performance measure defined in Equation (8.5), a relative measure suitable for the comparison of values with different magnitude. To get a global comparative view of the performance we computed the summary statistics (mean, standard deviation, minimum, maximum) of the 200 MRD values for each pattern, imputed versus ground truth. The summary statistics for cluster 1 can be found in Table 8.1, for cluster 2 in Table 8.2, and for cluster 3 in Table 8.3.

For cluster 1, the imputations are quite accurate and the MRD is usually between 1 and 3%, with a few exceptions. The best performance is obtained with MSSA and Amelia, but the other techniques produce comparable results. The patterns in cluster 1 have relatively few missing values (1.5% on average) and they come in short stretches such that the imputation is fairly straightforward.

A more challenging situation occurs for the patterns in cluster 2, which have a larger missingness fraction of 13% on average. The MRD results in the second table

TABLE 8.1   Summary statistics for MRD metrics for cluster 1 in comparison:
Random Forest (RF), DINEOF, MSSA, and average result out of 5 imputations for
Amelia, MICE.

	Amelia	DINEOF	MICE	RF	MSA
mean	0.017	0.024	0.031	0.019	0.016
std	0.010	0.019	0.032	0.014	0.011
min	0.002	0.001	0.002	0.000	0.001
max	0.057	0.141	0.374	0.077	0.102

TABLE 8.2   Summary statistics for MRD metrics for cluster 2.

	Amelia	DINEOF	MICE	RF	MSA
mean	0.035	0.064	0.052	0.046	0.048
std	0.035	0.053	0.056	0.057	0.056
min	0.005	0.011	0.009	0.002	0.005
max	0.328	0.384	0.497	0.483	0.492

TABLE 8.3   Summary statistics for MRD metrics for cluster 2 where patterns were
filtered out if they have rows entirely missing.

	Amelia	DINEOF	MICE	RF	MSA
mean	0.028	0.064	0.046	0.037	0.041
std	0.015	0.054	0.052	0.032	0.041
min	0.005	0.011	0.009	0.002	0.005
max	0.104	0.384	0.497	0.256	0.342

are also still quite accurate, with typical values 2–7%. Amelia shows the strongest
performance, followed by RF and MSSA. The matrix factorization approach
(DINEOF) is less successful imputing the patterns here. We will study this in more
detail later, when we directly compare the imputations with the ground truth values.

Cluster 2 contains 20 patterns, which have stretches where observations are missing for all maturities for a number of consecutive time steps. These cases are particularly difficult to impute with the methods discussed here. An imputation based on a
proxy (i.e. external data that is directly related) is likely to be more successful. It is
of interest to look at the metrics when these patterns are filtered out. The summary
statistics for this are shown in Table 8.3. We can see that the performance improves
a little bit for all the techniques except for DINEOF.

The patterns in cluster 3 typically have more missing values (about 19% on average) and long stretches of missing values for the long maturities. The summary statistics for MRD can be found in Table 8.4. The values for MRD are spread typically
between 3 and 20%, with means of the order of 10%. As in cluster 2, Amelia shows the

TABLE 8.4   Summary statistics for MRD metrics for cluster 3 in comparison.

	Amelia	DINEOF	MICE	RF	MSA
mean	0.093	0.141	0.111	0.098	0.128
std	0.135	0.121	0.158	0.103	0.125
min	0.009	0.012	0.010	0.014	0.008
max	0.980	0.728	1.522	0.650	0.739

TABLE 8.5   Summary statistics for MRD metrics for cluster 3, where patterns were filtered out if they have rows entirely missing.

	Amelia	DINEOF	MICE	RF	MSA
mean	0.061	0.135	0.950	0.920	0.126
std	0.084	0.124	0.155	0.104	0.129
min	0.009	0.012	0.010	0.014	0.008
max	0.705	0.728	1.522	0.650	0.739

strongest performance with an average of about 9%, followed by RF, MICE, MSSA, and DINEOF.

Cluster 3 contains 23 patterns that have stretches where observations are missing for all maturities for a number of consecutive time steps. The results for when we remove those are shown in Table 8.5. The performance improves considerably for Amelia and moderately for the others. Both EOF-based approaches depend on the starting values. We have also tested a combined Amelia+MSSA approach, where Amelia predictions are used as starting values for the MSSA algorithm. For cluster 3 we found mean MRD of 0.099, which is a considerable improvement over the pure MSSA approach (0.128) with naive mean starting values.

We now compare, in more detail, the predictions of the different techniques. As an example, we choose ticker 1 (cluster 2) for which the complete data and the missingness mask were shown in Figure 8.3. It misses a lot of consecutive values for the longer maturities and the total missingness fraction is around 17%. The Amelia imputations are shown in Figure 8.4 (top). From the 5 imputations we computed the average values shown as dots, and the shaded region indicates the spread between maximum and minimum for the imputation range. The full line shows the ground truth. We can see that the imputed data follows relatively well the general structure of the data, which is inferred from the correlation with the other series. The spread for the higher maturities is a bit larger. Hence, Amelia learns the correlations with the other (more complete) time series well and imputes both the temporal structure as well as the magnitude of the values accurately. The value for MRD is only 0.02.

The MICE imputations for the same time series are shown in Figure 8.4 (bottom) and are quite similar to the Amelia results in this case. We can see again that the imputed data follows relatively well the general structure of the data. The spread

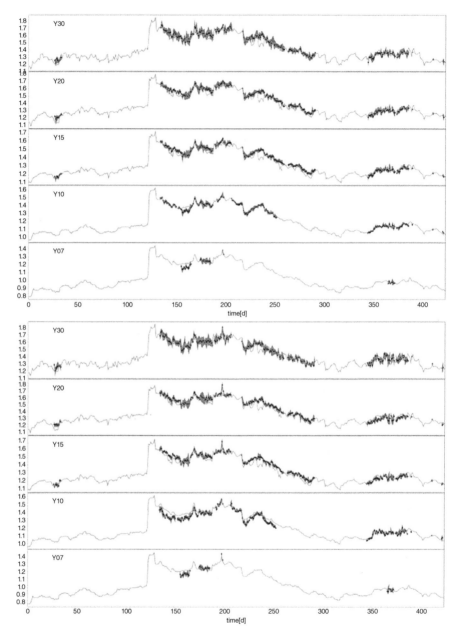

FIGURE 8.4   Amelia (top) and MICE (bottom) imputed time series for data in Figure 8.3 (dots), compared with the ground truth (lines) for the longer maturities. The shaded region indicates minimum and maximum for 5 imputations.

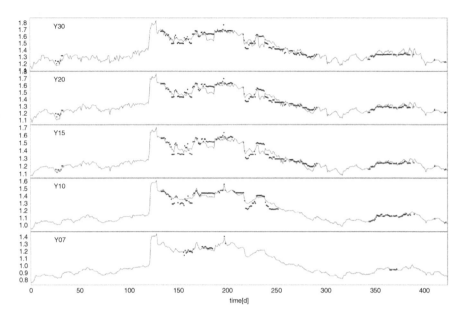

FIGURE 8.5   RF imputation (dots) for data in Figure 8.2-3, compared with the ground truth (lines) for the longer maturities.

appears to be a bit larger than in the case of Amelia. The value for MRD is with 0.024 slightly worse than for Amelia.

The imputations for RF, DINEOF, and MSSA are collected in Figure 8.5 and Figure 8.6. The values for MRD are 0.025, 0.044, 0.019, respectively. A number of observations can be made. RF imputes the magnitudes of the values relatively well; however, it does not follow the temporal structure very faithfully, and produces somewhat artificial results. These can be nearly constant over certain periods or possess unexpected discontinuities. In contrast, the DINEOF approach reproduces the overall temporal structures quite well, but does not predict the magnitude of the values as accurately as the other techniques. DINEOF systematically underestimates the magnitude of the values in many cases. EOF-based matrix interpolation techniques work best when there are enough data points in the vicinity of the missing values and the data has clear enough structure with variations on not too short scales. As shown in Section 8.2.5.2, this can work very well for images; however, the CDS data and missingness patterns here possess different features, for which DINEOF does not perform so well. Finally, MSSA reproduces the structures and values most accurately and performs competitively with the MI technique Amelia. Since it is based on an EOF basis expansion, it tends to smooth the curves somewhat.

For this example belonging to cluster 2, the overall performance of the imputations is quite strong. Since we have patterns that are alternating between missing and

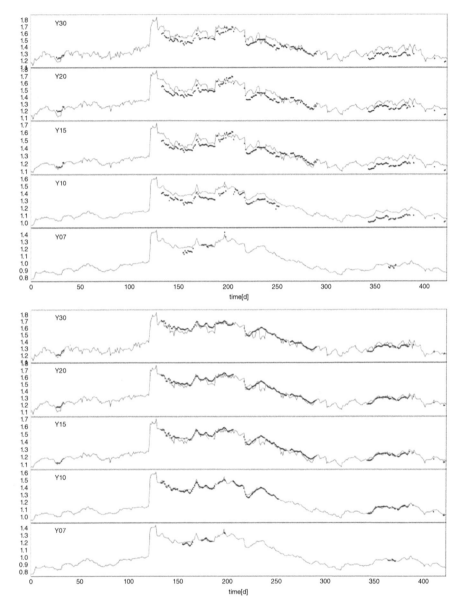

FIGURE 8.6   DINEOF (top) and MSSA (bottom) imputation (dots) for data in Figure 8.3, compared with the ground truth (lines) for the longer maturities.

observed data the algorithms can learn the structure very well. The situation is different in cluster 3, where we have much longer streaks of missing values. We show an example in Figure 8.7. The data for the long maturities is missing over almost the entire time period and partially for shorter maturities. The total missing fraction is 45%, which is rather high.

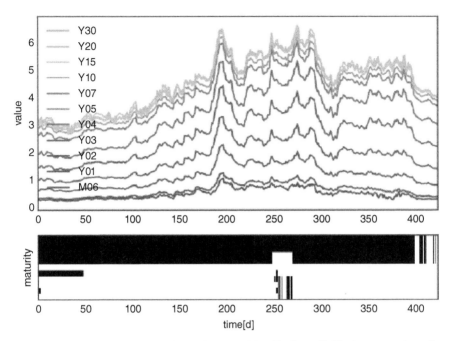

FIGURE 8.7   Example of complete time series data (ticker 40, cluster 3). The lower part shows the missingness pattern that is imposed on the complete data.

The Amelia imputation is shown in Figure 8.8 for the longer maturities;[5] MRD is 0.166, comparatively high. We can see that in contrast to the previous case the short periods toward the end, where all time series are observed, are not enough to learn the correlation pattern well enough to impute the long stretches of missing data in the past. For the maturities Y07 and Y10, which are closer to the observed data of shorter maturities, the time period between 280 and 400 is imputed quite well, whereas for the longer maturities (Y15, Y20, and Y30) the imputations systematically underestimate the true result. The imputations for the time period 0–180 are not satisfactory in all cases, and do not describe the trend correctly. This demonstrates limitations for cases where correlations cannot be learned well enough from the observed data. It is worth noting that some of the temporal structure is described fairly well while the overall values are estimated inaccurately in many cases.

For the same data, we also show the result for the MSSA imputation in Figure 8.9 MRD is 0.22, even higher than Amelia's result. We find that the intermediate maturities where some observations are present in the middle of the time period give satisfactory results for the time period between 280 and 400, whereas for the longest maturities the correlations have not been learned well enough from the few observed

---

[5]The shorter maturities are imputed accurately and are not shown.

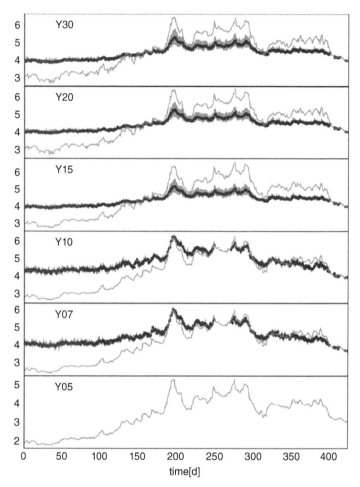

FIGURE 8.8 Amelia imputed time series for data in Figure 8.7 (dots), compared with the ground truth (lines) for the longer maturities.

values and thus the imputations yield too little variation. The other techniques (MICE, RF, DINEOF) have similar difficulties to impute this dataset and are not shown.

In summary, we therefore conclude that when there are few common observations and long stretches with missing data, the generic methods used here do not perform very well. One therefore has to accept inaccuracies of about 20%. Domain-specific techniques, including prior knowledge about the data, can be more per-formant then.

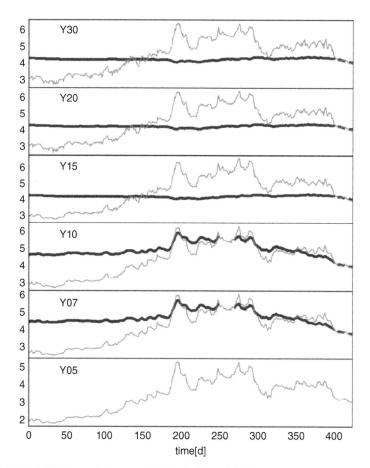

FIGURE 8.9 MSSA imputed time series for data in Figure 8.7 (dots), compared with the ground truth (lines) for the longer maturities.

8.3 CASE STUDY: SATELLITE IMAGES

In this section we will show how to apply the DINEOF technique to satellite images subject to missing pixels. We highlight again that this approach works quite well when there is enough structure in the data, and P must not be too small. For illustration, we give an example of DINEOF imputation for car park image data. Here, we take an image of a car park and randomly remove 50% of its pixels.[6] We then impute the

---

[6]This is a situation that could occur in reality if we were to lose 50% of data packets received from a satellite, or any other reason.

missing values via the DINEOF technique. The process can be split into two steps: (1) removing random pixels, and (2) imputing missing values. Step 1 can be split into two parts:

1. Generate a mask for the image where 50% of the values are set to true, 50% to false.
2. Wherever there is a true value in our mask, set the pixel intensity to 255 (i.e. set the value to white).

Step 2 can then be broken down into:

1. Set all locations where the mask is true (i.e. our missing values) to some naïve estimate of their true value (e.g. fill all missing values with the mean pixel intensity of all non-missing pixels in the image or fill all missing values with the mean pixel intensity of all non-missing pixels in some $m \times n$ window around the missing pixel). This would be our first estimate for the true image; denote it $X_0^{(n_{EOF})}$. Set $i = 0$.

2. Apply DINEOF to $X_i^{(n_{EOF})}$, setting $\widetilde{X}_{i+1}^{(n_{EOF})} = \sum_{k=1}^{n_{EOF}} \sqrt{\lambda_k} \boldsymbol{u}_k \boldsymbol{v}_k^T$, where $\lambda_k, \boldsymbol{u}_k$ and $\boldsymbol{v}_k$ come from the singular value decomposition of $X_i^{(n_{EOF})}$.

3. Define a new matrix (image), $X_{i+1}^{(n_{EOF})}$ to be equal to $X_i^{(n_{EOF})}$, but with all pixels where our mask is true to be equal to the corresponding values from $\widetilde{X}_{i+1}^{(n_{EOF})}$ (i.e. fill the missing points in our image with our i^{th} DINEOF-based guess). Go to step 2.

An example of this procedure can be seen in Figure 8.10.

Two comparisons are shown, both having 50% of the pixels randomly removed. In the first we start by filling the missing points by the mean of all non-missing points in the image before proceeding with the DINEOF procedure with 100 EOFs.[7] In the second we fill each missing point with the mean value of all non-missing points in a 5-by-5 window around the point, again performing DINEOF with 100 EOFs. As we can see, in both cases we can reproduce the image with a fairly good level of reconstruction. More precisely, for the first, we have an RMSE of 42.4[8] after our naïve guess using all non-missing pixels, decreasing to 12.8 after DINEOF. For the second we start with an RMSE of 16.8 after our naïve guess of using all non-missing pixels in a 5×5 window around each missing point, decreasing to 11.3 after DINEOF. Although it is not easy to see here,[9] it appears that the post-DINEOF images have sharper edges than the pre-DINEOF ones, appearing less noisy. This would likely help any image detection methods we apply. Note that the DINEOF approach aims to include EOFs only as long as they add signal.

---

[7] Because our image is 480 by 955 pixels, we have 480 EOFs.
[8] RMSE is measured using pixel intensities from 0 to 255.
[9] For larger versions of these images, see Figures 8.11–8.16.

Actual Image

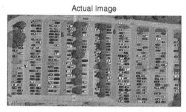

Image with 50% missing

Image with 50% missing mean filled

Image with 50% missing mean filled after DINEOF

Image with 50% missing local 5x5 window mean filled

Image with 50% missing local 5x5 window mean filled after DINEOF

FIGURE 8.10   Example of DINEOF imputation for car park data.

Actual Image

FIGURE 8.11   Car park image.

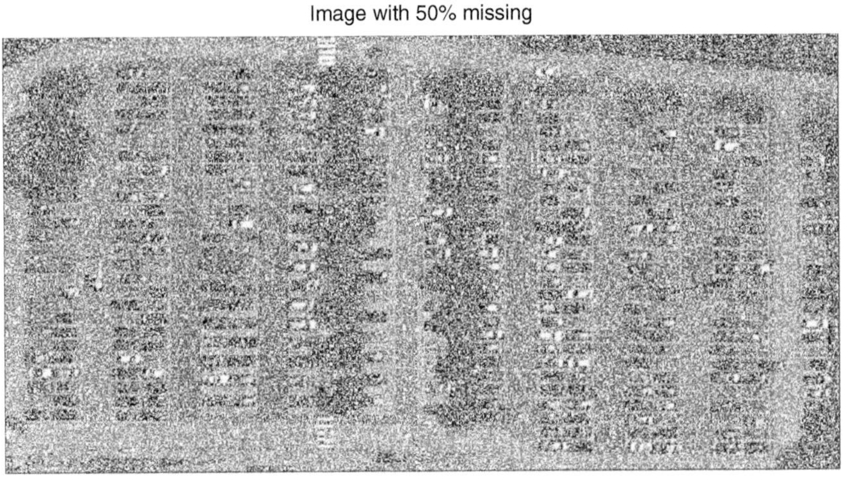

Image with 50% missing

FIGURE 8.12   Car park image with 50% removed.

Image with 50% missing mean filled

FIGURE 8.13   Car park image with missing pixels mean filled, pre-DINEOF.

8.4   SUMMARY

We have introduced a structured framework for approaching and benchmarking the problem of filling missing data for multivariate time series and images. As an example, we used a large sample of CDS daily quotes over a period of nearly two years and a set of satellite images. We introduced and described a variety of state-of-the-art stochastic MI techniques and deterministic, mainly EOF-based techniques.

Image with 50% missing mean filled after DINEOF

FIGURE 8.14 Car park image with missing pixels mean filled, post-DINEOF.

Image with 50% missing local 5x5 window mean filled

FIGURE 8.15 Car park image with missing pixels local mean filled, pre-DINEOF.

We ran imputations on the CDS data for three different clusters with different missingness characteristics for 200 samples each. For the patterns in the first cluster with small overall missingness fraction (1.5%), the performance of all methods was comparable and values for MRD of about 0.02 could be achieved. For missingness patterns with higher missingness fractions, the performance of the techniques varied considerably. We found strong and robust performance for the EM-based algorithm, Amelia. It has good time series support natively, including leads and lags, and as such is easier to apply for multivariate time series than MICE, the other MI package tested thoroughly.

Image with 50% missing local 5x5 window mean filled after DINEOF

FIGURE 8.16   Car park image with missing pixels local mean filled, post-DINEOF.

8.5   APPENDIX: GENERAL DESCRIPTION OF THE MICE PROCEDURE

As introduced in Section 8.2.4 the MICE framework in based on multiple imputations by chained equations. Chained equations refers to an iterative procedure by which features and parameter values are generated in series of steps. We describe them in the following.

The general assumption is that the (complete) data is generated from a multivariate distribution function, $p(X|\theta)$, where θ is a collection of parameters that are not known. In certain cases, the distribution function p can be assumed to have a particular form (e.g. MVN), which we discussed in more detail in Section 8.2.4.1. If not specified explicitly, it must at least implicitly be accessible for sampling. In the following, we describe a generic procedure by which parameters are estimated from the data, and in turn new data estimates are generated from the corresponding distributions (see Buuren & Groothuis-Oudshoorn, 2011). To keep the description very generic in this section, it is described as a pure Monte Carlo sampling approach. In particular, the description is a type of sampling, where, at each step, we draw values from a multivariate conditional distribution function $p(X_1, X_2, \ldots, X_p|\theta)$. This procedure is known as a Gibbs sampler. It is a member of the Markov Chain Monte Carlo (MCMC) family. This chained equation procedure can be described as follows.

At iteration t we determine $\theta_1^{(t)}$ by sampling from a distribution:

$$p_\theta(\theta_1|X_1^{obs}, X_2^{(t-1)}, \ldots, X_P^{(t-1)}) \tag{8.33}$$

where $X_i^{(t)} = (X_i^{obs}, X_i^{imp,(t)})$ includes both observed and imputed data, and $X_2^{(t-1)}, \ldots, X_P^{(t-1)}$ were determined at step $t - 1$. For the first step some initial guess must be used. We can imagine the distribution in Equation (8.33) as being derived from a prior and a likelihood function in a Bayesian framework.

We call the value sampled from Equation (8.33) $\theta_1^{(t)}$. New imputation values for the first feature X_1 are then obtained by sampling from the distribution:

$$p_x(X_1|X_1^{obs}, X_2^{(t-1)}, \dots, X_P^{(t-1)}, \theta_1^{(t)}) \tag{8.34}$$

This means that we take into account the previously sampled parameter vector $\theta_1^{(t)}$. The next step is to sample for θ_2 and X_2 in similar fashion as above. The only difference is that we take the imputed values for X_1, i.e., $X_i^{(t)}$ into account. Hence, the order in which imputations are made matters. This continues for all P features; that is, we sample θ_P from:

$$p_\theta(\theta_P|X_P^{obs}, X_1^{(t)}, \dots, X_{P-1}^{(t)}, \theta_P^{(t)}) \tag{8.35}$$

and the new values for X_P from:

$$p_x(X_P|X_P^{obs}, X_1^{(t)}, \dots, X_{P-1}^{(t)}, \theta_P^{(t)}) \tag{8.36}$$

Once this is finished, we can start with iteration $t + 1$.

A particular case for this procedure is when we can assume that the complete data is generated by an MVN, that is, $X \sim N(\boldsymbol{\mu}, \Sigma)$. Then all the distribution functions can be derived analytically, and the procedure becomes more explicit, as shown in Section 8.2.4.1.

8.6   APPENDIX: SOFTWARE LIBRARIES USED IN THIS CHAPTER

We used a number of software packages for the imputations performed in this chapter. Most of them that we detail and reference below are freely available. For multiple imputation there are two packages based on chained equations **MI** (see Su et al., 2011) and **MICE** (see Enders, 2010). We initially tested both but for the more involved performance studies we focused on **MICE**, due to the slightly simpler API. The standard R package for MI based on EM is **Amelia II** (see Honaker et al., 2011).

8.6.1.1 MICE

MICE is an R package that is available from the comprehensive R repository CRAN. Its functionality is documented in Buuren and Groothuis-Oudshoorn (2010). We used it for the multivariate time series data as specified in Section 8.2.6, explicitly including leads and lags. We also used an option to choose predictor variables for the imputation based on availability and aimed at using only variables that are present in more than 50% of the cases. Predictor models such as Bayesian linear regression and predictive mean matching have been discussed in the main text.

8.6.1.2   Amelia II

The R package **Amelia II** is available from CRAN and follows the algorithm described in Section 8.2.4.2. It has direct time series support with a number of different options. One of them is to include time polynomials up to third order as additional variables in the covariance matrix. Another option is the ability to use time-lagged variables (lead, lagged). The way this works is by using not only the variables at hand but also variables shifted by one unit of time into account and thus enlarge the covariance matrix accordingly. Amelia II uses a bootstrap approach to account for the variance of the parameters $\theta = (\mu, \Sigma)$.

8.6.1.3   MissForest: Random Forest Imputation

Random Forest (RF) is a very successful technique for regression and classification, which learns feature interactions well and naturally handles different data types (see Breiman, 2001). It has been proposed as a suitable tool for data imputation as well (see Stekhoven & Bühlmann, 2012). The algorithm proceeds as follows: we start with an initial guess for the missing values. Then for each feature (or time series component) p that contains missing values we train a RF prediction model from the available data. This can be used to generate improved imputations. We iterate through all the p features that contain missing values. In the next iteration we use the imputed values of the last iteration. The iterations stop once the imputed values do not change much from iteration to iteration. These converged values are used as imputations for the missing data.

Random Forest data imputation is available as the R library **MissForest** (Stekhoven & Bühlmann, 2012), which is obtainable from CRAN. It is well documented. It is noteworthy that the default setting for the subset of features used for the imputation is $\sqrt{P}$. For the imputations in this chapter, we increased it to $\sim P/2$ to improve the accuracy.

8.6.1.4   DINEOF

The matrix interpolation approach DINEOF is based on SVD of the data matrix and a suitable reconstruction. We used the R package **sinkr**, which is available from the repository https://github.com/menugget/sinkr. It is worth pointing out that this package assumes that the data has zero mean. Therefore, we subtracted the mean from the input data and added it again after the imputation.

8.6.1.5   MSSA

As discussed in the main text, the MSSA approach is based on SVD of the trajectory matrices and reconstruction employing the EOFs. This can be technically achieved by the R package **RSSA** (see Golyandina et al., 2013). To treat the multivariate time series, we found it better to use the "2dSSA" option rather than the "MSSA" option, even though the latter also works. We are not aware of a full implementation to treat the general missing data problem. Therefore, we wrote our own routine performing the imputations with the algorithm described in Section 8.2.5 and in Kondrashov and Ghil (2006).

CHAPTER 9

Outliers (Anomalies)[1]

9.1 INTRODUCTION

We discussed briefly in Section 3.3.4 that sometimes outliers can be an issue when dealing with (alternative) data. They can be of technical nature (e.g. a glitch) or simply a property of the data. In this latter case, we might either want to model them (e.g. fraud detection) or simply discard them as we might want to focus on modeling the "normal" portion of the data only.

The first step to treating outliers is, of course, to find them. In this chapter we will delve more into the details of how outliers can be detected. Preferably, the next step is to explain them, if required by the business application. A potential[2] third step is to treat them. This means we either remove them (and in this case we fall back to the missing data problem of the previous chapter) or model them. Again, this depends on the specific problem at hand.[3]

In this chapter we will show some techniques to outliers' detection and explanation. The techniques – like in the missing data chapter – cannot be exhaustive for all the problems encountered in practice. However, they will be a selection of what we have seen working broadly in practice in a breadth of applications. We will finish the chapter by illustrating a use case focused on detecting outliers in Fed's communications.

---

[1] Special thanks to Kate Lavrinenko for her contribution to this chapter.

[2] "Potential" because we might well want to stop at the second step.

[3] We must note that some data vendors might want to treat the data themselves (e.g. missing data imputation, outliers' removal, etc.) before selling it onwards, as discussed previously in Section 5.4. Some more sophisticated buyers might prefer data vendors not to perform this step for them but rather to buy the raw preprocessed data directly. They fear is that by preprocessing the data, data vendors might discard precious information that can be useful for them later at the modeling stage.

9.2   OUTLIERS DEFINITION, CLASSIFICATION, AND APPROACHES TO DETECTION

Outlier detection is the process of finding those observations in data that are different from most of the other observations. Hawkins's definition of an outlier (Hawkins, 1980) states that the points must be different enough from the rest of the observations to suggest that they were produced by a different mechanism or model. There is an intuition behind this definition. While normal observations are generated by some process, abnormal points deviate from this pattern and were likely generated by a different data generating process. In these situations, they are considered to be noise, measurements errors, deviations, or exceptions. There is no single definition. In different settings the underlying meaning of an exceptional object could, of course, be different.

There are numerous situations in which anomaly detection is important: in medical data analysis, industrial production monitoring, bank fraud and network intrusion prevention, financial markets activities regulation, public health, ecosystems disturbance, and so on. One particular case relevant to trading is trying to identify anomalies within high-frequency tick data, so-called "fat-finger" data points. In Chapter 19, we discuss using high-frequency tick data from FX markets to understand market liquidity.

Recent interest in anomaly detection is mostly driven by the particular case where outliers themselves are the main problem (Tan, Steinbach, & Kumar, 2006). In fact, anomalies were historically viewed as those observations that should be found and removed from the dataset being studied in order not to disturb the patterns of normal data. Even a few outliers can distort statistical properties (such as means and standard deviations) of a set of values or the outcome of a clustering algorithm that is aimed at grouping similar observations. Therefore, anomaly detection and removal are part of data processing and, when computationally feasible, it is combined with using statistics robust to outliers.

In the context of regularity-based tasks where the normal instances are of interest, outliers are considered to be noise that should be eliminated since it can worsen the predictive or descriptive capabilities of algorithms. However, "one man's noise is another man's signal."[4] Hence, there are applications in which outliers themselves represent useful knowledge of interest, and not something to be removed. These types of outliers are frequently dealt with in telecom or credit card fraud prevention, in intrusion detection, in medical analysis, in marketing and customer segmentation, in surveillance systems, in data cleaning, in biological data analysis, and in many other fields. Within financial markets, we also need to be careful to make a distinction between fat-finger data points, which we can think of as outlying points that are likely to be reversed, and price moves that result in exceptionally volatile outcomes for other perfectly valid reasons, rather than invalid data entry.

---

[4]This quote is commonly attributed to Edward W. Ng (1990), though its variations go back to Lucretius, around the first century BCE.

One example of such exceptionally volatile price moves that were not the result of fat-finger errors were those of EUR/CHF on January 15, 2015. On that day, the Swiss National Bank (SNB) stopped intervening in the market to maintain a floor in the price of EUR/CHF at 1.20. The SNB had previously been trying to prevent apprecia-tion in CHF, which would have negatively impacted Swiss exporters. However, they removed the floor following the ECB's move to begin quantitative easing. On the day the SNB removed the floor, EUR/CHF traded as low as 0.85, in the subsequent incredibly volatile price action. EUR/CHF settled in the area of 1.00 by the close of the day. It took over three years till it traded back above 1.20, hardly the sort of quick reversion we would associate with a fat-finger print.

If we think specifically about alternative data (and the structured datasets derived), it isn't always the case that outliers have a temporal structure, as we might expect in the time series for market data. There are many potential examples of outliers in alternative datasets. We may have outliers in sentiment scores based on news text, which might be unusual for a particular set of features like topic, type of article, or text length. We might either choose to remove this article, or indeed in other circum-stances to flag it specifically to the user, as the unusual news could be of particular market relevance. In Section 9.8, we have a specific case study on flagging outliers in a text-based dataset for FOMC communications.

When structuring satellite imagery, we might infer various features such as the car counts, which seem anomalous compared to other similar days and locations, which could be related to many factors such as cloud cover, holidays, and so on. Later, we shall discuss the concept of local outliers, which can be "contextual."

9.3 TEMPORAL STRUCTURE

Intrusion detection analyzes a data stream and is primarily focused on finding behav-ioral patterns in the data. When the pattern unexpectedly changes, an anomaly should be detected in nearly real-time, because the longer the lag, the higher the damage. In this sense, anomaly detection has a temporal connotation. A similar situation arises with fault detection systems in production line settings and in credit card fraud detec-tion. In the latter case, the spending pattern of the cardholder is continuously checked against the attempted activity so that in case a transaction is suspicious, an alarm is raised as soon as possible.

In many fraud detection settings, historical data logs are analyzed in order to label cases that could be associated with fraudulent accounting, suspicious inter-net payments, or misused credit cards. Also, there are specialized situations when a post-incident or predictive analysis is conducted in order to provide early warn-ings of undesirable situations in the future. These specialized problems can have very efficient solutions. In a vast number of real-world situations, though, there is no distinct time structure in the data, so other methods for anomaly detection must be used.

9.4 GLOBAL VERSUS LOCAL OUTLIERS, POINT ANOMALIES, AND MICRO-CLUSTERS

An observation in a dataset can be considered anomalous with respect to just one of its attributes or a combination of several features. Since in most cases an object has multiple attributes, it can be anomalous with respect to one of them, but can be normal with respect to others.

An outlier can be classified as global when that observation is different from the whole dataset (also known as the population) with respect to a particular attribute. It can be an unusually high, low, or just a rare value. However, an observation can have a common value for each of its attributes, but still be an outlier. For example, a high salary can be quite normal with respect to the whole population, but when restricted to 18-year-olds it is an outstanding observation. When the point is different from its neighborhood while its value is not exceptional for the whole dataset, it is classified as a local outlier. In the book on data mining by Han, Kamber, and Pei (2011), a local outlier is also called "contextual," such as our unusual news article example discussed earlier.

When using an approach of grouping similar observations (in a clustering setting) a separate category of micro-clusters can be introduced. These small groups of observations may consist of outliers, but also may consist of normal objects. Another name for a small group of outliers is "collective outliers." In order to deal with collective anomalies, correlation, aggregation, and grouping are often used to generate a new dataset with a different representation – a "data view" (Goldstein and Uchida, 2016). In the resulting dataset, micro-clusters are represented by single points and the problem is again formulated as point outliers' detection. This chapter focuses on single-point anomaly detection, assuming that there are no groups of anomalous observations or they are small enough to recognize each point as an outlier.

9.5 OUTLIER DETECTION PROBLEM SETUP

As we discussed in Section 3.3.4, anomaly detection problem setup is traditionally divided into supervised, semi-supervised, and unsupervised. In the supervised setting, labeled data is available for training and testing outlier detection algorithms. Usually, in these cases the data is highly unbalanced (the number of normal observations far exceeds the number of outliers) because anomalies are rare by definition. Therefore, not all traditional classification methods work equally well.

Nevertheless, some of them work well with unbalanced datasets. These methods include Random Forests, Support Vector Machines (SVMs), Neural Networks, and many other methods combined with tools that address the unbalanced structure of datasets (for instance, special sampling techniques). These approaches are extensively covered in the book on statistical learning by James et al. (2013) and in the book on data mining by Witten et al. (2011).

However, in most cases, a fully labeled dataset is not available because anomalies are not known in advance. If there exists a sufficiently large dataset of normal instances (without outliers), then the problem is called semi-supervised. It is also called a one-class classification problem. Commonly used methods in this setting are One-Class SVMs (Schölkopf et al., 2001), auto-encoders, and a wide range of statistical methods where algorithms learn the normal class distribution. Hence, any new observation is assessed with respect to the probability to observe its value for the normal class. For example, Kernel Density Estimation (Rosenblatt, 1956) or Gaussian Finite Mixture Models can be employed in this case.

In an unsupervised learning setup, there is no data that is labeled normal or anomalous. It means that the outlierness scores or probabilities assigned to observations depend solely on the pattern of the data distribution in this same dataset. By the nature of unsupervised learning, there are a variety of ways to define outlying objects and methods of dealing with them.

In what follows we will look at the case of unsupervised anomaly detection. This contrasts to a more mainstream classification task. Approaches for outlier detection can be roughly classified into model-based techniques, distance-based, density-based, and methods based on different heuristics. For a detailed description of these approaches, please refer to Appendix 9.10.

9.6   COMPARATIVE EVALUATION OF OUTLIER DETECTION ALGORITHMS

Numerous algorithms can be used for anomaly detection. In order to make the knowledge practical, it is important to compare their performance, at least on a few publicly available real-life datasets from different fields of studies. These datasets (for example, from the UCI Machine Learning Repository[5]) provide typical data for the unsupervised machine learning setup while they are the rare cases when true labels for outliers are also available.

Goldstein and Uchida (2016) implemented the most popular anomaly detection algorithms and compared them. Table 9.1 shows real-life datasets that authors used in their study.[6]

The datasets were designed or preprocessed to address only point outlier detection, so the anomalies are rare, not collective, and different from normal observations. This data selection covered a range of applications for unsupervised machine learning and had different properties such as size, number of outliers, and attributes. The authors

---

[5]UCI Machine Learning Repository, available from: https://archive.ics.uci.edu/ml/index.php. Retrieved July 17, 2018.

[6]Datasets used are available from: https://dataverse.harvard.edu/dataset.xhtml?persistentId=doi:10.7910/DVN/OPQMVF. Retrieved: July 17, 2018.

TABLE 9.1   Datasets used in comparative analysis of outlier detection algorithms.

Dataset	Observations	Outliers	Attributes	Comments
b-cancer	367	10	30	Breast Cancer Wisconsin (Diagnostic): features extracted from medical images; the task is to separate cancer from healthy patients.
pen-global	809	90	16	Pen-Based Recognition of Handwritten Text (global): handwritten digits of 45 different writers, in the "global" task only the digit 8 is kept as the normal class and digits from all of the other classes as anomalies.
letter	1,600	100	32	Letter Recognition: the UCI letter dataset contains features from the 26 letters of the English alphabet, where three letters form the normal class and anomalies are sampled from the rest.
speech	3,686	61	400	Speech Accent Data: contains data (i-vector of the speech segment) from recorded English language, where the normal class comes from persons having an American accent and outliers come from seven other speakers.
satellite	5,100	75	36	Landsat Satellite: comprises features extracted from satellite observations of soil from different categories, where anomalies are images of "cotton crop" and "soil with vegetation stubble."
pen-local	6,724	10	16	Pen-Based Handwritten Text (local): here all digits are the normal class, except for the anomalous digit 4.
annthyroid	6,916	250	21	Thyroid Disease: medical data, preprocessed to train neural networks, known as the "annthyroid" dataset, where normal instances are healthy non-hypothyroid patients.
shuttle	46,464	878	9	Statlog Shuttle: the shuttle dataset describes radiator positions in a NASA space shuttle with the normal "radiator flow" class and different abnormal situations.
aloi	50,000	1,508	27	Object Images: the aloi dataset represents images of small objects taken under different conditions and broken into feature vectors using HSB color histograms.
kdd99	620,098	1,052	38	KDD-Cup99: contains simulated normal and attack traffic, designed to test intrusion detection systems, where attacks constitute anomalies.

Source: Goldstein and Uchida (2016).

implemented the most popular algorithms with different approaches toward outlier detection. Some of them are:

- **KNN** is an algorithm for global outlier detection (Ramaswamy et al., 2000). It takes the distance to k-th nearest neighbor of the observation in the features space and based on this measure assigns scores of outlierness to every point in the dataset. Usually, k is in the range from 10 to 50, and a threshold for outlierness is set individually for a given dataset. Please also refer to Chapter 4 for a broader discussion of KNN.

- **LOF**, local outlier factor, searches for local outliers (Breunig et al., 2000). In order to get a local outlierness score, the k nearest neighbors are found for each observation. Then the local density in the neighborhood of the observation is estimated. The last step is to compare this local density with the ones for the nearest neighbors of the point. The resulting score is an average ratio of local densities. If it is around 1, the point is considered normal; if it is high, it is an anomaly. An example of LOF score visualization is shown in Figure 9.1.

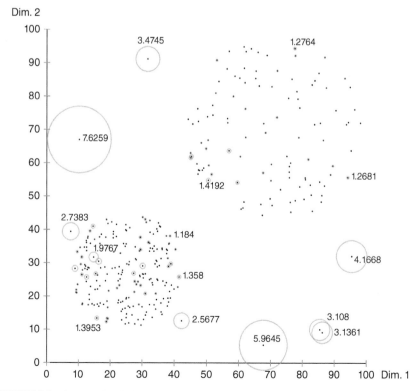

FIGURE 9.1 An example of LOF score visualization in 2 dimensions: radius of a circle around each point represents its score.

Source: Wikipedia, https://commons.wikimedia.org/wiki/File:LOF.svg. Public Domain. Retrieved: 6 August 2018.

- **CBLOF** is a cluster-based outlier factor algorithm (Goldstein, 2014). Clustering (usually, k-means) determines areas in the attributes space where observations are grouped. The outlierness score is calculated based on the distance of an observation toward the nearest cluster center. It depends on parameter k and gives different results for different runs due to the randomness of k-means.

- **HBOS** is a histogram-based statistical outlier detector (Goldstein and Dengel, 2012). For each attribute a histogram of values is built and for an observation its score is equal to the inversed product of histogram heights across all histograms. This method ignores dependence between attributes, but it is fast and works particularly well in high-dimensional sparse datasets. Parameters in HBOS determine the way bins are formed, which can affect outcomes.

- **One-Class SVM** (Schölkopf et al., 2001) estimates the area in the attributes space where normal observations are concentrated. This method is usually used in semi-supervised setup, but it is also applicable to unsupervised problems as by assumption outliers are rare and the soft margin optimization procedure allows the model to be trained to have only a few outliers. The outlierness score is based on the distance of an observation to the boundary of the area of normal cases. Please see Chapter 4 for a more general discussion of SVM.

An industry standard for comparison of unsupervised machine learning techniques is to rank all observations by scoring outputs and then iteratively apply a threshold from the first to the last rank. This results in a collection of pairs of true positive and false positive rates, which forms an ROC curve. The area under this curve is denoted AUC and represents the performance measure. The AUC can be interpreted as the probability that an algorithm assigns a randomly chosen normal instance a lower score than a randomly chosen anomalous instance (Fawcett, 2006).

Findings in Goldstein and Uchida (2016) show that local anomaly detection algorithms, such as LOF, perform poorly on datasets containing only global anomalies because they generate many false positives (they label normal observations as outliers). At the same time, global anomaly detection algorithms perform average or better than average on problems where only local outliers are present. Therefore, if the context of the data is not known *a priori*, it is better to choose a global anomaly detection algorithm.

Goldstein and Uchida (2016) infer that in most cases KNN-type algorithms perform better and are more stable than clustering approaches. On the other hand, clustering algorithms have lower computation time, which is crucial for large datasets or in near real-time setting, but can be detrimental for small datasets. It is shown that a variation of CBLOF performs well on average and can be used as a cluster-based method where appropriate. The final recommendation is to implement KNN, LOF, and HBOS, which shows good results in the comparative evaluation and works fast, especially for large datasets. We should be careful to note that some of these techniques might be amenable only to non-temporal numeric datasets.

9.7 APPROACHES TO OUTLIER EXPLANATION

There are numerous approaches to anomaly detection in an unsupervised setup with hundreds of algorithms implemented. But even when an expert from a particular field of study gets output from these methods, it may be unclear exactly why these observations have been chosen as outliers.

Some of the methods provide intuitive explanations as a byproduct of the anomaly detection process, but those explanations are applicable only to the observations picked by the methods. For example, a decision tree would give a set of rules as an output, stating that when some of the attributes exhibit values above or below particular thresholds, then an observation is classified as an outlier. Otherwise, it is classified as a normal instance. Such a method cannot explain outlierness of an observation if it does not consider this observation to be an outlier.

On the contrary, the outlier explanation task is aimed at describing what distinguishes an observation from the rest of the dataset. If attributes of the dataset are meaningful to the subject expert, then an explanation can help him or her to understand the underlying reason for outlierness, regardless of whether an algorithm has labeled that instance as an anomaly. It implies that an explanation should be intuitive and concise. A classical approach to explanation is to plot the dataset, where a point outlier or an outlying micro-cluster can be seen. But visualization requires an attribute subspace, where other objects are distributed around the labeled outlier in the way that demonstrates its anomalousness. Moreover, multiple subspaces might be provided to aid explanation.

Recently, a number of studies suggested other approaches to outlier explanation, where some methods return a combination of attributes that distinguishes an outlier while others derive different kinds of association rules (like in Agarwal et al., 1993). An explanation could be a byproduct of outlier detection as well as a separate problem. In what follows we summarize the works of Micenkova et al. (2013), Duan et al. (2015), and Angiulli et al. (2009, 2017). These solutions were chosen based on their comprehensiveness, applicability in different situations, ease of implementation, and computational complexity.

Similar to the outlier detection task, it is important to compare and evaluate explanation algorithms. Considerations in the article by Vinh et al. (2016) laid the base of the analysis. After a primary approach is selected, it is always possible to leave an opportunity to switch to another one in case the results do not meet expectations.

9.7.1 Micenkova et al.

The method of Micenkova et al. (2013) suggests separating an outlier from the normal instances in its neighborhood by a linear boundary and then turning the problem of separation into a classification task. Under the assumptions of the method, features that have the highest importance in classification are those that demonstrate the outlierness of the observation. This method is claimed to work well, but appears to be "local." According to Angiulli (2009), its locality makes a difference in case there is a small cluster of observations that are different from the vast majority of others

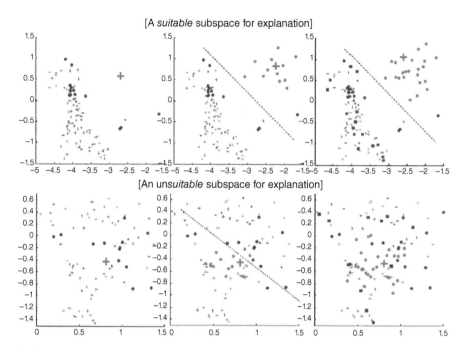

FIGURE 9.2 An illustration of potential difficulties in choosing a normal neighborhood (subspace) around an outlier in order to separate them with a linear boundary. Normal instances chosen to represent the neighborhood are highlighted with dark while lighter circular points around the outlier-cross represent a synthetic normal distribution generated to be an outlier class in the classification task.
Source: Adapted from Micenkova et al. (2013).

that do not fall into the small neighborhood of an outlier in focus. Also, in some cases outliers and the normal neighborhood cannot be separated by a linear boundary (see Figure 9.2).

Making a comparative evaluation of different approaches to the problem of outlier explanation, Vinh et al. (2016) notes that, while the feature selection–based approach works well, there are two important points. First, the k-nearest neighbors in the full attribute space may be significantly different, or even totally different, from the k-nearest neighbors in a subspace. It means that the neighbors in the full space are not necessarily representative of the locality around the outlier in subspaces. Therefore, an object can be well separated from its k-nearest full-space neighbors while in fact not being well separated from its subspace neighborhood.

The second potential drawback of this approach based on feature selection is concerned with the spread of the synthetic distribution that represents an outlier in the classification task. It depends on the k-nearest neighbors distance in the full features space and does not take into account differences among subspaces. Although some subspace can be a good explanation (the point being a local outlier), the feature selection approach may eventually rule out this subspace as the synthetic distribution heavily overlaps with the normal neighborhood.

9.7.2 Duan et al.

A different paradigm for outlier explanation is suggested in the work by Duan, Tang, and Pei (2015). The problem of explaining outlierness is defined as a search for a subset of the attributes space where the observation is outlying the most. In order to measure outlierness, the authors rank probability densities of all observations in a subspace of features. Roughly speaking, they rank all the observations with respect to how rare their combination of values for the chosen features are. A minimum in terms of dimensionality subspace where the anomalous object is ranked the best (the most exceptional) is returned as an explanation.

The approach of Duan et al. (2015) seems to be more comprehensive for a subject expert who conducts outlier explanation. Its drawback is in computational complexity of estimating probability density functions for all attribute subsets of the dataset. And, as mentioned in Vinh et al. (2016), rank statistics do not always choose the subset that describes outlierness of an object in the best possible way. For example, density rank may be high in a subset even though the point is not far away from the rest of the observations while in another subset the object could be an obvious outlier, but its rank can be lower (see Figure 9.3).

It is interesting to note, that in Vinh et al. (2016) a thorough exploration of outlierness measures is conducted with a focus on the fact that a proper measure should not depend on the dimensionality of the subspace where it is employed. According to the study, good candidates for the role of outlierness measure would be: the Z-score (normalized density function for an observation in a subset, as suggested in Vinh et al., 2016), isolation path length (a normalized length of a path to an outlier in an isolation

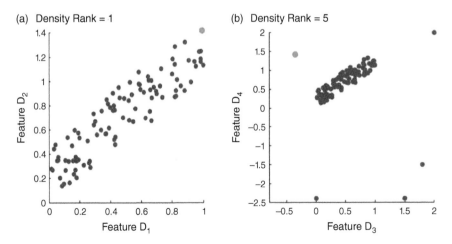

FIGURE 9.3 An illustration of a case where rank statistic does not provide the best explanation of an outlier (shown as a light shade of grey). It returns features D_1 and D_2 while the best explanation would be to return features D_4 and D_3.
Source: Adapted from Vinh et al. (2016).

tree, as suggested by Liu et al., 2012), and LOF score (as introduced by Breunig et al., 2000) formally satisfy dimensionality unbiasedness.

It is noted that the density Z-score exhibits good performance but is computationally expensive, so it is only applicable for small numeric data sets. On the other hand, the isolation path score is an effective measure that also demonstrates good performance, making it suitable even for large datasets. Its limitation is that isolation path is not designed to detect local outliers, though it is likely that no measure is optimal in all possible settings.

The techniques (Micenkova et al., 2013 and Duan et al., 2015) are representatives of two different categories of approaches: those based on features selection and those based on score and search. Vinh et al. (2016) discuss the connection between these two approaches and propose a hybrid solution.

9.7.3   Angiulli et al.

The last of the three approaches considered in this chapter is suggested by Angiulli et al. (2009, 2017). It focuses on modeling outlierness relative to the whole dataset or a homogeneous (that is, consisting of similar observations) subset around an outlier. It is a more technical, but also the most contextual, way of explaining outliers.

For a dataset with categorical attributes and a given outlier, Angiulli et al. (2009) find the top best subsets in which the outlier receives the highest outlierness scores with respect to a single attribute. The outlierness measure is calculated as a linear combination of the frequency and an analog of a Gini index of statistical variability of the attribute values in the subset. In the later work, Angiulli et al. extend and change the framework to deal with continuous numeric features, too.

The fact that the outlierness is always calculated with respect to a single attribute while the subset of observations (neighborhood of an anomaly) is always in the full feature space makes a consistent comparison possible. It results in that the problem set-up satisfies the desired properties of outlierness measures, summarized in Vinh et al. (2016).

If the abnormality of a given outlier is established with respect to the entire dataset, it is a global outlier. Otherwise, if the value is outlying for a subset, it is a local outlier. In the first case, the explanation is that an attribute exceeds its abnormality threshold. The second case is more complicated. A data point that is not an outlier relative to the whole dataset is considered an outlier relative to a subset containing it. In this setting, if an outlier is not rare compared to the rest of the objects in the dataset, no outlying features are detected.

A dataset on skills/age in Angiulli et al. (2009) provides an example of a situation where this approach gives a meaningful explanation of outlierness while the Duan et al. (2015) and Micenkova et al. (2013) do not. In the example, skills developed by employees are measured against their age. An outlier in focus is a young 18-year-old individual who exhibits a high level of skills. Under Micenkova's approach, local separability may be misleading because the nearest neighbors of the outlier can actually be anywhere below or to the right of the observation. It means that weights of age and skill features in a separation task would be misleading. The approach by Duan

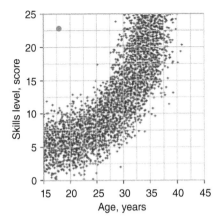

FIGURE 9.4 Outliers explanation in problematic situations: measuring skills versus age of employees. The outlier is highlighted in a light shade of grey in the top left corner.
Source: Adapted from Angiulli et al. (2009).

would return a subset of attributes equal to the whole set because low probability density of the object is exhibited only in the joint space of skills and age.

At the same time, if the explanatory subset under the Angiulli framework is the subset of people who are 18 years old, and the outlying attribute is the skills level, then the considered individual becomes a clear outlier, as demonstrated in Figure 9.4.

Besides other technical details, there are some substantial differences between the approaches suggested by Micenkova, Duan, and Vinh, and the approach devised by Angiulli (2009, 2017). Angiulli assumes that outlierness is relative to the whole dataset in the full attributes space. Other methods return individual subspaces where the query object is outlying the most compared to the other subspaces.

Keeping this in mind, it becomes clear that the approach suggested by Angiulli et al. (2009, 2017) can turn out to be the most applicable. First, it is developed both for categorical and numerical data, even though the approaches are not exactly the same. Second, it measures outlierness only with respect to a certain attribute, so calculations are always univariate (involving a single variable). The only point where subsets matter is when a subset of the whole dataset is taken as a neighborhood of an outlier. And last but not the least is that the explanation provided is the most contextual among peers.

The "contextual" approach to explanations mining is covered in two articles by Angiulli et al. In the 2009 work the authors focus on the case of categorical attributes, introduce an outlierness measure, build a general framework for further explanations mining, and develop a tree-based search to get the top pairs of explanatory subsets and outlying attributes. In the 2017 work the authors concentrate on tackling continuous numerical data, introducing probability density function estimation for an outlying attribute, amending the outlierness measure so that it is applicable to probability density functions rather than frequencies, and introducing a novel method to prune subsets when building explanations for outliers.

9.8   CASE STUDY: OUTLIER DETECTION ON FED COMMUNICATIONS INDEX

In this section, we show a practical use case of using outlier detection on an alternative dataset related to financial markets. We use as our dataset a preliminary version of Cuemacro's Fed communications index. The raw data consists of various Fed communications events. These events are speeches from the Fed's Board of Governors and Regional Fed presidents, FOMC statements, FOMC minutes, and various other types of Fed communications. These Fed communications to the market are collectively referred to as Fedspeak. The Fed regularly provides information to the market through these methods in an effort to be more transparent in how they operate. This approach is also consistent with the way many other central banks also interact with the market.

For each Fed communication event, we have a number of other fields, which have been tagged. These include:

- Date of the Fed communication
- Event type of Fed communication (e.g. a speech, an FOMC statement, etc.)
- Speaker (e.g. Chairman Powell)
- Audience (or location) of the communication
- Text of the communication
- Title of the text
- Length of the text
- CScore of the text

A proprietary algorithm is run on the text of each communication to create a CScore for that text, which is indicative of the underlying sentiment of that text. These CScore values are then aggregated across all the various Fed communication events, to create an index representative of overall Fed sentiment based on Fed communications. In Chapter 15, we discuss the index in more detail, showing how it can be used to understand the moves in UST 10Y yields.

While the text data is publicly available on the web, there are various challenges when collecting it. In particular, the sources are from a diverse array of websites. It requires a lot of maintenance to do such web parsing on an ongoing basis. It involves both updating code and performing manual checks. While this is a time-consuming and labor-intensive process, the problem of maintenance is tractable.

Another potential problem is that when backfilling the history of Fed communication events, we need to read a large number of archived websites. Their formatting can be substantially different, and often does not have a consistent format with the newer pages on the same websites. Hence, we face having to deal with myriad different webpage formats, even if they appear to be from the same website. This might result in problems in web parsing some of the history, and additional time spent to check anything we parse, as well as more time writing code.

The volume of historical texts in our dataset of Fed communication events is around 4000, and covers approximately 25 years of Fedspeak. While the history

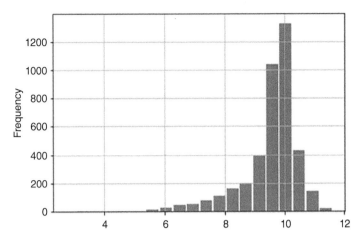

FIGURE 9.5 Histogram plot of log(text length).
Source: Federal Reserve, Cuemacro.

is quite comprehensive, we note that it does not include absolutely every Fed communications event during this period. From the outset, we have excluded a number of texts from any further analysis. This includes any text for which we do not have any license and access to such as those behind paywalls. We also excluded video interviews from Fed speakers. In fact, in order to extract text from video interviews, we would need to have access to the video data (and appropriate licenses).[7] Regardless, often text on a webpage relating to video interviews comes with a text summary. However, it is only a short summary, which may be insufficient to gauge sufficient meaning.

After this initial process of excluding various Fed communication events, we need to be able to historically identify outliers in the dataset in a relatively automated way. Any outliers that are flagged in this way would need further manual investigation, to assess whether these Fed communication events should be included in our final dataset. We have the problem of wanting to include relevant Fed communications events in our index while excluding those that are spurious.

Our first attempt at outlier detection involved creating features for what we thought identified "unusual" Fed communication events. We shall explain how we created these now. First, we created variables for measuring log(text length). Figure 9.5 shows a histogram plot for the log(text length). We have used the logarithm as the variation of text lengths of the various Fed communication events is substantial. From Figure 9.5, we could define unusually short texts as those with log(text length) being those less than 6.

---

[7]In case we had access, we would need to extract text from any video to create our own transcripts. Even if we were able to download the video interviews, we would subsequently need to do speech-to-text transcription of this data. This would not be difficult because there are many APIs, some of them available at almost no cost, able to do the transcription (e.g. from Google, AWS, IBM Watson).

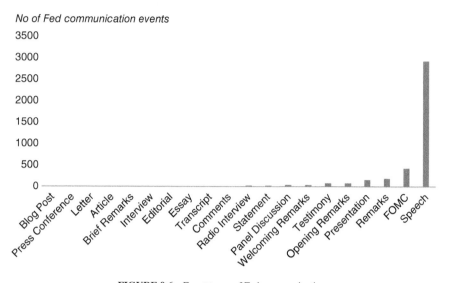

FIGURE 9.6 Event types of Fed communication.
Source: Federal Reserve, Cuemacro.

We also counted the event types of these Fed communications, which we report in Figure 9.6. This could help us assess whether there were any event types that were particularly "unusual." In around 4000 Fed communication events around 75% are speeches by Fed speakers. The next most common Fed communication events were FOMC statements/minutes/press conferences, at around 12%. The rest were made up of events such as panels, essays, and the like, which are more "unusual."

In Figure 9.7, we have plotted the histogram of CScores, which as we noted earlier represent the sentiment of the text associated with each Fed communication event. We can see that the vast majority of the scores are roughly in the range of −2/+2. Hence, a simple way to identify unusual CScores is just to flag anything outside that range.

We also counted the number of Fed communication events that were associated with specific Fed speakers. Figure 9.8 reports the 20 most "talkative" Fed speakers during our 25-year history of Fedspeak. Top of the list is the FOMC, which encompasses Fed communication events such as the release of FOMC statements and also FOMC minutes. Following that, we see that President Bullard has the largest number of Fed communication events. Among market participants, Bullard is known for communicating to the market quite often, so this perhaps is not surprising. Note that Yellen appears twice, once for her tenure as Fed chair and also for her tenure as president of the San Francisco Fed prior to that.

By contrast, there are some speakers historically who only appear a handful times in our Fed combinations dataset such as Gov. Lindsey. There can be a number of reasons. One can be the duration of their tenures. A fairer way to show this data, to adjust for this, could be to annualize the figure, calculating the number of Fed communications events per year for each speaker, than for their entire tenure. However,

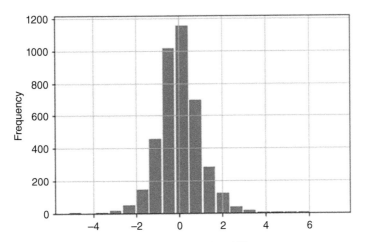

FIGURE 9.7   Histogram plot of CScores.
Source: Federal Reserve, Cuemacro.

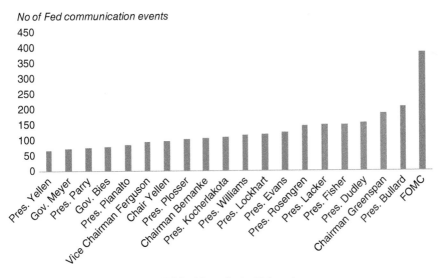

FIGURE 9.8   Most talkative Fed speakers.
Source: Federal Reserve, Cuemacro.

despite this, even if we adjusted this data, there can be a wide variation in how often Fed speakers communicate to the market.

Another complicating matter is that in practice, the market impact of Fed speakers is not always consistent. This can make it trickier to define if a Fed communications event is an outlier by examining the speaker. For example, we might expect that those Fed speakers who are voting members of the FOMC would have more impact on the market from what they say. Voting members of the FOMC have a more active role in changing Fed policy. The FOMC has 12 members. There are 7 permanent members from the Federal Reserve Board of Governors, which includes the Fed chair. The president of the New York Fed is also a permanent member. There are then 4 rotating members of the FOMC, drawn from the presidents of the regional Fed banks. These rotating members serve for 1 year. It should be noted that regional Fed bank presidents still take part in the meetings of the FOMC and take part in discussions around Fed policy and the Fed's assessment of economic conditions. We would also expect more focus from market participants on communications given by the Fed chair.

To summarize the above points, our rules-based approaches for identifying if Fed communications were "unusual" were based on the following:

- Unusual Fed speakers (such as Governor Lindsey who only appeared a handful of times in history as speaker)
- Unusual event type of Fed communication (such as "Editorial," which only appears very rarely in the history)
- Unusual CScores – i.e. extreme values (outside of −2/+2)
- Unusual log(text length) – i.e. very short texts (less than 6)

Hence, based on these various heuristic measures we have used, outliers are likely to consist of those Fed communication events that have characteristics such as shorter texts, extreme CScores, unusual event types, and are also from a speaker who communicates comparatively rarely to the market. It can be trickier, though, to precisely articulate the relative impact of each variable when combining these flags. Note that we avoided using some variables such as the audience/location of Fed communication events when flagging for an outlier. In this instance, it is difficult to think of an intuitive reason why the geographical location of a Fed speaker's speech would necessarily make it an "outlier" from the perspective of how the market interprets the communication. Furthermore, there are a very large number of locations and audiences that are not repeated in the dataset and are unique, making it difficult to come up with specific rules for flagging which are outliers.

Obviously, in all these cases where we are creating outlier flags, we are attempting to use our own domain knowledge of Fed communications in order to create indicators by hand to help identify unusual Fed communication events to be labeled as outliers. However, in practice, we might wish to have a more automated way of identifying outliers, particularly when backfilling the history, when the volume of communications is too high to check manually. Such automated methods can also take into account a combination of different variables tagged for each Fed communication event. We earlier noted that it might be difficult for us to formulate precisely how combinations of input variables are indicative of outliers.

In order to do a more automated approach, we used unsupervised ML techniques for detecting outliers, namely:

- k-means
- HBOS (histogram-based outlier score)

- HDBSCAN (hierarchical density-based spatial clustering of applications with noise)
- KNN (k-nearest neighbors)
- ISO (isolation forest)

In each instance, the algorithms were set to identify the most unusual 1% of cases, which corresponded to around 40 Fed communication events from our dataset of around 4000. These methods search for points that appear to be outliers away from the main cluster of points. We should note that in a production environment, such outlier analysis would need to be done on a rolling basis, rather than looking at the entire history. In order to use these techniques, as with our rules-based approach earlier, we needed to select input variables for each Fed communication event. Unlike in our rules-based approach, we did not specifically create cutoff points to define when each of these input variables constituted an outlier. For those variables that were categorical, there are several ways to encode them. If the number of unique categories is below a threshold, they are one-hot-encoded. Essentially, the categorical variable is replaced by several binary variables. For example, if we are encoding speakers this way, we'd have a binary variable to represent if Chair Yellen is the speaker (or isn't), another one for Chairman Bernanke, and so on. In other instances, the categorical variables are reduced to an analog of "value-of-information," which is a single column with values based on frequencies of a corresponding category.

We used the following input variables, which were a mix of both categorical and continuous variables:

- The speaker – categorical variable
- The event type of Fed communication – categorical variable
- Log(text length) – continuous variable
- CScore of the associated text – continuous variable

In general, most of the outliers flagged by these various unsupervised ML techniques or when flagging by extreme CScores tended to be associated with shorter texts. This seems intuitive, as it can be more difficult to ascertain the sentiment of the text when we have less text to parse. These events included presentations that typically have only a short summary of text associated with them. In some cases, Fed communication events were flagged as outliers because the texts were incomplete due to problems in parsing. Other reasons included mislabeling of various tags such as spelling mistakes on the speaker's name or an incorrect event type (which include slightly different labels for what are essentially similar events). In these instances, the "outlier" issue can be solved by parsing the text again, by modifying the approach to web parsing and also changing the tags. Once this is done, the newly read text would also need to be manually checked. Any new tags would also need to be checked. Such Fed communication events could be updated in the history, with the cleaned fields.

Roughly half of outliers were explained by variables associated with the text themselves (such as the length or the CScore) and/or combinations. For example, it might

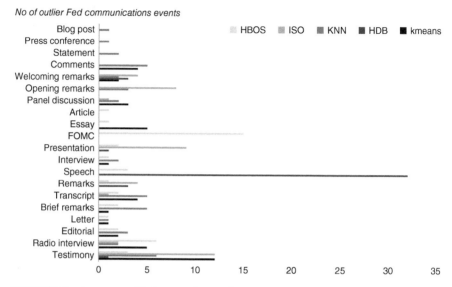

FIGURE 9.9 Event types of Fed communications flagged as outliers by unsupervised ML techniques.

be that the CScore was unusual for the text that was provided. Most of the remaining strong explanations were related to speeches being unusually long texts or a rare CScore for such a long text.

In terms of the unsupervised techniques, k-means tended to work best for flagging outliers, which seems understandable given the relatively wide spectrum of Fed communication events that are present in our dataset.

In Figure 9.9, we tally the total number of event types of those Fed communications events that were flagged as outliers by the various unsupervised models we discussed earlier. We note that k-means tended to flag unusual event types of Fed communications such as testimonies, which did not appear often in the dataset. Many of those events flagged as outliers would likely be considered as unusual or as special events by a domain expert such as an economist who reads Fed communications on a regular basis. Typically, testimonies are widely followed by the market, in particular when given by the Fed chair, as they can give a wide-ranging insight into Fed policy, given their length and also because of the many questions they face from lawmakers during such testimonies. One particular, noteworthy example of a Fed testimony which moved markets was Chairman Bernanke's testimony to Congress where he hinted at the winding down of quantitative easing. The resulting "taper tantrum" saw bond yields rising significantly.

This contrasts to HDB, which seemed to flag mostly event types such as speeches, which as noted earlier appear very regularly in the Fed dataset. This is also true of HBOS, which appeared to flag quite a few FOMC events that are again quite common in the dataset. While it is difficult to make any generalization about other datasets, in practice many of these Fed communication events, which were judged to be outliers by HDB and HBOS, would be less likely to be flagged as outliers by domain experts. Indeed, it would be extremely unusual to remove FOMC events such as statements and minutes, given that these are events where Fed policy changes are announced and explained to the market.

We should also note in closing that we could try combining both approaches, such as flagging outliers that satisfied our rules-based approach (such as those we have flagged as short texts), while also picking texts that were deemed to be outliers by an unsupervised approach such as k-means.

9.9 SUMMARY

We have examined a series of techniques for outlier detection and explanation. Again, the no-free-lunch theorem applies here as well – there is no universally best-performing algorithm but everything depends on the context and the specific problem at hand. Sometimes outliers are the result of technical glitches and/or recording mistakes – something that we said is occuring a lot in the alternative data world. In this case, they can be eliminated and will be again in the missing data domain. Sometimes, they are properties of the data-generating process and need to be explained and modeled separately. Hence, having the right toolkit of techniques is essential in the alternative data world. We glimpsed some of them but we are aware that there are many more with each application calling for its own best method.

We examined a real-world case study focused on a dataset of Fed communication events such as speeches, FOMC statements, and minutes. Each event had associated fields such as the text of the communication, the date of the communication, and the like. We approached the problem of finding outlying Fed communication events in two ways. First, we tried a simple rules-based approach. We created our own indicators to flag outliers based on extreme values of variables such as sentiment score of text, the length of each text, and so on. We then defined extreme values of these based on fairly simple approaches such as looking at the tails of histograms when plotting these variables.

Second, we used unsupervised ML techniques for detecting outliers on the dataset, rather than specify specific rules. This approach could more easily pick out outliers based on combinations of variables. Furthermore, we did not necessarily need to define what we thought was an extreme value for each input variable. Instead, we defined the proportion of values that we wanted the algorithm to define as outliers. We found that k-means was best to pick out more unusual Fed communication event types, such as testimonies, which do not appear that commonly. This contrasts to other methods, such as HDB and HBOS, which seemed to pick out speeches and FOMC events respectively. Typically, FOMC events such as statements and minutes are the most widely followed Fed communication events. Many domain experts would agree that these are very important for understanding Fed policy, and generally these should not be classified as outliers to remove from such a dataset.

9.10   APPENDIX

Approaches to do outlier detection can be roughly classified into model-based techniques, distance-based, density-based, and methods based on different heuristics. We describe them in detail in what follows.

9.10.1   Model-Based Techniques

In a semi-supervised or supervised setup, a model of the data can be built. Under supervised learning the data labeled as normal/anomalous is used to train the model to recognize outliers. In a semi-supervised setting, data that does not fit the model of normal data is the target.

For example, a statistical approach would generally estimate the data distribution and any object whose value has low probability within the framework is considered an anomaly. Most of the classical methods assume Gaussian or mixture of Gaussian distributions for the normal data and use tests based on the properties of this distribution, like Grubb's Test for Outliers, Dixon's Q Test, Chauvenet's Criterion, or Pierce's Criterion. Barnett and Lewis (1978) listed about a hundred discordancy tests for different distributions, with known/unknown parameters, different numbers of expected outliers, and their types.

In some cases, it is difficult to build a model because the underlying distribution of the data is hard to estimate or when no training data is available. In this case other approaches must be employed.

Many modern approaches to outlier detection involve statistical methods. They estimate the probability of observing an attribute value compared to any other value for the dataset in focus. Also, they often rely on association rules mining (as in Agrawal, 1993) where the key measures are support – how often a combination of values is observed, and a measure of dependence – how often two values occur together. This type of analysis is called rules-based, as opposed to classical model-based approaches.

9.10.2   Distance-Based Techniques

If a distance measure can be defined in the multidimensional space of attributes, then anomaly detection can be implemented by finding objects that are distant from their neighborhoods or from centers of nearest clusters. In cases where data can be visualized in 2D, outliers are the points that are best separated from other points. Separability is an alternative measure of outlierness – how easy it is to distinguish the point from its neighborhood.

Distance-based anomaly detection has been introduced by Knorr and Ng (1996) to overcome the limitations of statistical methods. An object is called a distance-based outlier with respect to parameters k and R if less than k objects in the dataset lie within distance R from it. This approach is based on density in a fixed-size neighborhood of the observation in the attributes space with Euclidean distance. This definition was later modified by different authors to relax reliance on the fixed radius. For instance, by taking the k-th neighbor distance instead of fixed radius, or taking an average distance toward k neighbors, and so on.

Distance-based approaches make no assumptions on the distribution of the data, as opposed to model-based statistical techniques. It makes them more flexible and universal. Moreover, in the case where the underlying distribution is known and a statistical approach is used, distance-based anomaly detection methods are a generalization of the definition of outliers in statistics, so that the larger the distance measure toward an observation, the less likely it comes from normal observations distribution (Angiulli et. al, 2009).

Distance-based methods can work well even when there is no geometric intuition behind the distance metric used. Another valuable property of these techniques is that outlierness scores are monotonic nonincreasing with respect to the amount of the data used to calculate them. This results in effective pruning rules and highly efficient algorithms.

9.10.3 Density-Based Techniques

In cases where the attribute space has a distance measure, it is possible to estimate the density of an object's neighborhood in the dataset. Based on this density and the density of the neighborhood, it is possible to pick the observations that are rare with respect to others and hence can be considered to be anomalous. (This idea was introduced by Breunig et al., 2000, with the Local Outlier Factor measure, LOF, and discussed earlier in this chapter.) The basis for high outlierness score is low relative density around an observation.

In contrast to distance-based definitions that declare as outliers the points where data density is low, density-based approaches score points on the basis of the degree of unbalance between density around an observation and the estimated density of its surrounding points. As a result, these approaches are more focused on detecting local outliers, for example, lying on the border of a cluster. If the dataset consists of groups of observations that are clustered and have different densities, density-based techniques prove to be effective in finding anomalies in the space between clusters.

Density-based approaches can rely on any adequate dissimilarity function even in case there is no usual distance measure available. However, quite often the resulting outlierness score lacks explanatory power and calculations become restrictively complex in higher-dimensional spaces. Moreover, density- and distance-based approaches are susceptible to the "curse of dimensionality," as with the growth of dimensionality it becomes harder to find adequate neighborhoods of an observation. Ideally, outlierness measures should not depend on data dimensionality.

9.10.4 Heuristics-Based Approaches

In high-dimensional datasets, angles between vectors (cosine distance) are more robust and convenient to use than distances (Kriegel et al., 2008). This is particularly true in case of sparse datasets, for instance, in text processing problems. Angle-Based

Outlier Factor (ABOF) method scores observations by the variability of the angles between a point and all other points in a pairwise manner.

Isolation-Based Outliers, introduced by Liu et al. (2012), are defined as observations in a dataset that are prone to be isolated quickly under random successive splits of a random feature until all points are isolated in separate leaves of the resulting random tree. Since anomalies are few and different from the rest of the data, they are more susceptible to isolation. This approach is fast and works surprisingly well on real-life data. Moreover, it suggests a valuable measure of outlierness, equal to the normalized length of an isolation path. This measure is dimensionality-independent, and together with Z-score (analog of Mahalanobis distance) is a decent choice to use in subset mining problems, whether it is outlier detection or outliers explanation (suggested by Vinh, 2016).

Isolation Forests can be applied only to ordered attributes and are not designed for use with categorical data. Also, they tend to lack explanatory power. But in an ensemble of outlier detection methods they are highly recommended to provide results independent from those obtained from other methods.

Another class of anomaly detection methods relies on clustering techniques, where a small cluster can consist either of outliers or not (Kaufman & Rousseeuw, 2008). High- and low-density clusters are first identified. Then the data is divided into two non-overlapping sets of outliers and non-outliers and a ranking is assigned to each observation, reflecting its degree of outlierness.

CHAPTER 10

Automotive Fundamental Data[1]

10.1 INTRODUCTION

In Chapter 6 we argued that alternative data can be used to predict company fundamentals, which in turn can be used in a Fama-French spirit to predict equity returns (Model A and C of Chapter 6). We also argued that alternative data can be used to predict returns directly by circumventing the fundamentals (Model B of Chapter 6). In this chapter we will illustrate the two approaches, which we call Approach 1 and Approach 2, respectively. Approach 1 requires one additional modeling step (i.e. first linking alternative data to company fundamentals, and then linking fundamentals to company returns). Hence, this approach brings in a greater methodological and operational complexity when put in production. It could be, however, more economically intuitive and could have greater explanatory power. Approach 2 is, in principle, more straightforward because the model behind it is simpler and uses alternative data with fewer transformations. But let's see now which approach yields better results before deciding on the trade-off.

Our focus will be on a set of companies belonging to the automotive sector. Nevertheless, the procedures, the methodology, and the backtests that we will show in this chapter are applicable to any industrial sector.

The automotive industry is one of the world's largest drivers of economic growth and change and is frequently a catalyst for new technologies. At the time of writing, the industry is facing an accelerated transformative period as four key technologies converge: ride sharing, connectivity, autonomous driving, and electrification. However, large-scale disruption from technological and social change has increased

---

[1]This chapter is based on the work of Henry Sorsky in IHS Markit in the team of the first author of this book. We are thankful to Henry for allowing us to share his work, part of which has become a thesis in Mathematical Finance at Imperial College, London. Most of the data in this chapter has been given to us by IHS Markit.

the difficulty of predicting the future of the automobiles sector and, in particular, its stocks performance. Although we can reasonably expect that automobile sales and production results will remain key components to auto stock performance, it has also become more challenging to find and incorporate other relevant information. For instance, the changing importance of electrification, trade tariffs, and emerging markets has led to stock prices being driven by factors that may not be captured in standard financial statement ratios. However, these hidden factors are likely to become more important components in determining the stock price behavior in the long term. Hence, access to such additional insights can help to estimate the potential trends among automobile manufacturers and provide a key competitive advantage. This is a justification for looking at alternative data sources beyond financial statements.

10.2 DATA

The chosen universe consists of 30 automotive companies. It has a total market cap of approximately $1 trillion, covers companies based in 8 different countries, and captures roughly 91% of global car sales. We chose this set of companies because of the nature of the proprietary dataset that IHS Markit (IHSM) owns. As we will try to show, this dataset contains information relevant for ranking predicted stock returns and, hence, creating a strategy.

The exact list of companies we consider can be found in Appendix 10.7.1. For the proprietary data, thanks to IHS Markit (IHSM), we have monthly reports for a variety of sales/production-based metrics for each of 30 automotive companies in our dataset.[2] It contains information on sales volumes, production volumes, estimated sales revenues, production plant utilizations, fleet ages, and market shares, among others.

Let us provide a more detailed description of the alternative dataset and the data provider. IHS Markit provides historical and forecasted automotive industry insights for the US and global markets. Traditionally used for decision-making by Original Equipment Manufacturers (OEM) and suppliers, the data provides market-driven intelligence on historical production and sales volumes across segments (light vehicles, medium- and heavy-duty vehicles, and commercial vehicles). Alongside it is analysis on various technologies and components in the industry. On a global level, IHSM also collects statistical data on new and used vehicle registrations, vehicles in operation, and predictive consumer behavior with granularity down to transaction type, brand loyalty, and other metrics.

For this research, we have utilized the following three different IHS Markit databases:

- Light vehicle production (global). Light vehicle production data offers an in-depth view of historical production levels across 50 countries, 600 plants, and 2300 models, plus information about alternative-propulsion-powered light vehicles.

---

[2]Given the sale of assets from "Old GM" (Motors Liquidation Company) to "New GM" (General Motors Company) in July 2009, in terms of the alternative dataset, these companies are considered the same. As for the stock, New GM's stock is not traded until its IPO in November 2010 and there is no traded Old GM's stock at all.

- Light vehicle sales (global). With 10 years of historical data, the light vehicle sales data provides geographic coverage of model sales in 70+ countries across 11 regions. This represents more than 97% of global light vehicle sales volume.

- US and global new vehicle registrations/sales. National monthly new registration/sales data for various markets provides various technical details, pricing and specification data, sales channel, and emissions details. This data varies from market to market.

These datasets have a deep history, going back to 2008 in most cases, with global coverage. They are updated monthly, which is much more timely than the update frequency of standard financial statement reports.

Data collection in IHS Markit is performed by analysts who have expertise in the automotive space. They work hand in hand with OEMs and members of the supply chain. An internal team collects automotive insights from a variety of sources, including OEMs, suppliers, industry associations, ancillary businesses, and government entities.

As a next step, IHS Markit have taken care to map the automotive data to the appropriate companies and equity securities. This mapping accounts for joint ventures and merger and acquisition activity that has occurred historically. In other words, it adjusts for point-in-time issues. Additionally, appropriate lags have been applied to the data to ensure there is no look-ahead bias in the factors. The data collected by the automotive analysts is published monthly with different lags for each country and/or OEM. Conservative lags are applied to the data in our backtests, as appropriate, to account for data availability in different markets. For example, due to different times of publication, US sales data is lagged one month while China sales data is lagged two months.

As an example, imagine we are collecting data on March 1, 2010. If we were to look at the aggregate of Ford's sales volume data for the month of January 2010 that we have available on March 1, 2010, we would be looking at the Ford sales data for only the countries that have a 1-month lag. This is because events occurring January 1, 2010, to January 31, 2010, could therefore be known on February 1, 2010, but with a 1-month lag can only be known on March 1, 2010. If we now move to April 1, 2010, and look again at the data of January 2010, we would now see the accumulation of data from countries with 1- and 2-month lags. The point we wish to stress is that there is, therefore, a trade-off to make between using the most recently available data and gaining a more complete picture of the situation by waiting more time. As an example, we illustrate in Figure 10.1 and Figure 10.2 the mean percentage of sales/production volume by company known x months after the end of the relevant period.

As we can see, the amount of information known x-months after the event varies greatly by company. This is likely due to the fact that many automotive companies will both sell and produce most within their home country/region. We do see, however, that for all but four companies,[3] we know more than 90% of both their sales and production data after 3 months.

Figure 10.3 summarizes collection and mapping processes.

---

[3]Hyundai, Mahindra & Mahindra, Suzuki and Tata.

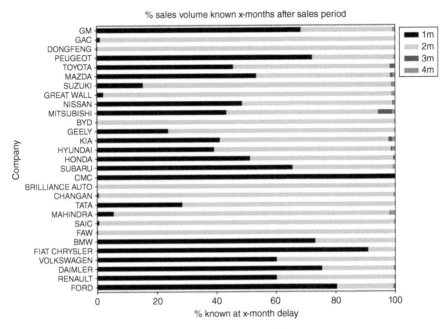

FIGURE 10.1   Mean percent of sales volume known x-months after the end of the relevant sales period by company.

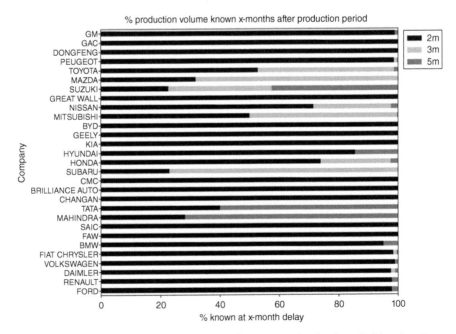

FIGURE 10.2   Mean percent of production volume known x-months after the end of the relevant production period by company.
Source: Based on data from IHS Markit.

Data collection

- Statistical data on sales and production history
- Aggregated registration information
- Vehicle pricing insight
- Collected by industry experts, sourced from:
  - OEMs and suppliers
  - Government and industry sources

Mapping and cleansing

- Adjust for M&A
- Adjust for joint ventures
- Lagged historically by country

FIGURE 10.3 The process followed.
Source: Based on data from IHS Markit.

As an example of the granularity of some of the data available from IHS Markit, we show in Table 10.1 the historic unit sales/registrations of the Chevrolet Cruze across the top 10 countries in 2017.

The data that we use, however, does not include all the information and variables from the databases listed above but rather a sample of it. We will use information on the companies' sales volumes; production volumes; estimated sales revenues;[4] model lifecycles; fleet ages; production plant utilizations; US, Chinese, and worldwide market shares; and the companies' exposures to electric cars. More information on this is in Section 10.4.

For the fundamentals data, we use the Thomson Reuters Worldscope database, including its daily FX data, to convert all values to USD, as reports are made in the parent company's home country's currency. Furthermore, because not all companies adhere to the same reporting frequency (varying from annual to quarterly reporting) for income statement and cash flow items, a trailing 12-month (TTM) amalgamation is applied. For example, if, on January 1, 2010, the last four quarterly reports stated revenues of $1,000,000 for each quarter over the past year, we would sum this to be $4,000,000 in revenues for the previous 12 months and use this as our January 1, 2010, revenues figure. This both allows companies with lower-reporting frequencies to be compared to those with higher reporting frequencies and accounts for seasonality in data (e.g. car sales are higher in spring and autumn in USA). Any missing data

---

[4]Sales revenues are estimated using average sales prices by model by region along with sales volumes by model by region.

TABLE 10.1 Chevrolet Cruze: Top 10 countries unit sales/registrations in 2017.

Country	Jan	Feb	Mar	Apr	May	Jun	Jul	Aug	Sep	Oct	Nov	Dec	Total
United States	19,949	15,368	18,608	21,317	17,120	12,828	12,278	16,500	15,268	11,129	10,982	13,407	184,754
China	8,558	3,589	3,402	5,333	3,273	6,191	6,720	5,056	7,228	7,938	10,165	11,882	79,335
Canada	1,884	1,715	2,711	3,174	4,097	2,843	2,233	1,995	2,202	1,724	1,892	1,487	27,957
Brazil	1,513	1,278	2,152	2,256	2,498	2,308	2,571	2,789	2,284	2,300	2,386	2,168	26,503
Argentina	1,563	1,289	1,552	1,236	1,239	1,435	1,325	1,710	1,590	1,506	1,387	735	16,567
South Korea	232	6	2,147	1,518	1,160	1,434	1,050	429	416	297	821	1,076	10,586
Mexico	477	450	1,045	1,333	663	578	488	341	141	262	266	305	6,349
Vietnam	283	254	325	170	261	187	211	148	220	208	186	194	2,647
India	171	188	192	68	71	219	48	48	—	—	—	—	1,005
Israel	129	125	95	62	94	62	117	59	80	61	69	6	959

Source: Based on data from IHS Markit.

values are forward filled from the last known value.[5] As we might be rebalancing more frequently than each company's reporting frequency, we construct a monthly timeseries by forward filling last known values (e.g. if we were rebalancing on March 1, 2018, but the last BMW report was January 24, 2018, we would use the values from January 24, 2018, as the March 1, 2018, values).

10.3   APPROACH 1: INDIRECT APPROACH

In this section we will use alternative data together with fundamentals to predict future fundamentals and rank stocks accordingly. In order to have the best investment strategy, the questions now are:

- Which fundamentals (or functions thereof) do we wish to predict?
- How far in time do we want to predict?

The methodology that we will use in this section is based on the intuition behind the paper of Alberg et al. (2017), which uses *future* values of fundamentals (as though they possessed an oracle) to prove that clairvoyance can be beneficial for a trading strategy. Although slightly more complicated, their method essentially consists of the following, for each year:[6]

1. Rank all stocks on the NYSE, AMEX, and NASDAQ exchanges based on some ratio of fundamentals (e.g. book-to-market).[7]
2. Buy those stocks that fall in the top 50 by investing equal amounts of capital in each of them, holding them for 1 year.

They then take from their historical dataset the value of the chosen ratio x-months (with $x \in \{1, \dots, 36\}$) in the future[8] and rank on that instead. They test to see if the returns generated by a strategy that uses this ratio from the future are better than in the case of using currently known ratios. Their results show that, for book-to-market, EBIT-to-EV,[9] net-income-to-EV, and sales-to-EV, the further ahead their values are known, the better CAGR[10] the strategy achieves. The greatest gain using future information is for EBIT-to-EV, increasing from 14.4% CAGR at 0-clairvoyance (i.e. using today's data) to around 70% CAGR at 3-years-clairvoyance.

---

[5]If a company has no price on a day attempted to trade on (e.g. due to it being a public holiday for that market), prices are filled backwards to emulate a trade occurring on the next available day. Of course, we can opt for more sophisticated missing data imputation algorithms along the lines of that discussed in Chapter 8. However, for the sake of simplicity, we will stick to this straightforward filling scheme.

[6]It also accounts for reinvesting dividends, funds from acquisitions, and so on.

[7]They exclude all financial sector companies, companies not based in the United States, and all with an inflation-adjusted market-cap below $100 million. The final list contains 11,815 stocks.

[8]In the future with respect to the rebalancing point of the portfolio.

[9]EV – enterprise value defined as EV = Common Shares + Preferred Shares + Market Value of Debt + Minority Interest – Cash and Equivalents.

[10]CAGR – Compounded annual growth rate.

After that, Alberg et al. try to predict (i.e. instead of using an oracle) the future value of EBIT-to-EV at a 1-year-clairvoyance horizon for which the CAGR is 44% and rank on that predicted factor instead. They do this by using a deep learning model[11] trained on trailing time series of 5 years of fundamental data. They manage to attain a consistently superior mean-squared-error through their modeling than a naive model assuming $x_{t+k} = x_t$, with the CAGR increasing from 14.4% to 17.1% and Sharpe ratio increasing from 0.55 to 0.68. Although they don't attain the hypothetical upper limit of 44% CAGR with perfect future knowledge of fundamentals (i.e. the oracle), even a 2.7% increase over the naïve strategy is quite remarkable given the use of only publicly available, relatively cheap data.[12] Given that such an improvement in CAGR and Sharpe ratio is attainable using publicly available, easily attained data, we will test here whether, with the particularly relevant, proprietary alternative dataset we possess, it is possible to reap even greater returns.

10.3.1 The Steps Followed

Our aim will be to show superior returns based on forecasting company fundamentals with alternative data compared to using current fundamentals alone. The approach will consist of three stages, which we now describe.

Stage 1, factor identification: Find if there are any transformations of fundamentals[13] for the companies in our dataset that, if known in advance, yield returns in excess of those we experience without knowledge of the future. It is important to note that, for this stage, no alternative data is used; we are simply using standard fundamental data, in advance of the dates it is known to the public, in order to ascertain whether it is worth forecasting future values of fundamentals using alternative data.

Stage 2, factor modeling/forecasting: If there are any factors that, given knowledge of the future, yield excess returns, attempt to predict them based on the alternative dataset in our possession. In doing so, we aim to attain better results than:

- ○ The naïve predictor of assuming no change over the prediction horizon
- ○ The naïve predictor of assuming the average change as occurs in the training data

This is the first point in this approach where we would incorporate alternative data, doing so in order to forecast the factors we deemed worth forecasting from stage 1.

---

[11] They evaluate two classes of deep neural networks: MLPs and RNNs.

[12] It can actually be downloaded for free if one has an affiliation with a university, such as having an .ac, .edu, or similar e-mail address.

[13] These may be functions of a single fundamental or of combinations.

Stage 3, model backtesting: Given a suitable model to construct portfolios, run a backtest based on the model's predictions and assess its performance.

10.3.2   Stage 1

10.3.2.1   Process
In Stage 1 we will be following these steps:

1. Rank our universe on some ranking factor (e.g. book-to-market, 3 months in the future).
2. Buy those with a ranking factor above some threshold. If we are shorting, short all those with a value below some threshold (e.g. go long the top quantile and short the bottom quantile, when ranked on book-to-market). When going long/shorting assets, we will do so equally across all assets in the relevant portfolio (i.e. buy/sell $x of all assets in the portfolio).
3. Hold these portfolios for some period (e.g. 1 month).
4. Repeat steps 1 to 3 over the backtest timeframe.

For the backtests, we have several possibilities to play with:

Ranking factor: which factor we are using in our ranking (e.g. book-to-market). For a list of factors used, see Section 10.3.2.4.

Long threshold: the quantile above which we long stocks. We test over the set $\{0.66, 0.75, 0.8\}$ (i.e. long the top third, quarter, fifth).

Short threshold: the quantile below which we short stocks. We test over the set $\{0.33, 0.25, 0.2, 0\}$ (i.e. short the bottom third, quarter, fifth).

Holding period: how long we hold the assets for before rebalancing. We test over $\{quarterly, yearly\}$ or $\{Q, Y\}$.[14]

Clairvoyance: how far into the future we take our information from. Given the nature of the alternative data set, we test over the set $\{0, 3\}$ months. Furthermore, for quarterly strategies, it does not make sense to use data from beyond the rebalancing horizon (i.e. more than 3 months away) because, for example, the Q4 v Q3 percent change in sales would be reflected in the Q2 v Q1 change in stock price.

10.3.2.2   Example
Ignoring clairvoyance for now, let us assume we are ranking based on book-to-market, not shorting (short threshold 0), going long the top quantile (long threshold 0.8) and rebalancing quarterly (Q). Imagine it is July 1, 2017, and our universe is as follows:

---

[14]We do not test any higher rebalancing frequencies because the highest financial reporting frequency in our data set is quarterly. Otherwise, we are effectively rebalancing back to the same weights (for ratios of fundamentals) or based on how long after a quarter each company releases their reports (for change-based factors).

Company	Book-to-Market	Price (USD)
BMW	1.45	86.92
VW	1.35	74.48
TESLA	0.68	132.05
FIAT CHRYSLER	1.49	63.68
KIA	0.71	71.76
HYUNDAI	0.8	20.72
FORD	1.4	137.17
GM	1.36	113.93
HONDA	0.73	41.04
MITSUBISHI	0.69	144.31

We go through the following steps:

1. Rank the stocks by book-to-market and take the top 20%.

Company	Book-to-Market	Price (USD)
FIAT CHRYSLER	1.49	63.68
BMW	1.45	86.92
FORD	1.4	137.17
GM	1.36	113.93
VW	1.35	74.48
HYUNDAI	0.8	20.72
HONDA	0.73	41.04
KIA	0.71	71.76
MITSUBISHI	0.69	144.31
TESLA	0.68	132.05

2. Create a long portfolio from the selected stocks, weighting each stock equally.[15]

Company	Book-to-Market	Price (USD)	Weight
FIAT CHRYSLER	1.49	63.68	0.5
BMW	1.45	86.92	0.5

---

[15] Although we did not do so, it may be worth testing the difference between equal weighting, market-cap weighting, and factor weighting within each portfolio.

Assume that the universe on October 3, 2016 (the first weekday in October) is:

Company	Book-to-Market	Price (USD)
BMW	1.89	93.34
VW	1.28	80.89
TESLA	0.87	146.77
FIAT CHRYSLER	1.31	63.97
KIA	0.87	73.55
HYUNDAI	0.86	21.34
FORD	1.33	144.44
GM	1.73	119.81
HONDA	0.94	44.16
MITSUBISHI	1.06	154.21

Given that Fiat Chrysler went from \$63.68 to \$63.97 and BMW from \$86.92 to \$93.34, we have that our portfolio's return over the period July 1, 2016, to October 3, 2016, is $0.5 * \left(\frac{63.97}{63.68} - 1 \right) + 0.5 * \left(\frac{93.34}{86.92} - 1 \right) = 0.5 \times 7.38\% + 0.5 \times 0.46\% = 3.92\%$. We then repeat the above steps again, moving forward one month at a time.

10.3.2.3 Clairvoyance

When it comes to clairvoyantly using future data in our Stage 1 backtest, say three months, we first shift our fundamental data backwards by three months (e.g. April 3, 2016, would map to January 1, 2016, as these are the first business days in these months) before applying identical methods as when there is no clairvoyance (those explained above). If a stock cannot be traded on a given rebalancing date, we assume that it is traded on the next day that it is possible to do so (i.e. backfill prices when used for trade execution).

> **Note:** It is important to take note of what is happening at any point in time with respect to reporting delays and clairvoyance distance.

Example: Imagine we want to generate a signal on April 1, 2010. With no clairvoyance, the most recent information we would have for each company would likely have been reported sometime between January 1, 2010, and March 31, 2010. This would pertain to the period October 1, 2009, to December 31, 2009. With 3 months clairvoyance, still set on April 1, 2010, we are assuming that we know any information that has been reported up to July 1, 2010. The most recent point will likely be from the quarterly report pertaining to January 1, 2010, to March 31, 2010, which is usually released sometime in April 2010. So, although we are using 3 months clairvoyance, we may actually only be using data from a few days ahead. On the other hand, if a company does not release a statement in this time (which is uncommon but does happen within the data set, especially for some of the Asian companies), we are not using any clairvoyance for their statement items.

Still using April 1, 2010, as our signal generation date, we could try another approach. Imagine we know what the report pertaining to January 1, 2020, to March 31, 2010, will be and rebalance on that information, no matter how far in the future it is released. We decide to go with the former approach as the latter has the (not so obvious) side effect that you may preemptively rebalance before the market has had a chance to react to the information. As an extreme example, imagine you know (before the market) that Ford's net income has increased twofold in the period January 1, 2010, to March 31, 2010, so you go long Ford on April 1, 2010. Given the rebalancing period, you would hold Ford until July 1, 2010, and then (possibly) drop it from your portfolio. If Ford doesn't release the first-quarter 2010 report until July 15, 2010, there is every chance that you might drop Ford from your portfolio before it experiences a huge surge in stock price, when the market finds out about their increased new levels of net income. In the chosen strategy, however, we are only ever using future information for which we will hold the stock at the time of release of that information, effectively allowing us to get ahead of the market without causing us ever to miss any movements due to the information. Obviously, this is a somewhat simple example because we would just hold Ford until it inevitably experienced this surge. However, we have used this example more to illustrate possible shortcomings of the latter strategy, especially given the automated approach.

10.3.2.4 Ranking Factors Used

Given that we are following many of the methods outlined in Alberg (2017), we included three of the four factors they tested in our analysis as well, namely:

- EBIT-to-EV
- Net-Income-to-EV
- Sales-to-EV

However, we do not want to limit ourselves to just three ratios. Yan and Zheng (2017) perform a thorough data mining–based search of 18,000 ratios of functions of fundamentals. They report a table of the factors with the greatest magnitude of alpha (i.e. negative or positive). We select a subset of those reported for which we have the relevant data. For those with negative alpha, we perform an appropriate transformation in order to invert the ranking of the factor but still keep its meaning easy to understand, in the hope that the factors with negative alphas will have inverses that produce positive alphas. For example, percent change in liabilities since last quarter would become its own negative.

Finally, given that most literature is only focused on factors that are performant at 0 clairvoyance, we include some for which we deem it would make economic sense that they benefit from clairvoyance.

For the full list of factors tested, please see Section 10.7.3. For a full description of each of the financial reporting items, please see Section 10.7.2.

Note: At this point, no alternative data has been used, only commonly found financial reporting ratios, popularly used in many trading strategies. We are simply trying to assess whether it is worthwhile trying to forecast these, at which point we would incorporate the alternative data in order to do so.

10.3.2.5 Supporting Statistics

Although CAGR and Sharpe ratio are the main statistics we (and most investors) care about here, we also track a number of others to ensure we are not "fitting the noise." The most notable of these are:

- Information coefficient (IC): The mean (over the backtest) of the Spearman rank correlation coefficients obtained at each period between next period returns and the ranking factor. An IC value above (below) 0.3 (-0.3) is often considered good. For those below -0.3, simply invert the factor in some reasonable way. We want an IC as high as possible because this indicates a strong correlation between the factor and security returns.

- Mean quintile gap (MQG): The mean difference in next period returns between an equal weighted portfolio of securities ranked in the top quintile versus those of an equal weighted portfolio of securities ranked in the bottom quintile. Usually one hopes to see a monotonic increase in mean returns from bottom quintile to top. Again, we want a high MGQ because this indicates a strong correlation between the factor and security returns.

Although we do not mention them here, it is also worth taking note of the standard deviation of the above measures, along with similar variants.[16]

10.3.2.6 Other Info

Time frame. Due to data restrictions, we run the backtests from January 1, 2010, to January 1, 2017. We do not go beyond January 1, 2017, because we need to use 12 months clairvoyance, causing us to require data from beyond January 1, 2018, which we do not have.

Transaction costs. It is important to note that we do not take transaction costs into consideration; however, assuming we buy at 5bps above and sell at 5bps below the prices used in the backtest, given we only rebalance a maximum of four times per annum, this would (at worst) only reduce our CAGRs by somewhere between 0.4% and 0.6% (if pre-cost CAGR was 0% and 40% respectively). Furthermore, given that

---

[16]For example, taking Pearson or Kendall correlation, taking the mean quartile or tertial gap, or using medians instead of means.

our strategies are all compared to a benchmark, which would also experience these costs, this difference can be considered negligible.

Tesla. Although Tesla is definitely an automotive company, it also has strong association with the technology sector. As such, the way in which it behaves may be very different from the other companies in the universe. Furthermore, given much of Tesla's value was/is seen to be in its future potential, its financial statements may tell a different story to the market, with poor reports not causing the usual decrease in share price. Given that our approach is cross-sectional, this possible difference in relationship to factors could skew results and create anomalies.[17] As such, we decide to remove Tesla from our universe. Our universe is now reduced to 29 companies.[18]

Non-quarterly reporting companies. It is worth noting that not all companies adhere to the same reporting frequencies for each of the fundamentals. Ford, for example, reports every quarter; however, Peugeot only reports every half year for some of the fundamentals used. As many of our factors relate to percent changes in fundamentals, it, therefore, does not make sense to compare companies that report at different frequencies. If we were to do so, for those companies that report yearly, we would either have to set 3 of their 4 quarterly percent changes to 0, because the level won't have changed given there was no report, or try to "nowcast" using the most recent report. Because this would add more uncertainty and noise into our data, we decide instead to remove all companies that don't report quarterly from our universe. Our universe is now reduced to 22 companies, resulting in each long/short-portfolio having sizes according to Table 10.2, depending on how many companies were trading at each point in time in our backtest.

10.3.2.7 Results

In our results, we only quote those using a long threshold of 66% (i.e. long the top third) and short threshold of 0% (i.e. no shorting). We pick one long threshold as the story is much the same as if we had chosen any of the others (unless otherwise stated). We pick 66% specifically because, otherwise, we run the risk of having too small

TABLE 10.2   Long/short-portfolio sizes by number of tradeable companies.

		Long Threshold		
		66%	75%	80%
Tradeable companies	22	7	5	4
	21	7	5	4
	20	6	5	4

---

[17] In fact, this is exactly what we see. Factors related to changes in inventory perform extremely well when Tesla is included but not when it is removed. When performing the company removal robustness tests, we then see a large difference in the mean CAGR across tests and the actual CAGR, along with a large standard deviation of test CAGRs.

[18] Again, this is due to the fact that there is "Old GM" and "New GM" during the turbulent period experienced by the company in the wake of the Great Financial Crisis. They are again merged in the data as "New GM" given "New GM" subsequently bought all of the "Old GM" assets.

a portfolio; remember, our universe is sometimes only as big as 22 stocks, leading to portfolio sizes of 4, 5, and 7 stocks for long thresholds of 80%, 75%, and 66% respectively. We decide to analyze only strategies that do not use shorting due to the generally strong performance of all stocks in the universe, causing shorting to reduce CAGR in most cases. Not looking at strategies that short also has the added advantage that they are easier to implement in practice and, on average, incur lower costs.

In Table 10.3 and Table 10.4 we can see some statistics of interest for the top-performing strategies according to CAGR and our benchmarks chosen to be equally weighted indices of the stocks. We see that, of our top 10 performing strategies, just two of them outperform the best non-clairvoyant strategy and our best benchmark.

These results seem to be good, but we wish to be sure of our results and check that they have grounding in both economic and statistical theory. We therefore further perform five extra checks:

- Time removal. We randomly remove 12 months from our data[19] and recalculate all statistics. We do this 100 times and calculate means and standard deviations.

TABLE 10.3 Top 10 strategies when ranked by CAGR. L – long threshold, S – short threshold, R – rebalancing frequency (Y means we rebalance at business year start, Q means we rebalance at business quarter start), C – clairvoyance in months, CAGR – compound annual growth rate, as per the Python package ffn's calculations, DS – daily Sharpe ratio, as per the Python package ffn's calculations, WYP – winning year percent, as per the Python package ffn's calculations, TMWP – Twelve month win percent, as per the Python package ffn's calculations.

Factor	L	S	R	C	CAGR	DS	WYP	TMWP
Q_pct_delta_ffo	66	0	Q	3	0.143	0.75	0.67	0.69
Q_pct_delta_netincome	66	0	Q	3	0.133	0.74	0.67	0.75
Q_pct_delta_currliab	66	0	Q	0	0.125	0.69	0.56	0.68
sales_to_Q_lag_entvalue	66	0	Q	3	0.122	0.68	0.67	0.70
sales_to_Q_lag_entvalue	66	0	Q	0	0.122	0.67	0.67	0.71
Q_pct_delta_opincome	66	0	Q	3	0.112	0.63	0.78	0.72
sales_to_entvalue	66	0	Q	0	0.108	0.61	0.67	0.70
Q_delta_currliab_to_Q_lag_sales	66	0	Q	0	0.108	0.61	0.67	0.69
Q_delta_totassets_to_Q_lag_equity	66	0	Q	0	0.103	0.58	0.67	0.66
Q_delta_inventory_to_Q_lag_equity	66	0	Q	3	0.100	0.57	0.67	0.79

TABLE 10.4 Equal weighted benchmarks.

R	CAGR	DS	WYP	TMWP
M	0.123	0.72	0.67	0.7
Q	0.124	0.73	0.67	0.71
Y	0.128	0.74	0.67	0.69

---

[19]Not necessarily consecutive months.

We should hope that the sample mean is roughly the same as our observed value and that there is low variance in the sample.

- Company removal. We randomly remove six companies from our universe and recalculate all statistics. We do this 100 times and calculate means and standard deviations. Again, we should hope that the sample mean is roughly the same as our observed value and that there is low variance in the sample.

- Consistency across parameters. We check that we obtain similar results across our parameter set. Namely:
  - As we increase our long threshold, we would expect our CAGR to increase (or at least not decrease much).
  - As clairvoyance increases toward the point of consideration, we would expect CAGR not to decrease too much between any two points.

- Supporting statistics. We would hope that the IC and mean quintile gap statistics support that the factor should have strong performance.

- Economic theory thought test. We consider whether it is plausible that this factor could predict returns.

Both Q_pct_delta_ffo and Q_pct_delta_netincome pass the time and company removal tests, the consistency across parameters test, and the supporting statistics tests.[20] As for economic theory, we believe it makes perfect sense that future knowledge of a company's net income or funds from operations should help to be predictive of future stock returns.

Note: Although it does not affect the rest of our analysis, it is important to note the poor supporting statistics of Q_pct_delta_currliab at 0-clairvoyance. In fact, if we look at its performance at long thresholds of 75% and 80%, we observe CAGRs of just 6.7% and 7.2% respectively, both below the CAGRs of our benchmarks. It is for situations such as this that it is important to check a factor's supporting statistics and stability as we vary parameters slightly.

TABLE 10.5   Supporting statistics for top-ranked strategies by CAGR.

Factor	L	S	R	C	IC	MQG
Q_pct_delta_ffo	0.66	0	Q	3	0.119	0.150
Q_pct_delta_netincome	0.66	0	Q	3	0.106	0.161
Q_pct_delta_currliab	0.66	0	Q	0	0.029	−0.002
sales_to_Q_lag_entvalue	0.66	0	Q	3	0.017	−0.039
sales_to_Q_lag_entvalue	0.66	0	Q	0	0.023	0.041
Q_pct_delta_opincome	0.66	0	Q	3	0.049	0.050
sales_to_entvalue	0.66	0	Q	0	0.028	0.038
Q_delta_currliab_to_Q_lag_sales	0.66	0	Q	0	0.020	−0.014
Q_delta_totassets_to_Q_lag_equity	0.66	0	Q	0	−0.042	−0.063
Q_delta_inventory_to_Q_lag_equity	0.66	0	Q	3	0.032	−0.050

---

[20] Supporting statistics can be found in Table 10.5.

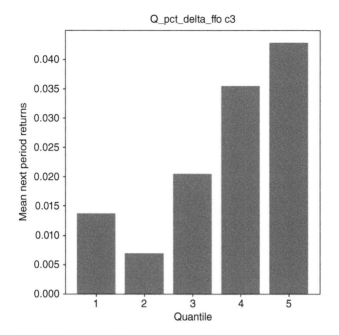

FIGURE 10.4 Q_pct_delta_ffo quintile CAGRs at 3-months clairvoyance.

As funds from operations and net income are fairly similar cash flows, we will just look at Q_pct_delta_ffo at 3-months clairvoyance here. First, we consider the factor's performance across each quintile it divides our universe into. Figure 10.4 shows the mean CAGR for each quintile if we were to create equal weighted portfolios based on the ranking induced by Q_pct_delta_ffo. For example, the third column represents the mean-over-time CAGR experienced over the next quarter by the middle fifth of companies when ranked by Q_pct_delta_ffo. As we are hoping that companies ranked higher by our factor would experience greater returns, the hope is that the plot below would show a monotonic increase from 1 to 5, suggesting that our factor is, indeed, indicative of future returns. Although we do not see absolute monotonicity from 1 to 5, there is a clear trend as we increase with just quintile 2 (or 1 depending on how you look at it) being an outlier. This is a good indication that Q_pct_delta_ffo at 3-months clairvoyance is a performant factor.

Next, Figure 10.5 assures us that the high CAGR is not simply due to one short period of extreme returns but rather a fairly consistent outperformance of the benchmark.

Finally, we look at Figure 10.6, which outlines which stocks are held at any point in time by our strategy. We see that it has fairly good coverage across the universe and does not just pick a select few stocks and hold them.[21]

---

[21] In fact, this is what happens if we include Tesla in our analysis; for inventory-based strategies, we pick Tesla plus some other companies and experience strong returns mainly due to Tesla.

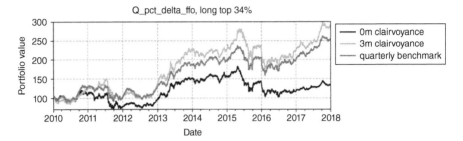

FIGURE 10.5   Q_pct_delta_ffo returns plot vs quarterly benchmark.

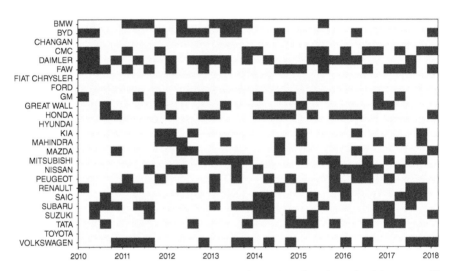

FIGURE 10.6   Heatmap of stocks held over time for Q_pct_delta_ffo at 3-months clairvoyance with long threshold of 66%.

Now that we have identified Q_pct_delta_ffo as a strategy that is potentially worth modeling, it is important to consider what this means. We have found that, with perfect knowledge of the future, the best CAGR we could hope for is 14.3% with a perfect forecast of ffo. Although the alternative data provides us with a breakdown of features that should relate to future values of ffo, at a time earlier than the market has it, it is unlikely we will be able to forecast it with 100% accuracy, especially once we account for the reporting delay for certain countries. Given that Q_pct_delta_ffo at 0-months clairvoyance performs far worse than the benchmark, we would have to get a fairly high prediction accuracy to be able to beat the benchmark using our forecasted factor. Before proceeding with modeling Q_pct_delta_ffo, given it will likely consume a fair amount of time engineering features and so on, it therefore makes sense to see if there is some other simple way that we can utilize the alternative data directly to see if we can beat these strategies.

10.4 APPROACH 2: DIRECT APPROACH

Similar to how we built factors from companies' financial statement reports (i.e. using their fundamentals), we can also use the alternative data to predict returns directly (Model B of Chapter 6) without bothering to predict fundamentals at all. This removes some complexities, although we could sacrifice some accounting and economic intuition in doing so, especially if the alternative data contains purely, say, engineering or logistic features. Luckily in our alternative dataset we have variables (e.g. production) that we can relate to our economic intuition about company performance.

Using the automotive statistical data, we produce factors that embody the operations of automotive manufacturers using industry-specific measures across a few categories. Sales-based factors measure historic sales, implied revenues, and market shares in key markets like the United States and China. Production factors look at the trend in production output and measure plant utilization. Vehicle trends factors look at changes in model life cycle and changes in a company's involvement in the electric vehicle market.

10.4.1 The Data

By using the historical set of automotive data back to 2008 as described in Section 10.2, we have created several factors that capture historical sales trends, production trends, market exposures, and electrification policies of the automobile manufacturers and analyzed the cross-sectional explainability of returns. This approach differs from the pure data mining we have adopted previously as it is more informed by expert opinion of IHS Markit analysts. For reporting purposes, we have selected key factors (see Table 10.6) that are representative of the factor group while the others, which we do not report, are highly correlated to these factors. The core factors from which we build all others are as follows:

- Previous month's sales volume
- Estimated trailing-3-month sales revenues
- Previous month's production volume
- Previous month's plant utilization levels
- Previous month's worldwide market share
- Previous month's US market share
- Previous month's Chinese market share
- Current electric ratio
- Current average time to EOP
- Current average age
- Current average lifecycle

Descriptions for what each of these factors represents can be found in Appendix 10.7.4.

10.4.2 Factor Generation

Given that we have reports for each of these features for each company every month, there are two ways we can use our data:

1. "Freshest" data (e.g. all the data reported on sales volume that we find out about, say, in January 2010)
2. "Delayed" data (e.g. all the data reported on sales volume pertaining to January 2010 that we know later, say, by March 1, 2010)[22]

We decide to use freshest data as, otherwise, we must decide on the balance between using data as quickly as possible after it becomes available and having a better understanding of the whole picture[23] of the whole company set.

From these "core" factors we then generate a larger set of factors. The process is as follows:

1. Aggregate each core factor into a trailing x-month sum, for x in $\{3, 12\}$.[24] We do this to account for natural splits that occur within the year, namely that we view things in months, quarters, and years. For example, we would then have sales volume figures for the previous quarter.
2. For each factor that we have after step 1, calculate the x-month Δ-difference and x-month %Δ-difference, on itself, for x in $\{1, n_{sum}\}$, where n_{sum} represents the number of months summed over to create the factor in step 1. Similar to step 1, we do this because it may be useful to know how each of these factors has changed since some previous natural breakpoint of the year. For example, we could then compare the most recent year's sales volumes to 12 months previously.
3. For each feature generated in step 2, we take the trailing 2-month mean as a rudimentary way of identifying a trend component (similar to SMA strategies). This allows us to see the average growth trend for each of the factors generated in steps 1 and 2.
4. We then remove factors that could not be used cross-sectionally – for example, any that pertain to differences (rather than percent differences) in volumes – because these will vary by company size and don't give much indication of the strength of a company when compared to companies of different sizes.

As for the naming convention, the structure of each factor's name is: <core factor>-<aggregation>-<difference>-<mean>. For example, sales_volume_prev_3m_sum_prev_1m_pct_change_prev_2m_mean would correspond to, taking the sales volume and:

1. Applying a trailing 3-month sum to it
2. Calculating the %Δ -difference from 1-month previously on the result of 1
3. Taking a trailing 2-month mean of the result of 2

---

[22] A table of these delays by country can be found in Appendix 10.7.5 in Table 10.12.
[23] Not to say our chosen method is better, but it removes another choice we would have to make.
[24] As estimated sales revenues are already in trailing-3-month form, we only add trailing-12-month form.

The hope is that those companies that, for example, have a more positive production volume growth trend (e.g. prod_volume_prev_3m_sum_prev_3m_pct_change_ prev_2m_mean) will experience greater returns in the following month than those with less positive ones.

Because this process generates some 2,000 factors, and many of them will be highly correlated, we choose a select few to discuss here, from those that we and expert analysts at IHS Markit deemed as sensible factors for such a strategy. Descriptions of these factors and what they try to capture can be seen in Table 10.6.

10.4.3   Factor Performance

Next, we analyze factor performance for the "freshest" factors of those we selected previously. To test factor efficacy, we again track each factor's IC and MQG, along with the CAGR attained from trading, using a long threshold of 66% with no shorting, rebalancing quarterly, similarly to how we did with the fundamental-based factors approach. Results can be seen in Table 10.7.

Because this is a large amount of information, we present just the top 10 strategies according to CAGR in Table 10.8.

Of those top 10 strategies, 8 of them outperform our equal weighted Y benchmark from Table 10.4. Furthermore, all but 2 of them have MQGs above 1%. Finally, half of them have ICs above 0.03. The top 3 strategies are particularly strong performers all having CAGRs above 16%, ICs above 0.03, and MQGs above 2.4%.

It is also worth noting that all the above strategies pass the time and company removal robustness tests mentioned in Section 10.3.2.7, along with the stability in parameters test. They also seem to make economic sense that they could be predictive of future returns, namely because they all predict company growth or a relative increase in size versus the other companies in some way.

Finally, in the case of both the fundamental-based factors in Section 10.3 and the alternative data–based factors mentioned here, it is worth noting that we can observe larger CAGRs by increasing our long threshold in most cases, at the cost of having a smaller portfolio size, likely increasing volatility. Furthermore, there are a number of other factors created from the alternative dataset that also outperformed the benchmark; however, they are all closely related to – and, therefore, have high correlations with – those mentioned above.

We have, therefore, shown that, using the alternative data to create factors directly, we can attain superior performance to even those strategies that used perfect knowledge of future fundamentals. As this method requires no further modeling and is "ready to trade" as is, we decide not to model any of the factors from Section 10.3.2.7 but rather continue our analysis of those presented above.

It is interesting to note that many factors that split the universe by US or Chinese sales-based factors perform well. It is not obvious why this should be the case, but it is possibly down to the facts that (1) most non-Chinese companies do not see large (if any) sales **outside** of China, when compared to the sales volume of manufacturers from other countries; (2) many non-Chinese companies do not see large sales **inside** of China, when compared to the sales volumes of Chinese manufacturers;

TABLE 10.6 Automotive factors created from the alternative data set.

Factor type	Factor	Description
Production	prod_volume_prev_12m_sum_prev_12m_pct_change	Yearly change in yearly production volume
Production	prod_volume_prev_12m_sum_prev_12m_pct_change_prev_2m_mean	Yearly production volume yearly growth trend
Production	prod_volume_prev_12m_sum_prev_1m_pct_change	Monthly change in yearly production volume
Production	prod_volume_prev_12m_sum_prev_1m_pct_change_prev_2m_mean	Yearly production volume monthly growth trend
Production	prod_volume_prev_12m_sum_prev_3m_pct_change	Quarterly change in yearly production volume
Production	prod_volume_prev_12m_sum_prev_3m_pct_change_prev_2m_mean	Yearly production volume quarterly growth trend
Production	prod_volume_prev_1m_pct_change	Monthly change in monthly production volume
Production	prod_volume_prev_1m_pct_change_prev_2m_mean	Monthly production volume growth trend
Production	prod_volume_prev_3m_sum_prev_12m_pct_change	Yearly change in quarterly production volume
Production	prod_volume_prev_3m_sum_prev_12m_pct_change_prev_2m_mean	Quarterly production volume yearly growth trend
Production	prod_volume_prev_3m_sum_prev_1m_pct_change	Monthly change in quarterly production volume
Production	prod_volume_prev_3m_sum_prev_1m_pct_change_prev_2m_mean	Quarterly production volume monthly growth trend
Production	prod_volume_prev_3m_sum_prev_3m_pct_change	Quarterly change in quarterly production volume
Production	prod_volume_prev_3m_sum_prev_3m_pct_change_prev_2m_mean	Quarterly production volume quarterly growth trend
Production	ave_utilization	Average production plant utilization
Production	ave_utilization_prev_1m_pct_change	Monthly change in production plant utilization
Production	ave_utilization_prev_1m_pct_change_prev_2m_mean	Monthly production plant utilization growth trend
Sales/Registration	revenues_sales_prev_3m_sum_prev_12m_pct_change	Yearly change in quarterly sales revenues
Sales/Registration	revenues_sales_prev_3m_sum_prev_12m_pct_change_prev_2m_mean	Quarterly sales revenues yearly growth trend
Sales/Registration	revenues_sales_prev_3m_sum_prev_1m_pct_change	Monthly change in quarterly sales revenues
Sales/Registration	revenues_sales_prev_3m_sum_prev_1m_pct_change_prev_2m_mean	Quarterly sales revenues monthly growth trend
Sales/Registration	revenues_sales_prev_3m_sum_prev_3m_pct_change	Quarterly change in quarterly sales revenues

Category	Variable	Description
Sales/Registration	revenues_sales_prev_3m_sum_prev_3m_pct_change_prev_2m_mean	Quarterly sales revenues quarterly growth trend
Sales/Registration	sales_volume_prev_12m_sum_prev_12m_pct_change	Yearly change in yearly sales volume
Sales/Registration	sales_volume_prev_12m_sum_prev_12m_pct_change_prev_2m_mean	Yearly sales volume yearly growth trend
Sales/Registration	sales_volume_prev_12m_sum_prev_1m_pct_change	Monthly change in yearly sales volume
Sales/Registration	sales_volume_prev_12m_sum_prev_1m_pct_change_prev_2m_mean	Yearly sales volume monthly growth trend
Sales/Registration	sales_volume_prev_12m_sum_prev_3m_pct_change	Quarterly change in yearly sales volume
Sales/Registration	sales_volume_prev_12m_sum_prev_3m_pct_change_prev_2m_mean	Yearly sales volume quarterly growth trend
Sales/Registration	sales_volume_prev_1m_pct_change	Monthly change in monthly sales volume
Sales/Registration	sales_volume_prev_1m_pct_change_prev_2m_mean	Monthly sales volume growth trend
Sales/Registration	sales_volume_prev_3m_sum_prev_12m_pct_change	Yearly change in quarterly sales volume
Sales/Registration	sales_volume_prev_3m_sum_prev_12m_pct_change_prev_2m_mean	Quarterly sales volume yearly growth trend
Sales/Registration	sales_volume_prev_3m_sum_prev_1m_pct_change	Monthly change in quarterly sales volume
Sales/Registration	sales_volume_prev_3m_sum_prev_1m_pct_change_prev_2m_mean	Quarterly sales volume monthly growth trend
Sales/Registration	sales_volume_prev_3m_sum_prev_3m_pct_change	Quarterly change in quarterly sales volume
Sales/Registration	sales_volume_prev_3m_sum_prev_3m_pct_change_prev_2m_mean	Quarterly sales volume quarterly growth trend
Sales/Registration	usa_sales_volume_prev_12m_sum_prev_3m_pct_change	Quarterly change in yearly US sales volume
Sales/Registration	china_sales_volume_prev_12m_sum_prev_3m_pct_change	Quarterly change in yearly Chinese sales volume
Market Share	china_market_share_prev_3m_sum_prev_3m_pct_change_prev_2m_mean	Last quarter average Chinese market share quarterly growth trend
Market Share	china_market_share_prev_1m_pct_change	Monthly change in Chinese market share
Market Share	usa_market_share_prev_3m_sum_prev_3m_pct_change_prev_2m_mean	Last quarter average US market share quarterly growth trend
Market Share	usa_market_share_prev_1m_pct_change	Monthly change in US market share
Market Share	ww_market_share_prev_3m_sum_prev_3m_pct_change_prev_2m_mean	Last quarter average worldwide market share quarterly growth trend
Market Share	ww_market_share_prev_1m_pct_change	Monthly change in worldwide market share
Electrification	electric_ratio_prev_1m_pct_change	Monthly change in electric ratio

TABLE 10.7   Freshest automotive factors summary statistics.

Factor	CAGR	IC	MQG
prod_volume_prev_12m_sum_prev_12m_pct_change	0.102	0.028	0.0075
prod_volume_prev_12m_sum_prev_12m_pct_change_prev_2m_mean	0.102	0.033	0.0085
prod_volume_prev_12m_sum_prev_1m_pct_change	0.091	−0.020	−0.0149
prod_volume_prev_12m_sum_prev_1m_pct_change_prev_2m_mean	0.107	0.023	−0.0050
prod_volume_prev_12m_sum_prev_3m_pct_change	0.103	0.020	−0.0229
prod_volume_prev_12m_sum_prev_3m_pct_change_prev_2m_mean	0.119	0.014	−0.0187
prod_volume_prev_1m_pct_change	0.058	−0.048	−0.0241
prod_volume_prev_1m_pct_change_prev_2m_mean	0.136	0.059	0.0203
prod_volume_prev_3m_sum_prev_12m_pct_change	0.110	0.016	−0.0189
prod_volume_prev_3m_sum_prev_12m_pct_change_prev_2m_mean	0.111	0.014	−0.0168
prod_volume_prev_3m_sum_prev_1m_pct_change	0.110	−0.004	−0.0144
prod_volume_prev_3m_sum_prev_1m_pct_change_prev_2m_mean	0.110	0.030	0.0077
prod_volume_prev_3m_sum_prev_3m_pct_change	0.061	−0.009	−0.0029
prod_volume_prev_3m_sum_prev_3m_pct_change_prev_2m_mean	0.006	−0.010	−0.0122
ave_utilization	0.105	0.007	−0.0099
ave_utilization_prev_1m_pct_change	0.078	−0.070	−0.0379
ave_utilization_prev_1m_pct_change_prev_2m_mean	0.120	0.039	0.0268
revenues_sales_prev_3m_sum_prev_12m_pct_change	0.093	−0.012	0.0022
revenues_sales_prev_3m_sum_prev_12m_pct_change_prev_2m_mean	0.082	−0.010	−0.0034
revenues_sales_prev_3m_sum_prev_1m_pct_change	0.146	0.027	0.0275
revenues_sales_prev_3m_sum_prev_1m_pct_change_prev_2m_mean	0.121	0.027	0.0221
revenues_sales_prev_3m_sum_prev_3m_pct_change	0.115	0.017	0.0070
revenues_sales_prev_3m_sum_prev_3m_pct_change_prev_2m_mean	0.092	−0.016	−0.0245
sales_volume_prev_12m_sum_prev_12m_pct_change	0.120	−0.010	−0.0076
sales_volume_prev_12m_sum_prev_12m_pct_change_prev_2m_mean	0.107	−0.014	−0.0039
sales_volume_prev_12m_sum_prev_1m_pct_change	0.127	0.031	0.0153
sales_volume_prev_12m_sum_prev_1m_pct_change_prev_2m_mean	0.093	0.003	0.0055
sales_volume_prev_12m_sum_prev_3m_pct_change	0.098	−0.017	−0.0054
sales_volume_prev_12m_sum_prev_3m_pct_change_prev_2m_mean	0.091	−0.020	−0.0102
sales_volume_prev_1m_pct_change	0.104	0.004	0.0287
sales_volume_prev_1m_pct_change_prev_2m_mean	0.147	0.024	0.0261
sales_volume_prev_3m_sum_prev_12m_pct_change	0.096	−0.020	−0.0047
sales_volume_prev_3m_sum_prev_12m_pct_change_prev_2m_mean	0.093	−0.028	−0.0152
sales_volume_prev_3m_sum_prev_1m_pct_change	0.109	0.000	0.0307
sales_volume_prev_3m_sum_prev_1m_pct_change_prev_2m_mean	0.122	0.020	−0.0005
sales_volume_prev_3m_sum_prev_3m_pct_change	0.128	0.007	0.0066
sales_volume_prev_3m_sum_prev_3m_pct_change_prev_2m_mean	0.124	−0.008	−0.0046
usa_sales_volume_prev_12m_sum_prev_3m_pct_change	0.187	0.081	0.0326
china_sales_volume_prev_12m_sum_prev_3m_pct_change	0.137	0.025	−0.0008
china_market_share_prev_3m_sum_prev_3m_pct_change_prev_2m_mean	0.077	−0.003	−0.0168
china_market_share_prev_1m_pct_change	0.141	0.003	0.0106
usa_market_share_prev_3m_sum_prev_3m_pct_change_prev_2m_mean	0.162	0.032	0.0377
usa_market_share_prev_1m_pct_change	0.085	−0.014	−0.0051
ww_market_share_prev_3m_sum_prev_3m_pct_change_prev_2m_mean	0.121	0.036	−0.0035
ww_market_share_prev_1m_pct_change	0.169	0.065	0.0242
electric_ratio_prev_1m_pct_change	0.118	0.047	0.0203

and (3) companies are likely measured on their growth within their major market(s). As such, Chinese companies are likely to be measured on their growth within China and non-Chinese companies (certainly US-based ones) are likely measured on their growth in USA (or within Europe, for which we do not have the data). Factors based upon these geographical markets, therefore, are likely to have more indication of how the stock market treats the companies' stocks.

10.4.4 Detailed Factor Results

In this section we show detailed results for 3 of the top 10 factors from Table 10.8, namely:

- revenues_sales_prev_3m_sum_prev_1m_pct_change
- ww_market_share_prev_1m_pct_change
- usa_sales_volume_prev_12m_sum_prev_3m_pct_change

10.4.4.1 *revenues_sales_prev_3m_sum_prev_1m_pct_change – monthly change in quarterly sales volume*

The first factor, revenues_sales_prev_3m_sum_prev_1m_pct_change (see Figure 10.8), measures our current best estimate of the monthly change in the quarterly sales revenues. As such, it is a measure of short-term sales growth, which we therefore deem makes economic sense as a predictor of future returns. We see that beats our quarterly rebalanced benchmark's, attaining a CAGR of 14.6% compared to the quarterly rebalancing benchmark's 12.4% (see Table 10.4 and Figure 10.7). Backing up this superior performance is an MQG of 2.75%, with an IC of 0.027, which is below but close to the value of 0.03 considered to be strong. Furthermore, we see that the quintile plot shows a definite increase from Q1 to Q5, with just Q4 standing as a slight outlier (see Figure 10.8). Finally, we note that the strategy obtained an average 12-month hit rate (i.e. the average number of months per year that we experience positive returns) of 75%.

TABLE 10.8 Top 10 alt data strategies according to CAGR.

Factor	CAGR	IC	MQG
usa_sales_volume_prev_12m_sum_prev_3m_pct_change	0.187	0.081	0.0326
ww_market_share_prev_1m_pct_change	0.169	0.065	0.0242
usa_market_share_prev_3m_sum_prev_3m_pct_change _prev_2m_mean	0.162	0.032	0.0377
sales_volume_prev_1m_pct_change_prev_2m_mean	0.147	0.024	0.0261
revenues_sales_prev_3m_sum_prev_1m_pct_change	0.146	0.027	0.0275
china_market_share_prev_1m_pct_change	0.141	0.003	0.0106
china_sales_volume_prev_12m_sum_prev_3m_pct_change	0.137	0.025	−0.0008
prod_volume_prev_1m_pct_change_prev_2m_mean	0.136	0.059	0.0203
sales_volume_prev_3m_sum_prev_3m_pct_change	0.128	0.007	0.0066
sales_volume_prev_12m_sum_prev_1m_pct_change	0.127	0.031	0.0153

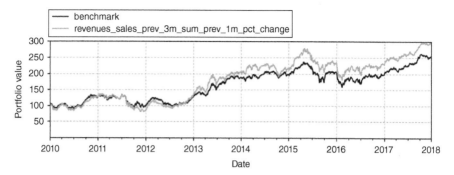

FIGURE 10.7   revenues_sales_prev_3m_sum_prev_1m_pct_change returns plot vs quarterly benchmark.

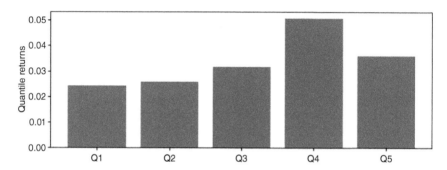

FIGURE 10.8   revenues_sales_prev_3m_sum_prev_1m_pct_change quintile CAGR.

10.4.4.2   *ww_market_share_prev_1m_pct_change – monthly change in worldwide market share*

The second factor, ww_market_share_prev_1m_pct_change, measures our best estimate of the monthly change in each company's worldwide market share of sales. This is, therefore, again a measure of sales growth, but this time taking into account performance versus other companies. Given that it takes into account each company's sales growth relative to other companies, it again makes sense that it could predict future returns and that it could be a more performant factor than individual sales growth alone. We see that this factor's strategy remains above our benchmark for nearly our whole backtest, attaining a CAGR of 16.9% (see Table 10.4 and Figure 10.9). Complementing this is its strong performance in terms of both IC and MQG, attaining 0.065 and 2.42% respectively, both very strong. The quintile plot is also promising, with a definite increase from the lower quintiles to the upper, although not monotonic (see Figure 10.10). Finally, we note the strategy attained a 12-month hit rate of 74%.

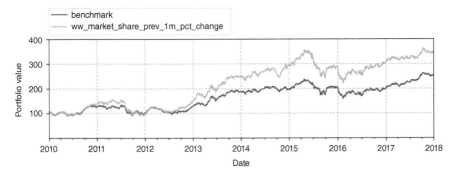

FIGURE 10.9   ww_market_share_prev_1m_pct_change returns plot vs quarterly benchmark.

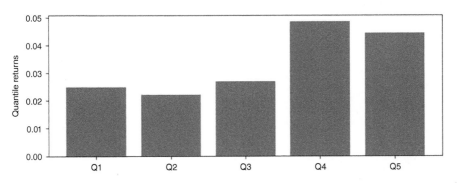

FIGURE 10.10   ww_market_share_prev_1m_pct_change quintile CAGR.

10.4.4.3   *usa_sales_volume_prev_12m_sum_prev_3m_pct_change – quarterly change in yearly US sales volume*

The third and final factor we analyze in detail is usa_sales_volume_prev_12m_sum _prev_3m_pct_change, which measures the change since the last quarter of the previous year's US sales volume. As such, it is another sales growth measure; however, it is important to note that this factor would likely always rank Chinese automotive manufacturers somewhere in the middle, due to the fact that they don't sell in the United States and therefore would experience 0 growth. The associated strategy attains the highest CAGR of those we consider at 18.7%, backed up by an IC of 0.081 and an MQG of 3.26%, making it our strongest performer in terms of IC and second strongest in terms of MQG. Both the returns plot (Figure 10.11) and the quintile plot are also promising (Figure 10.12), with the returns plot showing our strategy's cumulative returns to always be above those of the benchmark, and the quintile plot showing a clear increase from Q1 to Q5, with Q5 far outperforming the other five quintiles. Finally, we note the strategy's 12-month hit rate of 72%.

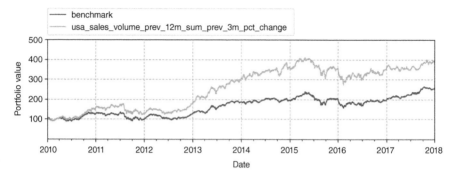

FIGURE 10.11   usa_sales_volume_prev_12m_sum_prev_3m_pct_change returns plot vs quarterly benchmark.

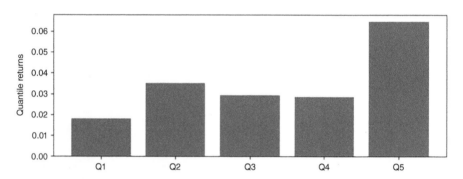

FIGURE 10.12   usa_sales_volume_prev_12m_sum_prev_3m_pct_change quintile CAGR.

10.4.4.4   Factor Correlations

In terms of diversifying one's portfolio, we may wish to take a smart beta approach to factor investing and invest in multiple factors together. When doing so, we need to ensure that our factors are not representative of the same information/compensating us for the same type of risk. As such, we look at how our factors correlate with one another in two important ways. To begin with, for each of:[25]

1. ww_market_share_prev_1m_pct_change
2. sales_volume_prev_1m_pct_change_prev_2m_mean
3. prod_volume_prev_1m_pct_change_prev_2m_mean
4. revenues_sales_prev_3m_sum_prev_1m_pct_change
5. usa_sales_volume_prev_12m_sum_prev_3m_pct_change

we investigate the Pearson correlation of each strategy's portfolio's weekly returns in excess of the equal weighted quarterly rebalanced benchmark, against the excess returns of the other factors from Table 10.6. These correlations can be found in Table 10.9.

---

[25]These represent 5 of the top performers from Table 10.8.

TABLE 10.9 Long top 33% strategy excess returns vs equal weighted benchmark, Pearson correlations.

	1	2	3	4	5
prod_volume_prev_12m_sum_prev_12m_pct_change	0.14	0.29	0.01	0.10	0.16
prod_volume_prev_12m_sum_prev_12m_pct_change_prev_2m_mean	0.13	0.26	-0.02	0.08	0.18
prod_volume_prev_12m_sum_prev_1m_pct_change	0.26	0.27	0.17	0.21	0.24
prod_volume_prev_12m_sum_prev_1m_pct_change_prev_2m_mean	0.29	0.36	0.21	0.26	0.16
prod_volume_prev_12m_sum_prev_3m_pct_change	0.23	0.30	0.12	0.19	0.17
prod_volume_prev_12m_sum_prev_3m_pct_change_prev_2m_mean	0.23	0.26	0.08	0.17	0.16
prod_volume_prev_1m_pct_change	0.18	0.19	0.21	0.14	0.27
prod_volume_prev_1m_pct_change_prev_2m_mean	0.33	0.43	N/A	0.35	-0.01
prod_volume_prev_3m_sum_prev_12m_pct_change	0.27	0.30	0.13	0.24	0.21
prod_volume_prev_3m_sum_prev_12m_pct_change_prev_2m_mean	0.25	0.29	0.09	0.18	0.18
prod_volume_prev_3m_sum_prev_1m_pct_change	0.38	0.31	0.37	0.55	0.14
prod_volume_prev_3m_sum_prev_1m_pct_change_prev_2m_mean	0.34	0.18	0.24	0.48	0.18
prod_volume_prev_3m_sum_prev_3m_pct_change	0.22	0.10	-0.01	0.33	0.13
prod_volume_prev_3m_sum_prev_3m_pct_change_prev_2m_mean	0.12	0.01	-0.05	0.25	0.17
ave_utilization	0.22	0.22	0.30	0.10	0.29
ave_utilization_prev_1m_pct_change	0.34	0.24	0.20	0.18	0.31
ave_utilization_prev_1m_pct_change_prev_2m_mean	0.27	0.39	0.64	0.21	0.16
revenues_sales_prev_3m_sum_prev_12m_pct_change	0.23	0.32	0.09	0.16	0.30
revenues_sales_prev_3m_sum_prev_12m_pct_change_prev_2m_mean	0.26	0.27	0.10	0.22	0.25
revenues_sales_prev_3m_sum_prev_1m_pct_change	0.46	0.37	0.35	N/A	0.19
revenues_sales_prev_3m_sum_prev_1m_pct_change_prev_2m_mean	0.31	0.35	0.38	0.79	0.10
revenues_sales_prev_3m_sum_prev_3m_pct_change	0.38	0.20	0.26	0.63	0.11
revenues_sales_prev_3m_sum_prev_3m_pct_change_prev_2m_mean	0.26	0.14	0.13	0.32	0.09
sales_volume_prev_12m_sum_prev_12m_pct_change	0.11	0.25	0.07	0.02	0.15

(continued)

TABLE 10.9 (*Continued*)

	1	2	3	4	5
sales_volume_prev_12m_sum_prev_12m_pct_change_prev_2m_mean	0.14	0.25	0.09	0.04	0.14
sales_volume_prev_12m_sum_prev_1m_pct_change	0.29	0.36	0.10	0.26	0.27
sales_volume_prev_12m_sum_prev_1m_pct_change_prev_2m_mean	0.20	0.32	0.10	0.11	0.21
sales_volume_prev_12m_sum_prev_3m_pct_change	0.24	0.36	0.13	0.16	0.21
sales_volume_prev_12m_sum_prev_3m_pct_change_prev_2m_mean	0.20	0.34	0.12	0.11	0.16
sales_volume_prev_1m_pct_change	0.62	0.41	0.18	0.64	0.24
sales_volume_prev_1m_pct_change_prev_2m_mean	0.44	N/A	0.43	0.37	−0.04
sales_volume_prev_3m_sum_prev_12m_pct_change	0.22	0.36	0.10	0.14	0.21
sales_volume_prev_3m_sum_prev_12m_pct_change_prev_2m_mean	0.20	0.34	0.12	0.12	0.16
sales_volume_prev_3m_sum_prev_1m_pct_change	0.46	0.41	0.36	0.90	0.13
sales_volume_prev_3m_sum_prev_1m_pct_change_prev_2m_mean	0.34	0.42	0.33	0.70	0.07
sales_volume_prev_3m_sum_prev_3m_pct_change	0.31	0.24	0.19	0.57	−0.01
sales_volume_prev_3m_sum_prev_3m_pct_change_prev_2m_mean	0.18	0.13	0.11	0.29	0.07
usa_sales_volume_prev_12m_sum_prev_3m_pct_change	0.18	−0.04	−0.01	0.19	N/A
china_sales_volume_prev_12m_sum_prev_3m_pct_change	0.08	−0.02	−0.04	0.16	0.28
china_market_share_prev_3m_sum_prev_3m_pct_change_prev_2m_mean	0.06	0.04	0.12	0.27	0.10
china_market_share_prev_1m_pct_change	0.34	0.20	0.13	0.32	0.33
usa_market_share_prev_3m_sum_prev_3m_pct_change_prev_2m_mean	0.26	0.03	0.12	0.25	0.43
usa_market_share_prev_1m_pct_change	0.14	−0.17	−0.06	0.13	0.44
ww_market_share_prev_3m_sum_prev_3m_pct_change_prev_2m_mean	0.23	0.10	0.24	0.37	0.15
ww_market_share_prev_1m_pct_change	N/A	0.44	0.32	0.46	0.18
electric_ratio_prev_1m_pct_change	0.15	0.03	−0.01	0.06	0.16

As we expected, some of the factors do, indeed, correlate highly, at least with those five we chose to analyze here. Of particular interest, however, are the low correlations between:

- ww_market_share_prev_1m_pct_change and china_sales_volume_prev_12m_ sum_prev_3m_pct_change = 0.08
- sales_volume_prev_1m_pct_change_prev_2m_mean and usa_sales_volume_ prev_12m_sum_prev_3m_pct_change = -0.04
- sales_volume_prev_1m_pct_change_prev_2m_mean and china_sales_volume_ prev_12m_sum_prev_3m_pct_change = -0.02
- sales_volume_prev_1m_pct_change_prev_2m_mean and usa_market_share_ prev_3m_sum_prev_3m_pct_change_prev_2m_mean = 0.03
- prod_volume_prev_1m_pct_change_prev_2m_mean and usa_sales_volume_ prev_12m_sum_prev_3m_pct_change = -0.01
- prod_volume_prev_1m_pct_change_prev_2m_mean and china_sales_volume_ prev_12m_sum_prev_3m_pct_change = -0.04

Each of these pairs has a very low correlation, with each individual factor's respective strategy, producing a CAGR that outperforms our benchmark.

Next, we consider the correlations between the factors themselves (e.g. between prod_volume_prev_12m_sum_prev_12m_pct_change and ave_utilization), rather than between the returns of the portfolios they induce. After the excess returns their strategies produce, the rankings these factors induce are the next most important matter to consider when trying to assess orthogonality of factors. For this purpose, we calculate the mean Spearman correlation over time between each factor. That is to say, we calculate the Spearman correlation between each factor at times t_0 to t_n and take their average. We report the results in Table 10.10.

Again, although we see there exist some quite strong correlations between factors, it also seems that we have at our disposal some that do not correlate at all. In particular, we have:

- ww_market_share_prev_1m_pct_change and usa_sales_volume_prev_12m_ sum_prev_3m_pct_change = 0.00
- ww_market_share_prev_1m_pct_change and china_sales_volume_prev_12m_ sum_prev_3m_pct_change = 0.04
- ww_market_share_prev_1m_pct_change and usa_market_share_prev_3m_ sum_prev_3m_pct_change_prev_2m_mean = -0.03
- sales_volume_prev_1m_pct_change_prev_2m_mean and usa_sales_volume_ prev_12m_sum_prev_3m_pct_change = 0.04
- sales_volume_prev_1m_pct_change_prev_2m_mean and china_sales_volume_ prev_12m_sum_prev_3m_pct_change = 0.04
- sales_volume_prev_1m_pct_change_prev_2m_mean and usa_market_share_ prev_3m_sum_prev_3m_pct_change_prev_2m_mean = 0.00

TABLE 10.10   Time averaged Spearman rank correlations.

	1	2	3	4	5
prod_volume_prev_12m_sum_prev_12m_pct_change	0.00	0.02	0.00	0.01	0.27
prod_volume_prev_12m_sum_prev_12m_pct_change_prev_2m_mean	0.01	0.02	-0.01	0.00	0.26
prod_volume_prev_12m_sum_prev_1m_pct_change	0.05	0.11	0.23	0.13	0.20
prod_volume_prev_12m_sum_prev_1m_pct_change_prev_2m_mean	0.02	0.09	0.16	0.11	0.23
prod_volume_prev_12m_sum_prev_3m_pct_change	0.02	0.05	0.05	0.09	0.25
prod_volume_prev_12m_sum_prev_3m_pct_change_prev_2m_mean	0.01	0.03	0.00	0.06	0.26
prod_volume_prev_1m_pct_change	0.11	0.27	0.54	0.14	0.01
prod_volume_prev_1m_pct_change_prev_2m_mean	0.11	0.40	N/A	0.29	0.03
prod_volume_prev_3m_sum_prev_12m_pct_change	0.02	0.05	0.06	0.08	0.25
prod_volume_prev_3m_sum_prev_12m_pct_change_prev_2m_mean	0.01	0.03	0.01	0.06	0.26
prod_volume_prev_3m_sum_prev_1m_pct_change	0.09	0.29	0.56	0.37	0.02
prod_volume_prev_3m_sum_prev_1m_pct_change_prev_2m_mean	0.10	0.23	0.37	0.37	0.04
prod_volume_prev_3m_sum_prev_3m_pct_change	0.05	0.15	0.11	0.28	0.05
prod_volume_prev_3m_sum_prev_3m_pct_change_prev_2m_mean	0.02	0.07	-0.04	0.19	0.06
ave_utilization	0.03	0.06	0.19	0.18	0.10
ave_utilization_prev_1m_pct_change	0.03	0.20	0.34	0.12	0.01
ave_utilization_prev_1m_pct_change_prev_2m_mean	0.06	0.29	0.66	0.23	0.05
revenues_sales_prev_3m_sum_prev_12m_pct_change	0.03	0.02	0.02	0.19	0.44
revenues_sales_prev_3m_sum_prev_12m_pct_change_prev_2m_mean	0.01	0.00	0.00	0.12	0.43
revenues_sales_prev_3m_sum_prev_1m_pct_change	0.29	0.44	0.29	N/A	0.05
revenues_sales_prev_3m_sum_prev_1m_pct_change_prev_2m_mean	0.05	0.33	0.22	0.73	0.09
revenues_sales_prev_3m_sum_prev_3m_pct_change	0.09	0.11	0.09	0.60	0.12
revenues_sales_prev_3m_sum_prev_3m_pct_change_prev_2m_mean	-0.02	-0.02	0.01	0.31	0.14
sales_volume_prev_12m_sum_prev_12m_pct_change	0.00	0.03	0.02	-0.01	0.32
sales_volume_prev_12m_sum_prev_12m_pct_change_prev_2m_mean	0.00	0.02	0.01	-0.01	0.31

(continued)

sales_volume_prev_12m_sum_prev_1m_pct_change	0.14	0.22	0.14	0.22	0.31
sales_volume_prev_12m_sum_prev_1m_pct_change_prev_2m_mean	0.04	0.16	0.10	0.17	0.34
sales_volume_prev_12m_sum_prev_3m_pct_change	0.03	0.08	0.07	0.13	0.36
sales_volume_prev_12m_sum_prev_3m_pct_change_prev_2m_mean	0.00	0.03	0.04	0.07	0.36
sales_volume_prev_1m_pct_change	0.67	0.52	0.20	0.38	0.01
sales_volume_prev_1m_pct_change_prev_2m_mean	0.34	N/A	0.40	0.44	0.04
sales_volume_prev_3m_sum_prev_12m_pct_change	0.03	0.07	0.07	0.12	0.36
sales_volume_prev_3m_sum_prev_12m_pct_change_prev_2m_mean	0.00	0.04	0.04	0.07	0.36
sales_volume_prev_3m_sum_prev_1m_pct_change	0.32	0.52	0.33	0.85	0.02
sales_volume_prev_3m_sum_prev_1m_pct_change_prev_2m_mean	0.08	0.40	0.27	0.63	0.05
sales_volume_prev_3m_sum_prev_3m_pct_change	0.10	0.17	0.14	0.51	0.06
sales_volume_prev_3m_sum_prev_3m_pct_change_prev_2m_mean	−0.01	0.02	0.04	0.25	0.08
usa_sales_volume_prev_12m_sum_prev_3m_pct_change	0.00	0.04	0.03	0.05	N/A
china_sales_volume_prev_12m_sum_prev_3m_pct_change	0.04	0.04	0.03	0.08	0.13
china_market_share_prev_3m_sum_prev_3m_pct_change_prev_2m_mean	0.03	0.09	0.09	0.18	0.05
china_market_share_prev_1m_pct_change	0.23	0.25	0.12	0.14	0.01
usa_market_share_prev_3m_sum_prev_3m_pct_change_prev_2m_mean	−0.03	0.00	−0.01	0.07	0.29
usa_market_share_prev_1m_pct_change	0.36	0.19	0.04	0.13	0.01
ww_market_share_prev_3m_sum_prev_3m_pct_change_prev_2m_mean	−0.02	0.02	0.05	0.25	0.07
ww_market_share_prev_1m_pct_change	N/A	0.34	0.11	0.29	0.00
electric_ratio_prev_1m_pct_change	0.00	0.01	−0.01	0.02	−0.02

- prod_volume_prev_1m_pct_change_prev_2m_mean and usa_sales_volume_ prev_12m_sum_prev_3m_pct_change = 0.03
- prod_volume_prev_1m_pct_change_prev_2m_mean and usa_market_share_ prev_3m_sum_prev_3m_pct_change_prev_2m_mean = -0.01
- revenues_sales_prev_3m_sum_prev_1m_pct_change and usa_sales_volume_ prev_12m_sum_prev_3m_pct_change = 0.05
- usa_sales_volume_prev_12m_sum_prev_3m_pct_change and china_market_ share_prev_1m_pct_change = 0.01

We will show in the next section a way to combine factors to achieve a more performant strategy.

10.5 GAUSSIAN PROCESSES EXAMPLE

Similar to Ghoshal (2016), we decided to see if Gaussian Processes (GP) used to combine some of our factors create even more performant ones. Why Gaussian Process Regression (GPR), you might ask? Why not a simpler, more understood method like Linear Regression (LR) or Principal Component Regression (PCR)? Here, we favor Gaussian Process regression for a few reasons:

- Orthogonality: With two factors, for example, if they are somewhat orthogonal (i.e. don't have any or a very small correlation), the two principal components would explain exactly the same amount of variance. Therefore, we don't have a single factor that encodes most of the information from the two individual ones. It is for this reason we do not pick PCR.
- Nonlinearity: Obviously we hope that, as each of our factors increases, the associated returns also increase. Who is to say, however, that there is no interaction between the two factors? Perhaps the surface of the returns given our two factors is not a plane, but some more complex, undulating shape. LR would impose/assume that the returns lie in the plane; GPR does not. It is for this reason we do not pick LR.

As an example, we decide to pool sales_volume_prev_3m_sum_prev_3m_pct_ change and prod_volume_prev_1m_pct_change_prev_2m_mean via a Gaussian Process to create a new factor. We choose these factors because they (1) are both at least as performant as the benchmark, and (2) have a relatively low correlation (0.19 Pearson correlation between excess returns from Table 10.9 and 0.14 time-average Spearman correlation from Table 10.10) with each other.

For the GP we use the cubic-dot-product kernel, defined by:

$$K(x, x') = (\sigma_0^2 + [x, x'])^3$$

which assigns high covariance to inputs that point in similar directions to one another in vector space. Because it is the relative values (within the universe) of our factors

TABLE 10.11 Factors CAGRs.

Factor	CAGR	Sharpe	Vol	Ave. Drawdown (Days)
sales_volume_prev_3m_sum_prev_3m_pct_change	12.8%	0.69	0.197	49
prod_volume_prev_1m_pct_change_prev_2m_mean	13.6%	0.72	0.200	40
Gaussian Process factor	16.7%	0.84	0.199	36

and the next period returns that we actually care about (given we pick the top $x\%$ as per our factor to hold the top $x\%$ of stocks as per next period returns), we decide to regress the quantiles induced by the next period returns on the quantiles induced by the factors. Given that the assumption of a Gaussian process is that everything lives within $\mathbb{R}^n$, we transform our quantiles from $[0, 1]$ to $\mathbb{R}$ via the inverse logistic transform before regressing. We then train our Gaussian process on the previous year's data in order to predict the following month's return's quantiles, optimizing σ_0^2 via k-fold (with k=5) cross-validation on the training set at each point, before rolling forward month-by-month to create a timeseries of predictions from January 1, 2010, to January 1, 2018. We then use the ranking of these forecasted next-period returns quantiles as our new factor that we rank on. The results can be seen in Table 10.11.

From these results it is evident that Gaussian Processes may be useful in combining multiple factors into one, obtaining superior CAGR and Sharpe than the individual factors, a similar volatility, and a shorter average drawdown. We stop here but the GPs open the door to the exploration of many more different factor mixes that could, in principle, enhance any strategy's returns.

10.6 SUMMARY

In this chapter, we have explored two approaches to generating a trading strategy based on both financial statements and alternative automotive data: Approach 1 using alternative data to forecast company fundamentals, and Approach 2 using alternative data directly. We showed that Approach 2 yields superior returns and that it is easier to implement. This conclusion should not be generalized to any strategy because it might be very specific to the problem we have just examined. Hence, an assessment on a case-by-case basis is warranted. The alternative IHS Markit dataset at our disposal contained both financial information (e.g. sales by specific market, production etc.), and hence already mimicking a financial statement, and additional information (e.g. electrification share, market share by specific market). So, the granularity of the information and the additional factors helped unlock returns superior to those generated by financial statements ratios alone. Moreover, our alternative dataset is released at monthly frequency and we have not explored a monthly rebalancing strategy for the sake of comparison between Approach 1 and Approach 2. Finally, we could have explored an Approach 3 similar to Model C of Section 6.8, which is based on both alternative and financial statements data. For the sake of brevity, this is something that can be further investigated by the curious reader.

10.7   APPENDIX

10.7.1   List of Companies

1. BAYER MOTOREN WERKE AG
2. BRILLIANCE CHINA AUTOMOTIVE HOLDINGS LTD
3. BYD COMPANY LTD
4. CHINA MOTOR CORP
5. CHONGQING CHANGAN
6. DAIMLER AG
7. DONGFENG MOTOR GROUP CO LTD
8. FAW CAR CO LTD
9. FIAT CHRYSLER AUTOMOBILES NV
10. FORD MOTOR CO
11. GEELY AUTOMOBILE HOLDINGS LTD
12. GENERAL MTRS CO
13. GREAT WALL MOTOR CO LTD
14. GUANGZHOU AUTOMOBILE GROUP CO LTD
15. HONDA MOTOR CO LTD
16. HYUNDAI MOTOR CO
17. KIA MOTORS CORP
18. MAHINDRA & MAHINDRA LTD
19. MAZDA MOTOR CORP
20. MITSUBISHI MOTOR CORP
21. NISSAN MOTOR CO LTD
22. PEUGEOT SA
23. RENAULT SA
24. SAIC MOTOR CORP LTD
25. SUBARU CORP
26. SUZUKI MOTOR CORP
27. TATA MOTORS LTD.
28. TESLA INC
29. TOYOTA MOTOR CORP
30. VOLKSWAGEN AG

10.7.2 Description of Financial Statement Items

- **accpayable** (accounts payable). When a company purchases goods on credit that needs to be paid back in a short period of time, it is known as accounts payable. It is treated as a liability and comes under the head current liabilities. Accounts payable is a short-term debt payment that needs to be paid to avoid default.

- **cogs** (Cost of Goods Sold). COGS is the direct costs attributable to the production of the goods sold in a company. This amount includes the cost of the materials used in creating the good along with the direct labor costs used to produce the good. It excludes indirect expenses such as distribution costs and sales force costs.

- **currliab** (current liabilities). Liabilities are funds owed by the business and are broken down into current and long-term categories. Current liabilities are those due within one year and includes items such as:
  - Accounts payable
  - Wages
  - Income tax deductions
  - Pension plan contributions
  - Medical plan payments
  - Building and equipment rents
  - Customer deposits
  - Utilities
  - Temporary loans, lines of credit, or overdrafts
  - Interest
  - Maturing debt
  - Sales tax and/or goods and services tax charged on purchases

- **ebit** (earnings before interest and tax). EBIT = Net Income + Interest + Taxes or EBIT = Revenue − Operating Expenses.

- **equity** (common equity). Common equity represents common shareholders' investment in a company.

- **ev** (enterprise value). EV is a measure of a company's total value, often used as a more comprehensive alternative to equity market capitalization. Enterprise value is calculated as the market capitalization plus debt, minority interest, and preferred shares, minus total cash and cash equivalents. EV = market value of common stock + market value of preferred equity + market value of debt + minority interest − cash and investments.

- **ffo** (funds from operations). FFO represents the sum of net income and all non-cash charges or credits. It is the cash flow of the company.

- **inventory.** Inventory includes amounts for raw materials, work-in-progress goods, and finished goods. The company uses this account when it reports sales of goods, generally under cost of goods sold in the income statement.

- **netincome** (net income). Net income is equal to net earnings (profit) calculated as sales less cost of goods sold, selling, general and administrative expenses, operating expenses, depreciation, interest, taxes, and other expenses.
- **opincome** (EBIT and depreciation). EBITDA represents the earnings of a company before interest expense, income taxes, and depreciation. It is calculated by taking the pretax income and adding back interest expense on debt and depreciation, depletion, and amortization and subtracting interest capitalized.
- **sales** (sales/revenues). Revenue is the amount of money that a company actually receives during a specific period, including discounts and deductions for returned merchandise. It is the top line or gross income figure from which costs are subtracted to determine net.
- **totassets** (total assets). Total assets represent the sum of total current assets, long-term receivables, investment in unconsolidated subsidiaries, other investments, net property, plant, and equipment and other assets. An asset is a resource with economic value that an individual, corporation, or country owns.

10.7.3   Ratios Used

Alberg and Lipton:

- EBIT-to-EV
- Net-Income-to-EV
- Sales-to-EV

Yan and Zheng:

- Sales to current-liabilities
- Negative change in inventory to lagged sales (i.e. is positive if inventory is decreasing)
- Negative change in current-liabilities to lagged equity (i.e. is positive if current-liabilities is decreasing)
- Negative change in current-liabilities to lagged total-assets (i.e. is positive if current-liabilities is decreasing)
- Negative change in inventory to lagged cost-of-goods-sold (i.e. is positive of inventory is decreasing)
- Negative change in inventory to lagged total-assets (i.e. is positive of inventory is decreasing)
- Negative change in inventory to lagged current-liabilities (i.e. is positive of inventory is decreasing)
- Negative change in inventory to lagged equity (i.e. is positive if inventory is decreasing)

- Negative change in total-assets to lagged equity (i.e. is positive if total-assets is decreasing)
- Negative % change in current-liabilities (i.e. is positive if current-liabilities is decreasing)
- Negative % change in inventory (i.e. is positive if inventory is decreasing)
- Negative change in current-liabilities to lagged sales (i.e. is positive of current-liabilities is decreasing)
- EBIT to enterprise-value
- Net-income to enterprise-value
- Sales to enterprise-value

Our own:

- % change in sales
- % change in EBIT
- % change in net-income
- % change in cost-of-goods-sold
- % change in funds-from-operations
- % change in operating-income
- % change in total-assets

10.7.4 IHS Markit Data Features

- Sales volume: number of units sold/registered
- Estimated sales revenues: estimated sales revenues based on sales volume and average sale price per model in the country of sale
- Production volume: number of units produced
- Plant utilization levels: production output as a % of total possible production output, averaged across countries
- Worldwide market share: share of automotive sales worldwide
- US market share: share of sales within US automotive market
- Chinese market share: share of sales within Chinese automotive market
- Electric ratio: electric vehicle share as measured by weighted average electric vehicle exposure
- Average time to EOP: time to end of product (end of life) averaged across all models, weighted by model production volume
- Average age: average age of unit in automotive company's fleet
- Average lifecycle: lifecycle of each model averaged across all models, weighted by model production volume

10.7.5 Reporting Delays by Country

TABLE 10.12 Lags applied in automotive factor calculations.

Country	Sales Lag	Production Lag
Argentina	1	1
Australia	1	N/A
Belgium	1	2
Brazil	1	1
Canada	1	2
China	2	2
France*	1	2
Germany	1	2
India	2	5
Indonesia	2	2
Iran	2	2
Italy	1	2
Japan	2	3
Malaysia	2	2
Mexico	2	2
Netherlands	1	2
Philippines	3	2
Poland	1	2
Russia	2	2
South Africa	1	2
South Korea	2	2
Spain	1	2
Sweden	1	2
Taiwan	1	2
Thailand	2	2
Turkey	2	2
United Kingdom	1	2
United States	1	2

* **Varies by producer.**
Source: Based on data from IHS Markit.

CHAPTER 11

Surveys and Crowdsourced Data

11.1 INTRODUCTION

Later, in Chapter 12, we will analyze and discuss the use of PMI data. In essence, PMI data is collected from surveys of managers in the industry concerning their economic expectations. Essentially, PMIs can be utilized as a proxy for more traditional macroeconomic datasets, such as GDP, which tend to be released on a heavily lagged basis, as we already discussed in Chapter 1. However, there are many different contexts where survey data can be utilized by investors. In this chapter, we will discuss the use of other types of survey data that can be gathered from sources such as consumers or subject matter experts. We will discuss two case studies to show how they can be utilized to understand consumer products (in this case produced by computer games firms) and also to estimate crude oil production.

Later in this chapter, we will examine alpha capture data. These datasets essentially consist of sell-side broker recommendations. In the final part of this chapter, we will look at survey data for corporate earnings releases and macroeconomic data releases. We will show how crowdsourcing can be used to compile these datasets.

11.2 SURVEY DATA AS ALTERNATIVE DATA

Data obtained by surveying people who have a view on a company (or any other entity of interest) or an asset (physical or financial) may turn out to be very insightful. This is particularly the case when information is not obtainable in other ways, or is obtainable with a delay or at prohibitively high price (e.g. on-site visits and travel, satellite images, credit card transactions acquisition). This information can be used to monitor a current position, evaluate a trade that will be performed, extract trading signals, or assess a risk situation.

In this context, the "people" surveyed are not "insiders." The survey would instead involve respondents whose background allows them to express an informed opinion with regard to, for example, the current and/or potential future performance of a company and/or the industry it operates in and the broad market context. These relevant "people" to include in a survey can also mean scouts and researchers. They can collect visual or other types of information about company assets such as the condition of buildings and facilities, quality of its products, foot-traffic, and so on. A deep domain expertise in this latter case is not needed.

In general, a survey leverages not one person but a multitude of people. Their opinions can be averaged to provide a wisdom-of-the-crowds view. Hence in principle this is likely to provide better information than the view of single person. Figure 11.1 shows a hierarchy of potential contributors to a survey. From people on the ground (scouts) it can be narrowed up to managers and senior company executives.

Current technology allows identifying, contacting, and onboarding contributors through mobile applications. Features like geolocation, image uploading functionality, and rating of contributors allow us to control the veracity of this type of data source. A sample of contributors can be set up quite quickly, usually in a few days or even hours, and the results of a survey can be available shortly after that. The universe of potential contributors – defined by those individuals who have access to a mobile device – is estimated to be around 3bn people. The coverage is global, including remote areas not accessible or monitored by other means.

A survey can be conducted in anticipation of an event such as product launch, earnings report (we'll talk about crowdsourcing earnings forecasts later in this chapter), or election results. It can be also conducted as a confirmation of already

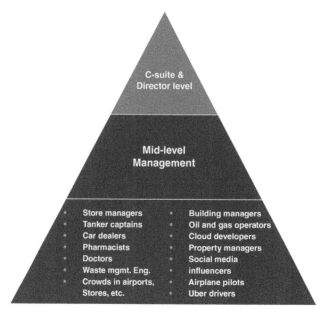

FIGURE 11.1   Hierarchy of contributors.
Source: Based on data from Grapedata.

public information or any private beliefs. They may not always be linked to any specific event. Instead they can be conducted to understand trends better, such as the switch to generic (and cheaper) medicines of a population, intention of a population to opt for an electric vehicle for the next purchase, and so on. All this information can be of invaluable help to investors and asset and risk managers.

11.3 THE DATA

In the first case study we will be using data from Grapedata. The company provides an alternative data-sourcing platform through which one can instantly connect with any individual or group of individuals globally and perform on-demand surveys. This offers an opportunity to unlock offline information that can be important in financial decision making and due diligence. This information may not be available from other sources. It makes use of an online mobile phone platform on which more than 70,000 contributors are currently onboarded. The platform provides compliance oversight, aggregation, and anonymization.

Key tasks include targeted survey data on precise demographic cohorts and seeking out specific individuals who would be inaccessible via traditional routes. Once connected, dialogue channels allow ongoing information sharing in real time. It is synced to the mobile device of a client who can enter queries at any time, 24/7, via an encrypted application.

To get a sense of a typical timeline of a survey conducted by Grapedata, an example is shown in Figure 11.2.

The process followed by Grapedata in a survey is illustrated in Figure 11.3. After a client query, Grapedata checks that contributors are screened for geolocation. They are also passed through a background check, which is intended to increase the veracity of the dataset that will later be delivered to clients. After the answers stage, respondents are rated. The rating is based on the quality and the promptness of the answers. Low-rating respondents' answers are not incorporated in the final dataset and those respondents are no longer employed for future surveys.

11.4 THE PRODUCT

Grapedata provides geolocated surveys in a fully digital way through its online platform. It engages with respondents in three ways:

- Pooled surveys
- Q&A surveys
- Reports

Scouts are employed in **pooled surveys** to collect information where deep domain expertise is not needed. For example, these can be shopping mall customers who can be asked to express an opinion on the changes in traffic. In order to get better insights,

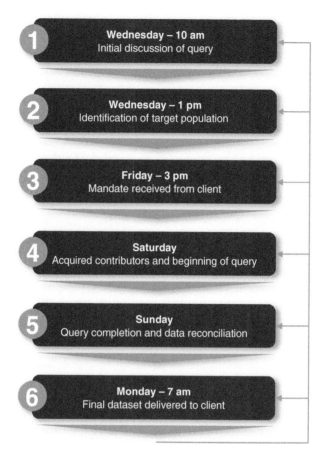

FIGURE 11.2   Typical timeline of a survey.
Source: Based on data from Grapedata.

this information can sometimes be augmented or cross-checked with foot-traffic data providers who use other means to collect information. In other cases, pooled survey data can be the only way to get certain information. For example, an investor might want to detect the foot-traffic changes in a chain of pharmacies and/or the changes of their sales, but these stores are out of the reach of satellites or out of the focus of mobile phone tracking companies. The questions asked in pooled surveys are specific, but deep expertise and detailed answers are not required. For example, questions could be something like "How has the total sales changed in the last six months?" with a simple set of answers "Up/Neutral/Down," "Has the number of customers declined?" with answers "Yes/No," and so on.

Q&A surveys are generally based on a smaller sample of respondents with a specific domain knowledge. The elicited responses can be much more detailed and elaborated. Q&A surveys are required by clients who want a more detailed background and justification to the answers provided by the respondents. The answers are for very

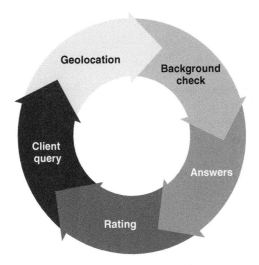

FIGURE 11.3   The process followed in a survey.
Source: Based on data from Grapedata.

specific questions, such as "What is the daily oil production in a region?" These require deeper expertise and domain knowledge than in the pooled survey.

Apart from pooled surveys and detailed Q&A sessions, if required by a client, respondents can be asked to compile detailed **reports** on specific queries like company performance and evaluation.

In contrast to pooled surveys, respondents to Q&A surveys and reports are onboarded after undergoing automated background checks through "World Check-One." They are given preliminary assignments to test their knowledge. In this case, data is screened by Grapedata and Optima Partners (for compliance sensitive cases) before it is shared with a client.

11.5   CASE STUDIES

11.5.1   Case Study: Company Event Study (Pooled Survey)

Grapedata conducted a pooled survey on January 31, 2019, on the market attitude toward the imminent release of a new game (JX Mobile III) in Q2 2019 by Kingsoft, a Chinese software company based in Beijing.

The survey was commissioned by an asset manager with a long position in Kingsoft. They wanted to check whether the attitude of the gaming community to the new release was positive. They also wanted to know how much customers would be willing to spend on it. This survey would have helped the asset manager to estimate several metrics, including the future earnings of Kingsoft and hence the impact on its share price. This information would be used to assess whether they should maintain a long position in the stock. Grapedata kindly provided us with this survey data.

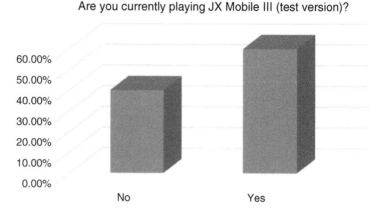

FIGURE 11.4   Are you currently playing JX Mobile III (test version)?
Source: Based on data from Grapedata.

Kingsoft operates four subsidiaries: Seasun for video game development, Cheetah Mobile for mobile internet apps, Kingsoft Clouds for cloud storage platforms, and WPS for office software, including WPS Office. All these business lines determine the earnings of Kingsoft. The launch of JX Mobile III is a major event for Kingsoft because the JX game line is a substantial source of revenue for it. Scheduled for release in late Q4 2019, JX Mobile II was expected to have limited overall contribution to 2019 results, so it was not included in the survey.

Grapedata devised a survey on a carefully selected subset of the gaming population in China. Latest estimates report 3.3 million online JX I and JX III players playing at any given time.[1] The total sample of the conducted survey was 700 respondents. Of these, 350 players funneled down to either JX PC III or JX Mobile I players, or players of both. These are the people likely to play JX Mobile III. Respondents who were not already registered on Grapedata's platform were acquired online on diverse gaming platforms, blogs, and social media. The questions of the survey appear in Appendix 11.10.

The distribution of the answers to three of the questions is plotted in Figures 11.4, 11.5, and 11.6.

The results of the survey helped the asset manager raise the Kingsoft 2019 earnings estimate by 14% on higher gaming revenue estimates. Upside risks to this estimate included earlier-than-expected launch of JX Mobile II and JX Mobile III. Downside risks included: (1) weaker-than-expected performance of JX Online III, and (2) stronger competition in the office application and public cloud market – another significant revenue source for Kingsoft. The downside risk (1) above was considered low by the asset manager thanks to the insights from the Grapedata survey.

---

[1]M. Lu, October 5, 2016, US Video and Computer Game Industry Overview Report, UBC.

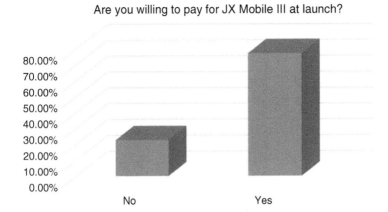

FIGURE 11.5 Are you willing to pay for JX Mobile III at launch?
Source: Based on data from Grapedata.

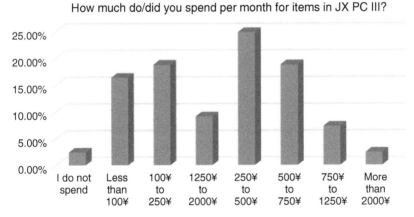

FIGURE 11.6 How much do/did you spend per month for items in JX PC III?
Source: Based on data from Grapedata.

The performance of the Kingsoft share price after the survey (conducted around January 3, 2019) and the performance of the market (Hang Seng index) is plotted in Figure 11.7.

Since the survey was performed, the share price of Kingsoft appreciated around 100%, compared to the market increase of around 20%. An investor would thus have been able to lock into a profit with the aid of some reassurance about the prospects of JX Mobile III from the gaming community before the other market participants. The obvious caveat to this analysis is that this is a single stock over a relatively short time period.

FIGURE 11.7   Performance of the share price of Kingsoft (top) and the Hang Seng index (bottom) after the survey (3/1/2019).
Source: Adapted from Grapedata.

11.5.2   Case Study: Oil and Gas Production (Q&A Survey)

In this case study we will show the use of Q&A survey data to estimate the production of crude oil, natural gas liquids (NGL), and condensates from the OPEC countries before this information is made available by other data providers. The survey was conducted for a commodity trader who is actively involved in the trading of oil products and futures. Grapedata kindly provided us with this survey data.

The OPEC oil supply is one of the driving factors of oil prices. In fact, the OPEC countries provide around 40% of world global oil and OPEC's oil exports represent about 60% of the total petroleum traded internationally. Hence, it is a well-known fact that OPEC's actions around increasing/decreasing oil production targets have influence on oil prices. In particular, indications of changes in crude oil production from Saudi Arabia, OPEC's largest producer, frequently affect oil prices. Other factors that have an influence are the non-OPEC countries' production and the demand for oil. All these are components of a typical commodity trader's balance model.

OPEC countries publish official production figures on the 15th of each month for the previous three months. There is belief among traders that the figures can be understated or overstated for some countries, because governments either consider them to be confidential and do not publish the data, or publish numbers that do seem untrustworthy. Hence, the OPEC Secretariat publishes production data on the basis of estimates produced by "secondary sources."[2]

An expert survey can invariably provide insights in this context both as a sanity check for other data sources or as a timely primary source of information. For this purpose, Grapedata has set up a network of respondents (~200) in the OPEC countries with oil and gas industry knowledge in charge of providing their estimates 15 days before the official date of publication of OPEC. Figure 11.8 shows a plot of the production numbers estimated through the Grapedata methodology. Alongside this are estimates by OPEC, S&P Platts, Wood Mackenzie, and the International Energy Agency (IEA).

The estimates are close. However, there are some differences even between the numbers of well-established data providers, especially in the last months of the sample. The discrepancies in the last few months are due to the situation in Iran, whose exports have become more opaque since the US sanctions on the country's oil sector took effect in November 2018. While most industry experts agreed they had dropped steeply, views on the amounts differed by as much as several hundred thousand barrels per day. Grapedata predicted a drop of lower magnitude than other providers, which positively affected its global supply estimates, as visible in Figure 11.8. Later,

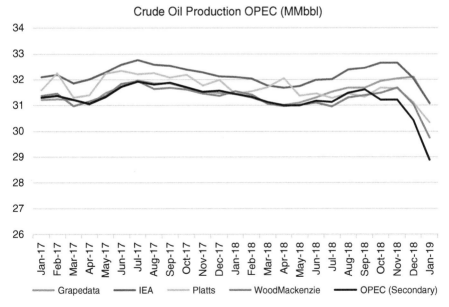

FIGURE 11.8 Crude oil production by OPEC as estimated by several data providers.
Source: Based on data from Grapedata.

---

[2]These include S&P Global Platts, Argus Media, Energy Intelligence Group, IHS Markit, the Energy Information Agency (EIA), and the International Energy Agency (IEA).

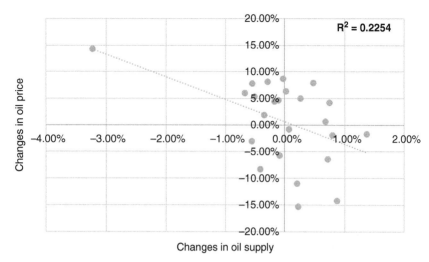

FIGURE 11.9   Monthly changes in oil prices versus changes in OPEC oil supply January 2017–January 2019.
Source: Based on data from Grapedata.

in line with Grapedata's estimates, industry experts confirmed that the drop was not indeed as steep as estimated by many data providers.[3]

Figure 11.9 is a plot of the correlation between oil price monthly changes and the monthly changes in supply based on Grapedata data. The relationship has the expected sign – negative changes in supply results and positive changes in the oil price. The R^2 is ~22%, but as mentioned oil supply is only one of the determinants of the oil price. A fully fledged balance model similar to one used by commodity traders must include demand as well. Surveys like the Grapedata's can be a reliable input to such balance models.

11.6   SOME TECHNICAL CONSIDERATIONS ON SURVEYS

Two important decisions must be made before starting a survey. The first one is how to select the sample in terms of size, coverage, and penetration to make it representative for the entire population – if this is required. This could be the case for political surveys or any other surveys where proportions that reflect the general population must be estimated. Of course, this is because the entire population cannot be covered due to costs and time constraints, and hence one has to settle for a smaller set of respondents. If the chosen sample is indeed representative (as Grapedata makes sure through well-established methods), then, by using statistical formulae, one can calculate the margin of error given the sample size. Hence, the client must select the

---

[3] https://www.reuters.com/article/us-iran-oil-exports/despite-sanctions-irans-oil-exports-rise-in-early-2019-sources-idUSKCN1Q818X.

sample size according to the error tolerance they are willing to accept. We note that representativeness might not be required if, for example, scouts are needed to assess the condition of a factory, or any other asset.

A second important decision is how to choose the optimal timing of conducting the survey. One usually wants to do it before an event, if the objective is to estimate the impact of that event (a new product release, earnings report, etc.). But how much in advance must be carefully pondered.[4] Too close to the event could be late because information about it might already be priced by the market. Too soon and other events, including systematic ones, could influence the share price to the extent of complete dilution of the information we gathered beforehand through the survey.

11.7   CROWDSOURCING ANALYST ESTIMATES SURVEY

Historically, the way to understand market consensus for specific events, such as earnings releases, has consisted of looking at consensus surveys made by data companies such as Bloomberg or Refinitv. This can cover macro data releases. It can also cover forecasts for traded assets like equities, FX, and fixed income. We have already seen an example earlier of similar surveys of experts for estimating crude oil production by Grapedata. Usually, the "crowd" has been subject matter experts at sell-side investment firms. As noted, these forecasts are compiled by data firms such as Bloomberg and Refinitiv. They are often used as a proxy for the crowd. Refinitiv's I/B/E/S dataset goes back to 1976 (Refinitiv, n.d.) and covers key performance indicators, including estimates of earning expectations, covering 22,000 firms.

Hence, traditionally analyst estimates of metrics like earnings forecasts tend to be over a "crowd" of sell-side contributors. What if we increase that crowd considerably to include many more participants from more diverse backgrounds, not just those analysts working on the sell side? Newer data firms such as Estimize crowdsource these estimates from a wider pool of market participants. Estimize is a platform that sources estimates from a diverse array of individuals for hedge funds, brokers, and independent and amateur analysts. They primarily cover earnings estimates for US stocks and certain macroeconomic data releases, as well as key performance indicators like subscriber numbers for Netflix. Jame et al. (2016) find that Estimize crowdsourced earnings forecasts provide additional information content to I/B/E/S estimates, which is the traditional source of consensus estimates. They note that the value of the crowdsourcing is a function of the crowd size. Drogen and Jha (2013) show how post-earnings drift is more pronounced for earnings surprises that are benchmarked against Estimize's data compared to the traditional Wall Street consensus. They also create a trading strategy that uses this observation, which accrues abnormal returns especially for large-cap stocks. Banker, Khavis, and Park (2018) suggest that the advent of crowdsourced estimates from Estimize has also changed the behavior of analysts contributing to I/B/E/S surveys resulting in earlier and more frequent forecasts. They also tend to issue more forecasts.

---

[4]These are decisions that also apply to more "traditional" surveys that have been around for many years in politics and marketing.

11.8 ALPHA CAPTURE DATA

As well as publishing longer-term forecasts for clients for asset prices and for specific events, such as earnings releases, sell-side brokers regularly generate trade recommendations in reports sent to their clients. One way for clients to keep up to date is to read every research report. Given the volume of research reports received by clients, this is likely to be very time consuming. It can be challenging for clients to aggregate these trade recommendations quickly and efficiently. Automating the process is challenging, given that there is not a standard format for research reports. An alpha capture system is a type of software that enables banks to submit trade recommendations in a standard format that are then communicated to the client. This approach was first devised by the hedge fund Marshall Wace (Greene, 2008). These trade recommendations can be aggregated and consumed by buy-side firms to help in their decision-making process. It can also be easier to track the value of these trade recommendations by specific contributors and firms. While alpha capture originally started as a way to standardize equity trade recommendations into a more structured form that is easier to ingest, these datasets are now being used by hedge funds to trade in other asset classes. Today there are a number of proprietary alpha capture platforms developed by individual hedge funds and also platforms from vendors like TIM Group and Bloomberg.

11.9 SUMMARY

We discussed some forms of surveys and crowdsourced datasets in this chapter. We began by making the point that survey data can be seen as an alternative data source. We described survey datasets from the firm Grapedata that are sourced from consumers and subject matter experts through a mobile phone platform. We gave specific examples of how they could be used, starting from an example for a consumer survey in the gaming industry. A second example showed how subject matter experts could be surveyed to help estimate metrics for crude oil production in parallel to OPEC estimates. In the two examples, the survey data provided insights that would not be easily and quickly obtainable by other means.

We talked about crowdsourcing consensus analyst estimates. We showed how crowdsourced estimates from a wider pool of contributed ones compared to the traditional Wall Street consensus. We also discussed alpha capture datasets, which can be seen as standardized and more structured versions of sell-side broker recommendations – something that is gaining momentum in the financial industry. In Chapter 12, we will go into some detail about PMI data, which is also derived from surveys.

11.10 APPENDIX

Questions asked in the Kingsoft survey are as follows:

1. Are you male/female?
2. What is your age?

3. Do you play MMORPG (massively multiplayer online role-playing games)?

4. Are you currently/were you a JX3 PC player?

5. How much time do/did you spend on JX3PC a day?

6. How much do/did you spend per month for items in JX3 PC?

7. Are you currently/were you a JX1 mobile player?

8. How much time do/did you spend per day on JX1 mobile?

9. How much do/did you spend per month for items in JX1 mobile?

10. Are you currently playing JXIII mobile (test version)?

11. How much time do you spend per day on JX3III mobile (test version)?

12. Are you willing to pay for JX III mobile at launch?

13. If you won't play JXIII Mobile, which game do you think you will play?

14. Please comment on JXIII Mobile.

CHAPTER 12

Purchasing Managers' Index

12.1 INTRODUCTION

As we discussed in Chapter 1, the ability to accurately predict changes in key economic indicators, such as GDP, can serve a wide number of groups, not only investors. We mentioned that PMI indicators could be a good proxy for this purpose. Given their importance, in this chapter we will elaborate more around them. We will present some quantitative analysis to justify their use.

GDP forecasting (or better nowcasting) can be used by policymakers to optimize changes to key macroeconomic management levers such as interest rates or fiscal policy. Likewise, by knowing the current macroeconomic context, investors and businesses can make investment allocation decisions with greater certainty and potentially better performance. As a result, in recent years, practitioners have focused on improving their understanding of economic performance in near "real time," rather than waiting for updates to slowly produced official figures, such as GDP, which are also numbers subject to notable future revisions. Performing such a task requires the use of other high-frequency datasets that are released in a timely fashion. This up-to-date information can be exploited to predict, or nowcast, slower-released, low-frequency macroeconomic variables such as GDP.

For example, the PMI series produced by IHS Markit in over 40 countries can be such a high-frequency and timely data source. It is derived from a questionnaire sent to a fixed panel of selected business executives across both manufacturing and service-sector industries. The PMI datasets provide monthly information on a wide variety of metrics such as output, new orders, employment, prices, and stocks. Hence, the PMI datasets provide an insight into countries' current and expected level of business activity. They can also be a leading indicator to forecast upcoming expansions or recessions.

The advantage of the PMI is that it is released earlier than other official indicators, such as the industrial production index or GDP. Typically, they are conducted in the middle of the month. Results from the surveys are released on either the first day (manufacturing) or third working day (services and composite aggregations of both sectors) following the reference period. However, for the eurozone (plus the US, UK, Japan, and Australia), PMI "flash" data is also available around 10 days before the "final" releases. These flash numbers are based on around 85%–90% of the final sample and the revisions between "flash" and "final" PMI data is typical but usually small. In the Eurozone, detailed flash PMI figures for France and Germany are also provided.

Figure 12.1 shows how the PMI data fit into a typical timeline for nowcasting GDP growth in a given quarter (in this example, Q2 2018).

To highlight the relative timing advantage of the PMI, the release formats of two closely watched indicators – the European Commission's Economic Sentiment Indicator (ESI) and official figures from Eurostat on industrial production – are also provided.

The Economic Sentiment Indicator, abbreviated as ESI, is a composite indicator made up of five sectoral confidence indicators with different weights: (1) industrials confidence indicator (40%), (2) services confidence indicator (30%), (3) consumer confidence indicator (20%), (4) retail trade confidence indicator (5%), and (5) construction confidence indicator (5%). The economic sentiment indicator is published monthly by the European Commission. The ESI is derived from surveys gathering the assessments of economic operators of the current economic situation and their expectations about future developments.[1]

The timeline in Figure 12.1-1 provides an indication of how data availability builds through a nowcasting cycle: during the first two months of a quarter, only survey (so-called "soft") data is available – the PMIs and the ESI. It is not until midway through the final month of the quarter that official "hard" figures (in this case industrial production) are available for the first month. So, until a certain point, economists, investors, and policymakers are reliant on soft data to gauge economic performance. Indeed, it is the non-synchronization of releases and subsequent timing advantages that the PMI tends to enjoy that provides the foundation for its use, especially in areas such as monetary policy.

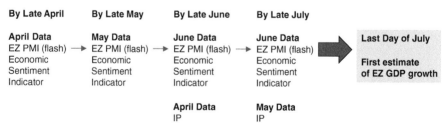

FIGURE 12.1   Nowcasting Eurozone (EZ) GDP Growth in Q2 2018.
Source: IHS Markit.

---

[1]For more information, visit the Eurostat website: https://ec.europa.eu/eurostat/statistics-explained/index
.php?title=Glossary:Economic_sentiment_indicator_(ESI).

12.2 PMI PERFORMANCE

Being of a higher-frequency and timelier nature than GDP statistics, PMI datasets can be a good candidate to meet the demands of continuous tracking of economic growth. In Figure 12.2 we can observe the relationship between quarterly changes in GDP and the PMI for the Eurozone.

Since 2006, the Eurozone Composite PMI (which combines the manufacturing and service sectors) has correctly indicated underlying changes in growth through the financial crisis in 2008–2009, the Eurozone debt-crisis intensification in 2011, and the 2017 upswing in economic performance. Table 12.1 shows correlation statistics for the Eurozone, and its three largest member states. The comparison period begins in January 2000, but to provide a sense of performance since the depths of the 2008–2009 global financial crisis, we also provide a subsample of results since January 2010.

Generally speaking, the PMI outperforms the ESI and is comparable to industrial production at the Eurozone and country level. Naturally there are some exceptions, with industrial production data in Germany notably a strong performer, perhaps not surprising given the structure of Germany's economy. These results also hold broadly true since January 2010, with the PMI performance for Italy especially eye-catching. France remains a laggard in terms of pure correlation statistics, although the PMI continues to perform better than the respective ESI and industrial production data series.

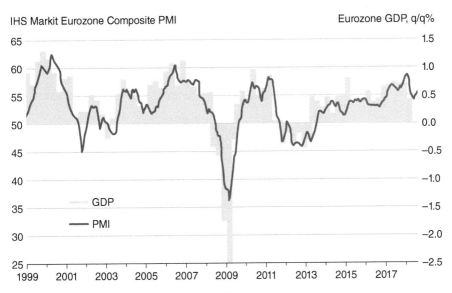

FIGURE 12.2 Eurozone GDP and Composite PMI.
Source: Based on data from IHS Markit, Eurostat.

TABLE 12.1   GDP Growth correlations with % changes of select indicators.

	Euro area	France	Germany	Italy
Since Jan 2000				
PMI Comp	0.87	0.57	0.76	0.79
EC ESI	0.76	0.41	0.61	0.7
IP	0.88	0.55	0.86	0.82
Since 2010				
PMI Comp	0.84	0.52	0.64	0.89
EC ESI	0.71	0.46	0.32	0.74
IP	0.74	0.41	0.79	0.7

Source: Based on data from IHS Markit.

12.3   NOWCASTING GDP GROWTH

We now turn to the short-term predictive power of the PMI (as well as the ESI and industrial production) in forecasting quarterly changes in GDP via a simple nowcasting exercise. To circumvent the issues of misaligned time frequencies (PMI data are released monthly and GDP quarterly), we base our nowcasting model on a simple AR-MIDAS (mixed-data sampling) style regression. It is a single-equation approach, where quarterly GDP is explained by specifically weighted observations of monthly predictors. In mathematical terms:

$$GDP_t = \alpha + \beta_1 GDP_{t-1} + \beta_2 \sum_{j=0}^{q_w-1} \omega_j X_{k,t-j} + \varepsilon_t \qquad (12.1)$$

In this broadly standard forecasting setup, current quarter GDP_t is predicted by using a lag of itself GDP_{t-1} and a weighted average ω_j of an explanatory variable $X_{k,t}$. There are $k = \{1, \ldots, m\}$ observations of X seen over the time period t (in this instance $k = 3$, which is the number of monthly observations of the explanatory variable recorded per calendar quarter).[2]

We run the model as an out-of-sample nowcasting exercise for the period 2010Q1 to 2018Q1. We use both the PMI and the ESI separately as the variable $X_{k,t}$. For industrial production data, the process is simplified by creating a quarterly series of 3m/3m changes and regressing this (along with a lag of the dependent variable) against GDP. Note, however, that the industrial production data is based on "pseudo-time," meaning that when predicting GDP growth, we assume that industrial production data are only available for the first two months of a quarter (as would be the case in a real-time GDP exercise). In essence, this means a time shift of a quarterly industrial production series is performed, whereby month-two observations are used in the regression exercise.

---

[2] We also have the option in this setup to incorporate j lags of $X_{k,t-j}$, the number of which is determined by q_w. For simplicity we stick to using the coincident readings of the explanatory variables over a quarter (e.g. January, February, March observations to predict Q1 quarterly GDP).

TABLE 12.2 Model performance (2010Q1–2018Q1).

	BM	PMI	ESI	IP
Euro area				
RMSFE	0.3	0.23	0.34	0.28
Correct (%)		82.8%	72.4%	65.5%
France				
RMSFE	0.39	0.32	0.42	0.21
Correct (%)		59.4%	56.3%	81.3%
Germany				
RMSFE	0.62	0.5	0.62	0.39
Correct (%)		68.8%	56.3%	78.1%
Italy				
RMSFE	0.31	0.29	0.34	0.44
Correct (%)		69.0%	69.0%	65.5%

Source: Based on data from IHS Markit.

To compare nowcasting performances, the Root Mean Square Forecasting Errors (RMSFE) and the percentage of correctly predicted changes in GDP are provided. In the case of RMSFE, readings closer to zero should be viewed as the most positive. For added context, we also provide the results of a simple benchmark model (denoted as "BM"), which is simply a "no-change" forecast (i.e. current quarter GDP growth is assumed to be unchanged since the previous observation). Table 12.2 provides a summary of the various model performances.

The results show that, in nowcasting terms, models that include PMI data generally outperform those based on the ESI when it comes to predicting quarter-on-quarter growth rates. This is especially the case at the Eurozone level, where the PMI-based model outperforms equivalent ESI and industrial production set-ups considerably in terms of RMSFE while also registering a near 25% average nowcasting gain over the benchmark model. Moreover, the PMI model correctly forecasts the direction of quarterly growth in the Eurozone over 80% of the time (again a better result than what is seen for the ESI and industrial production).

For France and Germany, PMI-based models again outperform the simple benchmark and ESI models – and indicate the value-added of using PMI when it comes to predicting GDP growth – but it is the industrial production–based models that perform the strongest in terms of RMSFE and forecasted direction (though of course the delay in the publication of the industrial production data relative to the PMI needs to be borne in mind here). In Italy, it is only the PMI that outperforms the benchmark based on the RMSFE statistic.

12.4 IMPACTS ON FINANCIAL MARKETS

Having shown the predictive power of PMIs for GDP, we now turn to examine their impact on financial markets, which is the main interest of investors.

As Gomes and Peraita (2016) point out, one of the main problems in measuring the effects of economic indicators on financial markets is that both sets of data are usually available at different frequencies. Although financial data can be obtained for daily, hourly, or even finer intervals, macroeconomic indicators are produced and released at most monthly. Historically this led to the formation of two strands of thinking when modeling the relationship between macroeconomic information and financial markets. One strand consists of the use of lower-frequency regression by aggregating the financial market variables to a less granular time scale (e.g. calculating stock returns at monthly frequency and then regressing on monthly macroeconomic variables). The other strand consists of performing an event study analysis of the impact of a macroeconomic announcement on financial markets at the moment immediately after this information is released. For example, this could be payroll data numbers publication and its effect on stock markets. Gomes and Peraita (2016) provides a good literature review of different studies belonging to the two strands. Their study, however, focuses on the second.

Gomes and Peraita (2016) analyze the effect of PMI announcements on stock market returns and sovereign bond yields for Germany, France, Italy, and Spain, and on the Euro exchange rate, for the period between 2003 and 2014. They find that all of the examined financial markets are affected by the Purchasing Managers' Index announcements, in particular by negative announcements during the Euro Area crisis. Markets that experience the greatest impact are the stock markets, and these are particularly impacted by negative surprises in the PMI announcement. They also find that the effect on bond markets is of a lower magnitude and is symmetric and that the impact of the PMI in most financial markets became significant after the beginning of the crisis in 2008.

Hanousek and Kočenda (2011) analyze the effect of PMI indices on the stock markets of three EU countries – Czech Republic, Hungary, and Poland. They find that PMIs impact the markets in an intuitive manner: a worse-than-expected outcome provokes a negative effect on stock returns and vice versa. The analysis in the papers of Gomes and Peraita (2016) and Hanousek and Kočenda (2011) are both based on the news "surprise" (i.e. the deviation between expectations and the announced PMI). More formally, following the approach of Andersen (2007), they use the following definition of "surprise":

$$Surprise_t = \frac{I_t - E_{t-1}[I_t]}{\hat{\sigma}} \tag{12.2}$$

where I_t denotes the announced value of an indicator and $E_{t-1}[I_t]$ refers to the market's expectation of that indicator at time $t - 1$. $\hat{\sigma}$ is equal to the sample standard deviation of the surprise component $I_t - E_{t-1}[I_t]$. The use of standardization allows a better comparison of coefficients arising when more than one indicator is used in a regression model.

Johnson and Watson (2011) find that PMI changes have a greater impact on the stocks of smaller market capitalization firms and industries such as precious metals,

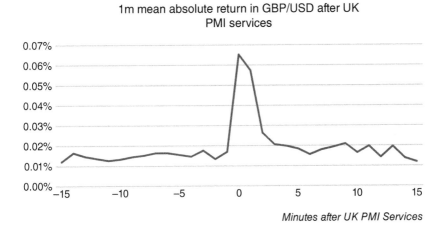

FIGURE 12.3   GBP/USD intraday volatility around UK PMI Services over past 5 years.

computer technology, textiles, and automobiles. The effects of PMI announcements on the commodity futures indices, S&P 500 index, and government bond indices, including those in the United States, has been established by Hess et al. (2008).

We can illustrate how GBP/USD reacts to UK PMI Services releases, by conducting a short event study. We use as our historical sample mid-2013 to mid-2019. We calculate the absolute return of GBP/USD in each of the 15 minutes before and after every UK PMI Services release in our historical sample. Typically, this is at 9:30 am London at the start of the month. Hence, our analysis encompasses 72 UK PMI Services releases. We then take an average of the absolute return for each minute across all the event releases in our sample. This gives us a simple estimate of volatility around each minute. Alternatively, we could have used range-based measures, which would also require high/low data for each minute. Another option was to calculate rolling intraday volatility. In Figure 12.4-1, we report this mean absolute return around UK PMI Services for GBP/USD. We note a very clear spike in intraday mean absolute returns of GBP/USD when UK PMI Services are released. However, this spike in volatility dissipates very quickly. After 5 minutes, the market returns to a normal level of volatility.

We note in closing that we have focused on the study of the impact of PMI data, measuring the supply side of the economy, on financial markets but there are also other important economic indicators. For example, a consumer confidence indicator measures how consumers – the demand side of the economy – expect their personal and general economic situation to evolve. This information could be gathered through the survey methods explained in Chapter 11. We expect in principle, similarly to what we have illustrated here, that the release of such information has impact on markets. However, we will not discuss consumer confidence indicators further in this book.

12.5 SUMMARY

Getting an understanding of the economic growth picture is an important considera-tion for both investors in macro assets, such as rates and FX, as well as for investors in more micro assets such as single stocks. However, GDP data is often released with a large lag; hence it can be quite backward looking. We have shown in the chapter that PMI data based on surveys of business executives can provide an effective timelier estimate for economic growth. In other words, PMI data can be used as a nowcast for GDP data. The release of such information also has impact on financial markets, as witnessed by the amount of literature on the topic, some of which we briefly discussed in this chapter.

CHAPTER 13

Satellite Imagery and Aerial Photography

13.1 INTRODUCTION

On October 4, 1957, the Soviet Union launched Sputnik I, the first artificial satellite in space. The first image of the earth captured by a satellite was made by NASA's Explorer VI Earth satellite (NASA, 2009) on August 14, 1959 (see Figure 13.1). The picture shows a sunlit area of the Central Pacific Ocean and its cloud cover. The photo was taken when the satellite was about 27,000 km above the surface of the Earth.

Of course, this was not the first time that Earth had been observed from the sky. During the First World War, for example, aerial photography became a significant weapon. While only a few hundred photos may have been taken in the first six months of the war, in 1918 Britain produced just over 5 million aerial photographs (Cable, 2015). And this was not the first example of aerial observation for military purposes. In the American Civil War, Thaddeus Lowe used a hot air balloon to perform aerial reconnaissance for the Union against the Confederate forces.

The most obvious difference between satellite imagery and aerial photography is the difference in altitude at which images are taken. From a much higher altitude, a satellite image will be able to capture a larger area. Furthermore, it can also capture weather patterns more easily and broadly. Satellites also regularly pass over the same spots, so they can potentially provide regular updates, and in effect in recent years this frequency has increased, given the number of satellites in the sky. At the same time, the cost of satellite imagery has come down. Overall, aerial photography tends to be more detailed. While in recent years the resolution of satellites has improved, there are limits to the resolution available on satellite images released to the public by law (Bump, 2017). Today there are many organizations in both the public and private domain that operate satellites for imaging purposes.

FIGURE 13.1   First picture from Explorer VI satellite.
Source: NASA.

There are difficulties associated with photographing the Earth from above, such as the vast amount of data generated, given the sheer size of the Earth's surface area and the resolution at which the images are captured. Also, we need to factor in issues like cloud cover, which at times can make some images less clear and usable. As with pretty much every other alternative dataset, the raw satellite imagery is essentially unstructured data. Hence, to be useful for investors it needs to be structured so it can be unified into a common format. Think about the way a human sees the world: we take in a large amount of information through our retina, then we dispense with much of that data and focus on just the important parts of the image.

Computer vision is the area that brings together many different techniques to help a computer see the world in a similar way to humans. There are several steps involved in computer vision, and we shall briefly describe some of these. The initial step deals with image acquisition, which involves the conversion of the world into a raw binary format such as through a digital camera. It should be noted that computer vision need not always deal with images that are observable to the naked eye. There could be data that includes wavelengths that are not visible to the eye, such as infrared wavelengths that allow night vision. There are also many transformations associated with computer vision that are used to enhance the original image, such as colorization, blur removal, or image reconstruction.

The second step is image processing. At this step the image is preprocessed and cleaned to prepare it for higher-level interpretation. This can include operations such as changing the contrast and sharpening the image, as well as the removal of noise and edge tracing. Applications that extensively use image processing algorithms include, for instance, Photoshop and Instagram. The final output of image processing is itself an image.

The next step involves analysis and understanding of the image, essentially being able to convert the image into text that can describe it. At the highest level, image recognition will try to understand the image as whole. Delving into specific parts of the image, object detection flags objects inside the image with a bounded box. Object classification and identification tags what the object is and its type respectively. For videos, these concepts can be extended to object tracking. Please see Chapter 4 for a more detailed discussion of computer vision.

From an economic or markets perspective, satellite imagery can give us a snapshot into the world in a relatively automated and cheaper manner that might be costly or difficult to gather using more traditional and manual methods. Obviously, the higher the resolution of a satellite imagery, the more content we will be able to detect and structure from an image. Furthermore, if we can capture the contents of a certain location repeatedly, we can build up a time series of data to measure changes in activity. Clearly, the more frequent our sampling of satellite imagery, the more expensive it will be to obtain and store the raw data. We also need to be aware of challenges like changes in weather, such as cloud cover, that affect how imagery is processed, and the fact that images are unlikely to be collected at regular intervals across every location of interest, given the way a satellite sweeps the ground.

In the following sections, we will discuss a number of different examples of using satellite imagery for economic applications. This will include the use of night light intensity to understand and forecast US export data, as well as more granular use of imagery to identify car park activity and estimate earnings for retailers' stocks.

13.2 FORECASTING US EXPORT GROWTH

Estimating export growth can be an arduous task. In practice, it is often measured by a proxy, namely the GDP of the foreign export partners of a country. As already discussed at length, the difficulty with GDP figures is that they tend to be recorded on a relatively infrequent basis, which is usually quarterly. There is also often a considerable lag associated with the release and subsequent revisions. Hence, by the time GDP data is released, this could be several months after the associated period it is actually measuring. If we can proxy foreign GDP with a timelier measure, we can in turn estimate foreign growth in the current quarter without a large lag (i.e. doing a timely nowcast). One proxy for GDP is to use PMI surveys (see Chapter 12). Here, we shall discuss an alternative approach.

Nie and Oksol (2018) discuss using satellite imagery as a proxy for foreign GDP and hence as a proxy for foreign US export growth. They focus on the measurement of nighttime lights from satellite imagery. The rationale is relatively intuitive. We would expect that as a country becomes richer and there is more economic activity, this is likely to be reflected in more night lights. They use a dataset of publicly available images through the Earth Observation Group at the NOAA (National Oceanic and Atmospheric Administration). They are filtered for specific "noise," such as clouds.

TABLE 13.1 Annual correlation between exports, lights, and GDP.

Variables	Advanced	Developing
Export growth and lights growth	0.29	0.28
Export growth and GDP growth	0.79	0.49
GDP growth and lights growth	0.17	0.14

Source: Federal Reserve of Kansas City, Haver Analytics.

Each pixel on the image represents an area of around 1 square km. This type of resolution might be insufficient for measuring specific objects, such as cars or buildings. However, the focus here is simply on light intensity of a relatively big area. Each pixel has a value that represents night intensity between 0 and 63. Once a particular geographical area is identified, it becomes possible to create an index for measuring the light intensity of that area, whether it is a city, country, or other region.

This way of proxying GDP, Nie and Oksol note, is particularly useful for emerging markets where official national statistics are likely to be less reliable. In Table 13.1, we present their results for annual correlations from 1993 to 2013, for export growth and light growth, export growth and GDP growth, as well as GDP growth and light growth. In advanced economies, there does appear to be a stronger correlation between export growth and GDP growth. However, this correlation is weaker for developing economies. The authors conjecture that this is because GDP is better measured in advanced economies compared to developing economies.

Later, Nie and Oksol construct quarterly models to estimate export growth in the current quarter: a random walk model, a GDP model, and a light-based model. They note that while GDP data is only available quarterly, light data in recent years has become available on a monthly basis (and since 2017 on a daily basis). Hence, they repeat the exercise for a monthly random walk model and also monthly light models to estimate export growth.

They then compute the average percentage derivation between the model estimates and actual data, which we show in Table 13.2. It is notable that the monthly-based lights model outperforms all the other models, across all economies, for forecasting

TABLE 13.2 Comparing model forecasts through the average percentage derivation at quarterly and monthly frequency.

Model Specification	All	Advanced	Developing
Random walk: quarterly	2.2	3.23	4.13
GDP: quarterly	2.89	3.06	4.06
Lights: quarterly	3.06	4.05	3.11
Random walk: monthly	2.28	2.14	3.27
Lights: monthly	1.33	1.28	2

Source: Federal Reserve of Kansas City, Haver Analytics.

US export growth. This suggests that night light data could indeed be a useful way to help estimate export growth in a timely fashion, in particular where GDP data is lagged.

13.3 CAR COUNTS AND EARNINGS PER SHARE FOR RETAILERS

Imagine that you want to understand the retail sales of a certain store or the number of diners frequenting a certain restaurant. One way to get an idea is to count the number of customers walking inside the store or restaurant. If a store has only one entry and exit, it might be feasible to do this manually. However, if we are talking about a large store with lots of entry points and many branches in different parts of the country, it ends up being a logistic nightmare. If we want to track the whole retail sector, it quickly becomes a very big undertaking to source such data and manage the processes behind. Alternatively, we can attempt to automate the problem by using satellite imagery. Satellite images of car parks attached to the stores can be used as input data for this purpose.

We have explained earlier in broad terms (see Section 4.5) how it is possible to classify an image or objects by using a number of techniques. In particular, we noted that using a convolutional neural network outperforms more traditional classification techniques. Whatever the chosen technique, the goal is to structure the images and extract the relevant information. This would usually involve identifying and counting the number of cars in each of these satellite images, using techniques such as convolutional neural networks. The hypothesis to be tested is that the number of cars at any one time would be a proxy for retail activity in a store or how busy a restaurant is. Potentially, we might expect that this could be a good indicator for the earnings reported by the firm. In order to do this, it is necessary to have satellite images of sufficiently high resolution. This contrasts with our earlier example of measuring nighttime light intensity, which may be possible using lower-resolution imagery. Furthermore, as with any satellite imagery, there can be the additional complications of factors such as cloud cover, which can impact the analysis and the conclusions drawn from an image.

The car counts are, of course, only going to be an approximation, given that we do not really know the spend per customer from a satellite image. Furthermore, this approach is also most appropriate for those retail outlets whose customers are mostly driving there by car. Of course, although we are here focusing on retail outlets or restaurants, we could apply the techniques to any other consumer-oriented business.

In order to make these car counts useful, extra data is required that is not contained in the image, such as address data, which we can join with the geospatial data. In particular, once we have the address of each car park in every image, we can focus on those car parks that are adjacent to particular retail outlets and ignore other car parks. If our goal is to use this data for trading purposes, we need to do some entity matching. In other words, we also need to be able to match the various retail brands of the car parks to their underlying equities, which we can trade. Indeed, this type of joining with other datasets and entity matching is a common feature of most alternative data use cases, as we have already explained in Chapter 3.

To test this hypothesis, we use a dataset from Geospatial Insight derived from satellite imagery data. Geospatial Insight has access to a network of more than 250 satellites in orbit for gathering their imagery. They primarily use Digital Global Worldview's network of satellites. The resolution of the images produced by these satellites is particularly high (26cm–51cm). This level of detail enables the identification of cars, but not, for example, number plates or people.

Our focus is on Geospatial Insight's RetailWatch dataset, which we shall use to estimate company performance for several European retailers. It consists of the number of cars parked nearby several retail outlets in Europe, with observations snapped on a regular basis. From the input images, areas bounded by the geofenced outlines for specific retailer car parks of interest are clipped. A convolutional neural network (CNN) predicts the likely location of cars within these clipped car park areas, which has been trained on a large dataset of manually annotated car positions. Post processing then extracts the individual car locations, and a car count is constructed from that for each car park area. While the process is automated, manual checks are also done to check the accuracy.

The dataset currently tracks a number of publicly traded companies, as well as a number of additional private companies. While there are a few datasets for the car parks of similar retailers based in the United States, such as Walmart, at the time of writing it is less common to find ones that are specifically focused on Europe. For obvious reasons such an approach is not going to be as useful for purely online-focused retailers. Instead, for those types of firms we would need to use other approaches, like examining consumer transaction data.

The focus of our study will be on the retail outlets attached to firms that are publicly traded on equities markets. For each company, the raw data provided by Geospatial Insight consists of the company name, the associated equities' Bloomberg ticker, as well as the name and location of the retail outlet car park. There is a timestamp for each observation, with the area of the car park and the number of cars counted. The dataset is relatively sparse, since we do not necessarily have observations every single day. As we might expect from satellite data, the observations on a particular day are not all snapped at the same time. Given the way that satellites sweep over the sky, they will be covering different parts of the earth at different times. It is also the case that the number of car parks photographed can vary significantly at any day. There can also be issues associated with cloud cover. Chapter 8 presented a case study of how to impute missing points in satellite imagery of car parks.

We go through several steps to compute an indicator based on car counts:

- We compute the total amount of area photographed and the number of cars counted during that period on a rolling basis.
- In order to adjust for the fact that the images will vary in terms of the car parks being photographed for a certain retailer, we compute the ratio of the cars counted divided by the total car park area photographed. If we do not do this, then we will end up overcounting those days when more images happened to be collected.

- Obviously, there are other ways to combine the data. At present we are ignoring any store-by-store differences, and we instead aggregate all these observations into one variable. We could instead try to combine the car count data at the store level first, and then include these as separate variables in any model. We could also try to classify stores according to the relative size of their car parks, and aggregate them for "small," "medium," and "large" stores, using these car counts as different variables in our model.

Our current approach does take into account the relative size of the car parks for each store (as proxied by the total car park area). However, it does not use any other metadata associated with the store, such as location. We also do not bucket specific stores together by other metrics, such as the car park size. The difficulty with aggregating at a very high granularity is that our dataset might become too sparse. Hence, any sort of bucketing would need to take this into account. It is also the case that the irregularity of snapshots might pose problems. For example, it is unlikely to be a good approach to compare a specific store with snapshots taken at very different times of day. Other issues such as cloud cover could also prove more problematic for this type of approach.

Given our hypothesis that car count data can be a good proxy for earnings, we can take a rolling average that matches with the official earning announcements for each firm. This will also help to smooth out the sparseness of the data. Typically, a publicly traded firm will have earnings announcements at quarterly intervals, twice a year or annually. The benefit of our car count dataset is that we will have it as soon as the period has finished, well before the official announcement. It has been well known for many decades that equities experience a post-earnings announcement drift, so if earnings are better than expected, typically the stock goes higher in the immediate aftermath and falls on disappointing earnings (Ball & Brown, 1968).

Hence, if our car count measure can be used to enhance earnings forecasts, we can potentially trade the associated equity around earnings announcements. If we forecast higher earnings than the market consensus, we buy the stock before the announcement and take profit afterwards. Alternatively, our car-count-enhanced earnings forecast could potentially be used as an additional factor in cross-sectional long/short equity baskets.

In our case, the European retailers within our car park dataset generally report semi-annually. Therefore, we create 6-month rolling averages of our adjusted car count measure. We can then snap the value that corresponds to the reported earnings periods. A major benefit of using the car count data is that it is available as soon as the earnings period ends. This contrasts to the reporting of earnings, where there is likely to be a lag of a few weeks. The earnings consensus is also available before the actual official earnings announcement. However, it is likely that it will change in the leadup to the announcement, as analysts update their estimates. Hence, earnings consensus estimates are unlikely to give you as early an indication as measures purely based on car count.

However, does our car counting measure have any relationship with the actual earnings per share announcement and the earnings consensus, as compiled by

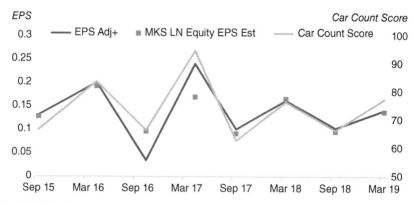

FIGURE 13.2   Car count for Marks & Spencer versus earnings (actual and estimate).
Source: Based on data from Geospatial Insights, Bloomberg.

Bloomberg, for example? Figure 13.2 plots our car count measure for Marks & Spencer, against both the announced earnings per share and the estimate. At least in this stylized example, it does appear that our car count measure derived from satellite imagery of Marks & Spencer's car park does appear to be strongly correlated with both the consensus estimate and the actual announcement. Admittedly, we have relatively few data points in our history. One way to help expand our study is to look at more companies, which we shall do later.

Does using the car count data have additional insight compared to using the consensus? To check this historically, we look at several companies in the dataset, where we also have a full set of Bloomberg consensus data. We create several full sample linear regressions, to help predict the earnings per share, which is our dependent variable y. The first regression uses only consensus data as its independent variable x_1. The second regression uses the car count score x_2 as its independent variable. The last regression uses both consensus data x_1 and car count score x_2 as its independent variables. In Figure 13.3-2, we report the adjusted R^2 of these regressions for several UK retailers.

We see that, in all cases, adding car count data to consensus helps to increase the adjusted R^2, compared to using the consensus alone. This suggests that there might indeed be value in using car counts as an additional variable to consensus when forecasting earnings.

Of course, there are some caveats to our analysis that we need to mention. The data history in the study is relatively small from 2015 to 2019. In Figure 13.3, we have only three companies. We could source consensus estimates from other sources to help add other companies within the Geospatial Insight dataset into our study. Furthermore, another caveat is that we are trying to use the data to help forecast only a handful of points and then calculating our in-sample regressions with a very small sample set. However, as history accumulates, this is going to be less of a problem.

We have seen that adding car count data to consensus estimates can be helpful for explaining earnings per share. What if we explore combining car count measures with

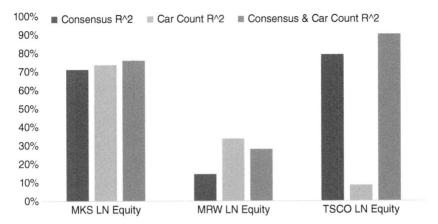

FIGURE 13.3 Regressing consensus and car count data with earnings per share for the period September 2015–March 2019.
Source: Based on data from Geospatial Insight, Bloomberg.

another alternative dataset, such as news? Furthermore, this will enable us to compare car counts with news. As with car counts, news-based measures will be available as soon as the earnings period ends, rather than being lagged, or only being fully updated close to actual earnings release. This contrasts to consensus data that is only going to be fully updated very close to the earnings call. If we want an earlier forecast for earnings, we need to focus on those datasets that are available well before the actual earnings announcement.

For a news-based measure, we use indicators that record the number of news articles from Bloomberg News for given publicly traded equity tickers. The indicators are split between the number of positive and negative news articles published for each company. We compute a rolling average of the number of positive stories minus the number of negative stories, which corresponds to the length of report period to create a news sentiment metric.

We snap the value of the rolling news metric indicator at the end of each reporting period. Hence, the approach is somewhat similar to the way we treat our car count measure. We expand our universe for all the publicly traded companies in the Retail-Watch dataset, even those for which we do not have a full set of consensus data, given that we are not using that in this instance.

We again create several full sample linear regressions, to help explain the actual earnings per share, which is our dependent variable y. The first regression uses only our news indicator as its independent variable x_1. The second regression uses only our car count as its independent variable x_1. The last regression uses both the news indicator x_1 and the car count score x_2 as its independent variables. In Figure 13.4, we report the adjusted R^2 of these regressions for a number of European retailers. We note that since publication, Geospatial Insight have added a large number of additional tickers to the RetailWatch dataset.

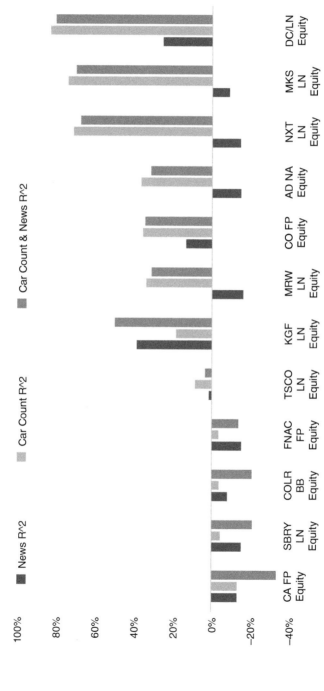

FIGURE 13.4 Regressing news sentiment and car count data with earnings per share for the period September 2015–March 2019.
Source: Based on data from Geospatial Insights, Bloomberg.

For a small number of companies such as Carrefour (i.e. CA FP Equity), both car count and news sentiment metrics have quite low adjusted R^2. There can be many explanations for this. It might be the case that many customers visit their stores by public transport, or indeed that news sentiment is relatively neutral; hence it is difficult to extract a directional signal.

In the majority of cases the adjusted R^2 of car counts is higher than the adjusted R^2 news sentiment, when regressing each variable separately against earnings per share. We find that, in general, adding news does not help to increase the adjusted R^2 of car counts alone, other than Kingfisher (KGF LN Equity). Later in the book we will show that there are instances where news can be used to trade markets profitably, in particular FX, on a historical basis. However, this is typically by aggregating the news on a shorter time horizon, rather than using it to forecast EPS by looking at it over a very long period of time (6 months).

In summary, we have used relatively simple techniques for aggregating the car count data and even with these very few basic and intuitive steps we have seen that the car count method shows promise. Further work could include using the same technique but on other datasets, covering, for example, other developed economies like the United States and Canada. Also given that the dataset reports for individual car parks for each company, it would be worth investigating whether certain car parks act as leading indicators for the broader company. We have also noted that augmenting the car count indicator with other metrics such as the consensus earnings estimates or news sentiment–based indicators can increase in certain cases the overall explanatory power when it comes to understanding earnings per share. However, the lack of plentiful history in the dataset impedes drawing strong statistical conclusions for the time being.

It is also worth exploring whether consensus earnings estimates can be combined with other alternative datasets (in addition to news as we have done), such as consumer transaction data or mobile phone location, to create more accurate forecasts for earnings. In practice, all these measures are only taking partial samples of consumer spending patterns or general sentiment toward a firm. Hence, by increasing the size of our sample using more alternative datasets, we are likely to increase accuracy provided the samples do not totally overlap.

13.4 MEASURING CHINESE PMI MANUFACTURING WITH SATELLITE DATA

In Chapter 12, we discussed PMI data at length, noting that this survey-based "soft" data can be a leading indicator for GDP, which is "hard data." One question we may wish to ask is whether we can create a leading indicator for PMI data using another alternative dataset, such as satellite imagery. Such an estimate is likely to be available before PMI data is compiled and released.

For certain types of economic activity, like industrial activity, it seems intuitive that a physical imprint could be left behind that can be profitably exploited. After all, manufacturing processes often require the ingesting of raw materials, which are likely to be stockpiled, in order to create finished goods that can also be tracked. This contrasts to an industry like finance, which is less likely to leave behind a physical imprint as an exhaust of its activity. Also, for some parts of the world, official economic data might not be as reliable or may be released with very large lags. Hence these alternative ways of measuring economic activity could be particularly useful, as we already discussed at length.

Eagle Alpha (2018) discusses the usage of satellite imagery by SpaceKnow to estimate Chinese PMI manufacturing data. SpaceKnow tracks specific signs of industrial activity, such as new construction sites or the accumulation of inventory. Over the 14-year history, 2.2 billion observations have been collected to generate the dataset over an area of over half a million square kilometers.

The Normalized Difference Vegetation Index (NDVI) has been created to understand how much vegetation covers the Earth's surface (Weier & Herring, 2000). Vegetation absorbs visible wavelengths of light, for use in photosynthesis, but tends to reflect infrared light to reduce the chances of overheating. By contrast, soil tends to absorb less visible light. Clearly, as a result, vegetation tends to appear lighter to the naked eye while soil is darker. The Enhanced Vegetation Index (EVI) works in a similar way but corrects for distortions in reflected light because of particles in the air.

SpaceKnow uses a similar approach in their algorithm, albeit for identifying the coverage of man-made structures as opposed to vegetation. The general idea behind their algorithm is that cement and steel reflect on the surface light of different wavelengths in a specific way. Hence, just like with the NDVI, it is possible to identify how much of the surface is covered with cement and steel structures. The algorithm also adjusts for various atmospheric factors that are likely to impact the image, such as cloud cover or aerosols. The algorithm compares the images from over 6000 industrial facilities to create SpaceKnow's satellite manufacturing index (SMI). The SMI is released every Monday, Wednesday, and Friday with a 10-day lag, compared to both official and Caixin PMI indices, which are published monthly with a 1-month lag.

The focus of China's official PMI manufacturing is larger firms, including state-owned enterprises. Caixin's PMI, on the other hand, focuses on small and medium-sized firms. Figure 13.5 shows China's official PMI manufacturing index, Caixin PMI manufacturing, alongside SpaceKnow's satellite manufacturing index. At least from a cursory glance, there does appear to be a good relationship between SMI and the other the other PMIs, despite the fact that the source data is, of course, very different. The correlation between SMI and China's official PMI manufacturing is 64% in our sample.

From a trading perspective, if we are forecasting an economic indicator, such as PMI, we might be interested in understanding how it compares with consensus forecasts, compiled by firms such as Bloomberg from a number of market economists, usually in sell-side firms.

At least in the very short term, the market reacts to surprises versus market expectations. If the market is already expecting a very bad number, and the release is indeed a very bad number, it is likely that the market reaction will be muted. We illustrate this point in Figure 15.5, where we give an example of how USD/JPY reacts

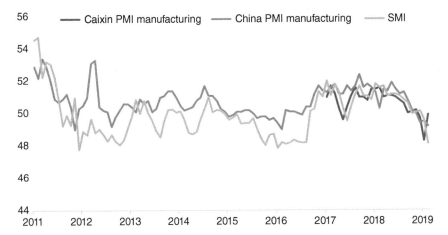

FIGURE 13.5 China SpaceKnow's satellite manufacturing index versus official Chinese PMI manufacturing and Caixin PMI manufacturing.
Source: Based on data from SpaceKnow, Bloomberg.

to the surprise in nonfarm payrolls. In this instance, the relationship is broadly linear between short-term returns and the surprise (at least for relatively small surprises). Hence, it suggests that if we are able to understand the nature of the data surprise, we might be able to monetize it.

Does the SMI give us any further information compared to using the consensus forecast in isolation? Our focus is on forecasting the official China PMI manufacturing dataset, given that it has a much longer history available both for the actual data and the consensus forecast from Bloomberg.

In order to answer our question, we create a hybrid model. Our model uses a rolling linear regression, as seen in Equation (13.1), which has an expanding window. Our independent variables are the consensus forecast x_1 and the SMI x_2. Our dependent variable y is the actual Chinese PMI manufacturing data release, β_0 is the constant of the regression, and ε is the error. Thus:

$$y = \beta_0 + \beta_1 x_1 + \beta_2 x_2 + \varepsilon \qquad (13.1)$$

We use last month's coefficients from this model to create a forecast of the current month of Chinese PMI manufacturing. We use current month points for SMI and the consensus forecast for our independent variables.

In Figure 13.6, we plot the surprises in China PMI manufacturing versus the consensus from Bloomberg, SMI and also our hybrid model, during our sample, which runs from 2011 to early 2019. The worst performer is SMI, which has a mean absolute error of 1.05. The mean absolute error for the consensus surprise is 0.42, which is virtually the same as the hybrid model.

We might therefore question why we would use the satellite data, if the consensus model provides virtually the same mean absolute data with or without including it. We

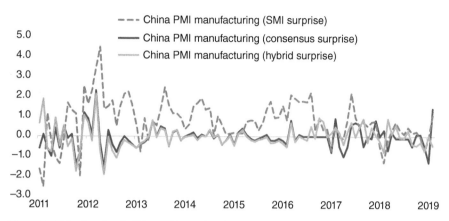

FIGURE 13.6 Surprises in China PMI manufacturing versus consensus, SMI and hybrid.
Source: Based on data from SpaceKnow, Bloomberg.

noted earlier that the satellite data is available ten days before the actual China PMI manufacturing release. We have used the final consensus number, which is updated just before the actual release. The consensus number will often change as we approach the actual economic release, as economists update their forecast in the survey. Hence, it is likely that ten days before the event we would not have a fully updated consensus number whereas we would have the SMI data point. Furthermore, the SMI data is also published on a high-frequency basis, every Monday, Tuesday, and Wednesday. By contrast, China PMI is only published once a month.

It also is possible that in practice we could improve upon the hybrid model by adding more variables to reduce the mean absolute error. In other words, it may be possible to augment observations made from existing datasets, rather than using them as a replacement. We would, of course, caution that mean absolute error should not be the only metric by which we judge a forecast. We could also try to backtest a trading strategy based on the SMI indicator, too, as another way to test its value. Furthermore, we could try to use SMI to model other indicators, in particular hard data, which are released later.

13.5 SUMMARY

Data derived from satellite imaging and aerial photography has been used for many years, particularly in the military sphere. In more recent years, alternative datasets have been developed by using satellite and aerial photography for investors. We have described several such datasets, including Geospatial Insight's dataset for car counts in the parking lots of European retailers, which we have used to estimate earnings per share data with good results. We also showed how using several datasets together could help to improve the explanatory power of a model for estimating earnings per share (for example, here with news sentiment data on the same retail stocks).

Key to all these image-based datasets is the use of efficient structuring techniques to convert the satellite image into a more usable, usually numerical form that can be more easily consumed by investors. Techniques such as convolutional neural networks have proved very effective for tasks such as object detection in images (see Chapter 4, for a further discussion on using machine learning to structure images).

However, the usage of satellite data as an alternative dataset is a pretty recent phenomenon that translates into short-length datasets. This issue is, of course, temporary, and soon we will have enough imagery data to make statistically robust models and conclusions.

CHAPTER 14

Location Data

14.1 INTRODUCTION

Satellites have not only had a profound impact on the ability to produce imagery, as discussed in Chapter 13. They have also made it easier to find our location using GPS (global positioning system) and similar systems like Galileo. GPS capability is now built into many devices installed in cars, ships, and airplanes, as well as in mobile phones.

The location of mobile phones can also be tracked by triangulation of a mobile phone's signal from different mobile phone transmitters. This can be particularly important within buildings where GPS might be inaccessible. Location data from mobile phones can be collected in a number of ways, including through the use of different mobile phone apps.

There are many examples of how location data can be useful for investors. Specifically, in this chapter, we will look at research on the movement of ships to monitor the seaborne exports of crude oil. Later, we will talk about how mobile phone location data can be used to understand retail activity. We will also discuss a study that examines taxi ride data in New York City to the New York Fed around the time of the FOMC meetings to shed light on the flow of market information around these periods. There is also a section on using corporate jet activity as a leading indicator for M&A activity.

14.2 SHIPPING DATA TO TRACK CRUDE OIL SUPPLIES

It is possible to obtain global trade statistics using sources like UN Comtrade or from national government statistics agencies. They will typically be standardized using specific conventions, so we can easily measure the flow of trade between various countries for all sorts of goods or commodities. There are standard codes for each specific type of trade such as crude oil and some of these codes can be very granular. The difficulty with trade statistics obtainable from UN Comtrade and similar organizations is that they are not updated very frequently. Hence, there can often be a large lag in their publication that varies across countries. One alternative is to look at the voyages of ships carrying goods or commodities between countries, then aggregating this data to create a proxy of UN Comtrade and similar datasets. Historically, this information has usually been collated by ship brokers but it is difficult to do it at high frequency.

However, with the advent of AIS (automated identification system), high-frequency monitoring of vessel traffic has become more feasible. Adland et al. (2017) discuss using AIS data to understand flows of crude oil. We will quote some results from their paper in this section and summarize their results. All vessels with a gross tonnage of 300 tonnes or more and all passenger vessels have AIS transmitters. These AIS messages record the location of a ship, speed, and current course, alongside various details such as the ship name, the vessel type, draught, destination of the current voyage, and so on. It is possible to collect these signals to create a history of ship movements. Receivers can be land-based beacons, those carried by air to sweep the oceans periodically, or satellite-based receivers. There is obviously likely to be a discrepancy in how frequently a vessel's position is tracked, depending on its proximity to a receiver. The AIS messages sent by ships out in the open ocean and only being tracked by a satellite AIS receiver will only be picked up every couple of hours. Hence, the only way to evaluate their position at a higher-frequency basis would be to infer the position from the last available AIS message from the speed and direction of motion. This large lag in receiving messages by satellite AIS receivers contrasts to land-based AIS receivers, which can pick up signals of ships within their range on a real-time basis.

Raw AIS datasets can be very large and difficult to decipher. There are also complications in trying to understand if certain fields in AIS data have been deliberately faked, such as the destination of the current voyage. Abbreviations might also be used that need to be correctly entity-matched. Button (2019) notes that there are instances of AIS data where captains have used multiple ways to write Rotterdam, including R'dam, Rdam, Roterdam, and R-dam. In summary, AIS data requires a large amount of structuring to convert them into a more usable form, if we are to use it to answer questions such as quantifying the flow of commodities by sea.

A number of data firms, such as IHS Markit, have data products based upon AIS data. Typically, data firms spend a lot of time to structure the AIS data, summarizing the most important parts of the dataset from a trader's perspective. Data firms will usually add tags such as the port of departure and arrival for each ship voyage, alongside the commodity they are carrying and a number of other details. They summarize these details in a number of records available on a regular basis (e.g. daily). In order to define ports, it is necessary to do geo-fencing of the maps to point out these areas. It is possible to make an educated guess about the commodities carried by ships by using draught data and having an understanding of the relative density of each commodity.

Tankers are specifically designed to carry crude oil and they cannot carry other commodities. Similarly, only certain types of ships can carry LPG (liquefied petroleum gas). For dry bulk ships, it is more difficult to understand what they are carrying (e.g. coal and grain). More granular data based upon the type of berths those ships use to offload are needed. The port authority will have this berth-level data. GPS data might not be sufficient to ascertain precisely which berth has been used (and you would also need to geo-fence every single berth in order to do this). Certain berths can only accommodate certain types of commodities.

This data can also be combined with other datasets, such as port agent reports. This structured data can then be aggregated to understand trade flows for certain goods and commodities. Typically, the final structured shipping dataset will be orders of magnitude smaller than the raw AIS data collected.

This approach might be particularly amenable for commodities that are typically carried by ships, such as crude oil. Admittedly, this will fail to capture trade flows via other methods. This would include crude oil carried by a pipeline without any seaborne leg of the route. It can be problematic for ships that are carrying multiple types of goods, such as those in containers, where the precise contents are not declared. It should be noted that such lower-level data can sometimes be available in certain cases, albeit through third parties. For example, in the United States, this data would be recorded in the Bill of Lading, as pointed out by Adland et al. (2017), but not every other country has an equivalent dataset. It is also tricky to track any sea-to-sea transfers.

IHS Markit's crude oil shipping dataset (IHS Markit, 2019) does model such transfers. Their data set shows the activity of ships and their journeys taking into account journeys that may have multiple legs. They use over 2600 AIS detectors, both on land and some based on satellites, to monitor ship movements combined with location data for ports and particular berths.

IHS Markit also aggregates crude oil import/export information. Crude oil flows are grouped by product type (over 300 variants) and by geography, from regional to port level. At any particular time, while oil might be stored in tanks on land, it is also the case that a substantial amount of oil is being carried at sea. Indeed, some ships might have stopped moving because they are essentially floating storage. IHS Markit provide data that indicates the volume of oil currently at sea. They also provide forecasts of crude oil flows up to 5 weeks ahead based on a number of alternative datasets, including satellite imagery.

Adland et al. (2017) use crude oil data that has been aggregated by another firm, Clipper Data. Their data is derived from AIS tracking of ship voyages with port agent reports (provided by Inchscape Shipping services). Certain voyages such as domestic journeys are excluded from consideration in the paper. In order to gauge how precise the AIS estimated exports are, the authors compare it with official oil export data from JODI (Joint Organizations Data Initiative Oil World Database), which are collected from a number of sources, including Eurostat, OPEC, and IEA. We quote the crude oil exports for the top 20 seaborne crude exporters from Adland et al. (2017) in Figure 14.1, for both AIS-derived and JODI figures.

As Adland et al. note, there are wide disparities in the accuracy of the data across the various countries. We shall try to summarize a few of the reasons they give for this. They note, for example, that some countries without any oil production appear to

Millions of barrels	2013 AIS	2013 JODI	2013 %diff	2014 AIS	2014 JODI	2014 %diff	2015 AIS	2015 JODI	2015 %diff
Saudi Arabia	2486	2753	−9.7	2326	2592	−10.2	2352	2698	−12.8
Russia	1360	1565	−13.1	1282	1640	−21.8	1393	1787	−22
UAE	835	945	−11.7	937	934	0.4	941	468	101.1
Iraq	688	867	−20.7	868	920	−5.7	980	1097	10.6
Venezuela	667	468	42.8	698	539	29.5	713	530	34.6
Nigeria	584	755	−22.6	729	765	−4.6	709	777	8.8
Kuwait	663	751	−11.8	672	730	−7.9	681	661	3
Angola	591	595	−0.8	572	577	−0.9	598	607	1.6
Iran	352	606	−42	422	506	−16.6	439	496	11.6
Mexico	417	464	−10.2	410	445	−7.9	413	455	9.3
Qatar	436	218	99.5	401	217	84.7	406	179	126.5
Norway	206	437	−52.9	373	439	−15	339	451	24.8
Turkey	292	–	249	–		368		–	
Oman	271	306	−11.4	280	294	−4.6	307	287	7
Egypt	266	35	657.7	253	43	492.4	281	57	396.7
Colombia	245	257	−4.6	267	264	1.2	263	156	68.8
UK	224	224	0.3	234	208	12.6	237	217	9.2
Brazil	133	133	−0.4	189	189	−0.1	228	269	15
Algeria	190	229	−17	170	206	−17.5	165	193	14.7
Neth. Antilles	142	–	161	–		189		–	
Total top 20	11,047	11,610	−4.8	11,493	11,506	−0.1	12,002	11,384	5.4

Source: Based on data from Clipper Data, JODI.

FIGURE 14.1   Comparing AIS versus official crude oil exports.

be oil exporters, such as the Netherlands Antilles (which are major staging posts for transshipment and storage of oil). Countries that mainly export oil by pipeline such as Canada do not appear at all, as we might expect.

On an aggregate basis, the differences are relatively small, even if there are some big disparities with individual countries. This suggests that AIS-based methods can be good for getting an idea of total exports by seaborne methods. Of course, for understanding specific country exports, we might need to augment with other datasets.

From a trading perspective, having a high-frequency picture for quantifying crude oil supply is likely to be advantageous, compared to having to use datasets such as UN Comtrade data, which are heavily lagged. While the example from Adland et al. (2017) we have discussed focuses on crude oil, it is likely that a similar approach can be used for other commodities. In particular, dry bulk commodities like grain, iron ore, and coal might be more amenable to this type of analysis, given that they cannot be carried by pipelines.

While our focus here has been on using shipping data to understand flows of crude oil, there are many other potential uses for AIS datasets. For example, the shipping datasets from Clipper Data have also been used to help forecast future freight rates for oil tankers (Olsen & Fonseca, 2017). Also, Button (2019) discusses how Marine-Traffic's AIS-derived dataset can be used to understand imbalances in the supply and demand of certain ships for freight, which can be useful for forecasting freight rates.

14.3 MOBILE PHONE LOCATION DATA TO UNDERSTAND RETAIL ACTIVITY

There are several ways to track people at a certain location. If we want to physically track people, we need to have a sensor installed locally. This could be a CCTV-based solution through which we count people in an automated fashion via recorded video or infra-red sensors. If we were able to install such sensors extensively, we would have a very large sample and good coverage. However, this approach is likely to be challenging unless we own all the venues of interest and we have the right to install such devices.

Another approach is to track devices carried by people, typically their mobile phones. Wi-Fi can be used to track individuals without the need to install anything on their phones. However, each Wi-Fi device has a unique MAC address and potentially this could fall under GDPR because individuals might be identifiable (Cobb, 2018). Such tracking does not require specific software to be explicitly installed on a phone. Hence, it is likely to be difficult for users to explicitly opt-in and consent to such Wi-Fi tracking.

We mentioned that mobile phone location can be tracked in a number of different ways. One way is via mobile phone apps that people have installed on their phone with location tracking enabled. This data can be recorded if users have explicitly accepted the opt-in on their apps. The position can be gauged using GPS, in combination with other measures such as distance from mobile phone towers and Wi-Fi access points. Obviously, such an approach requires that we have a sufficient number of app installations in order to make a sample large enough to be representative of the broader population of consumers that we wish to model. We must also take into account that some users will choose not to opt in to tracking.

As with most alternative datasets, in order to make such datasets usable for investors, a large amount of structuring is necessary. Simply looking at location data derived from mobile phones in isolation is not likely to provide many usable signals for investors. It is important to be able to combine datasets containing location data with databases of business addresses. It is also necessary to have sufficient geo-fencing for each address of interest and further metadata such as the business hours. From this we can identify which location an individual is visiting. The geo-fencing also needs to be recorded in a point-in-time fashion, because the nature of location can change over time; for example, new stores may open and other stores may close. For obvious reasons, it will be harder to ascertain whether individuals have visited smaller geo-fenced locations, like neighborhood stores, compared to larger areas, such as a theme park. It is also necessary to exclude individuals who are simply passing by the geo-fenced location, such as by car or on foot.

From an investor perspective, we might be interested in specific stores to see if they lead other stores of the same brand. Or we might simply want to aggregate the footfall, the number of people who have visited a store, across a specific store brand. We also need to do entity matching between brands and their parent companies that we want to trade and the associated ticker. As well as footfall, other variables of interest from location data that could be recorded include the time they spent there, so-called "dwell time." If customers are returning and spending more time in a store, then it could be a good sign for an uptick in revenue. By contrast, if there is a large amount of footfall but the dwell time is minimal, it suggests that customers are not spending a sufficient time to purchase any goods or services.

As with other datasets, it is important to note that the panel of the mobile phone location dataset is unlikely to be comprehensive, and is instead a sample. It is important that any sample be large enough to be representative. Furthermore, it is important that any observations are properly normalized. For example, any footfall metrics should not increase simply because the sample size is increased and should instead be adjusted for shifts in the panel size. In addition, normalization needs to account for other demographic, geographical, and behavioral biases. We do not want to overcount individuals who happen to be emitting more location data simply because they tend to be heavy users of apps. Typically, an app will record location information more often when they are actually using the app, as opposed to when it is running in the background.

It is also possible to join such a dataset with other retail-focused datasets to cross-reference our observations on retail traffic. These can include, for example, car counts from satellite imagery, which we discussed earlier. We could also join with consumer transaction data, which can give us more granularity on the actual spend per visitor. In addition, datasets related to sentiment can also be joined, as discussed further below.

Clearly, before any such data is distributed externally, it needs to be sufficiently anonymized and aggregated. From an investor perspective, aggregated data is more important in any case. While a major focus is likely to be on retailers, mobile phone tracking could be used for other purposes, such as tracking activity in industrial firms, such as the number of workers entering a particular facility.

14.3.1 Trading REIT ETF Using Mobile Phone Location Data

Thasos (2019) discusses the Thasos Mall Foot Traffic Index, which provides year-on-year changes in customer visits collated from mobile phone location data and is updated on a daily basis. The index examines visits to around 4000 properties that are owned or managed by the largest retail estate investment trusts in the United States. As a first step, we plot the Thasos Mall Foot Traffic YoY index against monthly official US retail sales YoY economic data in Figure 14.2. As we might expect, there does appear to be a correlation between the two datasets (21%). The benefit of using a metric such as Thasos Mall Foot Traffic index, however, is that it is available on a very timely basis compared to official data such as US retail sales.

If we calculate the correlation of the Thasos Mall Foot Traffic Index (YoY) with YoY returns from XRT,[1] the correlation is 63%. XRT can be seen as a way of getting exposure to the retail sector, which is being tracked by Thasos Mall Foot Traffic index. Thasos notes that the differences between these correlations likely suggests that the Thasos Mall Foot Traffic YoY index has orthogonal information, which is useful for

---

[1] SPDR S&P Retail ETF (XRT) is made up of large US retail estate investment trusts.

FIGURE 14.2 Thasos Foot Traffic Index YoY versus US Retail Sales YoY.
Source: Based on data from Thasos, Bloomberg.

understanding price moves in XRT, which is not contained in US retail sales data. The paper later presents a trading rule that uses Thasos index to trade XRT.

We follow Thasos (2019) by creating a trading rule based on the Thasos index to trade XRT. However, in our case, we create a somewhat a simpler trading rule. We shall apply the following trading rule:

- Go long XRT, when Thasos YoY index is above its 20D SMA.
- Go short XRT, when Thasos YoY index is below its 20D SMA.

The rationale is that if we have more customer visits, it like likely that revenue is higher, and hence the equity should outperform. We assume that the Thasos YoY data is available at the same close that we are trading. In Figure 14.3, we present the cumulative returns for such a trading strategy, including transaction costs. However, we do not include additional costs such as funding when going short. Alongside this active trading strategy, we also present the returns for a long-only XRT position. The active trading strategy has an information ratio of 0.96 while the long-only strategy has an information ratio of zero. Furthermore, returns are considerably higher, and drawdowns are significantly lower for the active Thasos-based strategy. This suggests that at least historically, Thasos's Mall Foot Traffic index derived from mobile phone location data does provide some useful insight for trading XRT on an active basis.

Note that in practice, we might need to lag the signal given delays in data processing and the time it takes to generate the signal. If we introduce a lag of one day for trading, it reduces returns to around 6% and the information ratio is cut to 0.35. We might also argue that a longer lag is necessary, because it can take time for the market to incorporate the data into prices. If we take a month lag, the information ratio is also reduced (0.6). However, these metrics still outperform the long-only benchmark by a significant amount, even with these various lags applied.

The visitation data from Thasos (2018) is also available on property level. This is of particular relevance to private equity investors who are directly invested in certain

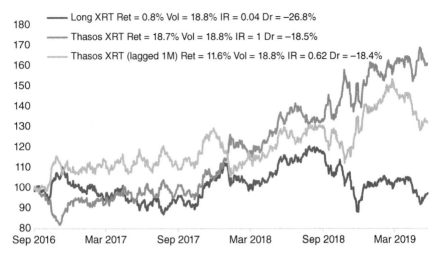

FIGURE 14.3   Trading XRT based on Thasos Mall Foot Traffic index.
Source: Based on data from Thasos, Bloomberg.

properties, or are seeking to invest in those properties. Also, from the perspective of an equity investor, we may find that certain malls are leading indicators for the broader health of the industry. Hence, having more granular data can help us forecast broader trends better.

In Figure 14.4, we plot the YoY changes in visits to two shopping malls that are relatively close to one another in California at Century City and Westside Pavilion. Alongside that we flag when various large stores have opened (1, 3, and 4) and also when they have closed (2 and 3). We see that the opening of new large stores in Century City was accompanied by a rise in visits. However, the rise began to tail off after this period. By contrast, in Westside Pavilion, visits began to drop over the same period, which was accompanied by store closures.

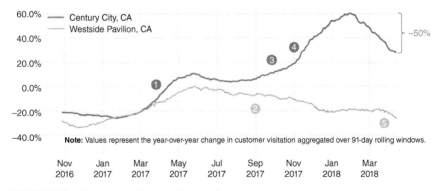

FIGURE 14.4   Comparing visits to particular malls.
Source: Thasos.

As well as visitation data, the paper also discusses other metrics derived from mobile location data, such as the distance traveled by visitors to the malls, which can be used as a measure of how much of a draw a mall is. Perhaps unsurprisingly, over the same period, the average distance traveled to visit Century City picked up, while it fell for Westside Pavilion.

14.3.2 Estimating Earnings per Share with Mobile Phone Location Data

We have seen how mobile phone data can be used to trade REIT-based ETFs. In this section, we will again use mobile phone data. This data is particularly applicable for those firms where a significant part of the customer transactions is done in person, as opposed to online.

In this instance, we use a more granular dataset from Thasos, which is broken down into visits for specific US retail outlets and restaurants. The dataset we use consists of daily data between 2016 and 2018. These companies include well-known consumer companies such as McDonald's and Walmart. In all cases, these firms report their earnings on a quarterly basis. We create a footfall score, which is an average of the daily observations of Thasos data across each quarter, which corresponds to an earnings period. The end points of this quarter period vary between the companies. The data from Thasos has been normalized in a number of ways to take into account all the various biases that could be present in location data. Typically, the panel in the dataset will be a small proportion of the entire sample (i.e. all individuals visiting a store). It needs to be normalized to make sure that the panel is representative in terms of various characteristics, such as the age or income group of visitors.

In Figure 14.5, we plot a stylistic example showing consensus earnings per share estimates, sourced from Bloomberg against actual reported earnings and the footfall score. We see that the footfall score, consensus earnings estimates are all heavily correlated (85% and 98% respectively) to actual earnings. At least in this example, it does appear that footfall is likely a useful metric for estimating earnings per share.

The next step is to see whether we see similar behavior for all companies in our dataset (from 2016 to 2018). To test this, we do a number of linear regressions with our

FIGURE 14.5 Comparing Walmart's actual earnings per share against consensus and footfall.
Source: Based on data from Thasos, Bloomberg.

dependent variable being the actual earnings per share, and our independent variables are:

- Consensus estimates
- Footfall score
- Consensus estimates and footfall score

For each of the three regressions, we report the adjusted R^2 and plot these findings in Figure 14.6. The adjusted R^2 is used, to help adjust for the number of variables in each regression and data points. We find that for some companies, such as Darden Restaurants (DRI US Equity), the consensus estimates exhibit a very high adjusted R^2, suggesting that the market is very good at forecasting these numbers. One possible explanation could be that many of the contributors to consensus estimates are using alternative datasets to help generate their forecasts. Adding footfall into the regression does not change the adjusted R^2 much. While the consensus number appears to be very good at explaining the actual earnings per share, it is not likely to be fully updated by all the contributors until much closer to the actual earnings announcement, as we mentioned in Chapter 13 on satellite data. This obviously contrasts to the mobile phone location footfall data that is available with minimal lag at the end of the earnings quarter and well before the official earnings release announcement.

Are there ways we can improve the adjusted R^2 of our footfall regression with other alternative datasets that are also available very early? It will also enable us to compare the explanatory power of footfall versus these other alternative datasets and to get good visibility before the consensus estimates were updated closer to the official release.

In Chapter 13, we used news sentiment data derived from news articles on individual stocks to see how it compared with car count data for European retailers. We used the reported number of positive and negative articles and we took an average of these for each earnings period as our news score. We will try the same approach here, augmenting our footfall score with a news score. In addition, we will also look at data that shows the number of positive and negative tweets on each company. Our Twitter score will be constructed in the same way as our news score, taking an average of positive and negative tweets over the corresponding earnings period.

To understand how beneficial it is to combine news, footfall, and Twitter data to explain the actual earnings number, we will do several regressions. As in the earlier regressions, our dependent variable is the reported earnings per share. Our five different regressions have the following independent variables:

- News score
- Footfall score
- Twitter score
- Footfall and news scores
- Footfall, news, and Twitter scores

We report the adjusted R^2 for each of these five regressions for all the US companies in our dataset in Figure 14.7. For some firms, such as Walmart (WMT US

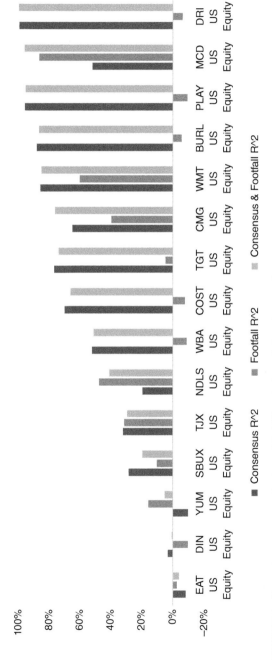

FIGURE 14.6 Regressing consensus estimates and footfall against reported earnings per share.
Source: Based on data from Thasos, Bloomberg.

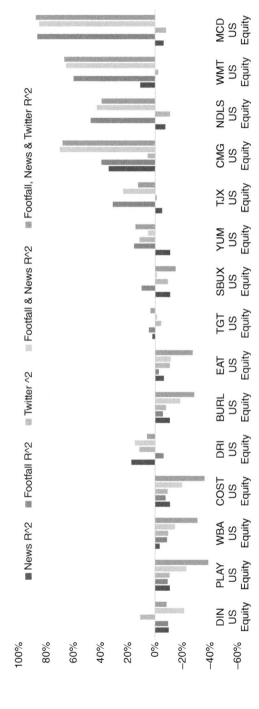

FIGURE 14.7 Regressing footfall, news, and Twitter data against reported earnings per share.
Source: Based on data from Thasos, Bloomberg.

Equity) and McDonald's (MCD US Equity), the adjusted R^2 shows a strong relationship between reported EPS and footfall. In most cases, the addition of news and Twitter-based sources does not seem to help increase the adjusted R^2.

For other firms in our study, we find that the adjusted R^2 values are not significant, using the various alternative datasets. We should note that later in the book, we will look at other use cases for news and social media data, which have been generally profitable historically. In general, these tend to involve looking at much shorter time frames, which are less susceptible to alpha decay.

In practice, if we wanted to create a tradable strategy out of these observations, we would not be able to use a full sample regression. Instead, we would need to use some sort of expanding window (or rolling regression) in order to estimate coefficients of any model. Also, we should note that if we want to model EPS in a trading environment, we would likely augment existing models with alternative data, as opposed to using alternative data in isolation. We could also try trading more high-frequency trading rules, using this retailer footfall data, similar to the REIT-based rule we looked at earlier using mall mobile phone footfall.

14.4 TAXI RIDE DATA AND NEW YORK FED MEETINGS

Taxis are often equipped with GPS devices to track their locations. Could this data be useful for market participants when aggregated together? One readily available free source of taxi ride data is available from NYC Taxi & Limousine Commission on an annualized basis. It lists details about each individual trip on for-hire taxis and also services like Uber and Lyft in New York City. Each record contains fields such as the pickup/drop off points, and their respective times, as well as the number of passengers. The data is also released on an annual basis; hence, it is unlikely to be useful to shed any insights for short-term trading. One obvious use case for shorter trading could be trading the stocks of companies like Lyft or potentially using taxi ride statistics as an input into overall economic activity estimates. However, despite the relatively lagged nature of the publication, the dataset could nevertheless be useful for doing longer-term analysis, for example, to understand the impact of services like Uber and Lyft on taxis.

Finer (2018) uses the same NYC Taxi & Limousine Commission rides dataset for somewhat different purposes. The objective here is to use it to understand information flow around dates of FOMC meetings between the Fed and market participants. The paper examines taxi rides in this dataset that are between locations near major banks in New York City and the area near the New York Fed in the period from 2009 to 2014. These taxi rides are used as a proxy for meetings between market participants and the New York Fed. Of course, it is impossible to say with certainty that every taxi ride between these locations can be mapped to such a meeting, even if the hypothesis seems plausible.

The paper notes that there is an increased number of taxi rides between locations near major banks and the area around the New York Fed around FOMC meeting dates, after the Fed communications blackout period, during lunchtime, and also later at night.

The Fed communications blackout period (or quiet period) occurs in the runup to FOMC meetings in which officials cannot make public comments on monetary periods. Even if we assume the majority of these taxi journeys result in private meetings between Fed officials and market participants, it is impossible to pinpoint the information flow during these meetings. Furthermore, such an approach will not capture trips that are made by other means of transport.

14.5 CORPORATE JET LOCATION DATA AND M&A

These days a lot of meetings are conducted virtually, whether it is over the phone or through videoconferences. High-speed communications can make calls crystal clear and it is also possible to share screens and media. However, in practice, it is unlikely that any amount of technology is going to eliminate the need to travel for business meetings. This is particularly the case for very important transactions. If we are able to track the travel of high-level executives, it might potentially provide an insight into any deals they might be planning. Given that high-level executives can often travel on private jets, it may give us an ability to track this type of activity, in particular if they are visiting relatively unusual locations.

Kamel (2018) discusses Quandl's Corporate Aviation Intelligence dataset, which tracks the activity of corporate jets. In order to make a raw dataset of aircraft location data usable, they note a large amount of entity matching needs to be done. In fact, it is necessary to map various private jets to their corporate owners and then on to the tradable ticker of that firm. Given that ownership structures of corporate jets can be complex, it often is not a straightforward exercise. For example, the aircraft may not be owned directly by the corporation, but may instead be leased or fractionally owned. Then further matching needs to be done to map a firm's ticker to a particular jet journey.

Adams-Heard and Crowley (2019) gives a specific example derived from the Quandl's dataset of how such corporate travel activity in a private jet can be a leading indicator for M&A activity. It showed a private jet belonging to Occidental Petroleum Corp present in Omaha, the home of Warren Buffett and the headquarters of his firm Berkshire Hathaway, in late April 2019. Researchers at Gordon Haskett Research Advisors LLC cited the data while acknowledging there was no way to tell with certainty why the aircraft was in Omaha ("It has occurred to us that it might be trying to bring Buffett into this deal and help with the cash portion of its offer"). The deal in question was Occidental's potential purchase of Anadarko Petroleum Corp. It was later confirmed that Buffett was indeed involved in the deal.

Strohmeier et al. (2018) uses data from the OpenSky network, which has positional data for aircraft. It was then combined with various metadata to provide some additional context, such as datasets on aircraft type and ownership. Thanks to this it is possible to exclude, for example, commercial aircraft. However, as the authors note, these datasets are quite noisy, which alludes to the point made earlier by Kamel (2018) about the difficulty of matching aircraft to corporate owners. Part of their study examines activity by government aircraft to understand relationships between governments. Another part discusses predicting M&A transactions and that is our focus here.

Strohmeier et al. work with a dataset detailing the activity of 88 corporate jets that were relatively easy to match in terms of ownership to large listed European or US firms. The vast majority of these jets were observed flying in the OpenSky dataset during the sample period between January 2016 and June 2017. Each jet had a median number of 91 flights completed. Strohmeier et al.'s focus was on European targets for M&A given the nature of the OpenSky dataset. This yielded seven identifiable M&A cases. There was also a control group of 31 firms whose flights were used for comparison. A table from Strohmeier et. al appears in Figure 14.8, which details the number of flights to takeover targets for each of these seven M&A cases.

For each instance, Strohmeier et al. calculated the number of flights to the target of M&A over different periods of time, a month before and after the M&A details as well as up to a year beforehand. They defined landings as those within 100km of the takeover target. Admittedly, the sample of M&A details is very small, given that the focus of the study is on easily identifiable corporate aircraft and also given the analysis is over a relatively short time period (1.5 years). However, their analysis does appear to show that in the month before a takeover, there is an average of around three visits to a takeover target versus an average of 0.40 for the control group where there was no takeover target.

Clearly, there are caveats to this type of analysis, namely that it is impossible to know with certainty the exact company visited within the vicinity of an airport, as with the above example. Hence, it seems reasonable that any sort of corporate jet data should ideally be used with other observations or datasets (perhaps based on news) to build a fuller picture. This would help to reduce the likelihood of "false positives" in a

Absolute visits	Monthly AVG 12-2 months before	Monthly AVG 2 months before	Month before	Month after	Monthly AVG 6 months after	Last seen before announcement (days)	Combined share price change (%)
Case 1 (EU/EU)	0.11	1	0	2	0.67	50	6.71
Case 2 (EU/EU)	2.56	2.5	2	0	0.75	25	1.1
Case 3 (EU/EU)	0	1	2	4	1.56	20	1.96
Case 4 (US/EU)	0	2.5	3	0	0	8	1.83
Case 5 (US/EU)	0.11	0	0	0	0	325	0.2
Case 6 (US/EEA)	0.22	6	12	2	5	1	20.29
Case 7 (US/EU)	0.29	1	2	0	1	1	23.18
Average	0.47	2	3	1.14	1.28	61.43	7.9
Control group	0.14	0.33	0.4	0.42	0.34	–	–

Source: Based on data from Strohmeier, Smith, Lenders, and Martinovic (2018).

FIGURE 14.8 Corporate aircraft visits at takeover targets.

live investment scenario, without the benefit of hindsight. Furthermore, it is also likely that such analysis of corporate jet activity is more amenable for firms in "unusual" locations, where the shortlist of potential takeoff targets for meetings is likely to be a lot shorter. The other difficulty with this sort of analysis is that it would not capture commercial jet travel by executives visiting takeover targets.

14.6   SUMMARY

In recent years there has been a huge increase in the devices that have location tracking enabled. When this data is aggregated and cleaned sufficiently, it can be used to provide investors with useful insights. Many data vendors now have products built on top of location data.

The use cases for location data can range from tracking ships to understanding the supply of commodities around the world and to aggregating mobile phone location data near retail outlets to help forecast earnings per share of those same firms.

We have discussed even more novel datasets encompassing location data, such as those of private jets, and given examples of how this has been used in the past to make an educated guess about possible M&A activity.

CHAPTER 15

Text, Web, Social Media, and News

15.1 INTRODUCTION

The notion that text-based data is useful for trading financial markets is not an unusual concept. After all, news has been a major driver of trader behavior and prices for centuries. What has changed in recent years is the sheer quantity of text-based data that a trader might need to look at, in particular driven by the advent of the web. There is simply too much text for any human to read and interpret. We need to turn to machines to help us extract value from this huge quantity of text for us to use in the investment process.

In this chapter, we begin by exploring how to read web data. We then give many use cases for text from an investor viewpoint. We look at social media and show how it can be used to understand ideas such as market sentiment and to help forecast US change in nonfarm payrolls. Later, we will focus on newswire data and develop systematic trading rules by using it for FX markets. We will also discuss how to aggregate Fed communications and apply NLP to it to understand the movement in US Treasury yields. Lastly, we will talk about making estimates for CPI using web-sourced data from online retailers.

15.2 COLLECTING WEB DATA

The web was invented in 1989 by Tim Berners-Lee while he was working at CERN. Obviously today, over 30 years later, the amount of content available on the web has mushroomed. The web can encompass content such as news, social media, blogs, corporate data, and so on, but it also contains non-textual content, such as images, audio, and video. Some of it is freely available while other parts have restricted access, such as newspapers behind paywalls. Because content on the web originates from so many disparate sources, it is perhaps not surprising that it is predominantly in an unstructured form and does not fit into some standardized formats. Hence, if we wish to aggregate data from a large number of web-based sources, a significant effort is required to structure different sources. The huge amount of text available means that to get a true sense of it, we need to use automated methods not only to collect the data but also to decipher its meaning.

To collect text content from the web we can use an automated program, a web crawler (or spider) that systematically browses through web pages to start download-ing the content. Obviously, there are too many websites to be able to browse the whole web, so typically we need to guide our web crawling. Even search engines (which seek to index the web with significant computational and bandwidth resources) using web crawlers are unlikely to be able to catalogue the entire web. Furthermore, content owners might choose to restrict the access of web crawlers and might have terms of usage that restrict automated processes. In Chapter 3, we discussed some of the legal points around the collection of data from the web.

Once we have found a specific web page of interest, the next step is understanding the content. Getting content from a specific web page utilizes "web scraping,"[1] which typically involves:

- Downloading the content of the web page into its raw form
- Assigning a time stamp for the time the web page was scraped (and also, if possible, another time stamp for when the content was created)
- Removing HTML tags
- Identifying metadata such as the page title, hyperlinks, and so on
- Capturing the body text of page
- Getting multimedia content (such as images)

We can then store each of these elements of content into different fields in a single record in a database. We can view each database record as a summary of the web page content. In practice, we are likely to want to structure the data further and add additional metadata fields to describe the content. For text content this will involve a large amount of natural language processing.

Of course, aside from the web, there are many other possible sources of text. Some of these might be publicly available sources such as newswires and books. There are also many text sources of private data, such as emails, text messages, and chat tran-scripts. Typically, in financial firms, these private sources of text will be particularly relevant for tasks such as trade surveillance or the collection of price data (such as in the transcripts of chat conversations between counterparties).

15.3   SOCIAL MEDIA

Perhaps the first social media was the scrawling in caves by our ancestors, or perhaps it was the graffiti written on walls in ancient Rome (Standage, 2014). Today, there

---

[1]See Section 3.1 for more details around the legal risks of web scraping.

are many sites on the Internet for social media. Some, of course, are very well known and have many users worldwide, like Twitter, Facebook, and Instagram. They have a broad audience and, due to this, a large number of topics discussed on them. Others, such as Stocktwits, are more specialized social media networks and the user base is much more focused on markets. Many social media sites will often have APIs allowing machines to read the messages posted by users that in themselves already contain some element of structuring. These partially structured messages will usually have a time stamp associated with them as well as other metadata such as the username of who posted and possibly their location. However, typically such a stream of messages will contain the raw text without any indication of topic or sentiment.

It is often left up to the consumer of the API stream to do this additional analysis, although there are many vendors who typically offer such a structuring service on top of social media streams (such as Social Media Analytics), which consume raw streams from social media sites like Twitter and Stocktwits and apply additional analysis to structure the stream to provide additional metadata like the topic and sentiment.

As mentioned earlier, trying to understand text can be very difficult. Social media has additional challenges that make it more difficult to gauge meaning compared to traditional newswires. Unlike text derived from newswires – which is often written in a consistent style – by contrast, messages posted on social media tend to be much noisier and more difficult to understand. Social media posts are generally much shorter than a typical news article and in the case of platforms like Twitter there is an explicit character limit. The language used in social media also tends to be much less formal and often contains slang and abbreviations. Sarcasm is another major problem in social media. One specific example can be seen on Twitter, where references to "buy gold" can often be sarcastic retorts to gold bugs rather than a true view of the author to buy gold. There might be hashtags, such as #chartcrime, that have a specific meaning. In this case, #chartcrime refers to very misleading bits of market analysis that have been tweeted.

There is also a lot of context dependency when it comes to interpreting social media. While hashtags are sometimes used to give some indication of a topic, they are often omitted. Hence, it can sometimes be difficult to understand a single tweet in isolation. Take, for example, tweets around an event such as an ECB meeting. People might tweet "what a dove!" around such times. Without having the context of knowing that there is an ECB meeting at the same time, such a tweet would be very difficult to decipher and is extremely ambiguous. After all, it could be referring to the "dovish" underlying policy of many central banks, or indeed something totally different, or an actual bird. One way to add context is to combine social media with another source such as structured data from a newswire. DePalma (2016) discusses how to combine social media buzz, namely the volume of messages on social media relating to specific equities, with the sentiment on machine-readable news of those same assets. The idea of the paper is to use social media buzz as a proxy for investor attention. We refer to DePalma (2016) for more details.

15.3.1 Hedonometer Index

Many measures give us an idea of how an economy is performing. However, what about trying to measure the happiness of people? One attempt to do this is the Hedonometer index developed by the University of Vermont. (Its construction is detailed in University of Vermont, 2013). It uses as raw data tweets posted on Twitter and randomly picks around 10% of the tweets posted each day, which constitutes around 100GB of raw JSON messages for processing. Words in English in these messages are then assigned a happiness score. There are around 5,000 common words in their corpus that have been assigned a "happiness" score. These happiness scores have been derived from Amazon Mechanical Turk,[2] which is essentially a service to crowd-source tasks to a large community of people. In this case, we can think of it as basically being a large survey. The words are rated between 1 and 9. Figure 15.1 presents some of the happiest and saddest words in Hedonometer's database (University of Vermont, 2013). Words like "laughter" score very high while words like "war" score very poorly, as we might expect. However, as noted by University of Vermont (2013), there are words where there is disagreement about their relative happiness. These words are "tuned out."

Of course, this approach is only measuring those people tweeting, in particular those tweeting in English, so it is not going to be totally representative of the general population sample, even if it does include a large number of people. However, we would argue that it does have the benefits of being updated very regularly and without a lag.

Figure 15.2 presents the Hedonometer index for the later part of 2018 and early 2019. The lowest point occurred around the mass shooting tragedy in Las Vegas in October 2018. By contrast, the happiness periods were around Christmas, New Year's, and Thanksgiving, which seems intuitive.

Can we glean any other observations from the Hedonometer dataset? One simple thing we can try is to take the average scores by day of the week. Figure 15.3

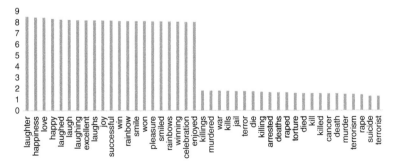

FIGURE 15.1   Happiest and saddest words in Hedonometer's corpus.
Source: Based on data from Hedonometer.

---

[2]https://www.mturk.com/.

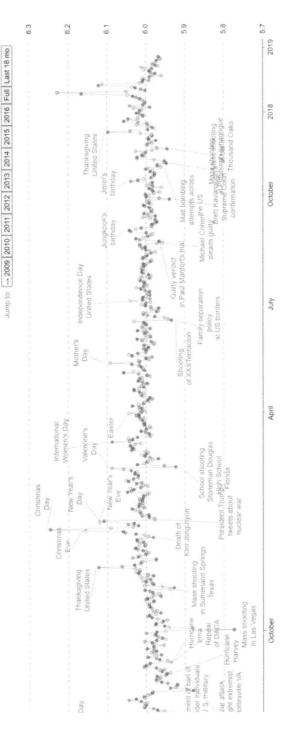

FIGURE 15.2 Hedonometer index for latter part of 2018 till early 2019.
Source: Hedonometer.

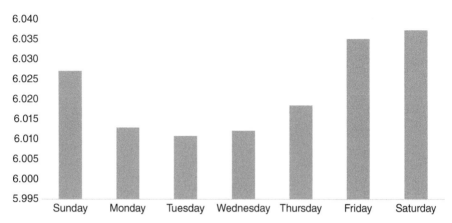

FIGURE 15.3   Average Hedonometer score by day of the week.
Source: Based on data from Hedonometer.

plots these average scores. Perhaps, as we might expect, it appears that peoples' happiness is least in the earlier part of the week on a Monday or Tuesday and rises throughout the week toward Saturday. Admittedly, from an investor perspective, this specific observation is difficult to monetize. However, it does illustrate how, from a very large raw dataset of tweets, we can derive what appear to be very intuitive results.

Can we make a connection between happiness and markets? After all, we would think that overall consumer confidence would be linked to happiness, and hence it could be a reasonable indicator for risk sentiment. In order to do this, we created the HSI (Happiness Sentiment Index) out of the Hedonometer Index. This first step involves stripping out weekends, given they are non-trading days. We also exclude outlier days (i.e. where there are significant jumps in the Hedonometer index, which we have defined at moves greater than 0.05). Furthermore, we exclude any US holidays, where people are generally likely to be happier; otherwise our model will simply be biased to suggesting good market sentiment because of holidays rather than for any other reason. Indeed, we already observed, for example, that the Hedonometer index is highest during the weekend.

A 1-month SMA is then applied to smooth the index. Finally, the scores are standardized between 0 and 1, using a rolling percentile rank with a 2-month window. Figure 15.4 plots the HSI against the 1-month changes in S&P 500 1st dated futures. At least from this specific example, there does appear to be somewhat of a relationship between moves in the S&P 500. If we regress the HSI against S&P 500 during our sample (February 2009–July 2019), the T-statistic of the beta coefficient is 7.7 (and has p value of $2.13*10^{-14}$), which shows a statistically significant relationship between S&P 500 and HSI. This suggests that the HSI could potentially be used as an indicator for trading markets. In practice, of course, it is likely that it would be combined with a number of other market sentiment metrics, which could, for example, include news sentiment or market positioning.

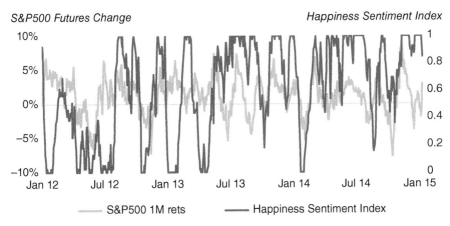

FIGURE 15.4 Happiness Sentiment Index against S&P 500.
Source: Based on data from Hedonometer Index, Bloomberg.

15.3.2 Using Twitter Data to Help Forecast US Change in Nonfarm Payrolls

We have seen that we can derive an indicator that gives a representation for the happiness of Twitter users from their tweets. Are there very specific ways we can use Twitter to help us understand the market? Social media gives us an idea of what people are talking about at any specific moment. Hence, it seems reasonable to assume that they might be able to give us insights into the economy at any particular time. One of the most keenly awaited economics releases is the US employment situation report, which usually happens on the first Friday of the month from the US BLS (Bureau of Labor Statistics) at 8:30 am EST. The report relates to the jobs market in the previous month. It is usually the first official release of actual "hard" US economic data in the month. Before that, much of the data tends to be "soft" data or from surveys based upon people's expectation about the economy. There is also the privately compiled ADP employment report, which is published before the BLS data, but the market tends to place less weight on its release.

The US employment situation report contains a number of different statistics relating to the labor market (Bureau of Labor Statistics, 2019), which are broken down into two parts: the household survey of around 60,000 households and the establishment surveys of businesses (around 142,000).

The statistics that are the most relevant to the market are the national unemployment rate (from the household survey) and the national monthly change in nonfarm payrolls (from the establishment survey). Market expectations for nonfarm payrolls are typically determined by consensus surveys (such as those conducted by Bloomberg) of US economists working in large financial institutions.

As the name suggests, nonfarm payrolls omit farm workers. Historically, measures of farm labor are collected by the US Department of Agriculture's Census of Agriculture. The release of the US employment situation report also includes revisions to the previous estimates, as well as many other statistics, such as average hours worked, earnings, and the participation rate. In many cases, there is a significant amount of granularity available in the underlying statistics, sometimes down to state level and subsectors. Indeed, at the time of publishing, ALFRED (n.d.) has over 8,500 time series sourced from the household survey and 811 time series sourced from the establishment survey.

There is usually a very strong relationship between the surprise in the change in nonfarm payrolls on the one hand, and the move in US Treasury yields and the move in the USD on the other. The rationale is that when economic data is stronger, it is more likely that FOMC will adopt a hawkish tone and yields will climb higher to reflect that. The converse is true when data is weaker. Typically, the USD also reacts in this way, moving with US Treasury yields after strong data. There have been occasions in the past, however – for example, following the financial crisis – that the USD actually strengthened after very poor payrolls releases. One rationale was that investors were flocking toward USD as a flight-to-safety trade given its status as the main reserve currency.

To illustrate this, in Figure 15.5 we plot the surprise in nonfarm payrolls between 2011 and 2016 versus the returns in USD/JPY in the 1 minute following the release of the US employment report. The surprise is simply the actual released number minus the consensus number. We note that with very large surprises the reaction tends to be nonlinear. When the surprise is positive then USD/JPY tends to move higher, and when it is negative it tends to move lower, which seems fairly intuitive for the reasons we have discussed.

Hence, if we could forecast the "actual" change in nonfarm payrolls better than consensus, we could potentially monetize it by entering the trade before 8:30 am EST on the day of the US employment situation report and exiting it shortly after. In other words, if our more accurate forecast was higher than consensus, we would buy USD; conversely, we would sell USD if our forecast was lower. As traders, our objective is

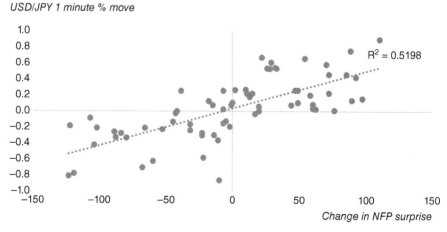

FIGURE 15.5   Surprise in nonfarm payrolls vs. USD/JPY 1-minute move after release.
Source: Based on data from Bloomberg.

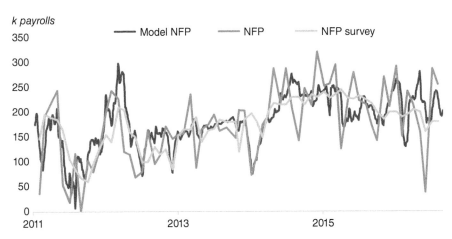

FIGURE 15.6 Twitter-based forecast for US change in nonfarm payrolls versus actual release & Bloomberg consensus survey.
Source: Based on data from Twitter, Bloomberg.

not necessarily to minimize the standard error of our forecast, but instead to generate alpha from a forecast. If a forecast has a smaller standard error but misjudges the direction of an event surprise, often it is of less use for a trader.

Note that we are not trying to use some sort of latency advantage attempting to be the first one to trade immediately after the release. There is likely to be very little liquidity at that time, and furthermore we would have to have very sophisticated and expensive technology to be able to engage in this type of latency arbitrage. So how can we try to get a more accurate forecast for payrolls? One approach can be to augment existing variables we use to forecast payrolls (typically related to variables that use existing labor market data). In our case, we shall attempt to use data derived from tweets related to chatter about the labor market as an additional Twitter variable to augment our model. Figure 15.6 plots our Twitter-enhanced payrolls model forecast alongside the first release of nonfarm payrolls and also the consensus survey of economist estimates from Bloomberg. Our model-based nowcast is available on a daily basis, given that we can have access to Twitter data on a high-frequency basis. Our sample is again from early 2011 to summer 2016. We see that there are certain periods where our model-based nowcast managed to pick up the actual NFP number very well, such as at the start of 2014, despite the survey number being way off. However, purely from this plot it is difficult to tell on aggregate whether you could trade our model NFP forecast profitably. In order to understand that, we need to do more work and backtest a trading strategy.

Basically, how useful is this enhanced nowcast for nonfarm payrolls for a trader? We can check this historically by doing a backtest using a very simple trading rule, which we described earlier:

- Buying USD when our estimate is better/higher than consensus
- Selling USD when our estimate is worse/lower than consensus

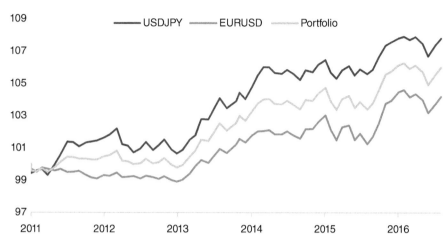

FIGURE 15.7   Trading EUR/USD and USD/JPY on an intraday basis around NFP.
Source: Based on data from Twitter, Bloomberg.

In Figure 15.7, we use our enhanced forecast to trade EUR/USD and USD/JPY on an intraday basis around payrolls, entering the trade a few minutes before the data release and exiting a few minutes after. The average returns on an annualized basis are 119 bps for USD/JPY and 59 bps for EUR/USD. An equally weighted portfolio of EUR/USD and USD/JPY has average return of 88 bps. Obviously, there are some major caveats to this type of analysis, given that our sample is relatively small. Indeed, we only have 68 data releases in our sample. Furthermore, we have to bear in mind that we would need access to good liquidity to execute such a strategy. With wider spreads, it would be difficult to monetize such a trading rule.

15.3.3   Twitter Data to Forecast Stock Market Reaction to FOMC

We have noted that Twitter can be used to improve forecasts for nonfarm payrolls. However, can it be used in other ways? Azar and Lo (2016), for example, discuss how to use tweets to forecast future returns around FOMC. The approach requires the filtering of tweets in the runup to FOMC meetings, specifically filtering on terms "FOMC" and "Federal Reserve" and the name of the Fed chair during their historical sample of 2007–2014 (i.e. "Bernanke," later "Yellen," and so on). Basic sentiment analysis was applied to each tweet, to give a score between −1 and +1 using a deterministic algorithm, dubbed "Pattern," which relies on a database containing positive/negative scores for each word. It also takes into account the use of adjectives and adverbs to "amplify" or "dampen" the score. Hence, it should capture that "not good" exhibits a negative sentiment. These scores are then weighted by the number of followers of the user tweeting. These weighted scores are aggregated into daily sentiment scores. In practice, the historical sample was curtailed to 2009–2014, given the relatively small volume of tweets in their sample between 2007 and 2009. The authors construct various portfolios that incorporate this sentiment information from tweets and then compare it to a market benchmark portfolio. They note that a model that includes these tweets – in particular immediately preceding an FOMC meeting – performs well. Just as with the example showing a trading rule applied to the US employment situation, we need to note that there are a relatively small number of FOMC meetings in the sample. Potentially, one way to increase the sample space could be to apply the same approach to other central banks, such as ECB or BoJ and examine whether tweets provide informational content for the reaction of domestic assets such as bonds and equities. To our knowledge, this has not been attempted yet.

15.3.4   Liquidity and Sentiment from Social Media

We have already given some examples of why understanding sentiment is an important component of trading. When sentiment is negative and hence the market becomes more risk averse, we might expect liquidity to be more constrained. Essentially, market makers need to be compensated for offering liquidity in environments where traders are scaling back their risk exposure. In contrast, when sentiment is good, we might expect liquidity to be more abundant and we should find it easier to transact. Agrawal, Azar, Lo, and Singh (2018) discuss the relationship between social media sentiment and equities market liquidity. To measure social media sentiment, they use a feed from PsychSignal that supplies a time series of sentiment scores related to equities based upon data from Twitter and Stocktwits. They compare this against a feed of sentiment scores from RavenPack's news dataset. They show that negative sentiment based on social media tends to have a bigger impact on liquidity than positive sentiment. They find that highly abnormal social media sentiment tends to be preceded by high momentum and this is followed by a period of mean-reversion. Using some of these observations they develop some equities-based trading strategies that use social media as an input and that outperform their benchmark with the caveat that their relatively high frequency makes them amenable only for those with access to lower transaction costs.

In terms of further study, they note that overall it can be difficult to identify the direction of causality in their study. Do price moves drive social media, or vice versa? They also note that not all social media users have the same impact, which seems entirely intuitive in particular, given the disparity in followers and general influence.

15.4   NEWS

News has always had an impact on markets and it is very much a traditional source of information. However, what has changed is that the volume of news has grown significantly over the years. In Figure 15.8, we illustrate this by plotting S&P 500 against the number of stories on Bloomberg News, whose text includes S&P 500. We note that in the late 1990s, the story counts were less than half where they are today. In this instance, we are examining a single source of news (Bloomberg News). In recent years the number of sources of news has also increased significantly, largely

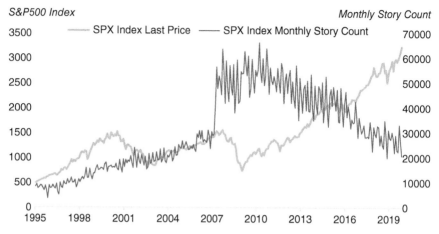

FIGURE 15.8   S&P 500 versus article count on it on Bloomberg News.
Source: Based on data from Bloomberg.

due to the web. It is clearly impossible for one human to read every single news article published about the market. However, what if that reader of news was not a human?

Recently, newswires that have been traditionally read by traders on their computers through proprietary applications, such as Bloomberg News, have begun to be distributed in machine-readable form. As the name suggests, news that is in a machine-readable form can be parsed by a computer. Typically, machine-readable news published by newswires will already have a large amount of structure, which makes it easier to discern content in them. Furthermore, vendors will typically add a significant amount of metadata, such as the topic of news article, its sentiment, and the entities referred to in the text. In addition, it will be written in a relatively consistent style.

A large amount of news is obviously also published on the web, both by traditional news outlets and in other forms such as blogs. We could also argue that a lot of social media itself is informed by news articles. In practice, web-based content gathered from disparate sources requires a significant amount of structuring into an appropriate and consistent form before it can be made into a form that is usable by traders. Other important sources of text data for markets include material published by companies about themselves, such as corporate call transcripts and interviews.

For high-frequency traders, a computer can obviously parse text and interpret it much more quickly than a human, and hence react faster. For longer-term strategies, automated parsing is also beneficial, allowing the parsing of vast amounts of news that can be aggregated together to give a more rounded view of what is being reported in the press.

15.4.1   Machine-Readable News to Trade FX and Understand FX Volatility

We have noted the general rationale behind using machine-readable news to understand and hence predict markets. A use case that we will examine in this section is how to extract sentiment from news to generate signals to trade FX from a directional perspective. Amen (2018) discusses how machine-readable news from Bloomberg News (newswire between 2009 and 2017) can be used to create sentiment scores for G10/developed market currencies. We will give a brief summary of the paper here and will illustrate its results. The rationale for using machine-readable news is that historically news has always been a key part of the decision-making process for traders. The dataset is structured such that each record has the time stamp of each news article as well as other fields, such as topic and ticker tags. The dataset is then filtered in a way that only articles related to each developed market currency are read. In Figure 15.9, we give the average daily number of news articles for each currency from the paper. We note that the most heavily traded currencies, such as EUR and USD, have more news articles as we would expect.

Amen (2018) applies natural language processing to each of these articles to ascertain the sentiment score. We need to be careful in understanding FX quotation conventions, which can sometimes require us to flip the score. For example, if we are trying to capture sentiment for JPY, and the currency pair is quoted in USD/JPY, we would need to invert the score. We calculate a daily sentiment score by creating a cutoff point at 5 pm EST each day and calculating an equally weighted average of all the sentiment scores for that currency over the past day. We then construct a Z score (Z_t) for each daily observation (d_t) by subtracting the mean of the daily observations (μ_t) and dividing by the standard deviation of the daily observations (σ_t). The mean and standard deviation of the daily observations are calculated over a rolling window. The Z score normalizes sentiment across different currencies.

$$Z_t = \frac{d_t - \mu_t}{\sigma_t} \tag{15.1}$$

We now have scores for each currency. To construct a score for a particular currency pair, we simply subtract one from the other. For example, the USD/JPY score is simply USD − JPY. We plot this specific metric in Figure 15.10 alongside weekly returns.

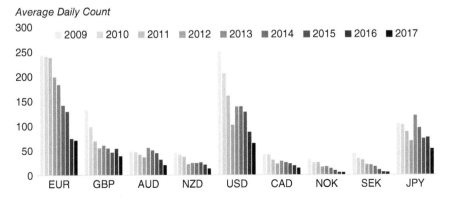

FIGURE 15.9 Average daily count of articles per ticker.
Source: Based on data from Cuemacro, Bloomberg.

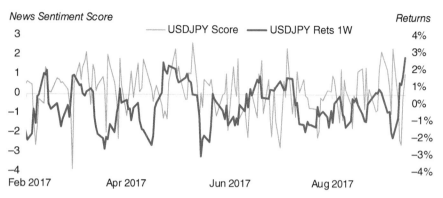

FIGURE 15.10   USD/JPY news sentiment score versus weekly returns.
Source: Based on data from Cuemacro, Bloomberg.

We now have a way of identifying the sentiment for any particular developed
market currency pair from underlying news data. We can apply a simple trading
rule, buying that currency pair when the sentiment is positive and selling when it
is negative. Of course, this approach of trading with the short-term momentum in
the news is just one approach to using news data. Another approach could involve
looking at news data over extended periods and then fading extremes as follows.
When there is very good news over a prolonged period of time, the market will
tend to be conditioned to it. The market has basically already priced in "good news"
in such a scenario. Hence typically the market will not react so positively to it.
Conversely, if we see something similar with extremely bad news, after a while the
market becomes used to it and has priced it in. Hence, it no longer reacts negatively.
We might even see the market bounce.

Does such a short-term news momentum trading rule, as described here, work in
practice? We can backtest this trading rule using historical data. The risk-adjusted
returns (i.e. information ratios) for this trading strategy for each currency pair are
presented in Figure 15.11 alongside returns for a generic trend-following strategy on
price data, which is one of the typical strategies used by FX traders historically. We
see that while trend following has underperformed in our sample, our news-based
approach has been profitable. In Figure 15.12 we plot the correlation between the
returns of these two strategies for each currency pair. We note that there is no consistent pattern, suggesting that the factor we are extracting from news adds value to
a trend-following strategy on prices.

We can also construct a basket of all these currency pairs using both our
news-based and trend-following trading rules. In Figure 15.13, we present the
returns of these baskets. As we would expect from our earlier currency pair–specific
example, the news-based basket outperforms trend (risk-adjusted returns of 0.6

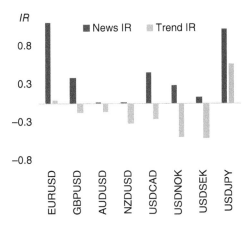

FIGURE 15.11 News versus trend information ratio.
Source: Based on data from Cuemacro, Bloomberg.

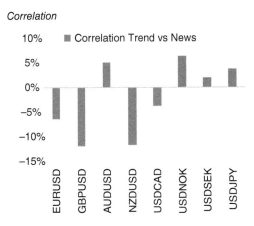

FIGURE 15.12 News versus trend correlation.
Source: Based on data from Cuemacro, Bloomberg

versus –0.3 respectively). In Figure 15.14, we show the year-on-year returns of both baskets. In most years, news outperforms, with the largest exception being 2010, where news heavily underperforms trend.

Another way we can extract value from news data is to understand how it can be used to understand FX volatility. Amen (2018) also shows how news volume on a certain asset can have a strong contemporaneous relationship with the volatility of that asset. In Figure 15.15, we see the news volume on USD/JPY plotted against the news volume score, which is essentially a standardized metric relating to the news volume

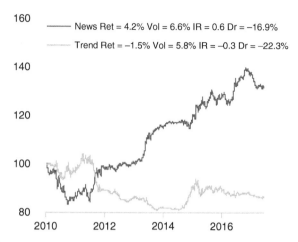

FIGURE 15.13   News versus trend model returns.
Source: Based on data from Cuemacro, Bloomberg.

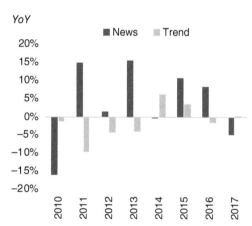

FIGURE 15.14   News versus trend model YoY returns.
Source: Based on data from Cuemacro, Bloomberg.

on articles tagged in the Bloomberg News (BN) newswire as relating to USD/JPY. At least from this single plot, it does appear that there is some link between news volume and volatility. This is of course intuitive – that there is more news written about an asset that is exhibiting more volatile price action.

In Figure 15.16, we report the T-statistics from a regression of daily returns against the news volume metric for that same currency pair using the same historical sample 2011–2017. We see that in every case (other than USD/NOK), the T-statistics are statistically significant, confirming our intuition that volatility and news volume are strongly linked. All the p-values are well below 0.05 (other than USD/NOK, which is 0.27), indicating statistical significance.

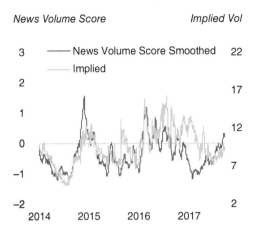

FIGURE 15.15   USD/JPY news volume versus 1M implied volatility.
Source: Based on data from Cuemacro, Bloomberg.

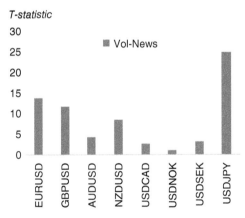

FIGURE 15.16   Regressing news volume versus 1M implied volatility.
Source: Based on data from Cuemacro, Bloomberg.

Are there potentially other ways we can utilize the observation that news volume is linked to volatility? One way is to understand the volatility around major scheduled events such as FOMC and ECB meetings. Obviously, before a scheduled economic event, there is no certainly concerning the outcome, but we do at least know the timing. Hence, before these meetings, volatility traders will typically mark up implied vol, given the expectation of heightened realized volatility over these events. This additional markup is typically known at the event volatility add-on and is expressed in terms of overnight volatility. For events like central bank meetings, the event vol add-on can be substantial. For lesser events, the event vol add-on can often be negligible.

In Figure 15.17, we plot the overnight implied volatility for EUR/USD just before an FOMC meeting, ignoring all other days (hence the option would expire just after FOMC). We also plot the add-on associated with EUR/USD ON, which has been generated by a simple model. Alongside this we plot the subsequent realized volatility on FOMC days and the volatility risk premium (VRP), which is simply implied minus realized volatility. Our first observation is that the implied volatility is nearly always more than realized volatility on FOMC days. This shouldn't be surprising, given that traders need to be compensated for selling "insurance." Typically, the times when buying options is profitable are during Black Swan events, when both the timing and the nature of the event are totally unpredictable. It can be argued that events like FOMC are not really Black Swan events, given that we at least know the timing. The add-ons are typically around 4 volatility points. In other words, EUR/USD overnight implied volatility is around 4 volatility points higher just before FOMC meetings.

However, what can news tell us about EUR/USD overnight implied volatility before FOMC meetings? One way to see this is to look at the normalized volume of FOMC articles on Bloomberg News, in the days in the runup to an FOMC meeting (we obviously ignore news articles written after FOMC). In Figure 15.18, we plot EUR/USD overnight implied volatility just before FOMC meetings against this normalized news volume measure. At least on a stylized basis there does appear to be some sort of relationship between the news volume on FOMC before a meeting and how volatility traders price implied volatility. This should seem intuitive. If there is a lot of chatter about a particular FOMC meeting, there are more expectations of significant policy changes (and hence volatility). Conversely when there is little chatter, it would suggest that the FOMC meeting is likely to be relatively quiet.

We can view the data in another way using scatter charts (see Figure 15.19). These charts show the normalized FOMC volume against the add-on, implied vol, and realized vol of EUR/USD. We also report the R^2 of these regressions. The R^2 are not negligible in all instances. This suggests that potentially using news volume as an indicator could be a useful addition when modeling volatility over major scheduled events.

The exercise can also be repeated for examining EUR/USD overnight volatility before ECB meetings (see Figure 15.20). We see a similar picture as we did for FOMC.

15.4.2   Federal Reserve Communications and US Treasury Yields

Historically, central banks have not always been open with how they operate. Indeed, Bernanke (2007) notes that Montagu Norman, the governor of the Bank of England from 1921 to 1944, had a personal motto: "Never explain, never excuse." However, as a whole, central banks have become far more open in the decades since that era. As Bernanke stresses, ultimately central bankers are public servants and their decisions can have a big impact on society. Thus, they have a responsibility to explain the rationale behind their decisions.

The Federal Reserve communicates in a number of different ways. The FOMC (Federal Open Markets Committee) consists of 12 members who vote on Fed policy. All seven members of the Board of Governors of the Federal Reserve System and

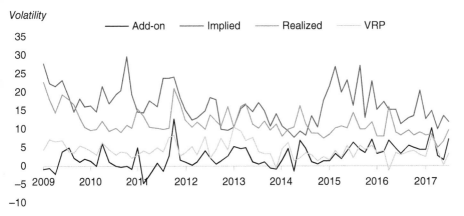

FIGURE 15.17 EUR/USD ON volatility add-on, implied volatility, realized volatility, and volatility risk premium (VRP) on FOMC days.
Source: Based on data from Cuemacro, Bloomberg.

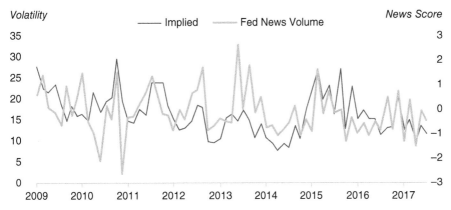

FIGURE 15.18 EUR/USD ON implied volatility on FOMC days against FOMC news volume.
Source: Based on data from Cuemacro, Bloomberg.

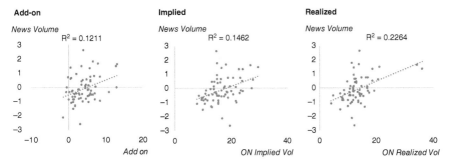

FIGURE 15.19 EUR/USD overnight volatility on FOMC days.
Source: Based on data from Cuemacro, Bloomberg.

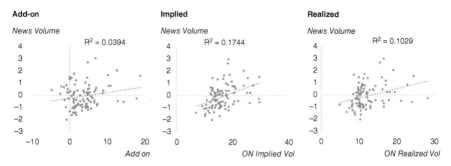

FIGURE 15.20   EUR/USD overnight volatility on ECB days.
Source: Based on data from Cuemacro, Bloomberg.

the president of the Federal Reserve Bank of New York are permanent members of the FOMC. The other four alternate members are chosen from the other 11 Reserve Bank presidents who serve rotating one-year terms. As noted in Chapter 9, nonvoting Reserve Bank presidents still take part in meetings of the FOMC and all the various discussions concerning Fed policy, as well as contribute to the Fed's assessment of economic conditions.

Communications from the FOMC can involve the statements and press conferences that accompany each FOMC meeting (of which there are 8 every year) where monetary policy changes can be made. There are also more detailed minutes that give further insights into the decision-making process, which are published several weeks after each meeting. Transcripts of FOMC meetings are published several years afterwards. While they might not be relevant from a market perspective, they nevertheless shed light on the general workings of the Fed. Voting members of the FOMC and nonvoting members also regularly give speeches to the public, sometimes concerning monetary policy and other subjects under the remit of the Fed, such as regulation. They also regularly appear in the media on TV, radio, in the press, and also even sometimes tweeting from their own social media accounts. Typically, market participants collectively refer to communications from the Fed as Fedspeak.

If the Fed becomes more hawkish, suggesting that it might have to increase the base rate, then we might expect yields in the front end of the US Treasury curve to rise. Conversely, if their communications are pessimistic about growth and expect inflation to fall, suggesting a more dovish outlook, we might expect front-end yields to fall. In a sense, we can view bond yields as proxies for monetary policy expectations, in particular those without significant credit exposure, such as US Treasury yields. In recent years, through quantitative easing, the Fed has also had a larger impact further along the yield curve.

As a result, for market practitioners, trying to understand how the Fed sees the economy and an understanding of how it views future monetary policy is crucial. Historically, economists have pored over Fed communications to see if they can glean an idea of future policy. Ultimately, the Fed, like everyone else, cannot see the future with perfect foresight. However, the Fed does have the power to change monetary policy.

The annual volume of communications from the FOMC, while it might encompass many pages of text, is ultimately "small data," which could comfortably fit in a few megabytes. So theoretically, it is possible for an economist to read a large amount of this text, if they are a "Fed watcher." However, in practice, many market participants will likely skim through only a small number of communications at best.

A large amount of FOMC communications is available from the various Fed websites, although some might only be available to subscribers of various news organizations. Hence, we can get a reasonable corpus of FOMC communications by parsing a number of websites. What steps need to be taken in order to do this?

In practice, we first need to do a substantial amount of work. We need to identify the specific web pages that have Fed communications. It is necessary to structure the raw text downloaded, so we dispense with HTML tags and the like and only capture the body text of the article. Once we have extracted the raw text, we can present that alongside metadata, such as the speaker and the time stamp of the communication. As a further step, we can use additional metadata related to sentiment for each communication. As a final step, we can create an index of the various sentiment scores. This will give us an idea of the general path of Fed communications, which can be useful from a longer-term trading perspective.

We are essentially "structuring" the Fed communications into a time series that is more easily interpretable by traders. So, after we have done all of this work, would such an index actually help us understand the moves in US Treasury yields?

In Figure 15.21, we have plotted Cuemacro's Fed communications index between 2015 and 2017, which has largely been constructed in the way we described, only using text as an input, and no other market variables such as bond yields, equity moves, and so on. While it does not encompass absolutely every single example of Fedspeak, it does capture a large proportion of it and in particular the various statements, press conferences, and minutes, as well as many of the speeches. Alongside the index, we have also plotted the 1M change in US Treasury 10Y yields. Note that we discuss the various aspects of the Fed communications in a large amount of detail in Chapter 9, in particular discussing ways of detecting outliers from a preliminary version of the dataset of Fed communications used in Cuemacro's Fed communication index.

We note that for the most part, at least from a stylistic perspective, there does appear to be a relationship between the two time series. If we do a linear regression of the Fed communications index and 1M change in US Treasury 10Y yields, using a sample between 2013 and 2019, the T-statistic of the beta of the regression is close to 4.8 with a p-value of $1.2*10^{-6}$, suggesting a statistically significant relationship between them. The correlation is around 11% during this same sample.

It is, of course, intuitive that there is a relationship between the sentiment of the Fed and moves in UST 10Y yields for the reasons we discussed earlier. We note there are periods in time where there are significant divergences between the Fed communications index here and the moves in UST 10Y yields. In particular, during November 2016, there was a significant rise in UST 10Y yields going against the move in the index. In this instance, bond yields were reacting more to the election of Donald Trump and the whole theme of "reflation" rather than the underlying message

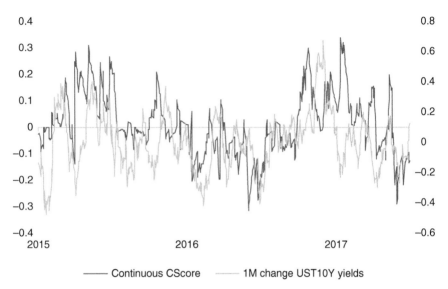

FIGURE 15.21 FOMC sentiment index and UST 10Y yield changes over the past month from 2015 to 2017.
Source: Based on data from Cuemacro, Federal Reserve.

from the Fed. This, of course, illustrates that markets move for many different reasons, and it is difficult to isolate a single factor that will always drive price action.

15.5   OTHER WEB SOURCES

The web obviously contains a large body of information that does not fall under either news or social media. There is also a substantial amount of content published on the web by individuals such as blogs. Corporate institutions also publish a large amount of data as part of their everyday business – for example, to promote themselves and also to interact with their clients, such as online retailers. Given the huge amount of data available on the web, it is likely that we can structure some relatively unique datasets from it.

We can use these other forms of web data to gain insights into financial markets. There are a number of data vendors focused on structuring data relevant for traders from the web, such as Import.io and ThinkNum. We can derive jobs data from the web. We can monitor corporate websites for current job openings data to get a specific picture on hiring by company. Expanding companies are likely to have more job openings. The health of a company can also be gauged by tracking store openings and closings that can be derived from web data. It is also possible to gauge consumer sentiment toward brands by looking at forum postings.

For many sectors there might not be "traditional datasets," and hence our only recourse is to use web-sourced datasets. For example, there are published metrics relating to the hotel industry, which give us an idea of the average daily rate, the revenue per available room, inventory, and so on. However, for location rentals that have recently been popularized by firms such as Airbnb, it is difficult to source such information. One solution is to derive these metrics from web data.

Next we discuss using data derived from online retailers to generate high-frequency inflation measures. We can derive many other datasets from websites for online retailers, aside from inflation. We can also get an idea of real-time inventory for products stocked by them. This can be particularly useful for product sectors where there are not similar existing datasets, and even for those where we have data it often is not as timely. Over time data history can be built up to construct time series of many of these web-sourced metrics. Having a longer time series can help with backtesting and understanding the effectiveness of the signal historically.

15.5.1   Measuring Consumer Price Inflation

Cavallo and Rigobon (2016) discuss using online prices to improve the understanding of consumer inflation, which they called "The Billion Prices Project." Consumer inflation price indices have typically been calculated by national statistics on a monthly or bi-monthly basis. It involves monitoring the price of a basket of goods and recording its changes. This data is collected manually by people from national statistics agencies visiting hundreds of stores. Over time the basket changes, as consumer preferences change. This data is aggregated into the consumer price indices.

Today, a large number of consumer transactions now occur online. In certain countries, official inflation data might be very unreliable or even simply not released, as Cavallo and Rigobon (2016) note for much of the period 2007–2015 in Argentina. Hence, it can be important to find alternative ways to measure consumer price inflation. Even for those countries where data is released regularly and is considered reliable by market participants, we might also wish to have a higher-frequency measure. It might also be useful in estimating the official release of inflation data and help us in trading decisions.

The prices of products sold by retailers can be scraped in a relatively automated way, as opposed to the traditional manual process of visiting shops, providing a much larger sample of price changes at a micro level. This is conditional on the items being relatively consistent over time. For example, we might have the situation where brands maintain the same price of their products but reduce their quality or size. One example of this is reducing the size of chocolate bars while maintaining the same price.

This data can then be aggregated into higher-frequency consumer inflation indices, which fit closely with many official time series. It is also possible to understand relative price levels across different countries with a different aggregation of the micro level information of similar products, which you cannot do by comparing consumer price indexes themselves. The authors give a specific example of products available globally, like those from Apple, IKEA, Zara, and H&M, which can be used to create such a consumer goods basket across different countries. The Big Mac Index, published by the *Economist,* attempts to do something similar, but of course just by examining a single item, the humble McDonald's Big Mac, and is more for illustrative purposes a PPP (purchasing power parity) model for estimating the long-term valuation of currencies. "The Billion Prices Project" evolved into a commercial entity, PriceStats, now owned by State Street, which distributes consumer inflation indices generated using this online approach on a daily basis.

15.6   SUMMARY

We have noted that the use of text to help traders make decisions is not new. However, what is new is that the amount of text available for investors has mushroomed in recent years. This is driven in large part by the advent of the web. Text can come in many different forms, ranging from newswire stories to social media and in many other forms, including the web pages of corporates. The sheer volume means that automated techniques are required to make sense of it all. Once structured and aggregated this text data[3] can be used to help inform the decisions of traders.

We have shown specific text examples, like using the social media chatter around labor markets to help forecast the change in US nonfarm payrolls. We have shown how to use the tone of social media posts to understand moves in S&P 500 (Hedonometer Index). Furthermore, more traditional datasets from newswire sources can be also used to understand sentiment in FX markets and also to help understand volatility. We also discussed how it is possible to collect Fed communications and apply NLP to them to understand the moves of US Treasury yields.

---

[3] See Chapter 4 for a discussion of natural language processing, which can be used to understand human language.

CHAPTER 16

Investor Attention

16.1 INTRODUCTION

As we have discussed, news volume can be an important metric to use to understand the market, and in particular market volatility. However, it should be noted that ultimately journalists (i.e. producers of news) are writing news they believe will be read by investors. It is not necessarily the case that because articles are written, they will attract investors' attention and be consumed. Hence, we can view news volume as broad proxy for investor attention, but with this obvious caveat.

Potentially, a closer proxy for investor attention can be seen in the way that investors actually consume information, such as their readership levels of news articles or their web search activity. Other metrics for attention can also include volumes of web traffic and page views. In this chapter, we give some specific examples of measures of investor attention, ranging from examining the readership of news articles related to payrolls, to looking at search data traffic, to Investopedia, to understanding investor anxiety. We will also create a trading strategy for EMFX based on combining measures of online attention with news volume.

16.2 READERSHIP OF PAYROLLS TO MEASURE INVESTOR ATTENTION

There are many market events that occur regularly. One of the most important of these repeated events is the US employment report, which features the release of the change in nonfarm payrolls statistics and we have discussed it many times already. While it is a repeated scheduled event, obviously some releases of the report are more important than others. The first issue is how we define "important." One measure can be the number of news articles written about the data release beforehand. However, as we have already established, just because news is written does not mean it will always garner attention. Another measure of importance can be related to readership statistics of news articles on payrolls.

Benamar, Foucault, and Vega (2018) discuss how it is possible to measure demand for information prior to release of nonfarm payrolls and use this metric to help understand the market reaction. Their dataset consists of clicks on Bitly links. Bitly provides a service where a long URL is converted into a short URL form. The shortened form can more easily be shared on social media where the number of characters you can post often has hard constraints (e.g. 280 characters on Twitter). It is also possible to keep track of statistics associated with the Bitly shortened link, such as number of clicks, the geographical location of the users clicking, and so on. Benamar, Foucault, and Vega (2018) examined a click-based dataset of about 10 TB associated with 10 billion clicks. While there are indeed many economic releases, they restricted their study to those on payrolls to reduce the complexity of the exercise. They filtered the clicks for URLs that contained the word "payroll." This yielded around 40,000 clicks for the period between January 2011 and June 2016. Unlike other measures of "attention," such as Google Trends, which might be available on a weekly or daily basis, they note that these click-based measures are available on a high-frequency basis. Benamar, Foucault, and Vega (2018) calculate the average number of readership clicks for "payrolls" article on the days of the US employment report by time of day (see Figure 16.1). They note an obvious spike at 8:30am EST, which is the time of the release of the US employment report.

Later in the paper they also discuss controlling for the supply of news articles and note that the correlation between news volume on payrolls (as measured on the RavenPack news dataset) and Bitly's click readership data for payrolls is around 13%. Hence, while news supply and demand might be related, they are certainly not

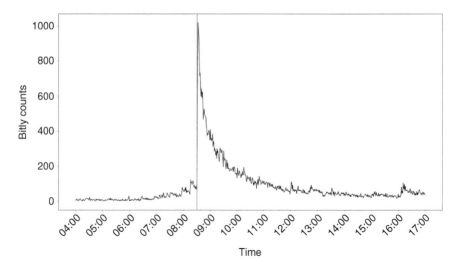

FIGURE 16.1   "Payrolls" clicks on the days of US employment report.
Source: Federal Reserve Board, bitly.

identical. One of the main discussions of the paper revolves around the relationship between payrolls clicks and the market reaction in US Treasury Note futures to a surprise in the change in nonfarm payrolls number. Surprise in this context is defined as the difference between the actual payrolls release number and median forecast of professional forecasters before it. Typically, these consensus forecasts are compiled by firms such as Bloomberg. Negative surprises are typically associated with falling Treasury yields (i.e. rising bond prices) while positive surprises tend be coincident with rising yields (i.e. falling bond prices). This is, of course, intuitive; when economic data is stronger (in the case of more jobs), you would expect yields to go higher, as the market expects tighter Fed policy. Conversely, poor data is seen as a sign of a more dovish Fed.

They show that when the number of payroll Bitly clicks is high, the price response in US Treasury note futures is nearly double. When payroll clicks are low, the market reaction is more muted. Hence, greater demand for information about payrolls can impact the market's reaction function to a surprise even when that demand comes before the actual event.

Later in this chapter we use a similar notion to adjust online attention from various Predata datasets, based on web traffic, with news supply as measured by the volume of articles about a similar topic published on Bloomberg News.

16.3   GOOGLE TRENDS DATA TO MEASURE MARKET THEMES

One commonly used measure for internet search traffic is Google Trends. Figure 16.2 shows an example of the search volume for "world cup" in the USA. We see an obvious spike every four years, which coincides with the FIFA World Cup. Obviously, this is not very surprising. However, could this type of internet search dataset be of use in financial markets? If we want to find out about something, typically the first port of call is an internet search, potentially before an action. Say we would like to buy a new car. Before doing so, it is likely that we might do some research on the internet concerning the various car brands. Hence, we might conjecture that internet search data can be useful for understanding what topics people are thinking about, and in particular it might be a leading indicator. This could potentially be a useful source of information if we were trading automotive stocks.

However, can we use internet searches to tell us something more broadly about the macroeconomic situation? Amen (2013) discusses how Google Domestic Trend indices can be used to develop systematic trading rules. Google Domestic Trend indices were historically produced by Google to measure the search traffic associated with various economically important themes. There was, for example, an index measuring "luxury," which was composed of searches related to brands like Prada, Gucci, and the like.

Figure 16.3 shows a chart from Amen (2013), which reports the T-statistics of the linear regressions of the year-on-year changes in Google Domestic Trend indices against year-on-year returns in S&P 500. Some of the search indices have a statistically significant positive correlation with stocks, such as "Business & Industrial."

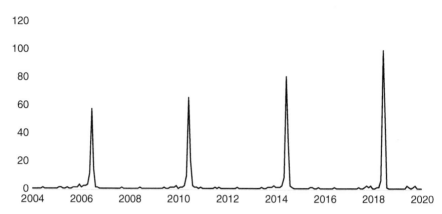

FIGURE 16.2   Search volume for "world cup" in the United States.
Source: Google.

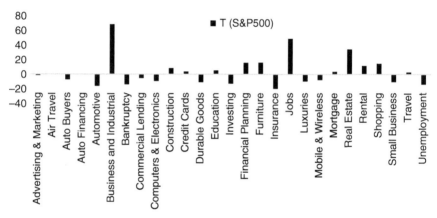

FIGURE 16.3   Regressing Google Domestic Trend Indices.
Source: Based on data from Thalesians, Google.

Others such as bankruptcy and unemployment have a negative correlation, which is not surprising, given that concern around these topics is likely to be associated with an economic slowdown and hence falls in stocks.

Amen (2013) then discusses the creation of a Google Shock Sentiment index, specifically using the (inverted) searches associated with bankruptcy and unemployment. In Figure 16.4, we plot this against the year-on-year changes in S&P 500 as a time series between 2005 and 2013 and in Figure 16.5 as a scatter plot over the same period. The R^2 of regressing these variables is 41%, which suggests that there is a strong relationship between these variables. Later, according to Amen (2013), the Google Shock Sentiment index is used to filter exposure to risky assets, namely S&P 500 and G10 FX carry trades. The author shows that cutting exposure to these assets during periods of high shock, as measured by the shock index, helps to improve

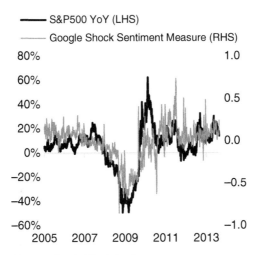

FIGURE 16.4   S&P 500 versus Google Shock Sentiment.
Source: Based on data from Thalesians, Google.

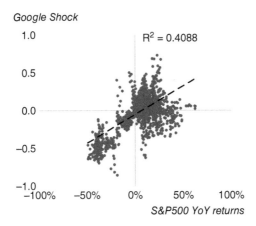

FIGURE 16.5   S&P 500 vs Google Shock Sentiment scatter.
Source: Based on data from Thalesians, Google.

risk-adjusted returns compared to a long-only strategy. There are caveats around using data from Google Trends, notably the fact that it is difficult to ascertain how it has been calculated. Also, in practice, the historical data can change over time, which can make it difficult to backtest, given the difficulty in having point-in-time data. There has also been the notable case of Google Flu trends, where Google search terms were used to predict the spread of flu. While it seemed to work effectively in-sample, it proved a failure out of sample (Salzberg, 2014). However, the difficulty is that many people doing web searching for "flu" might not actually have flu and effectively misdiagnose themselves.

16.4   INVESTOPEDIA SEARCH DATA TO MEASURE INVESTOR ANXIETY

Investopedia is a large financial education website that contains a huge amount of information concerning how the market and the economy work. If you do a Google search for a general financial term – for example, "bond market" – it is likely that a page from Investopedia will pop up on your search among the top results. Just as with our earlier example of Google searches, could the volume of web searches that end up at Investopedia provide us with actionable market insights? Investopedia created the Investor Anxiety Index (IAI), which specifically collects search traffic that ends up in specific pages on their website. These pages relate specifically to investor anxiety, and include topics such as "short selling," "bankruptcy," and "default." Amen (2016) discusses the IAI in some detail. An obvious parallel to the IAI is the VIX, which measures the implied volatility on a number of S&P 500 options and is commonly known as Wall Street's "fear gauge." The correlation of the level of VIX against IAI level in this sample is 30% and the R^2 is around 9% (see Figure 16.6). In Figure 16.7, we plot the IAI against the VIX, and we find that the two track each other, which seems like a broadly intuitive result.

The paper later discusses using the IAI as a filter for a long S&P 500 strategy as follows. The trading strategy involves having a flat position in S&P 500 when the IAI spikes higher. The idea is that when investor anxiety is high, investors should steer clear of stocks. The hypothesis is that when investors are anxious, they are more likely to liquidate their stocks and gravitate toward safer assets such as cash. When IAI is not spiking, we maintain a long position in S&P 500. The rationale is that during periods when investors are calm, they will be willing to invest in riskier assets such as stocks, or prioritizing returns over safety.

The paper also compares this trading strategy to one purely based on VIX spikes, to a strategy of being long only S&P 500 as a benchmark. Traditionally the VIX is

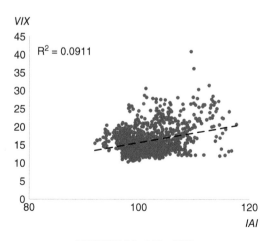

FIGURE 16.6   IAI vs VIX.
Source: Based on data from Cuemacro, Investopedia.

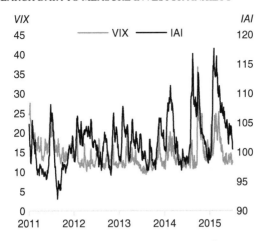

FIGURE 16.7   IAI vs VIX as a scatter plot.
Source: Based on data from Cuemacro, Investopedia.

referred to as Wall Street's "fear" index, and it is often used as a proxy of investor anxiety. The VIX is constructed from the implied volatility of various S&P 500 options. As investors become more anxious, they are likely to buy options to hedge their underlying cash positions, which feeds into a higher VIX.

In Figure 16.8 we show the cumulative returns of all three strategies from the paper. We see that the strategy with the lowest risk-adjusted returns in our sample is long-only exposure to S&P 500. Both active filters (VIX and IAI) outperform long only S&P 500. We note that the IAI-based filter has the highest risk-adjusted returns and lowest drawdowns of all three strategies. This suggests that there is additional value in using IAI as an indicator for investor fear compared to using VIX.

In the next few sections, we continue along this theme of using web-based traffic data to generate trading signals for financial markets, this time looking at page views on Wikipedia.

FIGURE 16.8   Trading S&P 500 with IAI and VIX.
Source: Based on data from Cuemacro, Bloomberg, Investopedia.

16.5   USING WIKIPEDIA TO UNDERSTAND PRICE ACTION IN CRYPTOCURRENCIES

One of the first tasks we might want to undertake when researching a topic is a web search. This very often results in coming to a page on Wikipedia, the crowdsourced encyclopedia. ElBahrawy, Alessandretti, and Baronchelli (2019) use data associated with Wikipedia pages devoted to cryptocurrencies to understand price action. In particular, they examine the edit history and page views of these articles. Edit history can be viewed as a proxy for news volume and the creation of information. This contrast to page views can be seen as proxy for interest in the subject for an audience of nonexperts.

They note that there is a significant correlation (42%) between the daily number of Wikipedia page views and the price of bitcoin, and these correlations are robust over time. They show that, by and large, there is a relatively small number of individuals editing cryptocurrency pages and the editors seem largely to be experts in the field, judging by the number of similar pages in the area they also edit. Hence, they note that it is likely that the audience of viewers of these cryptocurrency pages are likely to be different from those people who create this content.

The authors focus on using page views to develop a trading strategy, given that edits tend be fairly sporadic (roughly every 10 days), as opposed to page views, which are obtainable on a high-frequency basis. They use a relatively high-frequency trading rule examining the daily changes in page views to trigger trading rules. The Wikipedia trading rule outperforms a baseline strategy that examines purely the price as an input and another randomized strategy. However, the authors note that the backtested results do not include any trading fees. The introduction of transaction costs would likely significantly impact returns of a relatively high-frequency trading rule. One way to reduce the impact of transaction costs would be to reduce the trading frequency. In Chapter 19, we explore the subject of liquidity in some depth in the FX market using a dataset from Refinitiv.

Next, we assess how online attention can be used to understand the EMFX market.

16.6   ONLINE ATTENTION FOR COUNTRIES TO INFORM EMFX TRADING

We have seen how web traffic can be a way to understand if, for example, investors are focused on particular payrolls releases or seek to understand price moves in cryptocurrencies. The rationale for this is that metrics like page views can be a way of measuring concern or "attention" about a particular topic. In this section, we expand on the idea of using "attention" to inform decision making. Predata analyzes web-derived traffic data. In particular, they filter this data for specific subsectors, which are likely to be most closely followed by professionals and academics.

Time series are then constructed that are representative of interest in these subsectors. There are, for example, time series for countries that give an idea of the overall online attention in that country on a particular day, which is our focus here.

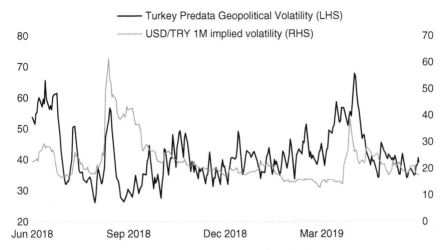

FIGURE 16.9   Turkey PVIX indicator vs USD/TRY 1M implied volatility.
Source: Based on data from Predata, Bloomberg.

Figure 16.9 plots the Predata geopolitical volatility index for Turkey alongside USD/TRY 1M implied volatility. The Predata geopolitical volatility index is based upon online attention on web traffic related to the political situation. In this stylized example, we see that there does appear to be some relationship between these metrics at times. We note that jumps in Predata's index are sometimes accompanied by jumps in the implied volatility. However, it is not a universal. Indeed, there are times when spikes in geopolitical concerns are not always reflected in the market. This is likely just a reflection of the fact that markets are not always purely driven by geopolitical concerns but can be driven by other factors as well. However, this example does suggest that it is worth delving further into the relationship between markets and online attention.

Next, we look at more granular online attention data. Each country has a different array of subsectors that have been curated by analysts and specialists. These subsectors can include "attention" related to, for example, macroeconomy, microeconomy, foreign policy, or military. However, not every subsector is tracked for every country. For example, the subsector for "terrorism" is tracked for Turkey, given that it has historically been an important area of concern for that country. This contrasts with South Korea, where there is no "terrorism" subsector, given that it has not been a significant issue there historically. The web sources used in the construction of the various Predata indicators include both the official languages of each country and also English.

In Figure 16.10, we plot the macroeconomy subsector for Brazil based on English content and also content in Portuguese. The dataset is normalized between 0 and 1. For comparison, we have also included the number of articles on Bloomberg News that mention Brazil, which is relevant to the supply of news.

We have applied a 20-day SMA (simple moving average) to smooth the data (excluding weekend data). We see that while the subsectors do appear to have some

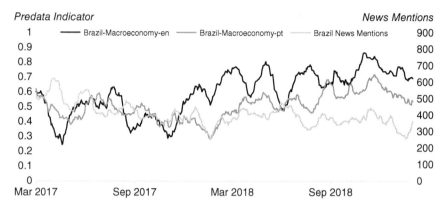

FIGURE 16.10   Comparing English attention with local content for Brazil.
Source: Based on data from Predata, Bloomberg.

sort of relationship, there are some divergences. The rationale is that English is likely to capture attention on a more international basis, whereas, obviously, Portuguese is likely to be more representative of local attention.

We see that the metric for news mentions does appear to have some sort of relationship with both Predata indicators, as we might expect, but again there are divergences. As we noted in the section on payroll article readership, the supply of information and the demand for information are likely to be different quantities. It is not necessarily the case that just because something has been written about, it will capture the interest of readers.

We can explore this idea further by investigating the difference between demand for information and the quantity of news that is written. In order to do this, we construct an indicator by calculating the ratio of attention on the macroeconomy versus news mentions for that same country. We use Bloomberg News as our source of news mentions. This ratio will therefore give us the attention, which has been normalized for the amount of news available for a country. We will use this ratio as a basis of a trading rule. We will apply the following rule to a number of emerging market currencies across a number of regions (IDR, INR, BRL, TRY, MXN, and RUB):

- When attention is **greater** than that suggested by the news mentions (i.e. the ratio is above its 20D SMA), we sell the currency of that country versus USD.
- When attention is **less** than that suggested by the news mentions (i.e. the ratio is below its 20D SMA), we sell the currency of that country versus USD.

The idea is that we can strip out the part of the attention that might purely be driven by the supply of news. Hence, when there is a lot of attention, when adjusted for the supply of news, it is likely to be bullish. Conversely, a lack of attention is likely to be bearish, when we have taken into account the amount of news available.

In Figure 16.11, we present the cumulative returns of a basket of IDR, INR, BRL, TRY, MXN, and RUB that have been actively traded based on this "attention"-based trading strategy between 2016 and 2019 versus USD. Carry and transaction costs are

FIGURE 16.11 Trading a basket of EM currencies using macroeconomy "attention."
Source: Based on data from Predata, Bloomberg.

included. We also assume an equally weighted notional across each currency pair. As a benchmark, the cumulative returns of a long-only EM versus USD basket are plotted alongside it.

The returns of both the active strategy and the long-only benchmark are relatively similar over the full sample. However, the information ratio of the active strategy is considerably higher. Furthermore, the drawdowns of the benchmark are considerably higher, compared to the actively traded strategy, as is the volatility. Hence, overall the risk-adjusted returns are much higher when adopting an attention-based strategy for EM. It does seem to suggest that measures of "attention" have been useful historically for trading emerging market currencies.

Further work could be done to investigate whether country-based attention measures can be useful in understanding currency volatility.

16.7 SUMMARY

It seems intuitive that being able to track investor interest should help us to understand what is driving the markets. The concept of investor attention is subtly different from that of news volume. Indeed, as discussed in the chapter, news demand is different from news supply. While journalists will endeavor to write what is likely to be read, it is not always the case that readership will tally with this.

In this chapter, we discussed several different ways of understanding investor attention, such as deciphering search data, looking at Google Trends data and also search traffic associated with Investopedia. Later, we looked at examining page views and edits on Wikipedia in the context of cryptocurrencies. We showed how combining different datasets on news supply (Bloomberg News volume) and online attention (based on, for example, Predata datasets) can be used to trade EMFX profitably on a historic basis.

CHAPTER 17

Consumer Transactions

17.1 INTRODUCTION

A large number of companies cater directly to consumers. These companies are present in many industries, including the retail, technology, and leisure sectors. If we can understand consumer spending at these firms through alternative data, this can provide insights into the financial health of these companies on a relatively high-frequency basis. This contrasts to existing ways that rely on quarterly earnings releases published by publicly traded firms. It might also be the case that digging deeper into consumer transaction data can give us more granularity about their spending behavior than a company's earnings release, and hence it can offer more insights.

An investor might wish to compare consumer spending patterns at different firms in a particular sector. Alternatively, economists could look at consumer spending as a whole to get a better understanding of the economy at a macro level. It is extremely unlikely that any consumer transaction dataset will include every single consumer. This is also true of other datasets that are seeking to measure the consumer activity such as footfall data. Instead, they are simply a sample of the population we are examining. Hence, it is key to ensure that the panel of consumers used in such a dataset is representative of the broader population. For example, if we are seeking to measure consumer spending in the United States and our panel is largely made up of coastal cities, such as New York and Los Angeles, our dataset is unlikely to be truly representative of the United States as a whole. The panel should also be suitably balanced around demographics, such as age, gender, income, and the like. Furthermore, it is likely that a considerable amount of time needs to be spent to ensure that the panel is maintained properly over time. If the panel is not balanced, and contains particular biases, it will be difficult to extrapolate observations to the broader population.

As with many other alternative datasets, entity matching is also a key issue in the context we are discussing. In particular, it is necessary to map the company names mentioned in consumer transaction data to tradeable assets. This can be particularly challenging for many different sectors, given that several brands often come together under the same parent company that is the traded entity. In practice, these mappings can change significantly over time and hence, any mapping needs to be continually maintained. Obviously for those firms whose customers are largely other businesses, consumer transaction datasets might be less relevant.

In this chapter, we will give examples of how to use credit card data to proxy official retail sales data. Later, we will go into some detail about consumer receipts data, showing how it can be used to understand Amazon earnings and also compare the relative performance of similar firms (in this instance for headphone manufacturers Sennheiser and Shure).

17.2   CREDIT AND DEBIT CARD TRANSACTION DATA

Gerdes, Greene, and Liu (2019) discuss patterns in noncash payments in the United States. They note that in recent years card payments have increased both in number and also value, by 10.1% and 8.4% respectively. Debit card payments made up 66.9% of total card payments in 2017. However, in value terms, credit cards actually made up just over half. Generally, credit card payments were higher on average at 88 USD versus 35 USD for debit cards in 2017 in the United States.

In 2017, the number of in-person payments by card was 75.3%. When broken down by value it was only just over half, 53.7%, indicating that remote payments were typical of higher value. Remote payments include those over the phone, online, and those involving a mobile device (such as via Apple Pay).

Kumar, Maktabi, and O'Brien (2018) look at consumer transactions in the United States from a different perspective, also comprising cash. They also include electronic payments that are typically for items like mortgages. The number of payments was higher for cash in 2017, as it has always been historically. They note how cash is generally used for lower-value items. For items up to 9.99 USD, cash was used in 55% of consumer purchases in 2017. However, this proportion quickly drops for larger-value items. For purchases greater than 100 USD, cash only makes up 7% of all consumer transactions. When looking at the total value of transactions in 2017, the value of cash transactions was less than half those of credit cards and debit cards.

Both these reports suggest that card payments form a large proportion of consumer transactions. Given the increasing prevalence of card payments, it seems reasonable to use data on payments made by consumers on credit and debit cards to understand the economy. Card transactions have the benefit of being easier to track than cash transactions. We should note that, given the different nature of the way cash is used, looking at card transactions alone might neglect some lower-value items. If we are most interested in high-value transactions, this might not matter. However, if we are tracking lower-value items, say to understand sales of a confectionary company, we might not necessarily capture a representative set of transactions.

There are a number of different sources for credit and debit card transaction data. Several data products are available directly from credit card companies.[1] These have

---

[1] As mentioned in Chapter 3, buying granular consumer transaction data hides the legal risk of obtaining involuntary personal information, which could lead to compliance issues.

FIGURE 17.1   Brazil YoY retail sales versus SpendingPulse Brazil retail sales YoY.
Source: Based on data from Bloomberg, MasterCard.

usually been aggregated from transactions by their own customers. There are also firms that aggregate credit card data from many different third parties. One example of credit card transaction data is MasterCard's SpendingPulse index, which creates retail sales statistics using consumer-level credit card transaction data at a national level. The advantage of this dataset is that it is typically available with a relatively short lag compared to official data.

On top of the United States, SpendingPulse also includes data on Australia, Brazil, Canada, Hong Kong, Japan, South Africa, and the United Kingdom. The dataset is also available at a more granular level, with availability for specific sectors like grocery or apparel. In Figure 17.1, we present official retail sales YoY data in Brazil, against data aggregated by SpendingPulse of credit card transactions. We can see that the SpendingPulse data is a relatively good fit for the official data, at least in the long term. We note that the official data is generally more volatile.

17.3   CONSUMER RECEIPTS

There are several different sources for e-receipts/consumer data. E-receipt data might give us a lot of granularity about purchases since these receipts often contain details of items bought. This contrasts to credit card transaction data, which will likely have only the name of the store where the purchase took place and the amount, as opposed to what was bought. Sometimes, if we want more granular information from credit card transaction data, we can try building models to infer missing fields, such as the location of the store.

In some cases, e-mail providers will have an ability to read the e-mails as part of their user service agreement. Users can opt to give third-party add-ins permission to "read" their e-mail to provide additional functionality. For example, there are accounting tools that can read through e-mail receipts of purchases to help give a summary of your expenditure. Typically, after we make an online purchase, we are sent an e-mail receipt as a confirmation.

Obviously, e-mail receipts will not necessarily capture many in-person transactions, because in most of these instances consumers are given paper receipts (although occasionally these can also be e-mail based, such as for Apple Stores). It is possible to use aggregated anonymized e-receipts to understand sales at a very low level, such as specific items, and also at a higher level for entire companies. Point-of-sale (POS) devices at cash registers can be used to record items purchased in shops. Datasets such as Nikkei POS aggregate this data. Datasets derived from POS will also be able to track cash payments.

Quandl has data on their data platform gathered from partnerships with a number of firms that have visibility of consumer e-mails to collect together a large corpus of millions of anonymized e-receipts. Thomas (2016) discusses Quandl's consumer transaction dataset with an example on how it can be used to forecast Amazon revenue. While quarterly revenue is available in 10Q filings, the idea is, of course, to see if it can be forecasted beforehand. The approach examines selecting a group of consumers who have spent at Amazon in the current quarter and the previous quarter, and then calculating the changes in spending over that period. The dataset uses data from Q2 2014–Q2 2016.

One caveat mentioned is that clearly this approach of using transaction data is only relevant for those firms whose business is largely directly to consumers, as opposed to businesses whose clients are also businesses. Hence, it is ideal for a firm like Amazon, whose revenue is heavily linked to consumer-driven purchases. In Figure 17.2, we plot the implied revenue changes according to Quandl's model. There appears to be a fit between the data points, although we should, of course, note that there is a relatively small number of points. This is an issue we often have with quarterly data, which by its nature is relatively sparse.

Clearly, consumer spending patterns are likely to be different, if we compare the period up into Christmas, versus, say, January. Hence, the Quandl model also includes other variables to help account for calendar effects and seasonality.

Admittedly, such an approach might not necessarily capture the revenue from Amazon Web Services (AWS). This is because AWS is likely to show up under business expenses, as opposed to a consumer transaction. Thomas (2016) suggests that this might explain why the line of best fit is not through the origin and suggests that incorporating other variables into the model might be helpful, such as guidance figures. Indeed, in Chapter 13, we adopted a similar approach augmenting an alternative dataset (on Chinese PMI manufacturing) with consensus estimates to increase accuracy.

The granular nature data of consumer receipts also means that the dataset can be used to understand metrics such as the cost of the average item, not purely the average amount spent by consumers. Thomas (2016) gives an example of how consumer receipt data can be used to understand the relative consumer spend on different brands. In Figure 17.3, we quote a result from the paper, comparing the month-on-month changes of different headphone brands, Sennheiser and Shure,

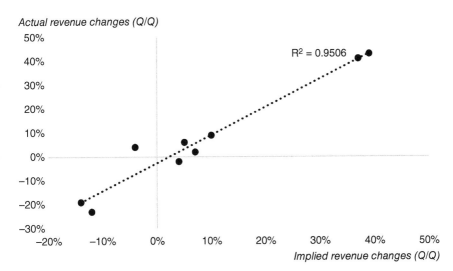

FIGURE 17.2 Alternative data forecasts for Amazon revenue versus actual revenue changes. (Q/Q)
Source: Based on data from Quandl.

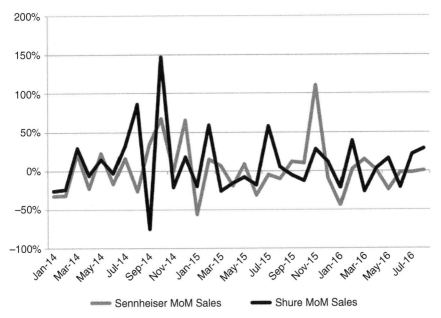

FIGURE 17.3 Comparing Shure versus Sennheiser (MoM) spend at Amazon.
Source: Based on data from Quandl.

on Amazon's marketplace. Both companies are privately traded in this instance, illustrating that this type of analysis need not be limited to public companies. In Chapter 20, we discuss how private equity investors might use alternative data to help identify company targets for investment and to assess their performance.

17.4 SUMMARY

Consumer transaction data can help us understand broader retail data and also spending in individual companies on a timelier basis than official data releases. Typically, this data is available from credit and debit card transactions, which can give us a broad insight into spending patterns. We showed how data derived from MasterCard can track official Brazilian retail sales data, which tends to be released much later.

For more granular information on precisely what consumers are buying, for example, on a product level, consumer receipts are useful. These can be derived from sources such as e-mail, which will help us to track online transactions. Meanwhile, point-of-sale devices at retailers' premises can track in-person transactions. This chapter gave examples of how investors can use consumer receipt data. We showed an example using consumer receipts to estimate quarter-on-quarter revenue changes for Amazon. We also gave an example of how a dataset of consumer receipts can be used to understand consumer spending patterns on headphones for different brands.

CHAPTER 18

Government, Industrial, and Corporate Data

18.1 INTRODUCTION

Governments and corporations publish a large amount of data on a regular basis. It is, in effect, exhaust data that is derived from the everyday activity of corporations, individuals, and governments. Some of this would not be regarded as alternative data. For example, headline data on the labor market, growth, and inflation has been used heavily by market participants. Corporations that are publicly trading have to report their earnings every quarter and various other statistics pertaining to their business.

In practice, many of these "common" datasets from governments and corporates are released at a very low frequency. One example is GDP data, which is typically released on a quarterly basis in most countries, albeit in the form of various estimates. Most economic datasets are released on a monthly basis, and only very occasionally on a weekly basis (such as US jobless claims data).

Such a large volume of this data is released that, in practice, most of it is rarely examined in all its entirety by many market participants. We can think of the US labor report, as an example. While market participants will tend to flag the headline figures, most of the underlying data in the report is ignored by the markets. We might consider some of these less commonly used data statistics as alternative data. Indices that aggregate some of these datasets in novel ways can also sometimes be considered as forms of alternative data.

Indeed, we will discuss several examples in this chapter showing how government data can be used to estimate how innovative firms are. We will also discuss some alternative datasets in this space for macro investors, one to quantify FX risk while the other seeks to estimate central bank intervention in FX markets on a high-frequency basis. There are also many datasets that are used internally by governments and corporations, but are generally not available externally.

It is also worth noting that in addition to "common" data (i.e. official quarterly earnings releases), corporates also regularly publish large amounts of much more granular publicly available data on their websites. This data can be useful from an investor perspective. One example of this is job postings. The advantage of this is that it is available on a higher-frequency basis. Furthermore, such data is available not only for publicly traded firms but also private firms. (See Chapter 20, where we discuss the use of alternative data by private equity firms.)

18.2   USING INNOVATION MEASURES TO TRADE EQUITIES

When it comes to headline economic data, these datasets have been used by market participants for many years. However, it should be noted that there is a vast quantity of data released by governments, in addition to economic data, that could be useful for investment purposes.

Earlier, we noted how the value of data held by a company can be difficult to measure. This is true of many intangible assets of a firm. For a company in an innovation-led sector, this can be quite problematic. Simply looking at a company's public financial filings may not give a full picture of the innovation value of a company. Are there any better ways we can measure innovation? One way could be to examine the number of patents filed by a company. However, without any sort of adjustment, this might not capture the dynamics of what precisely is innovation. Companies may simply file too many patents, many of which have little value. Hence, any such measure would somehow need to adjust any measure derived from patents. Such adjustments could be based on the size of the firm or also by scaling the number of patents filed by R&D spending. Even this might be imperfect as we might end up underweighting companies with large R&D expenditure.

Jha (2019) suggests an alternative way to measure innovation within companies that does not only entail examining patents filed. Rather than examining company financial statements, the paper instead looks at ExtractAlpha's ESGEvents Library. The dataset collects data on companies gathered from a number of different governmental organizations, including regulators. The sources include Consumer Financial Protection Bureau (CFPB), the Environmental Protection Agency (EPA), the Occupational Health and Safety Administration (OSHA), the Consumer Product Safety Commission (CPSC), the US Senate, the Federal Election Commission (FEC), the Department of Labor (DOL), the US Treasury Bureau of the Fiscal Service, and the US Patent and Trademark Office (USPTO).

As it can be expected, the entities are often recorded with different company names in the various sources. ExtractAlpha has mapped all the entities into a common reference data form that is mapped to its respective traded security. Jha (2019) specifically looks at a subset of the ESGEvents Library to proxy innovation at firms, in particular datasets from the Department of Labor (DOL), which relate to:

- Number of total workers for which the company has applied for H1B visas in the prior year
- Number of permanent H1B visas for which the company has applied in the prior year

The second source is from the US Patent and Trademark Office (USPTO) with the following information:

- Number of company patent applications in the prior year
- Number of patents granted to the company in the prior year

Thus, the measures not only examine patent applications and those granted, but they also cover the number of highly skilled individuals who require H1B visas and are likely to perform R&D.

There are some major differences in how the data is sampled. The DOL data is released quarterly and the USPTO data is released every week. Because of this, a suitable lag needs to be applied during any backtesting, given that in both cases the datasets are not immediately available for the period they cover. Companies used in the study are those stocks that are traded on US markets and with a market cap of $100 million or more and based upon sufficient trading volume.

Each of these four measures mentioned earlier is recorded both in terms of levels and of year-on-year changes for each of the companies in the universe, resulting in eight metrics. These metrics are then aggregated for every company in a specific industry to create industry-level measures that are then adjusted by market capitalization. Each of these eight metrics are then ranked across all the industries. A long-only portfolio of industries is then constructed. Those that have the higher innovation scores, as measured by the higher metrics, have a higher weighting. By contrast those industries with the lowest innovation score have a weighting zero. The weights are adjusted to sum to 1. In Figure 18.1, the backtested results are shown, excluding transaction costs for an in-sample period between 2003 and 2015.

Most of the risk-adjusted returns are positive. However, the major exception is year-on-year changes in permanent visa applications. One explanation is that visa applications are by implication already a change in the number of employees. Hence, taking a year-on-year change of this may not be necessary. The paper then discusses the construction of a composite innovation indicator. The composite indicator has

Factor		Excess Return	Information Ratio
Level	H1B visa	0.45%	0.17
	Permanent visa	0.39%	0.14
	Patent application	0.46%	0.28
	Patent grant	0.53%	0.3
YoY change	H1B visa	0.29%	0.2
	Permanent visa	−0.78%	−0.47
	Patent application	−0.02%	−0.02
	Patent grant	0.61%	0.5

Source: Based on data from ExtractAlpha.

FIGURE 18.1   Long-only portfolios derived from visa and patent data.

Factor		In Sample (2003–2015)		Out of Sample (2016–2018)		Full Sample (2003–2018)	
		Excess Return	Information Ratio	Excess Return	Information Ratio	Excess Return	Information Ratio
Level	H1B visa	0.45%	0.17	1.86%	0.66	0.71%	0.27
	Permanent visa	0.39%	0.14	2.12%	0.76	0.72%	0.26
	Patent application	0.46%	0.28	1.32%	0.68	0.62%	0.36
	Patent grant	0.53%	0.3	1.17%	0.6	0.65%	0.37
YoY change	H1B visa	0.29%	0.2	0.89%	0.41	0.40%	0.25
	Permanent visa	−0.78%	−0.47	0.25%	0.15	−0.58%	−0.35
	Patent application	−0.02%	−0.02	1.49%	1.02	0.26%	0.19
	Patent grant	0.61%	0.5	1.21%	1.22	0.73%	0.61
Composite Innovation score		0.47%	0.21	2.00%	0.87	0.75%	0.34

Source: Based on data from ExtractAlpha.

FIGURE 18.2   Long-only portfolios derived from visa and patent data (in and out-of-sample).

an excess return of 47 basis points, with information ratio of 0.21. Figure 18.2 shows results for risk-adjusted returns for each indicator, in-sample, out-of-sample, and during the full-sample. The results are also profitable out-of-sample. In particular, the paper notes that innovative industries have outperformed after 2013, although prior to 2009 there was not much difference between both more and less innovative industries.

Later the paper also discusses using the innovation measures to trade individual stocks within an industry, as opposed to at an industry level. However, the authors suggest that such measures are more effective when applying them at an industry level, as shown in the results above. In particular, implementing the trading strategy at an industry level could be more cheaply implemented using ETFs. In the rest of the chapter, we'll move away from single stocks toward macro assets. In particular, we'll focus on macro alternative datasets, constructed from a mixture of macro data released by governments and official organizations, together with market data.

18.3   QUANTIFYING CURRENCY CRISIS RISK

The volatility of currencies tends to be lower than that of single stocks. However, there are periods when currencies can move significantly, and we observe structural breaks in volatility. Understanding the likelihood of a currency crisis is important for both investors and risk managers. We define a currency crisis as a speculative attack on a currency. This attack results in a rapid sell-off in that currency. Typically, it results in central banks attempting to defend the currency through the selling of foreign currency, and also through the hiking of domestic interest rates to make shorting the currency punitive for speculators. It can also lead to shifts in policy, such as the introduction of capital controls. Glick and Hutchinson (2011) discusses currency crises in some detail, noting that even if these speculative attacks are not successful, defending against them can still have high costs. These include running down foreign currency reserves and the negative impact of very high interest rates on domestic growth. Some notable examples include sterling's devaluation when it was forced out of the ERM in 1992 and the Asian Crisis in 1997–98. The global financial crisis was also accompanied by large depreciations in a number of currencies as investors retreated to safe-haven currencies such as USD and JPY. In recent years, we have also seen the examples of RUB and TRY, which suffered large currency depreciations, albeit for more idiosyncratic reasons.

Glick and Hutchinson (2011) surveys the literature on currency crises and also ways to model them going through several generations of models. They suggest that any sort of forecasting requires several components. First, there needs to be a definition of what precisely a currency crisis is. In other words, what size of move would we want to flag? Then there is a need to select variables that are likely to be associated with such sharp currency depreciations. Lastly, a statistical model needs to be constructed.

Empirical analysis from Sleptsova, Tukker, and Fennessy (2019) suggests that there are several common factors that can be used to estimate the likelihood of currency crises. One is high interest rate differentials as well as overheating credit. Another factor is twin deficits – that is, when there is both a budget deficit and also a current account deficit. They also cite high levels of short-term debt relative to exports and FX reserves that could act as a buffer during a currency crisis. How these variables are weighted, however, depends on several factors, including the underlying currency regime (is it currently a floating, managed, or pegged currency). They develop Oxford Economics' FX Risk Tool, which covers 166 currencies in both developed and emerging market space, which is an alternative dataset aggregated from a large number of different raw datasets, ranging from market data to official macro data releases. The indicator is updated monthly and is scaled from 1 to 10, where 10 indicates the most vulnerability to a currency crisis. In Figure 18.3, we quote their analysis, which shows that those currencies with high risk scores have historically had more currency crises. Their out-of-sample results also suggest a high correlation between a high-risk score and high probability of a currency crisis or sharp sell-off.

There is also a high positive correlation between the FX risk score and realized volatility, as we might expect. From an investor perspective, having a method to forecast currency crises is clearly beneficial to avoid exposure to such currencies. For example, in an FX carry basket, we could decrease weights on currencies with the highest likelihood of a sell-off. We could also increase the weights on currencies with a lower likelihood. Typically, in an FX carry basket, we would want to buy the currencies with the highest yields and fund those with the lowest yield. However, as mentioned, the highest-yielding currencies will generally also be the ones most susceptible to sell-offs. Hence, the key is to try to find those outlier currencies that have both high yields and a lower risk of sell-offs. We might also seek to find a trade-off between the two factors, accepting a lower yield in exchange for reducing risk.

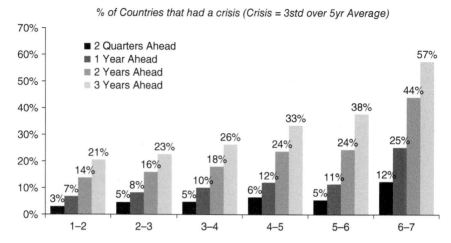

FIGURE 18.3   Average FX crisis rates, 2000–2017.
Source: Based on data from Oxford Economics.

Essentially, we would use "riskiness" as another way to rank currencies as well as the interest rate differential. Typically, one approach that is used for ranking currencies to include in a carry basket while taking into account risk is to examine the ratio of carry to implied volatility for each currency pair. Incorporating the FX risk index could provide additional information drawn from fundamentals that might not be fully incorporated into implied volatility quotes taken from the market. More risk-averse investors could weigh the riskiness factor more heavily than the yield differential in their model.

It is also likely that the FX risk index could also be useful from a speculative perspective to short those currencies, which are flagged as most likely to have a currency crisis. Of course, we need to be mindful of the costs associated with shorting high carry currencies when we do this. From a risk manager perspective, FX risk scores could be additional factors for forecasting volatility to enhance Value-at-Risk (VaR) estimates. Typically, VaR estimates take into account only historical market data, as opposed to augmenting them with insights from more fundamental datasets.

18.4   MODELING CENTRAL BANK INTERVENTION IN CURRENCY MARKETS

We noted that exhaust data can be derived from government activity. One area of particular interest for market participants is to understand the behavior of central banks. We noted earlier how central banks communications from the Federal Reserve can be used to understand moves in US Treasury yields in Chapter 15. Central banks obviously have a large impact on bond markets, both through their rhetoric and also through direct intervention in the market. This occurs not only in the short end but (because of quantitative easing) central banks have been in the market across many longer dated instruments. However, central banks are not active only in bond markets. Certain central banks have also become large holders of equities.

Central banks also trade in foreign exchange markets. This can be as part of managing their currency reserves. While the largest proportion of currency reserves are generally held in USD, the amounts across the various currencies do change over time, not only because of valuation effects, but also as central banks actively change the composition of their portfolios. Central banks may also intervene in their own currency to help manage volatility and also to keep their currency within certain bounds against USD or a basket of currencies. Typically, central banks in emerging markets will be more active in doing this, compared to central banks in developed markets who tend to allow their currency to float freely. One major exception to this has been CHF where the SNB had instituted a floor in EUR/CHF for several years through repeated intervention before abandoning the policy in January 2015. Historically, Bank of Japan has been more active in foreign exchange intervention than other central banks in developed markets.

Figure 18.4 plots quarterly COFER (Currency Composition of Official Foreign Exchange Reserve) data as an example of commonly used datasets in this area, which is compiled by the IMF from central bank data globally. COFER shows how the global composition of FX reserves has changed over time. The granular data by country that is used to construct COFER is strictly confidential and it is voluntary for central banks to be included in the COFER dataset. The difficulty with trying to understand the behavior of central banks within the FX markets is that data like COFER tends to be heavily lagged and also lacks a significant amount of granularity. The level of detail in FX reserves data provided can also vary significantly between the various central banks in official data. One way to try to fill in the gaps in the official data is to construct models.

One of the most widely followed managed currencies is CNY (Chinese yuan) where the PBoC frequently intervenes in the market. One question of particular importance for investors is to try to understand when the PBoC intervenes in the currency market and also what is the size of their intervention. If the PBoC sells large

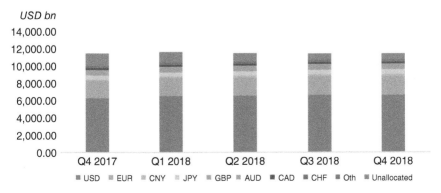

FIGURE 18.4   COFER data: Currency Composition of Official Foreign Exchange Reserve.
Source: Based on data from IMF.

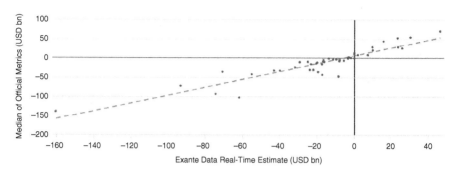

FIGURE 18.5   Comparing model estimates of CNY intervention versus official data.
Source: Exante Data, Macrobond, Thomson Reuters, PBoC, SAFE.

amounts of foreign currency versus CNY, we would expect their foreign currency reserves to be reduced. By contrast, if they bought foreign currency versus CNY, foreign currency reserves would obviously increase. We might be able to glean some of this information from China's official release of foreign exchange reserves. However, this data is only available publicly on a lagged monthly basis. Is there a way to estimate intervention without having to wait for this lagged data?

Exante Data (2018) constructed models to estimate PBoC intervention activity in CNY on a high-frequency basis. We give a high-level overview of the model here. The main rationale behind the model is that any intervention activity by PBoC is likely to have market impact that can be measured.

Exante Data use two separate models to do this. The first model detects market anomalies from unusually large trades, which are likely to be the result of PBoC activity. The second model meanwhile examines price and volume data from a number of different markets to identify PBoC footprint in price action. In both instances, intraday data is used as an input. The final signal is an average of both models.

In Figure 18.5, we show the results of comparing a monthly aggregation of the Exante Data intervention estimates against a measure computed from official Chinese data. We see that in general, the model-based estimates are quite close to those based on the official data that is released much later. While the data is plotted on a monthly basis here, it is also worth noting that a model-based approach can be used to estimate reserves on a high-frequency basis.

While this example is specifically for modeling PBoC intervention in CNY, it seems reasonable to conjecture that a similar approach could also be used for other central banks who regularly intervene in their own currency markets.

18.5 SUMMARY

Typically, investors tend to examine headline data published by governments and corporates. However, there is a wealth of information of more granular data that is published by them and that can also be utilized in the investment process. We have seen in this chapter that there are novel ways to examine published data from governments, industry, and corporates.

We have seen it is possible to use government data on visa applications and associated data to help understand how innovative companies are. We cited research from ExtractAlpha on how such innovation measures could be used to trade equities. On the macro side, we looked at FX risk indicators created by Oxford Economics, which seek to combine many economic variables to give us an idea of how susceptible a country is to defaulting and the potential for a currency crisis. We also described a dataset from Exante Data, which estimates central bank FX intervention on a timely basis.

CHAPTER 19

Market Data

19.1 INTRODUCTION

It might be unusual to include market data as "alternative." After all, if we consider market data such as daily closing prices, these are widely available to investors, in many cases for free from websites like Google Finance and Yahoo Finance. However, if we delve more deeply, we note that there is a wide discrepancy between the various asset classes, the frequency of data, and also the granularity. If we would like very high-frequency market data and in particular data that gives us an idea of quotes for different sizes (in other words market depth), this data is much more expensive. Furthermore, the sheer size of such datasets makes them more difficult to consume.

For very illiquid asset classes, which trade very infrequently, simply getting a daily time series of prices might be close to impossible. Even for very liquid asset classes, the breadth of information can vary. In equities, data such as volume traded is very common. This contrasts with FX, which is predominantly an OTC market and comprehensive volume data is more difficult to source.

In this chapter, we will talk about two examples of alternative datasets derived from market data in FX. First, we talk about aggregated FX flow data collected by CLS and show how it can be used to create systematic trading rules to trade FX. Later, we use high-frequency FX tick data to build up a picture of how liquidity has changed over the years and how it changes by time of day.

19.2 RELATIONSHIP BETWEEN INSTITUTIONAL FX FLOW DATA AND FX SPOT

We noted that the FX spot market is mostly traded on an OTC basis. Volume on exchanges is comparatively low. Some venues where it can be traded are open only to market makers. By contrast, other venues are open to all participants (so-called all-to-all venues). Many trades are done on a bilateral basis between price takers and market makers. Hence, it can be extremely difficult to obtain comprehensive volume and flow data on the FX spot market, given that the market is quite fragmented.

CLS Group was established in 2002, as a result of cooperation between a large number of firms involved in FX trading. CLS Group settles a large number of the trades on the FX spot market, whether they are transacted on venues or on a bilateral basis. For currency pairs that they settle, the proportion is over 50% of the market. As a result, they collect a lot of FX spot transaction data as part of their daily business operations. In the past few years, they have begun to distribute datasets that have been aggregated from this FX spot transaction data. These datasets include information on FX volume and FX flow, which has been split up into hourly buckets, to give a relatively high-frequency picture of the FX market. The CLS-IDHOF dataset consists of hourly FX flow data released with a relatively short lag of less than an hour. Meanwhile, the CLS-HOF dataset, which consists of similar data, has a release lag of a day. The flow data is split between corporate, fund, and non-bank financial accounts. There is also a buy-side designation, which includes all those accounts, as well as non-bank market makers. Amen (2019) discusses the dataset in some detail, first going through a few general results about the nature of the daily volume of these accounts and then developing trading strategies based on historical flow data. We will seek to summarize that paper, quoting some of these results. There are also a number of other papers on CLS FX data, including Ranaldo and Somogyi (2019), Hasbrouck and Levich (2018), and Gargano, Riddiough, and Sarno (2019).

Figure 19.1 shows the average daily volume of all four types of accounts trading EUR/USD from 2012 to 2018. In Figure 19.2, we show the average absolute net flow. We see that in general the buy-side flow consists of a lot of two-way flow, judging from the relatively small daily absolute net flow compared to the daily volume of those accounts. By contrast, the absolute net flow of fund trades is relatively high

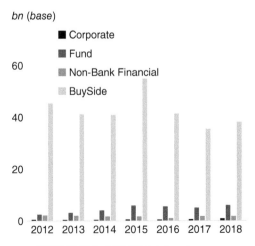

FIGURE 19.1   EUR/USD daily volume.
Source: Based on data from Cuemacro, CLS.

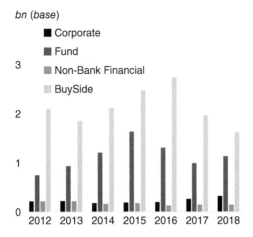

FIGURE 19.2   EUR/USD daily abs net flow.
Source: Based on data from Cuemacro, CLS.

as a proportion of their total volume. Hence, as a group they could exhibit more group-like behavior.

In Figure 19.3, we show the T-statistics from multiple regressions of the flow from each type of account for each currency pair against the returns of that currency pair. Our sample for the regression is from 2012 to 2018. We find that generally the coefficients tend to be positive for fund and non-bank financial accounts. We can infer that fund and non-bank financial accounts tend to have a positive contribution to spot returns. This contrasts to corporates and buy side on aggregate, which have a negative contribution. Of course, there are some caveats to this analysis, given that the constants terms are fairly large, suggesting that a large amount of price action cannot be explained by flow data alone.

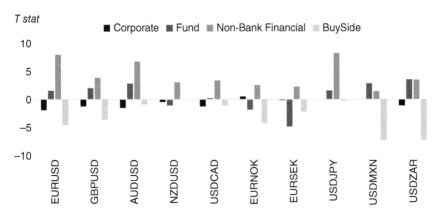

FIGURE 19.3   Multiple regressions between spot returns and net flow.
Source: Based on data from Cuemacro, CLS, Bloomberg.

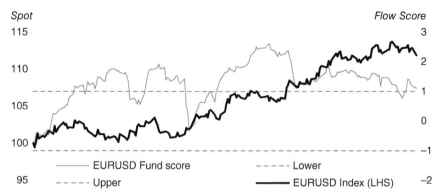

FIGURE 19.4   EUR/USD index versus EUR/USD fund flow score.
Source: Based on data from Cuemacro, CLS, Bloomberg.

Given that flow data from fund accounts tends to be quite directional and also given that it tends to have a positive contribution to FX spot returns, it seems a reasonable approach to create a trading rule based on this metric. Essentially, the trading rule used in the paper involves:

- Buying a currency pair when fund flow is heavily positive, and then holding till it turns more neutral
- Selling a currency pair when fund flow is heavily negative, and then holding till it turns more neutral

In order to measure funds' FX flow, we create a standardized score, which we illustrate in Figure 19.4, along with upper and lower lines to indicate trading point triggers.

Of course, other approaches can be used to fade extremes in the flow or positioning but in practice it can be tricky to time such points, given that positioning can remain extreme for long periods of time. In Figure 19.5, we present the risk-adjusted returns

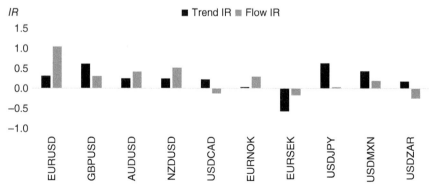

FIGURE 19.5   Risk-adjusted returns for trend and daily flow-based strategies.
Source: Based on data from Cuemacro, CLS, Bloomberg.

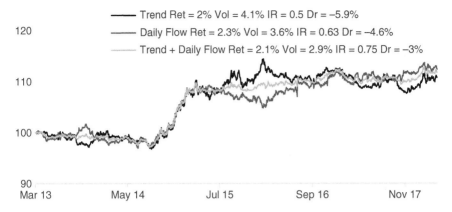

FIGURE 19.6 Daily flow and trend returns.
Source: Based on data from Cuemacro, CLS, Bloomberg.

for these trading rules for a number of G10 and EM currency pairs. For comparison, we also show the risk-adjusted returns for a generic trend-following rule.

The paper shows that this daily flow-based trading rule is profitable in the majority of cases, although it has been loss-making historically in USD/CAD, EUR/SEK, and USD/ZAR. The trend-following strategy seems to be profitable in the majority of cases other than EUR/SEK. In Figure 19.6, we create a basket based upon these rules. We find that the daily flow basket has higher risk-adjusted returns than the trend basket. Combining both, however, has the highest risk-adjusted returns, suggesting that for traders who already use a trend-following approach, adding flow data can help to diversify returns to some extent, at least when looking at historical returns.

The paper also later discusses using the FX flow data to construct hourly trading strategies for more liquid currency pairs. The risk-adjusted returns of the hourly FX flow data basket are 0.92, higher than either the trend strategy or daily flow trading rule. While we have focused on using FX flow data to create systematic trading rules, associated datasets like FX volume are important when it comes to understanding liquidity and cost of execution. In the next section, we'll shift to using FX datasets to quantify market liquidity and trading costs, which is relevant for both discretionary and systematic traders.

19.3   UNDERSTANDING LIQUIDITY USING HIGH-FREQUENCY FX DATA

A lot of the focus on alternative data is on how it can be used to increase the alpha of a strategy. However, it is worth noting for any time we might be seeking alpha, the cost of execution will act as a drag on trading and can impact the trading strategy capacity, particularly, for higher-frequency strategies. There are also significant costs of execution for larger notional sizes.[1]

---

[1]For a discussion on the capacity of trading strategy, see Chapter 1.

Hence, it is imperative to understand transaction costs and how liquidity changes over time and how it can impact our overall returns. Are certain liquidity providers typically charging us more than others? Are there certain times of day where liquidity is worst? Can we understand the impact of certain events on market liquidity? Indeed, the whole area of transaction cost analysis (TCA) has grown to help address these questions. In order to answer many of these questions, we need to have a high-frequency market data to act as a benchmark to compare against our executed trades. Furthermore, high-frequency market data can be used to understand market liquidity more broadly.

While high-frequency market data might not be strictly perceived as alternative data, it is used much less than other forms of market data, such as daily data. One reason is that it is much more unwieldly to work with given its size. Another reason is that typically these datasets can be much more expensive. This is especially the case if we are looking at data that provides market depth (i.e. quotes at different levels and sizes, rather than best bid/ask quotes).

In this section, we shall examine how high-frequency tick data can be used to understand liquidity changes in FX markets. We use indicative tick data from Refinitiv for our analysis, focusing on the best bid/ask indicative quotes for the two most traded currency pairs, EUR/USD and USD/JPY, with a sample between 2005 and 2017. It is likely that if we used executable data, we might get differing results and most likely tighter spreads. We will calculate the bid/ask spread in basis points as a simple way of representing liquidity. Figure 19.7 plots the average daily EUR/USD's bid/ask spread over time, excluding every Christmas and New Year's Day in the sample. We see that the peak is on June 24, 2016, just after the date of the Brexit vote. Spreads widen in the runup to that event. Widening of spreads also happened rapidly during the great financial crisis and Lehman bankruptcy.

Next, we calculate the average bid/ask spread for each hour of the day in London time. We then take the average spread by hour of the day across the full sample. We

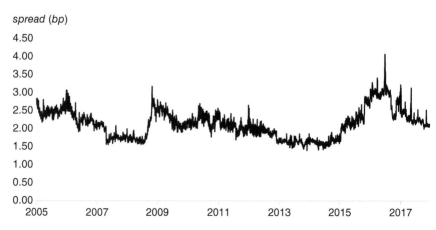

FIGURE 19.7   EUR/USD bid/ask spread over time.
Source: Based on data from Refinitiv.

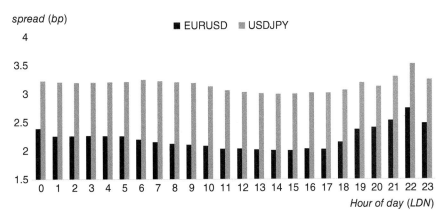

FIGURE 19.8 EUR/USD and USD/JPY bid/ask spread by time of day.
Source: Based on data from Refinitiv.

do this for both EUR/USD and USD/JPY, plotting the results in Figure 19.8. We note that the most illiquid time of day for both pairs is during the New York afternoon period. By contrast the most liquid period is when both London and New York desks are active. Asian hours tend to be comparatively less liquid. The bid/ask spread for USD/JPY sees less of a variation between London and Asian hours. Perhaps this is unsurprising, given that there are likely to be more local Japanese accounts actively trading JPY during Asian hours. By contrast for EUR/USD, Asian hours are outside of both European and American time zones when US and European investors and corporates are likely to be most active.

Having such liquidity profiles can be useful for traders in order to understand which times of day are likely to offer better liquidity. In practice, if we were forecasting liquidity, we would also need to factor in an event calendar for scheduled economic releases such as nonfarm payrolls or FOMC meetings. Obviously, it would be impossible to take into account unscheduled events, such as unscheduled statements from politicians crossing the newswires, which can often severely impact liquidity as traders scramble to react. While these examples are relatively straightforward, they nevertheless shed insight into how less used datasets can be useful for reducing the drag on returns associated with trading costs.

19.4 SUMMARY

Market data is rarely thought of as "alternative data," given that many of its forms are very commoditized. However, in practice, there are some datasets derived from the trading of market participants, which tend to be much rarer and more expensive. We discussed the relative scarcity of comprehensive FX flow and volume datasets. FX tends to be a very fragmented market; hence it is often difficult to get a full understanding of flows and volume that are transacted across the market. We examined a specific FX flow dataset from CLS, which gives an aggregated view of FX flows and used it to create some FX trading strategies. We also talked about how tick data can be considered as alternative data, particularly when it includes market depth information or actual trades. We showed how a tick dataset in FX space can be useful for understanding market liquidity, which is a key consideration for traders. A poor understanding of market liquidity can severely impact trading costs and hence the final returns delivered to clients. For readers interested in transaction cost analysis, one of the authors of this book has written tcapy, a Python based TCA library, which can be downloaded from https://www.github.com/cuemacro/tcapy.

CHAPTER 20

Alternative Data in Private Markets

20.1 INTRODUCTION

A lot of the focus on alternative data has been on its use within public markets. If a firm is publicly traded, it is required to disclose a significant amount of information, such as in the form of earning releases and annual reports. For macro traded assets, we also have many data releases from national statistical agencies. As we have already stated numerous times, alternative data can help us fill the gaps and it can give us an idea of the state of a firm or an entire economy on a much higher-frequency basis, such as daily and weekly, rather than quarterly. Alternative data can also help reduce the lag associated with "official" data. However, in both these instances, we often have an official yardstick of what "ground truth" is. We know what the earnings of a company will be at predefined intervals. We know that unemployment data will be released monthly and so on.

When it comes to understanding private companies, there is less data for us to establish the "ground truth." The level of disclosure required for private firms is much less than that required for public firms. In some countries, like the UK, we may at least have annual accounts for companies available from a public source such as Companies House. However, in many other countries, there might not be this level of granularity concerning the financials of private companies. At a macro level, the validity of official economic data is not consistent, especially for some less developed countries. The "ground truth" in private companies is much more difficult to quantify. This makes it more challenging for investors to do due diligence of private companies when deciding upon an investment, compared with public firms.

In this chapter, we will begin by describing what private equity firms and venture capital firms do. Later, we talk about datasets that track the performance of these firms. We will also discuss how alternative data can help investors plug the gaps in their due diligence of private companies and give some use cases.

20.2 DEFINING PRIVATE EQUITY AND VENTURE CAPITAL FIRMS

Typically, a private equity fund is made up of limited partners (LP), who own the vast majority of the shares. These can, for example, be pension funds. By contrast, the general partners (GP) in a fund own a very small amount of equity (in the order of 1%). However, they will be responsible for directing the fund and choosing the investments. Figure 20.1 plots the current AUM (assets under management) of some of the biggest GPs.

The GPs receive a management fee and carried interest, which is similar to a performance fee charged by a hedge fund. The shares in a private equity fund are not publicly traded; hence, the market in these funds tends to be illiquid and price discovery is more challenging.

There are many different types of approaches used in private equity investing. These include leveraged buyouts where a firm is taken over with a combination of debt and equity funding. The debt funding is then collateralized on the future income stream from the firm. The target firm is often private, although it can sometimes be a publicly traded company that is taken back into private markets through the transaction. Distressed funding involves taking over a firm that is under financial stress, often in bankruptcy. There are usually several objectives. One objective is to try to rescue the business by improving the way it is run, often through the changing of its management, and then to sell it on for a profit.

Alternatively, it can involve selling the firms' assets off for the highest price – in other words, asset stripping. Unsurprisingly, asset stripping is a much more controversial strategy, given it can often result in significant job losses.

Venture capital is also another form of private equity that involves funding entrepreneurs and their start-ups. In a sense, we can view venture capital funding as a way-out-of-the-money call option on a start-up. In most cases, that option will expire worthless. However, there will be those rare occasions when it will expire heavily in-the-money. As a result, a venture capital firm needs to make a large number of investments. The rationale is that although most investments may fail, they only need a small number of "successful" start-ups in order to offset all the failures and deliver substantial returns to their investors.

The pre-seed stage of a start-up often relies on self-funding from the founders themselves (and also friends and family). However, in order to expand more rapidly, external funding is usually sought over several rounds. Earlier stages of funding are obviously much riskier, given that the start-up is less established. However, the flipside is that valuations are much lower. The different rounds of funding after the seed stage are known as Series A, Series B, and so on.

The angel/seed funding stage tends to be the first infusion of outside capital. This stage can be focused on product development and understanding what the market is for the product through doing active research. Early-round funding will generally be larger and occurs once the business has got more traction. Late-stage funding is all about trying to scale an already successful business.

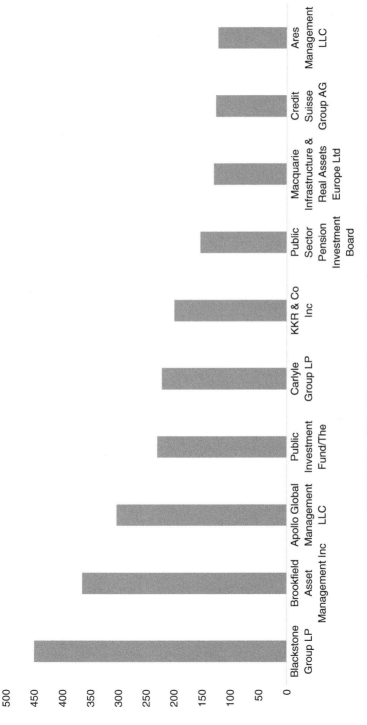

FIGURE 20.1 AUM of largest GPs (general partners) in billions USD.
Source: Based on data from Bloomberg.

20.3 PRIVATE EQUITY DATASETS

For publicly traded assets, market data is readily available. Hence, it is feasible for us to understand the historical returns we would have made from equity investments, once we have factored in dividends, funding costs, and so on. In private equity, by its nature "price data" is more difficult to understand, given that the shares are more illiquid and not publicly traded.

Kaplan and Lerner (2016) discuss the datasets associated with private equity and, in particular, with venture capital. They note that less information is available, given that venture capital firms typically do not have to disclose as much information to the SEC and other regulators, unlike, for example, mutual funds. As a result, there tends to be less data available about their transactions. Research on venture capital has therefore relied more on proprietary datasets.

As Kaplan and Lerner note, some of the oldest data available on venture capital has revolved around those firms that have had IPOs and have therefore produced IPO prospectuses. However, this type of approach ignores the vast majority of start-ups that never reach the public stage. Ultimately, if we are using a database of historical private equity transactions to inform our decision-making process when making new investments, it is insufficient to simply have the rare occasions when a start-up has become very successful. We also want company failures to be included in the dataset. This issue also affects databases for publicly traded companies where survivorship bias can also impact any sort of historical study or backtest.

Two of the oldest databases that chart venture capital transactions are VentureXpert (Refinitiv), which has a history going back to 1961, and Venture Source (Dow Jones), which starts in 1994. The authors note some challenges in both datasets. This includes understating the number of companies that have closed (thereby introducing survivorship bias whereby failed companies may disappear from the dataset, which would bias returns to the upside). There can also be some discrepancies between the datasets. However, there are some other recent datasets for private equity transactions, such as Preqin, Capital IQ, and Pitchbook. These datasets use a number of different sources such as disclosures from limited partners, SEC filings and also publicly available data. Another data source often used within venture capital circles is Crunchbase. It should be noted that, in terms of the biggest data providers, Bloomberg and FactSet also offer private equity transaction data.

When it comes to measuring the performance of private equity firms, there are a number of providers, including Burgiss Private I, Cambridge Associates, and Prequin. There can be a number of biases when it comes to venture capital performance data. There can also be a lack of completeness in the data because pension funds may face pressure from LPs not to disclose the performance of their venture capital investments to data providers. Also, there might be a lack of data on newer venture capital firms and poorly performing funds may prefer not to report. There might also be biases in the data reported by GPs and LPs such as valuations to data vendors. There might also be differences in how each data vendor reports their dataset.

20.4   UNDERSTANDING THE PERFORMANCE OF PRIVATE FIRMS

Let's say we have used a historical transaction dataset for private equity to find the characteristics of what have been "successful" private investments in the past. We might find that this approach can help us narrow down new private investment targets, whether they are start-ups or larger, more established private firms. However, what can we do in terms of additional research on private firms other than a high-level screening approach based on historical transactions data? As we noted earlier, private firms are generally not required to disclose as much data as public companies, which makes our task much more challenging. One approach is to use proxy companies in the same sector in public markets. We could have, for example, tried to proxy the performance of Shake Shack before it went to IPO by examining public firms such as Yum Brands (which includes brands such as Pizza Hut and Kentucky Fried Chicken) and McDonald's. This can at least give us some sort of bounds for the performance of our private company. If we have a situation where there are very few comparable companies in a sector, we can look at other characteristics, such as the country. In practice, it might not quite capture the idiosyncrasies of a certain firm using this peer-driven approach.

While private firms are not required to report as much information as publicly traded companies and we have less idea what "ground truth" is, alternative data can still help to create some sort of proxy. Just like public firms, private firms still need to interact with their clients and the external parties resulting in exhaust data. This can generate data such as credit card transactions, web traffic, satellite imagery, and so on. Hence, we can often use the same approaches that we would use to track the performance of public companies to delve into private companies.

We might be able to find a satellite imagery dataset that includes private retail firms capturing car counts in their respective car parks, as we did for public companies in Chapter 13. Hence, we could use the approach to give us an idea of how earnings are changing for private firms and it can also give us more granularity over how they differ from store to store. It is unlikely we could get such detailed information from annual private company accounts. What can be challenging is that many datasets designed for public companies may simply omit private companies.

Thomas (2016) gives an example of tracking Uber's performance before it became a public company, using consumer receipts data in the United States. Uber has often faced bans in cities by local authorities. In many instances, these bans have been revoked. How have these bans impacted Uber's revenues in these cities? Thomas uses consumer receipts on Uber transactions in San Antonio, where Uber was banned for 6 months in 2015. The data shows that the ban had no effect on the growth trajectory, suggesting that the impact of bans was temporary.

We can also track job postings on corporate websites of both public and private firms to seek an understanding of how they are growing and also which skills they are looking for. Firms such as ThinkNum and LinkUp have data products to track this sort of corporate web activity.

20.5 SUMMARY

Understanding private markets can be a lot more challenging than public markets. There are fewer datasets to understand the performance of private equity and venture capital firms historically. We have discussed some of the differences between such datasets.

Private equity and venture capital firms invest in private companies. Unlike public companies, these private firms do not need to publicly disclose as much information about themselves. It can be possible to track their performance by examining publicly traded peers. However, also alternative data can be used to track these private firms more directly. We gave an example of how consumer receipt data was used to understand consumer spending at Uber before the firm went public.

Conclusions

SOME LAST WORDS

The book has sought to provide an introduction to the topic of alternative data for investors. This is a new and rapidly growing topic that we certainly believed needed a book of its own.

In Part I, we looked at the area from a more general standpoint. In Chapter 1, we sought to define precisely what alternative data is and furthermore to define some statistics concerning the use of alternative data within the investor community. We then focused on the difficult question of how to value alternative data in Chapter 2, and how this could vary between sellers and buyers. We discussed the various risks associated with alternative data in Chapter 3, in particular, some of the legal questions that need to be asked when examining an alternative data set. Many of the challenges associated with alternative data, such as entity matching and structuring, were also discussed in Chapter 3.

We also explained in Chapter 4 that extracting profitable information from alternative data has become possible thanks to recent developments in the area of machine learning. We also argued that these developments alone are not sufficient for a successful investment strategy based on alternative data. This is why in Chapter 5 we went through the processes that need to be set up for an alternative data–based strategy.

In Part II of the book, we discussed the practical applications of alternative data. Chapter 6 introduced factor investing, and also explored how alternative data could be used in this context. We then moved on to discussing how to handle missing data and also anomaly detection in Chapters 7–9. The rest of the book then focused on specific alternative datasets, together with use cases, for investors, traders, and risk managers drawn from the many categories of alternative data and across multiple asset classes.

In Chapter 10, we gave a specific example of how alternative data could be used for factor-based investors, showing the use of automotive data to trade automotive stocks. In Chapter 11, we talked about survey data and also crowdsourced data. PMI was the subject of Chapter 12 where we showed how it can be useful for nowcasting less frequently released GDP data.

In Chapter 13, we gave use cases for satellite imagery, including an example for understanding the earnings per share metrics for European retailers using car count data from their car parks. This was followed by Chapter 14, where we did some similar analysis for US retailers, this time using mobile phone location data. The whole topic of using text data investing ranging from using social media to the web more broadly and newswire data was the subject of Chapter 15. We gave many use cases, including using Twitter data to help enhance payrolls forecasts to using Bloomberg News data to trade FX. The idea of investor attention was the focus of Chapter 16, where we talked about the different (but related) concepts of news demand and supply.

Consumer transaction datasets have become popular among analysts tracking retail stocks and we discussed these in Chapter 17. In Chapter 18, we gave a number of use cases that utilized government, industrial, and corporate data, including the idea of trading equities based in innovation measures based on government data such as work visa applications. We reverted to more market data–orientated alternative datasets in Chapter 19, for FX markets including flow data and also tick data. The last chapter of use cases, Chapter 20, addressed the benefits of using alternative data for private investing. Traditionally, there tends to be far less data available for private markets, hence alternative data could help plug that data gap in this area.

There can be challenges associated with the use of alternative data for investors. We have discussed many of these issues at length throughout the book. They can range from a relatively short history, to expense, to the difficulties in structuring the raw data. However, as we have noted, there are also many ways to mitigate these challenges and risks when incorporating alternative data within the investment process. Teams can also be structured to help overcome these obstacles. Ultimately, over time, more participants in financial markets will probably begin to use alternative data within their process to help find strategies that have an edge and are less susceptible to rapid alpha decay. It is likely that those investors who are late in using alternative data could face the risk of being left behind. At this point we are still at the relatively early stages of adoption of alternative data. Hence, there is still time to catch up!

References

Adams-Heard, R., & Crowley, K. (2019, April 29). *Occidental Jet Flew to Omaha This Weekend, Flight Data Shows*. Retrieved from Bloomberg: https://www.bloomberg.com/news/articles/2019-04-29/occidental-jet-flew-to-omaha-over-the-weekend-flight-data-shows

Adland, R., Jia, H., & Strandenes, S. P. (2017, March 28). Are AIS-based trade volume estimates reliable? The case of. *Maritime Policy & Management, 44*(5), 657-665. Retrieved from http://dx.doi.org/10.1080/03088839.2017.1309470

Agrawal, S., Azar, P., Lo, A. W., & Singh, T. (2018, July 12). *Momentum, Mean-Reversion and Social Media: Evidence from StockTwits and Twitter*. Retrieved from SSRN: https://papers.ssrn.com/sol3/papers.cfm?abstract_id=3197874

Alberg, J., & Lipton, Z. C. (2018, April 26). *Improving Factor-Based Quantitative Investing by Forecasting Company Fundamentals*. Retrieved from arxiv: https://arxiv.org/abs/1711.04837

ALFRED. (n.d.). *Categories*. Retrieved from ALFRED: Archival Economic Data - St Louis Fed: https://alfred.stlouisfed.org/categories

alternativedata.org. (2019). *Alternative Data Statistics*. Retrieved from alternativedata.org: https://alternativedata.org/alternative-data/

Amen, S. (2013, September 4). *Read All About It: Bloomberg News and Google Data to Trade Risk*. Retrieved from SSRN: https://papers.ssrn.com/sol3/papers.cfm?abstract_id=2439858

Amen, S. (2016, October 25). *Trading Anxiety*. Retrieved from Investopedia: https://i.investopedia.com/downloads/anxiety/20160921_cuemacro_trading_anxiety_index.pdf

Amen, S. (2018, January 2). *Robo-news reader - Using machine-readable Bloomberg News to trade FX*. Retrieved from Bloomberg: https://www.bloomberg.com/professional/blog/machines-can-profitably-read-news/

Amen, S. (2019, May 10). *Going with the FX flow*. Retrieved from Cuemacro: https://www.cuemacro.com/2019/05/10/going-with-the-fx-flow/

Azar, P., & Lo, A. (2016, March 31). *The Wisdom of Twitter Crowds: Predicting Stock Market Reactions to FOMC Meetings via Twitter Feeds*. Retrieved from SSRN: https://papers.ssrn.com/sol3/papers.cfm?abstract_id=2756815

Ball, R., & Brown, P. (1968). An empirical evaluation of accounting income numbers. *Journal of Accounting Research, 6*(2), 159-178.

Banker, R. D., Khavis, J., & Park, H.-U. (2018, March 25). *Crowdsourced Earnings Forecasts: Implications for Analyst Forecast Timing and Market Efficiency*. Retrieved from SSRN: https://papers.ssrn.com/sol3/papers.cfm?abstract_id=3057388

Benamar, H., Foucault, T., & Vega, C. (2018, May 3). *Demand for Information, Macroeconomic Uncertainty, and the Response of U.S. Treasury Securities to News*. Retrieved from SSRN: https://papers.ssrn.com/sol3/papers.cfm?abstract_id=3162292

Bernanke, B. (2007, November 14). *Federal Reserve Communications*. Retrieved from Board of Governors of the Federal Reserve System: https://www.federalreserve.gov/newsevents/speech/bernanke20071114a.htm

Bird, S., Klein, E., & Loper, E. (2009). *Natural Language Processing with Python*. Retrieved from NLTK: http://www.nltk.org/book_1ed/

Blei, D., Ng, A. Y., & Jordan, M. I. (2003, January). *Latent Dirichlet Allocation*. Retrieved from Journal of Machine Learning Research: http://www.jmlr.org/papers/volume3/blei03a/blei03a.pdf

Bojanowski, P., Grave, E., Joulin, A., & Mikolov, T. (2016, June 7). *Enriching Word Vectors with Subword Information*. Retrieved from arxiv: https://arxiv.org/abs/1607.04606

Briscoe, T. (2013, October 8). *Introduction to Linguistics for Natural Language*. Retrieved from Cambridge University: https://www.cl.cam.ac.uk/teaching/1314/L100/introling.pdf

Bump, P. (2017, April 21). *Here's why the resolution of satellite images never seems to improve*. Retrieved from The Washington Post: https://www.washingtonpost.com/news/politics/wp/2017/04/21/heres-why-the-resolution-of-satellite-images-never-seems-to-improve

Bureau of Labor Statistics. (2019, February 1). *Employment Situation Technical Note*. Retrieved from Bureau of Labor Statistics: https://www.bls.gov/news.release/empsit.tn.htm

Button, S. (2019, February 18). *Freight trading with MarineTraffic*. Retrieved from MarineTraffic: https://www.marinetraffic.com/blog/freight-trading-with-marinetraffic/

Cable, S. (2015, June 30). *Aerial photography and the First World War*. Retrieved from National Archives: https://blog.nationalarchives.gov.uk/blog/aerial-photography-first-world-war/

Cavallo, A., & Rigobon, R. (2016). The Billion Prices Project: Using Online Prices for Measurement and Research. *Journal of Economic Perspectives, 30*(2), 151–178.

Chapados, N., & Bengio, Y. (2007). *Forecasting and Trading Commodity Contract Spreads with Gaussian Processes*. Retrieved from: http://www.iro.umontreal.ca/~pift6266/A07/documents/gp_spreads_cef07.pdf

Cobb, J. (2018, October 10). *People Counting & Customer Tracking: Counters vs Wifi vs Apps*. Retrieved from crowdconnected: https://www.crowdconnected.com/blog/people-counting-customer-tracking-counters-vs-wifi-vs-apps/

Condon, S. (2019, September 9). *Appeals court: LinkedIn can't block public profile data scraping*. Retrieved from ZDNet: https://www.zdnet.com/article/appeals-court-linkedin-cant-block-public-profile-data-scraping/

Deloitte. (2017). *Alternative data for investment decisions*.

DePalma, E. (2016, June 15). *News & Social Media Analytics for Behavioral Market Mispricings*. Retrieved from Thomson Reuters: http://sanfrancisco.qwafafew.org/wp-content/uploads/sites/9/2016/07/QWAFAFEW.15Jun2016.ElijahDePalma.pdf

Devlin, J., Chang, M.-W., Lee, K., & Toutanova, K. (2018, Oct 11). *BERT: Pre-training of Deep Bidirectional Transformers for Language Understanding*. Retrieved from arXiv: https://arxiv.org/abs/1810.04805

Drogen, L., & Jha, V. (2013, October 10). *Generating Abnormal Returns Using Crowdsourced Earnings Forecasts from Estimize*. Retrieved from SSRN: https://papers.ssrn.com/sol3/papers.cfm?abstract_id=2337709

Dumoulin, V., & Visin, F. (2018, January 11). *A guide to convolution arithmetic for deep learning*. Retrieved from arxiv: https://arxiv.org/abs/1603.07285

Eagle Alpha. (2018). *Alternative Data Use Cases Edition 6*. Eagle Alpha.

ElBahrawy, A., Alessandretti, L., & Baronchelli, A. (2019, April 1). *Wikipedia and Digital Currencies: Interplay Between Collective Attention and Market Performance*. Retrieved from SSRN: https://ssrn.com/abstract=3346632

Exante Data. (2018). *Exante China FX Intervention Models*.

Finer, D. A. (2018, March). *What Insights Do Taxi Rides Offer into Federal Reserve Leakage?* Retrieved from Chicago Booth: https://research.chicagobooth.edu/-/media/research/stigler/pdfs/workingpapers/18whatinsightsdotaxiridesofferintofederalreserveleakage.pdf

Fortado, L., Wigglesworth, R., & Scannell, K. (2017, August 28). *Hedge funds see a gold rush in data mining*. Retrieved from FT: https://www.ft.com/content/d86ad460-8802-11e7-bf50-e1c239b45787

Gargano, A., Riddiough, S. J., & Sarno, L. (2019, April 18). *Foreign Exchange Volume*. Retrieved from SSRN: https://papers.ssrn.com/sol3/papers.cfm?abstract_id=3019870

Gerdes, G., Greene, C., & Liu, X. (. (2019, January 18). *The Federal Reserve Payments Study - 2018 Annual Supplement*. Retrieved from Federal Reserve: https://www.federalreserve.gov/paymentsystems/2018-December-The-Federal-Reserve-Payments-Study.htm

Ghoshal, S., & Roberts, S. (2016). *Extracting Predictive Information from Heterogeneous Data Streams using Gaussian Processes*. Retrieved from arxiv: https://arxiv.org/abs/1603.06202

Glick, R., & Hutchinson, M. (2011, September). *Currency crises*. Retrieved from Federal Reserve Bank of San Francisco: https://www.frbsf.org/economic-research/files/wp11-22bk.pdf

Greene, S. (2008, April 27). *Capturing ideas for the good of all*. Retrieved from FT: https://www.ft.com/content/220cbac0-12f1-11dd-8d91-0000779fd2ac

Greenwich Associates. (2018, December 6). *Alternative Data Going Mainstream*. Retrieved from Greenwich Associates: https://www.greenwich.com/blog/alternative-data-going-mainstream

Guida, T. (2019). *Big Data and Machine Learning in Quantitative Investment*. Wiley.

Hasbrouck, J., & Levich, R. M. (2018, March 2018). *FX Market Metrics: New Findings Based on CLS Bank Settlement Data*. Retrieved from SSRN: https://papers.ssrn.com/sol3/papers.cfm?abstract_id=2912976

Hastie, T., Tibshirani, R., & Friedman, J. (2009). *The Elements of Statistical Learning: Data Mining, Inference, and Prediction, Second Edition*. Springer.

Hirschberg, J. (2018). *Truth or Lie? Spoken Indicators of Deception in Speech*. Retrieved from EMNLP: https://emnlp2018.org/downloads/keynote-slides/JuliaHirschberg.pdf

IHS Markit. (2019, March). *Commodities at Sea: Crude Oil*. Retrieved from IHS Markit: https://cdn.ihs.com/www/pdf/0319/CommoditiesAtSeaCrude-Brochure.pdf

Jame, R., Johnston, R., Markov, S., & Wolfe, M. (2016, March 24). *The Value of Crowdsourced Earnings Forecasts*. Retrieved from SSRN: https://papers.ssrn.com/sol3/papers.cfm?abstract_id=2333671

Jha, V. (2019). *Innovation and industry selection*. ExtractAlpha.

Jia, Y., & Weiss, R. (2019, May 15). *Introducing Translatotron: An End-to-End Speech-to-Speech Translation Model*. Retrieved from Google AI Blog: https://ai.googleblog.com/2019/05/introducing-translatotron-end-to-end.html

Jones, C.I., and Tonetti, C. (2019). *Nonrivalry and the Economics of Data*. No. w26260. National Bureau of Economic Research, 2019.

Jurafsky, D., & Martin, J. H. (2019). *Speech and Language Processing* (3rd ed.).

Kamel, T. (2018, April 24). *Corporate Aviation Intelligence: The Sky's the Limit*. Retrieved from Quandl: https://blog.quandl.com/corporate-aviation-intelligence

Kaplan, S. N., & Lerner, J. (2016, August). *Venture Capital Data: Opportunities and Challenges*. Retrieved from NBER: http://www.nber.org/papers/w22500

Kolanovic, M., & Krishnamachari, R. T. (2017). *Investing, Big Data and AI Strategies: Machine Learning and Alternative Data Approach to*. JPMorgan.

Kumar, R., Maktabi, T., & O'Brien, S. (2018, November 15). *2018 Findings from the Diary of Consumer Payment Choice*. Retrieved from Federal Reserve Bank of San Francisco: https://www.frbsf.org/cash/publications/fed-notes/2018/november/2018-findings-from-the-diary-of-consumer-payment-choice/

Lassen, N. B., Madsen, R., & Vatrapu, R. (2014, December). *Predicting iPhone Sales from iPhone Tweets*. Retrieved from ResearchGate: https://www.researchgate.net/publication/282180382_Predicting_iPhone_Sales_from_iPhone_Tweets

LeCun, Y., Bengio, Y., & Hinton, G. (2015, March 15). *Deep learning*. Retrieved from Nature: https://www.cs.toronto.edu/~hinton/absps/NatureDeepReview.pdf

Lehalle, C.-A. (2019, January). *Some Stylized Facts On Transaction Costs And Their Impact on Investors*. Retrieved from CFM: https://amf-france.org/technique/multimedia?docId=e1841a80-2bce-4d6c-837a-f238626d192a

Lopez de Prado, M. (2016, July 17). *Building Diversified Portfolios that Outperform Out-of-Sample*. Retrieved from SSRN: https://papers.ssrn.com/sol3/papers.cfm?abstract_id=2708678

Mikolov, T., Chen, K., Corrado, G., & Dean, J. (2013, September 7). *Efficient Estimation of Word Representations in Vector Space*. Retrieved from arxiv: https://arxiv.org/abs/1301.3781

Mikolov, T., Sutskever, I., Chen, K., Corrado, G., & Dean, J. (2013, October 16). *Distributed Representations of Words and Phrases and their Compositionality*. Retrieved from arxiv.org: https://arxiv.org/abs/1310.4546

Montjoye, Y.-A. d., Hidalgo, C. A., Verleysen, M., & Blondel, V. D. (2013, March 25). *Unique in the Crowd: The privacy bounds of human mobility*. Retrieved from Scientific Reports: https://www.nature.com/articles/srep01376

Murphy, K. P. (2012). *Machine Learning: A Probabilistic Perspective*. MIT Press.

Muschalle A., Stahl, F., Löser, A., Vossen, G. (2013). *Pricing Approaches for Data Markets. In: Castellanos M., Dayal U., Rundensteiner E.A. (eds) Enabling Real-Time Business Intelligence*. BIRTE 2012. Lecture Notes in Business Information Processing, vol 154. Springer, Berlin, Heidelberg.

Naili, M., Chaibi, A. H., Hajjami, H., & Ghezala, B. (2017, Sep 6). *Comparative study of word embedding methods in topic segmentation*. Retrieved from ScienceDirect: https://www.sciencedirect.com/science/article/pii/S1877050917313480

NASA. (2009, August 20). *First Picture from Explorer VI Satellite*. Retrieved from NASA: https://web.archive.org/web/20091130171224/http://grin.hq.nasa.gov/ABSTRACTS/GPN-2002-000200.html

Ng, A. Y., & Jordan, M. I. (2001). On Discriminative vs. *Generative Classifiers: A comparison of logistic regression and naive Bayes. Advances in Neural Information Processing Systems 14*. Retrieved from https://papers.nips.cc/paper/2020-on-discriminative-vs-generative-classifiers-a-comparison-of-logistic-regression-and-naive-bayes

Nie, J., & Oksol, A. (2018). Forecasting Current-Quarter U.S.Exports Using Satellite Data. *Federal Reserve Bank of Kansas City* (Q II), 5-24. Retrieved from Federal Reserve Bank of Kansas City: https://ideas.repec.org/a/fip/fedker/00065.html

Norges Bank Investment Management. (2018). *Responsible Investment*. Retrieved from Norges Bank Investment Management: https://www.nbim.no/contentassets/e1632963319146bbb040024114ca65af/responsible-investment_2018.pdf

Olsen, M. F., & Fonseca, T. R. (2017). *Investigating the predictive ability of AIS-data: the case of arabian gulf tanker rates*. Retrieved from Semantic Scholar: https://www

.semanticscholar.org/paper/Investigating-the-predictive-ability-of-AIS-data-%3A-Olsen-Fonseca/e5499c28fc1c4189a282b8f0d862614115586c3c

Pardo, F. D. (2019, August 22). *Enriching Financial Datasets with Generative Adversarial Networks*. Retrieved from TUDelft: https://repository.tudelft.nl/islandora/object/uuid:51d69925-fb7b-4e82-9ba6-f8295f96705c?collection=education

Passarella, R. (2019, May 1). *If Data is the new Oil - we should think about the industry as: Upstream - Exploration & Production, Mid-Stream - Transport & Storage, & Down Stream - Refining & the Customer ... this way we know where the players fit*. Retrieved from Twitter: https://twitter.com/robpas/status/1123658427056705536?

Pearl, J. (2009). *Causal inference in statistics: An overview*. Statist. Surv. *3*, 96-146.

Petkar, H. (2016, October). A Review of Challenges in Automatic Speech. *International Journal of Computer Applications, 151*(3), 23-26.

Ranaldo, A., & Somogyi, F. (2019, April 19). *Heterogeneous Information Content of Global FX Trading*. Retrieved from SSRN: https://papers.ssrn.com/sol3/papers.cfm?abstract_id=3263279

Rasmussen C. E. (2004). *Gaussian Processes in Machine Learning. In: Bousquet O., von Luxburg U., Rätsch G. (eds) Advanced Lectures on Machine Learning. ML 2003*. Lecture Notes in Computer Science, vol 3176. Springer, Berlin, Heidelberg.

Refinitiv. (n.d.). *I/B/E/S Estimates*. Retrieved from Refinitiv: https://www.refinitiv.com/en/financial-data/company-data/institutional-brokers-estimate-system-ibes

Rocher, L., Hendrickx, J. M., & Montjoye, Y.-A. d. (2019, July 23). *Estimating the success of re-identifications in incomplete datasets using generative models*. Retrieved from Nature: https://www.nature.com/articles/s41467-019-10933-3/

Saacks, B. (2019, March 14). *Hedge funds closely watching LinkedIn lawsuit on web scraped data*. Retrieved from Business Insider: https://www.businessinsider.com/hedge-funds-watching-linkedin-lawsuit-on-web-scraped-data-2019-3

Salahat, E., & Qasaimeh, M. (2017, March 17). *Recent Advances in Features Extraction and Description Algorithms: A Comprehensive Survey*. Retrieved from arxiv: https://arxiv.org/abs/1703.06376

Salzberg, S. (2014, March 23). *Why Google Flu Is A Failure*. Retrieved from Forbes: https://www.forbes.com/sites/stevensalzberg/2014/03/23/why-google-flu-is-a-failure/#5613adcf5535

Schaffer, C. (1994). *A conservation law for generalization performance*. International Conference on Machine Learning, H. Willian and W. Cohen, Editors. San Francisco: Morgan Kaufmann, pp. 259–265.

Sleptsova, E., Tukker, M., & Fennessy, R. (2019, May 3). *A new tool for managing currency risk*. Retrieved from Oxford Economics.

Sugiyama, M., Suzuki, T., & Kanamori, T.. (2012). *Density Ratio Estimation in Machine Learning*. Cambridge University.

Standage, T. (2014). *Writing on the Wall: The Intriguing History of Social Media, from Ancient Rome to the Present Day*. Bloomsbury Paperbacks.

Strohmeier, M., Smith, M., Lenders, V., & Martinovic, I. (2018, April 24). *The Real First Class? Inferring Confidential Corporate Mergers and Government Relations from Air Traffic Communication*. Retrieved from IEEE: https://ieeexplore.ieee.org/document/8406594

TensorFlow Tutorials. (n.d.). *Vector Representations of Words*. Retrieved from TensorFlow: https://www.tensorflow.org/tutorials/representation/word2vec

Thasos. (2018). *Redefining Key Performance Indicators for Retail REITs*.

Thasos. (2019). *Trading SPDR S&P Retail ETF (XRT) Using Thasos Mall Foot Traffic Index*.

The Economist. (2017, June 6). *The world's most valuable resource is no longer oil, but data*. Retrieved from The Economist: https://www.economist.com/leaders/2017/05/06/the-worlds-most-valuable-resource-is-no-longer-oil-but-data

Thomas, A. (2016, October 13). *Email Receipts used to Forecast Amazon and Uber Revenues.* Retrieved from Quandl: https://blog.quandl.com/alternative-data-action-email-receipts

University of Vermont. (2013). *Hedonometer.* Retrieved from Hedonometer: https://hedonometer.org/about.html

Vapnik, V. (2000). *The Nature of Statistical Learning Theory.* Springer-Verlag.

Weier, J., & Herring, D. (2000, August 30). *Measuring Vegetation (NDVI & EVI).* Retrieved from NASA: https://earthobservatory.nasa.gov/features/MeasuringVegetation/measuring_vegetation_1.php

Wolpert, D. H. (2002). *NThe Supervised Learning No—Free—Lunch Theorems. In: Roy R., Köppen M., Ovaska S., Furuhashi T., Hoffmann F. (eds) Soft Computing and Industry.* Springer, London.

Wolpert, D. H., & Macready, W. G. (1996, Feburary 23). *No Free Lunch Theorems for Search.* Retrieved from Santa Fe Institute: https://pdfs.semanticscholar.org/8bdf/dc2c2777b395c086810c03a8cdeccc55c4db.pdf

Young, T., Hazarika, D., Poria, S., & Cambria, E. (2018, November 25). *Recent Trends in Deep Learning Based Natural Language Processing.* Retrieved from arXiv.org: https://arxiv.org/abs/1708.02709

Zuckerman, G. (2019). *The Man Who Solved the Market: How Jim Simons Launched the Quant Revolution.* Penguin.

About the Authors

Alexander Denev has more than 15 years of experience in finance, financial modelling and machine learning and is currently Head of AI – Financial Services, Risk Advisory, Deloitte LLP. Previously he led Quantitative Research & Advanced Analytics at IHS Markit, where he created and maintained a center of excellence for the development of analytics products.

He has also held roles at the Royal Bank of Scotland, Societe Generale, European Investment Bank and the European Investment Fund and has participated in the engineering of both the European Financial Stability Facility and the European Stability Mechanism.

Alexander Denev attained his Master of Science degree in Physics with a focus on Artificial Intelligence from the University of Rome, Italy, and he holds a degree in Mathematical Finance from the University of Oxford, UK, where he continues as a visiting lecturer. He has written several papers and books on topics ranging from stress testing and scenario analysis to asset allocation.

Saeed Amen is the founder of Cuemacro. For 15 years, he has developed systematic trading strategies and quantitative indices including at major investment banks, Lehman Brothers and Nomura.

Through Cuemacro, he now consults and publishes research for clients in the area of systematic trading. He has developed many popular open-source Python libraries, including finmarketpy, which is one of the most popular libraries for developing trading strategies on GitHub. His clients have included major quant funds.

He has also done numerous research projects for data companies on their alternative datasets, including for Bloomberg and RavenPack. He is also a co-founder of the Thalesians, a quant think tank, and is a visiting lecturer at Queen Mary University of London.

Saeed Amen graduated with a first-class honors MSci degree in Mathematics and Computer Science from Imperial College London.

Index

1M implied volatility
  regressing news volume, contrast,
    315*f*
  USD/JPY news volume, contrast,
    315*f*
50-day SMA, 82

A/B test, 35
accounts payable (accpayable), financial
  statement item, 241
ADP private payroll change, nonfarm
  payrolls (US change) (contrast),
  45*f*
ALFRED time series, 306
Algorithms
  feature detection algorithms,
    properties, 89*f*
  features/feature detection algorithm,
    87–89
  selection decision, 86–87
Alpha, 45–46
  capture data, 256
Alternative data, 3
  adoption curve, 16*f*
  brands, association, 24*f*
  buy side total spend, 25*f*
  capacity, 16–19

  characteristics, 6
  collection, cost, 6
  defining, 5–7
  dimensions, 19–23
  forecasts, 339*f*
  history, shortness, 6
  inputs, usage, 127–128
  maintenance process, 113–114
  process, 105–114
  reasons, 11–14
  risks/challenges, 47
  segmentation, 7–9, 8*t*
  strategies, 35–39, 229*t*
  survey data, comparison, 245–247
  team usage, structuring, 114–115
  usage, 6, 14*f,* 50–57
  use processes, 105
  users, identification, 15–16
  value, 27
  vendors, identification, 23–24
Alternative datasets
  buy side usage, 24–26
  commercial release frequency, 23*f*
  derivation, web scraping
    (usage), 25*f*
  maturing alternative datasets,
    advantages, 45–46
  usage, 226*t*–227*t*

Amazon
  Comprehend, 102
  Mechanic Turk, 53
  revenue, actual revenue changes
    (contrast/alternative data
    forecasts), 339*f*
Amazon Web Services (AWS), 79, 338
Amelia II (CRAN), 147
  usage, 180
Amelia imputed time series, examples,
  168*f*, 172*f*
Amelia+MSSA, 165, 167
Angle-Based Outlier Factor (ABOF),
  203–204
Anomalies, 181
  point anomalies, 184
Apache MXNet, 79
APIs, usage, 30, 71, 79, 91, 112
Approximate methods, rank, 142*f*
Approximate models, 139, 140
Arbitrage pricing theory (APT),
  122–123
Area under the ROC curve (AUC),
  mean/standard deviation/MSE
  values, 148*f*
Articles per ticker, average daily count,
  311*f*
Artificial Intelligence (AI), 4
Asian Crisis (1997), 86
Asset class
  breadth/depth, 20
  coverage, 20
  relevance, 19–20
Asset price, signals, 29
Assets under management (AUM), 16,
  360
  ranking, 361*f*
Auctions
  types, 43
  usage, 42
Auto-associative neural network
  (AANN), 143
Auto-correlation, absence, 64
Autoencoders, 71
  neural networks, 76–77

Automated identification system (AIS)
  crude oil exports, comparison, 286*f*
  data, collection, 285
  transmitters/messages, usage, 284
Automatic Identification System (AIS),
  117
Automotive company data
  alternative data strategies, CAGR
    basis, 229*t*
  company list, 240
  core factors, 223
    aggregation, 224
  delayed data, usage, 224
  direct approach, 223–238
  factors, 226*t*–227*t*, 229–238
  factors CAGRs, 239*t*
  financial statement items, description,
    241–242
  freshest automotive factors summary
    statistics, 228*t*
  freshest data, usage, 224
  Gaussian processes, example,
    238–239
  long top 33% strategy excess returns,
    equal weighted benchmark
    (contrast/Pearson correlations),
    233*t*–234*t*
  Q_pct_delta_ffo quintile CAGRs,
    3-months clairvoyance, 221*f*
  ratios, usage, 242–243
  reporting delays, country ranking,
    244
  stocks, holding (heatmap), 222*f*
  time averaged Spearman rank
    correlations, 236*t*–237*t*
Automotive fundamental data, 205,
  206–211
  book-to-market ranking, 214
  Chevrolet Cruze, country unit
    sales/registration, 210*t*
  equal weighted benchmarks, 219*t*
  IHS Markit databases, usage,
    206–207
  indirect approach, 211–222
  information, examples, 217–218

long portfolio, creation, 214
non-quarterly reporting companies, examination, 218
process, 209*f*
production volume, mean percent, 208*f*
sales volume, mean percent, 208*f*
Stage 1 process, 213–215
stages, 213–223
stocks, ranking, 214
strategies, CAGR ranking, 219*t,* 220*t*
supporting statistics, 217
Tesla, value, 218
tradeable companies, long/short-portfolio sizes, 218*t*
transaction costs, 217–218
universe, assumption, 215
Average percentage derivation, usage, 270*t*
Azure clusters, 79

Backtesting, usage/nonusage, 35–39
Backtests, 54, 213
Bagging, 67
Bag-of-words, 94
Bayesian principal component analysis (BPCA), 140
Bayes theorem, usage, 69–70
BeautifulSoup, 100
Benchmark model (BM), 263
Berners-Lee, Tim, 299
Bias, 60–61, 61*f*
Bidirectional Encoder Representations from Transformers (BERT), 95, 101–102
Big Data, 9–11, 50
Billion Prices Project, The, 321–322
Binned R^2 analyses, usage, 109
Bitly, 324–325
Blob-based feature detectors, 88*f*
Blockchain technology, usage, 31
Bloomberg News article count, S&P500 (contrast), 310*f*
Book-to-market ratios, 123

Brands, alternative data (association), 24*f*
Brazil
English attention, local content (comparison), 332*f*
YoY retail sales, SpendingPulse Brazil retail sales YoY (contrast), 337*f*
Buyers, data pricing perspective, 40–41

Caffe, 80
CAPEX, 38
Capital, allocation (increase), 18
Capital Asset Pricing Model (CAPM), 119–124
Car counts, 271–277
basis, steps, 272–273
data, 275*f,* 276*f*
earnings, contrast, 274*f*
Carhart model, 124
Car parks
data, DINEOF imputation (example), 175*f*
image, 175*f*–178*f*
Carry-based factor model, 125
Causality (machine learning assumption/limitation), 84–85
Central bank intervention, modeling, 346–348
Chevrolet Cruze, country unit sales/registration, 210*t*
China
GDP growth rate, PMI (contrast), 13*f*
SpaceKnow satellite manufacturing index, Chinese/Caixin PMI manufacturing (contrast), 279*f*
China PMI
China GDP QoQ, contrast, 13*f*
manufacturing (surprises), consensus/SMI/hybrid (contrast), 280*f*
manufacturing (measurement), satellite data (usage), 277–280

Chinese yuan (CNY)
intervention/official data (contrast),
model estimates (comparison),
347, 348*f*
Clairvoyance, 211–212
impact, 213, 215–216
Q_pct_delta_ffo quintile CAGRs,
3-months clairvoyance, 221*f*
Q_pct_delta_ffo returns plot,
quarterly benchmark (contrast),
222*f*
Classification methods, 139–140
CLS Group, establishment, 352
Cluster-based outlier factor (CBLOF)
algorithm, 188
Clustering-based unsupervised machine
learning techniques, 70–71
Collective outliers, 184
Commodity trading advisor (CTA),
risk-adjusted returns, 18
Common equity (equity), financial
statement item, 241
Company event study (pooled survey),
case study, 249–252
Company removal, example, 220
Compounded annual growth rate
(CAGR), 211–212, 217–222, 225,
229–230
factors CAGRs, 239*t*
production, 235
Q_pct_delta_ffo quintile CAGRs,
3-months clairvoyance, 221*f*
ranking, 219*t*
Concept most common/average (CMC),
140, 142
Consensus estimates (independent
variable), 292
Consumer Price inflation, measurement,
321–322
Consumer receipts, 337–340
Consumer transactions, 335
Content, topic/sentiment identification,
93
Continuous bag of words
(CBOW), 95

Convolutional neural networks (CNNs),
56, 69, 76, 272
convolutional/flat layers, inclusion,
76*f*
usage, 89–90
CoreNLP, 101
Corner feature detectors, 88*f*
Corporate aircraft, takeover target visits,
297*f*
Corporate data, 341
Corporate jet location data, 296–298
Corporate Sustainability Assessment
(CSA), RobecoSAM creation, 129
Corpus of Contemporary American
(COCA) English, 98–99
Cost of Goods Sold (cogs), financial
statement item, 241
Cost value (CV), 34
Cox regression models, 72
Credit default swap (CDS), 136, 151
data, usage, 111, 154–157
time series data, clustering, 156*f*
Credit transaction data, 336–337
Critical line approach
(Markowitz), 71
Cross-sectional trading approach, time
series trading approach (contrast),
126
Cross-validation (CV), 61–63
Crowdsourced data, 245
case studies, 249–254
contributors, hierarchy, 246*f*
product, 247–249
usage, 247
Crowdsourcing analyst estimates
survey, 255
Crude oil production, OPEC ranking,
253*f*
Crude oil supplies (tracking), shipping
data (usage), 283–286
Cryptocurrency price actions
(understanding), Wikipedia
(usage), 330
CScores, 198–199
histogram plot, 197*f*

Currency Composition of Official
  Foreign Exchange Reserve
  (COFER) data, 347*f*
Currency crisis risk, quantification,
  344–346
Currency markets, central bank
  intervention (modeling),
  346–348
Currency pair, purchase/sale, 354
Current liabilities (currliab), financial
  statement item, 241
CUSIP standard, 52

Daily flow returns, 355*f*
Data
  aggregation, 57–58
  assets, 33, 105
  availability, 21–22
  bias, 21
  clarity, 111
  delayed data, usage, 224
  external consistency, 111
  external marketing value, 44–45
  free data, 20
  frequency, 20–21
  freshest data, usage, 224
  fusion, 52
  internal consistency, 111
  legal aspects, 47–50
  markets, 29–31
  mining, 124–126
  missing data, 51, 54
  monetary value, 31–35, 39–45
  onboarding, performing, 106, 110
  originality, 22
  outliers, treatment, 51
  points, distinction, 182
  preprocessing, performing, 106,
    110–111
  pricing, perspective, 40–45
  protection laws, comparison, 48*f*
  quality, 21, 111
  science team, setup cost, 116*f*
  services, 30

  sources, entity identifiers (matching),
    51
  strategies, evaluation, 35–39
  structuring, 55–56
  team (creation), big bang hiring
    strategy, 115
  test data generation, 154–157
  timeliness/completeness, 111
  transformation, stages, 9*f*
  underusage, 15
  uniqueness, 111
  unstructured data, conversion, 51
  upside sharing, external sales, 43–44
  usage, limitations, 49
  validity/veracity, 111
  values, 32–33, 136
  vendors, 116–117
  view, representation, 184
Data-as-a-Service (DaaS), 117
Data interpolation with empirical
    orthogonal functions (DINEOF),
    152–153, 160–162
  application, 174
  imputation, 161*f,* 170*f,* 173, 175*f*
  usage, 180
Datasets
  identification, 107–108
  price, assignation, 27
  restricted information set, 86
  shift, types, 85
  time stamps, 110
  traditional datasets, 320–321
  usage, 186*t,* 269
Debit card transaction data, 336–337
Decision boundary, example, 68*f*
Decision trees, 67
Deep learning (DL), 72–80, 82–83
  defining, 77
  examples, 73–74
  high-level deep learning libraries, 79
  libraries, 77–80
  low-level deep learning libraries,
    77–79
  middle-level deep learning libraries,
    79
  usage, 89–90

Deletion (missing data treatment), 137–138, 143
Density-based techniques, 203
Deterministic techniques, usage, 160–164
Directionality factor, 82
Direct prediction, 129–132
Discretionary investors, 38–39
Distance-based techniques, 202–203
Diversification, factor investing benefit, 127
Do not impute (DNI), 140
Due diligence, performing, 105, 108
Dutch auction, 43
Dwell time, 288

Earnings before interest and taxes (ebit), financial statement item, 241
Earnings, car counts (contrast), 274f
Earnings per share (EPS), 271–277
   estimation, mobile phone location data (usage), 291–295
   examples, 275f, 276f
   news/Twitter data, contrast, 294f
   regressing footfall, contrast, 294f
EBIT and depreciation (opincome), financial statement item, 242
EBIT-to-EV ratio, 216, 242
Economic Sentiment Indicator (ESI), 260–262
Economic theory, test, 220
Economic value (EV), 35
Edge feature detectors, 88f
Efficient Market Hypothesis (EMH), 27
Emerging Market (EM) currencies basket (trading), macro-economy attention (usage), 333f
Emerging Market Foreign Exchange (EMFX), 323, 330–333
Empirical orthogonal function (EOF), 160–164
English auction, 43
Enhanced Vegetation Index (EVI), 278
Entities, identification, 93

Entity identifiers, matching, 51
Entity matching, 52–54
Environmental Social Governance (ESG) factors, 128–129
Equal weighted benchmark, long top 33% strategy excess returns, (contrast/Pearson correlations), 233t–234t
Equal weighted benchmarks, 219t
Equities (trading), innovation measures (usage), 342–344
Errors, types, 64
Eurozone
   Composite PMI, 261, 261f
   GDP, 261f
   model performance, 263t
EUR/USD
   bid/ask spread, 356f, 357f
   daily abs net flow, 353f
   daily volume, 352f
   ON implied volatility, FOMC news volume (contrast), 317f
   index, EUR/USD fund flow score (contrast), 354f
   overnight volatility, 317f, 318f
   trading, intraday basis, 308f
   ON volatility levels, 317f
Exhaust data, 7
Expectation conditional maximization (ECM), 149
Expectation maximization (EM) procedure, 143, 159–160
Explorer VI satellite, 267, 268f
Exponential MACD, 82
Exports/lights/GDP, annual correlation, 270t

Factor
   CAGRs, 239t
   correlations, 232–238
   factor-based strategies, 126–127
   generation, 224–225
   identification, 212
   modeling/forecasting, 212

performance, 225–229
removal, 224
Factor investing, 119
benefits, 127
cost, reduction, 127
usage, reasons, 126–127
Factor models, 120–126
approaches, 125–126
definition, 120
modeling sequences, examples, 130*f*–131*f*
types, 121–122
Fama-French 3-factor model, 123–124
Fear gauge, 328
Feature detection algorithms, properties, 89*f*
Feature detectors, types, 88*f*
Features/feature detection algorithm, 87–89
Fed communications, 316–320
Fed communications index
categorical/continuous variables, mixture, 199
CScores, histogram plot, 197*f*
event types, 196*f*, 200*f*
fields, tagging, 194
input variables, usage, 199
log(text length), histogram plot, 195*f*
outlier detection, case study, 194
rules-based approaches, 198
speakers, talkativeness (ranking), 197*f*
Federal Open Market Committee (FOMC), 111, 183, 194–198
communications, availability, 319
EUR/USD ON volatility levels, 317*f*
meetings, 66, 295–296, 316
news volume, EUR/USD ON implied volatility (contrast), 317*f*
sentiment index, 320*f*
stock market reaction forecast, Twitter data (usage), 308–309
Feed forward neural networks, 75–76

Financial markets
alternative data, relationship, 6
PMI, impact, 263–265
Financial problems, modeling techniques (suggestions), 83*t*
Financial ratios, usage, 129
First-Price Sealed-Bid auction, 43
Flat-fee models, 30
Footfall
regressing footfall, reported EPS (contrast), 294*f*
reported EPS, contrast, 293*f*
score (independent variable), 292
Foreign Exchange (FX), 5, 341
average crisis rates, 346*f*
daily flow returns, 355*f*
data, 6
flow data, institutional FX flow data (relationship), 351–355
spot returns, net flow (multiple regressions), 353*f*
trading, machine-readable news (usage), 310–316
trend returns, 355*f*
trend strategies/daily flow-based strategies, risk-adjusted returns, 354*f*
volatility (understanding), machine-readable news (usage), 310–316
Free data, presence, 20
Freemium models, free services/value-added services (combination), 30
Free services, value-added services (combination), 30
Freshest automotive factors summary statistics, 228*t*
Fundamental factor model, 121, 122
Funds from operations (ffo), financial statement item, 241
Fuzzy k-means clustering (FKMI), 140, 142
FX Risk Tool (Oxford Economics), 345

Gaussian distributions, 202
Gaussian Finite Mixture Models, 185
Gaussian mixture model (GMM), 143
Gaussian processes (GPs), 80–82
  example, 238–239
  orthogonality/nonlinearity, 238
  representation, 81
Gaussian Process Regression (GPR),
  238
GBP/USD intraday volatility, UK PMI
  Services (basis), 265f
General Data Protection Regulation
  (GDPR), 47, 50, 287
General partners, AUM ranking, 361f
Generative adversarial neural networks
  (GANs), 63, 77
Gensim, 101
Geospatial Insight dataset, usage, 272
GitHub, 79
Glmnet, 72
Global outliers, local outliers (contrast),
  184
Global Vectors for Word Representation
  (GloVe), 95
Google
  Cloud Natural Language, 102
  Cloud Speech-to-Text, 102
  Domestic Trend, 325–326
  regressing Google domestic trend
    indices, 326f
  search volume, example, 326f
  Shock Sentiment, 326, 327f
  trends data, usage, 325–327
Government data, 341
Grapedata, 247–256
Gross Domestic Product (GDP), 259
  exports/lights, annual correlation,
    270t
  growth correlations, 262t
  proxying, 270
  release, 11

Hang Seng index, share price
  (performance), 252f

Happiness Sentiment Index, 304, 305f
Hedonometer
  average score, 304f
  happiest/saddest words (ranking),
    302f
  Index, 302–305, 303f, 322
Heuristics-based approaches, 203–204
Hierarchical clustering, 70–71
Hierarchical density-based spatial
  clustering of applications with
  noise (HDBSCAN), 199
High-capacity strategies, properties, 18
High-frequency data, usage, 355–357
High-level deep learning libraries, 79
High-level neural network libraries, 79
Histogram-based outlier score (HBOS),
  198
Histogram-based statistical outlier
  (HBOS) detector, 188
Holding period, usage, 213
Homoscedastic errors, 64
HTML tags, removal, 300
Hyperspace, contents, 89

I/B/E/S dataset, 255
Ignore missing (IM), 140
IHS Markit (IHSM), 23, 259, 285
  databases, usage, 206–207
  data features, 243
  process, 209f
Images
  classification, deep learning/CNNs
    (usage), 89–90
  features/feature detection algorithm,
    87–89
  imaging tools, 91
  satellite image data, dataset
    augmentation, 90–91
  structuring, 87–91
Imputation methods, 152
  multiple imputation (MI) methods,
    157–160
  ranking, 143f
  values, computation, 148f

Imputation metrics, 154
Imputation-posterior (I-P) form, 158
Imputation step (I-step), 158
Imputation technique, classifiers
    (rank), 141*f*
Index market, evolution, 127–128
Indicator computation, car counts basis
    (steps), 272–273
Indirect prediction, 129–132
Induction learning methods, 140
Industrial data, 341
Information coefficient (IC),
    217, 230
Information ratios, 312
Innovation measures, usage,
    342–344
Input dataset error rates, LERS new
    classification (usage), 146*f*–147*f*
Institutional FX flow data, FX spot
    (relationship), 351–355
Interest rate swaps (IRSs), 71
Internal exhaust source, requirements,
    24
inventory, financial statement
    item, 241
Investment
    capacity, increase, 127
    management constituents, phase
        identification, 16*f*
    strategy, 22, 105
    value, decay, 27–29
Investopedia search data, usage,
    328–329, 328*f*
Investor Anxiety Index (IAI), 328
    usage, 329*f*
    Volatility Index (VIX), contrast, 328*f*,
        329*f*
Investors
    anxiety (measurement), Investopedia
        search data (usage), 328–329, 328*f*
    attention, 323–325
    discretionary investors, 38–39
    systematic investors, 36–38
Isolation-Based Outliers, 204
Isolation forest (ISO), 199

Joint Organizations Data Initiative
    (JODI) Oli World Database, usage,
    285
JX Mobile III, 249
    launch, payment willingness, 251*f*
    test version, usage question, 250*f*
JX PC III, monthly spending question,
    251*f*

KDB, usage, 110
Keras, 79
Kernel Density Estimation, 185
Kernels, usage, 81
Kernel trick, example, 69*f*
Kingsoft, 250
    share price, performance, 252*f*
    survey, questions, 256–257
k-means (K-means), 70, 143, 198
k-means clustering information (KMI),
    140, 142, 149
k-nearest neighbors (KNN) (KNNI),
    140, 147–149, 187, 199
    regression/classification, 149
    usage, 143
Kriging, 80–81

Lasagne, 79
Latency arbitrage, 307
Latent Dirichlet Allocation (LDA), 97
Latent semantic analysis (LSA), 97
Lazy learning, 139, 140
    methods, rank, 142*f*
Learning from Examples based on
    Rough Sets (LERS), 146–147
LERS new classification, usage,
    146*f*–147*f*
Licensees, number, 35
Lights/exports/GDP, annual correlation,
    270*t*
Light vehicle production (IHS Markit
    database), 206
Light vehicle sales (IHS Markit
    database), 207

Linear regression (LR), 64–65, 84, 87, 348
   neural network function, 73, 73*f*
   visualization, 65*f*
Liquidity
   social media, impact, 309
   understanding, high-frequency data (usage), 355–357
Local least squares imputation (LLSI), 140
Locally linear reconstruction (LLR), 149
Local outlier factor (LOF), 187, 203
   score visualization, example, 187*f*
Local outliers, global outliers (contrast), 184
Location data, 283
Logistic regression, 65–67, 82
   neural network function, visualization,74*f*
   single class logistic regression, neural network function, 73
   visualization, 66*f*
Log-likelihood, 159
Long-only portfolios (derivation), visa/patent data (usage), 343*f*
   in sample/out-of-sample, 344*f*
Long portfolio, creation, 214
Long short-term memory (LSTM), 76, 87
Long threshold, usage, 213
Long top 33% strategy excess returns, equal weighted benchmark (contrast/Pearson correlations), 233*t*–234*t*
Low-capacity strategies, 18
Low-level deep learning libraries, 77–79
Low-level neural network libraries, 77–79

Machine learning (ML), 4
   algorithms, calibration, 61
   bias/variance/noise, 60–61

   clustering-based unsupervised machine learning techniques, 70–71
   cross-validation (CV), 61–62
   deep learning, 72–80
   definitions, 60
   examination, 62–63
   fit, expected error (equation), 60
   Gaussian processes (GPs), 80–82
   libraries, 71–72
   neural networks, 72–80
   procedures, usage, 143
   processing layers, involvement, 40
   reinforcement learning, 63
   supervised learning, 62
   supervised machine learning techniques, 64–70
   techniques, 59, 60, 82–87
   unsupervised learning, 63
   unsupervised machine learning techniques, 71
Machine-readable news, usage, 310–316
Macro data, forecasting, 129–130
Macroeconomic factor model, 121, 122
Macro-economy attention, usage, 333*f*
Malls, visits (comparison), 290*f*
Market data, 351
Market participants, alternative data usage, 6
Market themes (measurement), Google trends data (usage), 325–327
Market value (MV), 34–35
Markov Chain Monte Carlo sampling, 157
Marks & Spencer, car count/earnings (contrast), 274*f*
Material non-public information (MNPI), 49, 109
Matlab ports, 72
Matplotlib, 91
Matrix factorization, 162–166
Maturing alternative datasets, advantages, 45–46
Maximization step (M-step), 159

Maximum likelihood estimation (MLE), 159

Mean absolute percentage error (MAPE), 154

Mean quintile gap (MQG), 217, 225, 230

Mean relative deviation (MRD), 154
metrics, summary statistics, 166*t*–167*t*

Mergers and acquisitions (M&As), 296–298

Metadata
addition, 93
identification, 300

Micro-clusters, 184

Middle-level deep learning libraries, 79

Middle-level neural network libraries, 79

Misclassification error rate, examples, 145*f*–146*f*

MissForest: Random Forest imputation, 180

Missing at Random (MAR), 137

Missing Completely at Random (MCAR), 136, 137, 148, 155–157

Missing data, 54, 135
case studies, 151
classification, 136–138, 143
classifier design, deletion, 143
deletion, 137–138
distinctions, 136–137
fraction, usage, 153
imputation/estimation, 143
inclusion, 144*f*
incomplete cases, deletion, 143
misclassification error rate, 145*f*–146*f*
predictive imputation, 138
replacement, 138

Missing data treatments, 51, 137–138
Farhangfar et al perspective, 148
Garcia-Laencina et al perspective, 143–146
Grzymala-Busse et al perspective, 146–147
Jerez et al perspective, 147–148

Kang et al perspective, 149
literature overview, 139–149
Luengo et al perspective, 139–143
Zou et al perspective, 147

Missingness patterns
imposition, example, 164*f*
occurrence, number (histogram), 156*f*

Missing Not at Random (MNAR), 137

Missing values
consecutive missing values, length statistics (usage), 153
total fraction, usage, 153

Mixture of Gaussians (MoG), 149

Mobile phone location data
independent variables, 292
usage, 287–295

Model backtesting, 213

Model-based nowcast, 307

Model-based procedures, usage, 143

Model-based techniques, 202

Model forecasts, comparison, 270*t*

Monopoly, impact, 42–43

Montreal Institute for Learning Algorithms (MILA) Theano development (cessation), 78

Multicollinearity, presence, 64

Multi-layer perceptron (MLP), 140, 143
hidden layer, inclusion, 75*f*
neural network, 75

Multiple imputation (MI) methods, 137, 138, 148, 157–160

Multiple imputation with chained equations (MICE), 153, 157
imputed time series, 168*f*
package, norm, 158
procedure, description, 178–179
usage, 179

Multiple singular spectral analysis (MSSA), 152–153, 162–164
imputation, example, 170*f*
imputed time series, example, 173*f*
usage, 180

Multi-task learning (MTL), 143

Multivariate credit default swap time series
  CDS data, 154–157
  deterministic techniques, 160–164
  EOF-based techniques, 160–164
  imputation metrics, 154
  missing data classification, 153–154
  missing values, imputing, 152
  MRD metrics, summary statistics, 166*t*–167*t*
  results, 164–173
  test data generation, 1540157
Multi-variate normal (MVN)
  assumption, 158–159
  distribution, 155, 157
  test, 155
MXNet (Apache), 79

Naïve Bayes (NB), 69–70, 140
Named entity recognition, 92–93
Natural language processing (NLP), 55, 78, 91–102
  challenges, 97–98
  defining, 91–93
  languages/texts, differences, 98–99
  normalization, 93–94
  speech, involvement, 99–100
  tasks, classification problem, 96
  tools, 100–102
  word embeddings, creation, 94–96
NDAs, negotiation, 30
Negative change, ratios, 242–243
Net flow, spot returns (multiple regressions), 353*f*
Net income (netincome), financial statement item, 242
Net-Income-to-EV ratio, 216, 242
Neural networks (NNs), 72–80, 184
  examples, 73–74
  frameworks, 79–80
  high-level neural network libraries, 79
  libraries, 77–80
  low-level neural network libraries, 77–79

middle-level neural network libraries, 79
  types, 75–77
News, 309–320
  articles per ticker, average daily count, 311*f*
  Bloomberg News article count, S&P500 (contrast), 310*f*
  trend correlation, contrast, 313*f*
  trend information ratio, contrast, 313*f*
  trend model returns, contrast, 314*f*
  trend model YoY returns, contrast, 314*f*
News data, 299
  reported EPS, contrast, 294*f*
newspaper3k, 101
News score (independent variable), 292
New York Fed meetings, 295–296
NLTK, 101
No-free-lunch (NFL) theorems, 82
Noise, 60–61, 88, 182
  cause, 60
Nonfarm payrolls (NFPs), US change
  ADP private payroll change, contrast, 45*f*
  Twitter-based forecast, actual release/Bloomberg consensus survey (contrast), 307*f*
  Twitter data, usage, 305
Nonfarm payrolls (surprise), USD/JPY 1-minute move (contrast), 306*f*
Non-negative matrix factorization (NMF), 97
Non-problems, modeling techniques (suggestions), 83*t*
Non-quarterly reporting companies, examination, 218
Non-stationarity (machine learning assumption/limitation), 85–86
Norges Bank Investment Management, 128
Normalization, 93–94
Normalized Difference Vegetation Index (NDVI), 278
Normally distributed errors, 64

Normal neighborhood, selection
(difficulties), 190*f*
Nowcasting
Eurozone (EZ) GDP growth, 260*f*
GDP growth, 262–263
NumPy, 77, 80

Official Foreign Exchange Reserve,
currency composition (COFER
data), 347*f*
Oil and gas production (Q&A survey),
case study, 252–254
Oil prices/supply changes, contrast, 254*f*
One-class SVM, 188
OPEC, 252
crude oil production estimates, 253*f*
oil supply changes, oil prices changes
(contrast), 254*f*
OpenCV, 91
OpenSky dataset, usage, 297
OPEX, 38
Optical Character Recognition (OCR),
55
Original Equipment Manufacturers
(OEM), decision-making, 206–207
Outliers
anomalies, 181
definition/classification, 182–183
flagging, 200*f*
global outliers, local outliers
(contrast), 184
local outlier factor (LOF), 187
temporal structure, 183
treatment, 51, 56–57
Outliers, detection
algorithms, comparative evaluation,
185–188, 186*t*
approaches, 182–183
case study, 194
density-based techniques, 203
distance-based techniques, 202–203
heuristics-based approaches, 203–204
model-based techniques, 202
problem, setup, 184–185

techniques, 57
unsupervised ML techniques, usage,
198–199
Outliers, explanations
Angiulli et al. explanation, 192–193
approaches, 189–193
Duan et al. explanation, 191–192
Micenkova et al. explanation,
189–190
rank statistic, usage (problem), 191*f*

Packaging models, 30
Pandas, 80
Passive investing, 127
Passive strategies, 126
pattern, 101
Pattern classification methods, missing
data (inclusion), 144*f*
Pay-per-use models, 40
Payroll readership, usage, 323–325
PDFMiner, 101
Percentage ratios, 243
Personal data, definition, 47
Pillow, 91
Point anomalies, 184
Point-of-sale (POS) devices,
usage, 338
Poisson regression models, 72
Pooled surveys
company event study (pooled survey),
case study, 249–252
usage, 247
Portfolio, effects, 22
Posterior step (P-step), 158
Predicted R squared coefficient, true R
squared coefficient (contrast), 154
Predictive imputation (missing data
treatment), 138
Predictive mean matching (PMM), 158,
165
Pricing
discriminatory pricing mechanisms,
42*f*
equation, 40

Principal component analysis (PCA), 71, 76
Principle Component Regression (PCR), 238
Private equity
  datasets, 362
  defining, 360
Private firms, performance (understanding), 363
Private markets, alternative data, 359
Probabilistic Graphical Model (PGM), example, 130*f*
Processed data (data transformation stage), 9*f*
Process expense, 34
Processing level, 21
Processing libraries, 80
prod_volume_prev_1m_pct_change _prev_2m_mean, 232, 235, 238
Proof-of-concept (POC), 106, 112
Pseudo-time, basis, 262
Publishing lag, 21
Purchasing Managers Indexes (PMI), 259
  China PMI, China GDP QoQ (contrast), 13*f*
  impact, 263–265
  indicators, appropriateness, 108
  manufacturing (measurement), satellite data (usage), 277–280
  performance, 261–262
  release, 11–12
  US GDP growth rate, contrast, 12*f*
Python ports, 72
PyTorch, 78

Q&A surveys
  oil and gas production (Q&A survey), case study, 252–254
  usage, 247
Q_pct_delta_ffo quintile CAGRs, 3-months clairvoyance, 221*f*
Q_pct_delta_ffo returns plot, quarterly benchmark (contrast), 222*f*

Q_pct_delta_ffo, stocks holding (heatmap), 222*f*
Quarterly benchmark
  Q_pct_delta_ffo returns plot, contrast, 222*f*
  revenues_sales_prev_3m_sum_prev _1m_pct_change, contrast, 230*f*
  usa_sales_volume_prev_12m_sum _prev_3m_pct_change returns plot, contrast, 232*f*
  ww_market_share_prev_1m_pct _change returns plot, contrast, 231*f*

Radial basis function network (RBFN), 140
Random forest (RF), 67–68, 184
  comparison, 166*t*
  imputation, 169*f*, 180
Ranking factor, usage, 213, 216–217
Raw data (data transformation stage), 9*f*
Real estate investment trust (REIT) ETF (trading), mobile phone location data (usage), 288–291
Rectified Linear Unit (RELU), 90
Recurrent neural networks (RNNs), 76, 87, 143
Regressing consensus, 275*f*
  estimates/footfall, reported EPS (contrast), 293*f*
Regressing footfall, reported EPS (contrast), 294*f*
Regressing Google domestic trend indices, 326*f*
Regressing news
  sentiment, 276*f*
  volume, 1M implied volatility (contrast), 315*f*
Regression, 62
  linear regression, 64–65
  logistic regression, 65–66
  models, 72
  softmax regression, 67
Reinforcement learning, 63

Replacement (missing data treatment), 138

Reported EPS, regressing consensus estimates/footfall (contrast), 293f

Reports, usage, 247

Research cost, 21

REST API, usage, 102

Restricted information set, 86

Retail activity (understanding), mobile phone location data (usage), 287–295

Retailers, car counts/EPS, 271–277

Returns, sensitivity, 18

Revenue, maximization (equation), 42

revenues_sales_prev_3m_sum_prev _1m_pct_change, 232, 238
    quarterly sales volume, monthly change, 229–230
    quintile CAGR, 230f
    returns plot, quarterly benchmark (contrast), 230f

RIPPER, 148

Risk-adjusted returns, 312

Risk managers, 39

Risk metrics, 39

Risks, pre-assessment, 106, 109

Risk tolerance levels, 36

Root mean square error (RMSE), 154
    computation, 161

Root Mean Square Forecasting Errors (RMSFE), 2643

Ross, Stephen, 122

R squared coefficient, differences, 154

RSSA, 180

Rule induction learning, 139
    methods, rank, 141f

Sales/revenue (sales), financial statement item, 242

Sales-to-EV ratio, 216, 242

sales_volume_prev_1m_pct_change _prev_2m_mean, 232, 235

Satellite data, usage, 277–280

Satellite images
    aerial photography, 267
    analysis, process (steps), 174
    case study, 173
    data, dataset augmentation, 90–91

Satellite manufacturing index, Chinese/Caixin PMI manufacturing (contrast), 279f

scikit-image, 77, 91

scikit-learn, 59, 71–72, 77, 101

SciPy, 77, 80

SciPy.ndimage, 91

Scrapy, 100

Search volume, example, 326f

Self-organizing map (SOM), 143

Sellers, data pricing perspective, 41–45

Semi-supervised anomaly detection, 57

Sentiment
    analysis, classification problem, 96
    identification, 93
    social media, impact, 309

Sequential minimal optimization (SMO), 140

Sharpe ratio, 128, 212, 239
    change, 18
    usage, 217

Shipping data, usage, 283–286

Short threshold, usage, 213

Shure, Sennheiser (MoM) (Amazon spend comparison), 339f

Signals
    data transformation stage, 9f
    existence, pre-assessment, 106, 109–110
    extraction, performing, 106, 111–112

SimpleCV, 91

Simple moving average (SMA), application, 331–332

Single class logistic regression, neural network function, 73

Singular spectral analysis (SSA), 162

Singular value decomposition (SVD), 71, 160

Singular value decomposition imputation (SVDI), 140

sinkr, 180
Siri, usage, 99–100
Smart beta indices, alternative data inputs (usage), 127–128
Social media, 300–309
    data, 299
    Hedonometer index, 302–305
Social Media Analytics, 301
Soft data, 260
Softmax regression, 67
    neural network function, 73–74, 74*f*
Software libraries, usage, 179–180
spaCy, 101
Spearman correlation, 235
Speech, involvement, 99–100
SpeechRecognition, 102
SpendingPulse Brazil retail sales YoY, Brazil YoY retail sales (contrast), 337*f*
SpendingPulse index (MasterCard), 337
Spot returns, net flow (multiple regressions), 353*f*
Standard and Poor's 500 (S&P500), 77, 265
    Bloomberg News article count, contrast, 310*f*
    Google Shock Sentiment, contrast, 327*f*
    Google Shock Sentiment scatter, contrast, 327*f*
    Happiness Sentiment Index, contrast, 305*f*
    trading, IAI/VIX (usage), 329*f*
Standard & Poor's 500 (S&P500) returns, 82
Statistical factor model, 121–122
Stochastic discount factor, definition/equation, 41
Stocks
    exchanges, stock ranking, 211
    heatmap, 222*f*
    market reaction (forecast), Twitter data (usage), 308–309
Stocktwits data/sentiment factor, 82, 309

Strategic risks, impact, 11
Strategy
    capacity, 16–19
    data transformation stage, 9*f*
    high-capacity strategies, properties, 18
    investment strategy, time frequency, 22
    loss making, 18
    low-capacity strategies, 18
    setup, 105, 106–107
Stride, 90
Structuring level, 21
Subject matter experts (SMEs), impact/usage, 107, 112
Supervised anomaly detection, 57
    example, 68*f*
Supervised learning, 62
Supervised machine learning techniques, 64–70
    assumptions, 64
Support vector machine (SVM) (SVMI), 68–69, 140, 142, 148, 162, 184
    one-class SVM, 185, 188
Survey data, 245
    alternative data use, 245–247
    case studies, 249–254
    contributors, hierarchy, 246*f*
    product, 247–249
    usage, 247
Surveys
    crowdsourcing analyst estimates survey, 255
    process, 249*f*
    technical considerations, 254–255
    timeline, example, 248*f*
Synthetic 2D data, DINEOF imputation (example), 161*f*
Systematic investors, 36–38

tabula-py, 101
Taxi ride data, 295–296
Technology, score, 22
TensorFlow, 59, 77–79, 101
    Tutorials, 94

Tesla, value, 218
TextBlob, 101
Text data, 299
TF-IDF, 94
TF Learn, 79
Thasos Mall Foot Traffic Index, 288
   YoY, US retail sales YoY (contrast),
     289*f*
Theano, 77, 78
The many, Big Data (contrast), 9–11
Tickers, usage (change), 18
TickerTags, 98
Time
   frame, impact, 217
   removal, 219
Time averaged Spearman rank
   correlations, 236*t*–237*t*
Time series data, examples, 164*f*, 171*f*
Time series trading approach,
   cross-sectional trading approach
   (contrast), 126
Topic
   identification, 93
   modeling, 96–97
Total assets (totassets), financial
   statement item, 242
Tradeable companies,
   long/short-portfolio sizes, 218*t*
Transaction cost analysis (TCA), 356
Transaction costs, 217–218
   impact, 18*f*
   increase, impact, 18
Transaction time, 54
Trend returns, 355*f*
Trend strategies/daily flow-based
   strategies, risk-adjusted returns,
   354*f*
Trial availability, 22
True R squared coefficient, predicted R
   squared coefficient (contrast), 154
t-statistics, report, 314
Turkey PVIX indicator, USD/TRY 1M
   implied volatility (contrast), 331*f*
Twitter data, 309
   reported EPS, contrast, 294*f*
   usage, 305–308

Twitter mood data, usage, 15
Twitter score (independent variable),
   292
Two-part-tariff models, 31

Unstructured data, conversion, 51
Unsupervised anomaly detection, 57
Unsupervised learning, 63
Unsupervised ML techniques, usage,
   198–199
usa_sales_volume_prev_12m_sum
   _prev_3m_pct_change, 229, 232,
   238
   quintile CAGR, 232*f*
   returns plot, quarterly benchmark
     (contrast), 232*f*
   yearly US sales volume, quarterly
     change, 231
USD/JPY
   bid/ask spread, 357*f*
   news sentiment score, weekly returns
     (contrast), 312*f*
   news volume, 1M implied volatility
     (contrast), 315*f*
   trading, intraday basis, 308*f*
USD/TRY 1M implied volatility, Turkey
   PVIX indicator (contrast), 331*f*
US employment report, payrolls clicks,
   324*f*
US export growth, forecasting, 269–271
US GDP growth rate, PMI (contrast),
   12*f*
US/global new vehicle registration/sales
   ((IHS Markit database)), 207
US ISM, US GDP QoQ
   (contrast), 12*f*
US retail sales YoY, Thasos Foot Traffic
   Index YoY (contrast), 289*f*
UST 10Y yield changes, 320*f*
US Treasury yields, 316–320

Value-at-Risk (VaR), enhancement, 346
Value-of-information, 199

Variance, 60–61
  bias, balance, 61*f*
  cause, 60
Vendors
  due diligence, performing, 105, 108
  identification, 23–24
  monopoly, impact, 42–43
Venture capital
  firms, defining, 360
  transactions, database charting,
    362
Vickrey auction, 43
Viscosity factor, 82
Vision, setup, 105, 106–107
Volatility Index (VIX), 63, 77
  Investor Anxiety Index (IAI),
    contrast, 328*f,* 329*f*
  usage, 329*f*
Volume, Variety, Velocity, Variability,
  Veracity, Validity, Value (Big Data
  characteristics), 9–10

Walmart, earnings per share
  (consensus/footfall contrast), 291*f*
Web data, 299
  collection, 299–300
  search volume example, 326*f*
Web page
  body text, capture, 300

content, downloading, 300
  time stamp, assignation, 300
Web scraping, usage, 25*f,* 300
Web sources, 320–322
Weighted k-NN (WKNNI), 140
Wikipedia, usage, 330
Word2vec, 94–96
Word embeddings, creation, 94–96
Words, frequency (example), 99*f*
Word tokenization/segmentation, usage,
  92
Wrappers, writing, 112
ww_market_share_prev_1m_pct
  _change, 229, 232, 235
  quintile CAR, 231*f*
  returns plot, quarterly benchmark
    (contrast), 231*f*
  worldwide market shares, monthly
    change, 230

XLNet, 96
XRT, returns/trading (Thasos Mall Foot
  Traffic index basis), 288–289, 290*f*

YARN clusters, 79

Z-score, 191–192, 204